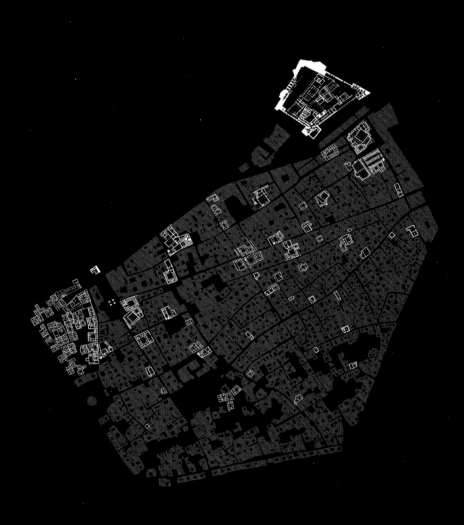

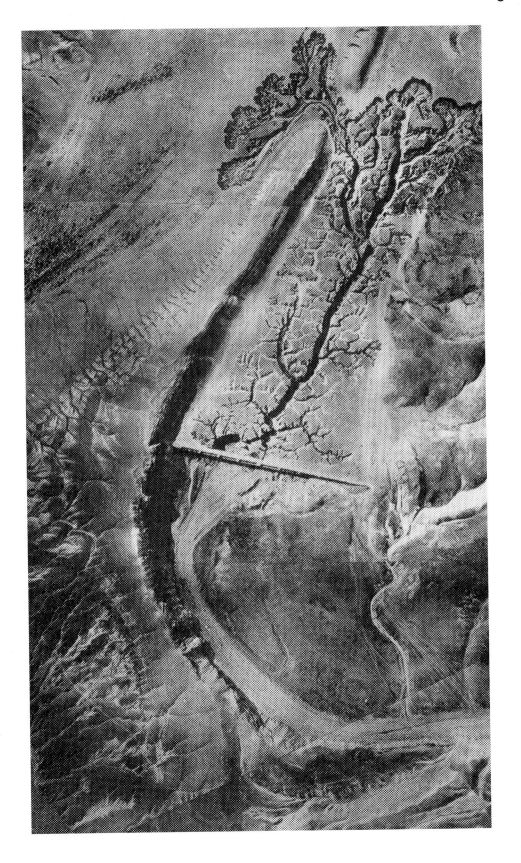

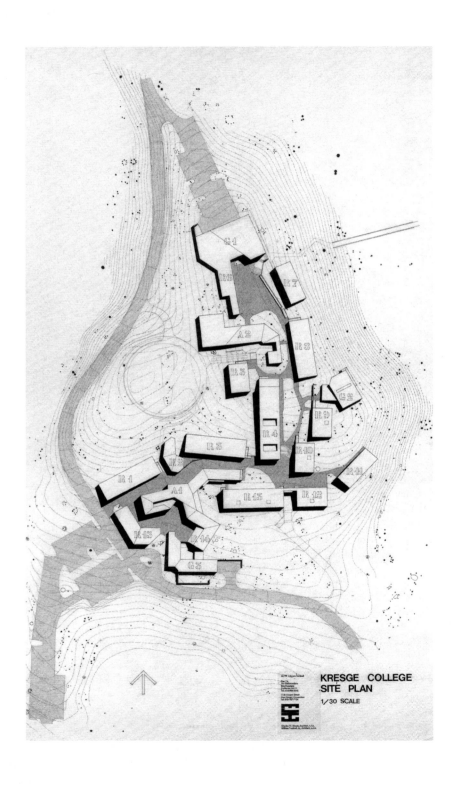

KRESGE COLLEGE
SITE PLAN

1/30 SCALE

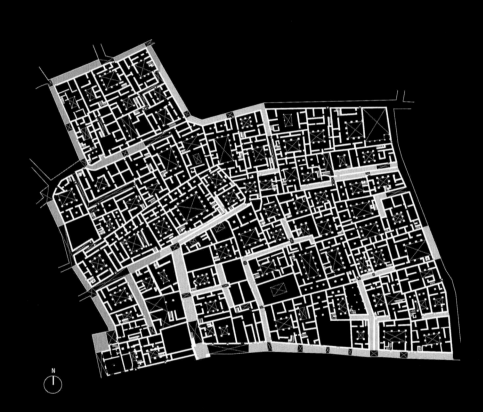

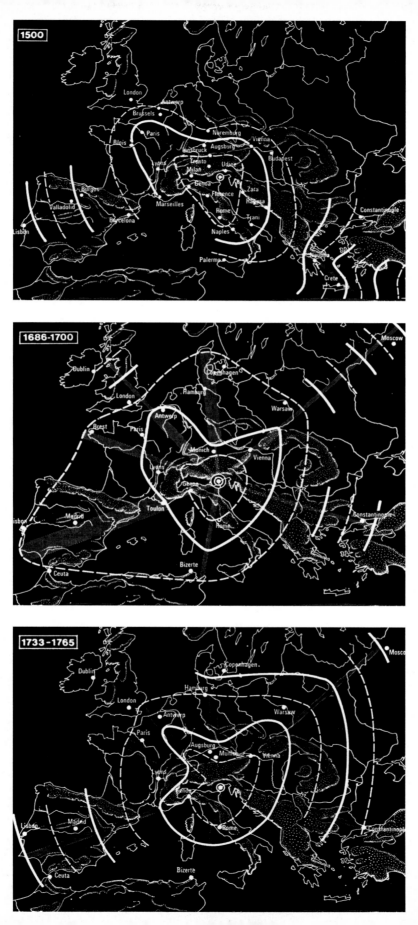

New Geographies 05
The Mediterranean

Worlds, Regions, Cities, and Architectures
Antonio Petrov

The central role of the Mediterranean in the development of global civilization cannot be denied. Situated at the intersection of Asia, Africa, and Europe, the Mediterranean — from the Latin mediterraneus, or inland or middle sea — is a region characterized by complex systems of urban and regional networks. The region's complexity is reflected not only in its diverse interrelations but also in endless debates about how to define it: Is the Mediterranean a space perceived as a binding geography, with a constellation of ports connected to hinterlands? Or is its expanded definition still based on seminal perspectives that come to us from historians such as Fernand Braudel, and Nicolas Purcell and Peregrine Horden, and from social scientists such as Henri Lefebvre and Michael Herzfeld?

The methodological postulation about it is important, as it reflects the struggle to understand and question the historic grounds and spatiality of a new emerging Mediterranean. Yet these sometimes overlapping and often contradictory conceptions of the Mediterranean find more possibilities of coexistence when considered in spatial terms. The "network of ports" definition versus the "complementary regions" approach may have generated heated debates in historiography, but in spatial terms these two views are quite compatible.

Although the Mediterranean has been able to resist an international architectural object fever and protect its cities from the seductive appeal of Dubaiization, globalization has nonetheless undermined the structures of Mediterranean cities and regions at a deeper level, influencing local configurations. Whether seen through the lens of early twentieth-century modernism or 1970s "critical regionalism," the Mediterranean is often still regarded from a perspective of idealism, which influences the spatial politics and the politics of Mediterranean identity and complicates twenty-first-century attempts to deal with globalization and its implications.

The superimposition of a universal logic driven by the economic and spatial politics of globalized actors and events obstructs the region's geographic logic, through which it might arrive at a renewed understanding of the contemporary Mediterranean. Despite the fact that the image of the Mediterranean is largely determined by stereotypes, a few countries dominate the identity, the brand, or what might be considered Mediterranean aesthetics. These claims on the brand drive the identity of the region as an image that has imposed itself on both reality and the imaginary,

Antonio Petrov received his doctoral degree in the History and Theory of Architecture, Urbanism, and Cultural Studies from Harvard University. Currently, he is teaching at the University of Texas in San Antonio. He is also program director at Archeworks in Chicago, cofounder and current editor-in-chief of the Harvard University Graduate School of Design publication New Geographies, the founder and editor-in-chief of DOMA, a bilingual magazine published in Macedonia, and the director of WAS, a think tank located in Chicago.

Antonio's research explores new discourses in regionalism and architecture with a focus on the Mediterranean. His research seeks to reconceptualize active processes of region making by dismantling prevailing geographic, spatial, and cultural meanings. His perspective on the Mediterranean recasts the region as a contemporary phenomenon and spatializes its region-making and region-formation processes as a larger geographic entity challenging conventional boundaries between the sea, cities, and hinterlands. Petrov is investigating new spatial paradigms to be presented in his forthcoming book, Superordinary: New Paradigms in Sacred Architecture. He traces evangelical architecture in the United States, arguing that postwar American Protestantism not only overcame the traditional signification of sacred architecture but also its dichotomy of form, function, and aesthetics.

Before coming to the University of Texas, Petrov taught at Harvard University, Wentworth Institute of Technology, Northeastern University, Iowa State University, the School of the Art Institute of Chicago, and the Illinois Institute of Technology. He is the recipient of a Fulbright fellowship and several other grants, fellowships, international prizes, and competition awards in architecture, planning, and design.

upsetting the balance between the two, leading to a new understanding of the whole, but with a contested meaning.

Although the Mediterranean's definition as a system of interrelated regions and identities is not easily apprehended, the speeds at which economic, political, and demographic shifts and resulting spatial consequences occur has made a clear reading even more challenging. The lack of awareness of "the emergence of indefinable, shapeless regions devoid of identity"[1] reflects how region-making processes are becoming increasingly transitory. Recent political changes have spawned new urban and regional morphologies, underscoring how the Mediterranean as a geographic entity is contributing to the understanding of what is at stake in regionalism and urbanism on an even larger scale.

Many essays in this volume recast the understanding of the Mediterranean city in much broader terms than the conventional port city definition ever allowed. In so doing, they expose patterns of urbanization that straddle national boundaries and challenge earlier topographically bound conceptions of the space. In some cases, mountains are no longer the defining backdrop and a limit to the Mediterranean city but are subsumed by its growth. In others, urban expansions along coastal areas are cordoning off the sea from the hinterland, but they are also creating new continuities and networks that could be folded into the Mediterranean model. These new urban behemoths and the hybrid modes of transportation serving them may have altered the Mediterranean model beyond recognition, but the related infrastructures and the new hinterlands are begging for refreshed morphological models, which some of the papers presented here seek to delineate.

It is at the architectural scale that the final set of interrogations emerge in this volume. What binds the "Catalan" house with the "Greek" house? As Barry Bergdoll has already proposed, the cyclical yearning for the Mediterranean has historically coincided with a desire for synthesis. Some of the featured projects propose new tropes, such as the island/colossus, that hybridize architecture with geography. Architecture has for too long been burdened with the responsibility of expressing place, of grounding itself in context. Some of the new responses suggest that the next synthesis may be between architecture and geography, helping us to find a more active role for architecture in shaping geography.

The featured projects by students in the New Geographies Lab at the Harvard Graduate School of Design explore a variety of possibilities: a new bridge between Africa and Europe; a master plan

1   Alain Thierstein and Agnes Förster, *The Image and the Region — Making Mega-City Regions Visible!* (Baden: Lars Muller Publishers, 2008), 228.

for the coastal area across nation-states, between Barcelona and Genoa; a new roll-on/roll-off harbor in a small Greek town that will serve as a major link between the Adriatic region and Asia Minor; an underwater network of conduits that transport gas, water, and electricity between countries around the Mediterranean; natural-gas rigs that punctuate the seascape; or constantly redrawn connections between public and virtual spaces that create the foundation for a permanent Arab Spring. The work in the New Geographies Lab reflects some of the major transformations that the Mediterranean region is undergoing today, placing these issues before architects and urbanists. A regional identity that had been tenaciously preserved over millennia, in part through its architectural tropes and stereotypes, is being radically revised.

This volume of New Geographies highlights these changes, their challenges, and their potentials. It aims to initiate new discussions that could extend to other transnational constellations, urban and regional forms, and the idea of region in architecture at large. We also hope to shed new light on the agency of architecture, which perhaps more than ever struggles to keep up with fast-changing regional structures that are morphing faster than the architecture making them. What role can architecture play in shaping large-scale territories that extend beyond the inhabited range of quotidian experience?

The Sea of Scales and Segments
Interview with Hashim Sarkis and Michael Herzfeld
Naor Ben-Yehoyada

Naor Ben-Yehoyada: We are here today to discuss region formation and region making in the Mediterranean with Michael Herzfeld and Hashim Sarkis. Michael Herzfeld is the Ernest E. Monrad Professor of the Social Sciences in the Department of Anthropology at Harvard University. Hashim Sarkis is the Aga Khan Professor of Landscape Architecture and Urbanism in Muslim Societies at the Harvard University Graduate School of Design. Thank you both for joining us today.

As the theoretical framework of this issue of *New Geographies* argues, in architecture and urbanistic literatures on the Mediterranean, cities are taken as emblems of ancient and medieval cross-sea connections, of early modern capitalism, and of modern cosmopolitanism. Cities like Naples, Thessaloniki, Izmir, Alexandria, and Tunis are often contrasted on the one hand to Atlantic cities, and on the other hand to the Mediterranean hinterlands. Recently this image of Mediterranean cities has been questioned. Some argue that the boundaries between cities and their hinterlands are exaggerated.[1] Others claim that Mediterranean hinterlands have actually been as connected to the worlds beyond their national boundaries as to their urban centers, if not more so.[2]

These developments in urbanistic scholarship on the Mediterranean raise several questions that may shed light not only on these cities but also on their relationships to the wider Mediterranean as well as the rest of the world. The Mediterranean is sometimes examined as an emblem or model for global interactions and connections.[3] Yet most historians agree that the Mediterranean world, however defined, died with the advent of modernity. How do megacities like Istanbul serve in the articulation of these tensions? What is the role of tourists, heritage projects,

1 Peregrine Horden and Nicholas Purcell, *The Corrupting Sea: A Study of Mediterranean History* (Oxford, [U.K.]; Malden, MA: Blackwell, 2000).

2 Henk Driessen, "Mediterranean Port Cities: Cosmopolitanism Reconsidered," History & Anthropology 16, no. 1 (2005): 129.

3 Ian Morris, "Mediterraneanization," *Mediterranean Historical Review* 18, no. 2 (December 2003): 30–55.

Naor Ben-Yehoyada (Ph.D. Social Anthropology, Harvard University, 2011) is a Research Fellow in Social Anthropology at Gonville and Caius (University of Cambridge) and Research Associate at the Consiglio Nazionale delle Ricerche (Istituto per l'Ambiente Marino Costiero). He specializes in Mediterranean maritime, political, and historical anthropology, specifically the maritime aspect of Israeli-Palestinian history and post–World War II region-formation processes between Sicily and Tunisia.

The Sea of Scales and Segments

migration, and cultural politics in the ways in which such tensions unfold?

This issue's thematic exploration frames this inquiry more generally: "What are the elements in the formula that determine Mediterranean regional formations? And how are they spatially manifested?" If the Mediterranean is not made of "cities and the routes between them," if cosmopolitan urban centers are not the main building blocks in this regional puzzle, what spatial-social constructions are?

Finally, the relationship of urban form and transnational constellations may help us distinguish also between region making and region formation — the former drawing our attention to projects and the latter to processes. Prima facie, anthropologists seem to reside safely on the "process" side of the fence, whereas urban planners seem to focus on the "project" side. But anthropologists and other social scientists have celebrated projects of "making," and scholars of the built environment have paid attention to the processes through which projects interact. How do you combine these approaches in your studies, and how does your work on the Mediterranean shape your approaches?

Michael Herzfeld: I find the question very disturbing, because that question presupposes a reification of the Mediterranean. It presupposes everything that I've argued against in the last thirty years and more, inasmuch as it seems to suggest that there is something that is identifiable as the Mediterranean other than a geographical fact. I would wonder what the purpose of this perspective is. Certainly the idea that the Mediterranean has, as a general region, included a lot of areas where cities have interacted with hinterlands, have drawn very heavily on the populations of those hinterlands, but also have emphasized the distinction between city and country holds true. But it's also true for many other parts of the world. As for the idea that it's a place where people now are beginning to construct cities that are specifically Mediterranean — perhaps because those who claim this have in mind a particular kind of climate — there again, what I fear is the domination of a set of stereotypes over individual planning and over the understanding of cultural processes. And this is particularly worrying, because Southern European countries and Middle Eastern countries, in very different ways, are now homes to new forms of violence. It would be easy for someone to say, "Ah, yes, this is typically Mediterranean behavior." Then we would be back to square one. All the stereotypes that were common in the 1960s and actually animated much of the anthropological and sociological thinking about the area, would move to a different

Hashim Sarkis is the Aga Khan Professor of Landscape Architecture and Urbanism in Muslim Societies at the Harvard University Graduate School of Design (GSD). He teaches courses in the history and theory of architecture, such as: Practices in Democracy; Constructing Vision: A History and Theory of Perspective's Applications in Architecture; Developing Worlds: Planning and Design in the Middle East and Latin America after World War II; and Green Modern: A History of Environmental Consciousness in Architecture from Patrick Geddes to the Present. His design studios include: The Architecture of Geography: Istanbul, Mixed-Use Development, and the Panoramic Condition; Makina/Madina: Reconfiguring the Relationship between Geography and Event in the City of Fez; Intermodal Istanbul; Square One: Martyrs' Square, Downtown Beirut, Lebanon; and A Field of Schools: Rethinking the Relationship between School and City in San Diego. Sarkis is a practicing architect between Cambridge and Lebanon. His projects include a housing complex for the fishermen of Tyre, a park in downtown Beirut, two schools in the North Lebanon region, and several urban and landscape projects.

He has authored and edited books and articles including *Josep Lluís Sert: The Architect of Urban Design, 1953–1969* (coedited with Eric Mumford, 2008), *Circa 1958: Lebanon in the Pictures and Plans of Constantinos Doxiadis* (2003), *CASE: Le Corbusier's Venice Hospital* (2001), and *Projecting Beirut* (coedited with Peter G. Rowe, 1998), He is executive editor of the CASE publication series. Sarkis directs the Aga Khan Program of Activities at the GSD. From 2002 to 2005, he was also Director of the Master of Design Studies (MDesS) and the Doctorate of Design (DDes) programs.

He received his Bachelor of Architecture and Bachelor of Fine Arts degrees from the Rhode Island School of Design, his Master of Architecture from the GSD, and his Ph.D. in Architecture from Harvard University.

plane, with the result that instead of focusing on the play of honor and shame in the villages we would be talking about the play of violence and refuge, or something of that sort, in the cities. So I worry about this kind of formulation. I think it would be much more useful to ask the question: Why is the idea of the Mediterranean so important to people who are looking at processes that have taken place in the area over a very long period of time?" If we approach the matter in that way, I think the answer will be clear and it will serve as an admonition to those who want to plan the future of the countries that sit around the rim of the Mediterranean Sea.

Hashim Sarkis: Let me start by situating the discourse on the Mediterranean within architecture and urbanism in relation to what I understand to be its reception, rejection, and criticism, in history and anthropology. I know I might be conflating two discourses that differ in their understanding and construction of the Mediterranean. However, I did see them conflated last year in the history/anthropology conference you organized.[4]

At the conference, I felt that we were at one level way behind you in our understanding of the Mediterranean as a region, and at another level way ahead of you. Let me start with where I felt we were behind. As much as our discourse has come to dismiss the issue of contextualism or regional expression in the last twenty years, we haven't yet critically assessed where we go from there. Because of the phenomena of globalization, the increasing mobility of architectural practices, and the waning interest in the expression of locality, we have lost interest in the past regionalist discourse, but we have not questioned it. We continue to operate with models that assume that architecture is indelibly bound to its region, even if we do not want to talk about it. We haven't asked the question: If architecture is in crisis in relation to the context, and this context is not going to go away, how are we going to be dealing with it? We understand region to be given rather than something that we are actively involved in constructing, which I saw both anthropology and historiography elaborate as a deep problematic at the conference last year.

However, I feel we are ahead of you because we are beginning to look at the Mediterranean differently, not with new eyes but because of the radical transformations that are happening in that region and that we as architects and urbanists have to deal with as projects. Irrespective of whether we define it, draw a line around it, to be corresponding to one of the lines of the different existing definitions or not, we are seeing radical transformations in the region, and we try to map and define them in different terms. And yet we keep resorting to our stereotypes because

4   "The Mediterranean, Criss-Crossed and Constructed"; 28–30 April 2011, Harvard University. See: http://isites.harvard.edu/icb/icb.do?keyword=k75136&pageid=icb.page378490, accessed October 10, 2012.

Michael Herzfeld   is the Ernest E. Monrad Professor of the Social Sciences in the Department of Anthropology at Harvard University. He was educated at the Universities of Cambridge (Bachelor of Arts in Archaeology and Anthropology, 1969), Athens (nondegree studies in Greek Folklore, 1969–70), Birmingham (Master of Arts in Modern Greek Studies, 1972; Doctor of Literature, 1989), and Oxford (Ph.D. in Social Anthropology, 1976).

Before coming to Harvard, he taught at Vassar College (1978–80) and Indiana University (1980–91), where he served as Associate Chair of the Research Center for Language and Semiotic Studies (1980–85) and as Chair of the Department of Anthropology (1987–90). He has taught and held visiting research appointments at various institutions around the world and is affiliated with doctoral programs at the University of Rome-I and Thammasat University (Bangkok). He holds honorary doctorates from the Université Libre de Bruxelles, the University of Macedonia (Thessaloniki), and the University of Crete.

His extensive ethnographic field research, much of it dealing in recent years with questions of historic conservation and its local social and cultural impact, has focused on Greece, Italy, and Thailand. The most recent of his ten books is *Evicted from Eternity: The Restructuring of Modern Rome* (2009). He is also a filmmaker whose work includes *Roman Restaurant Rhythms* (2011).

we haven't yet questioned them in the manner that you have. So we look at the littoral, at the coastal development of many of these cities, which have completely eradicated any sense of the Mediterranean port-city type, and yet we still seek to confirm this type in some implicit manner. So at the level of what constitutes the Mediterranean city, we are confronted with examples that are fantastically transforming it, if there ever was such an "it." We are still holding on to some grounding in a particular conception of the Mediterranean city, its history, and its evolution; evolution is very important for us in thinking about cities. We do not like cataclysmic shifts and breaks.

Herzfeld: Some of that presumably has to do with the fact that various nationalisms in the area are deeply conservative, both in the Middle Eastern area and in the Southern European segment, and that kind of conservatism is being radically enhanced by the pressures that those countries are under. Think of your own country, Lebanon, now with the pressure that is being produced by the events in Syria. I am thinking very much of Greece at the moment, where the policies of the leaders of the European Union have clearly intensified the violence in the streets, not because the Greeks are given to violence — in fact Athens used to be one of the most peaceful cities of the world — but because the new unrest is a response to structural violence. And these factors are operated by global forces that lie way outside the Mediterranean, so where I see the danger is that sometimes those forces actually use the idea of Mediterranean fecklessness against the countries in question. The classic case is Angela Merkel's way of talking about the Greeks as lazy; it turns out that the Greeks work the longest hours in Europe, the same number of hours as the Austrians on average. The Germans are way down on that list. The Greeks may be working less efficiently. They may be less efficient according to norms created elsewhere. But in terms of actual hours worked, they are considerably ahead of the Germans!

I certainly would recognize that there are strong cultural tendencies that lead to the production of differences. Where I see the danger is in how those differences become exaggerated. And I see that happening sometimes also in town planning and architecture, as in the case of Israeli architects who try to produce something that looks generically Mediterranean. To me some of what they produce looks very much like Greek island architecture. Unintentionally or otherwise, their work is a way of erasing the fact that there is tremendous ethnic and national conflict going on. It's a way of saying, "We are part of this landscape" — so that the architecture of urbanism itself becomes a piece of a mode of operating stereotypes to make claims on the land.

Sarkis: If I were to list these stereotypes and how we are dealing with them in architecture and urbanism today, I feel that here again we are observing things that are transformed radically. But in our nostalgia to those stereotypes that we have not yet questioned deeply, we are still trying to recover a certain connection to them as if this is the natural or the correct way of developing things. For example, in much of the literature about the Mediterranean city, we see the persistence of the idea of the city as being made of a weak public sector and a strong private sector. We see it as having a pulse that is very fine, that there is a kind of rhythm to the street life, to the façades of the buildings, to the interchange between inside and outside, that is different from other places. The term "the Mediterranean pulse" or "the pulse of the Mediterranean city" comes from Henry Lefebvre, who also holds on to that stereotype.[5] There is also this notion of the lax connection to the hinterland, even though the hinterland provides a "beautiful backdrop." The city and the hinterland are understood to have a loose connection. And then in terms of the internal composition of the Mediterranean city, we always look for, and somehow find, that the city is made out of a series of enclaves — ethnic or otherwise — that are more connected to enclaves in other Mediterranean cities than to each other. That is at least the stereotype. Now if we go back to the Mediterranean today, many of these attributes are not there, and we seek them to find them and to either restore them or, as you said, exercise a form of reification in relation to those stereotypes. And yet, as our students in the GSD New Geographies Lab are doing, we are discovering that many of these attributes may have never existed, but more important, that the transformations that are going on today are too radical to leave the stereotypes unstirred.

5 Henri Lefebvre and Catherine Régulier, "Attempt at the Rhythmanalysis of Mediterranean Cities," in *Rhythmanalysis : Space, Time, and Everyday Life* (London: Continuum, 2004), 85–100.

Herzfeld: There you have the problem that if you pursue that policy to its logical conclusion, you would probably eradicate a very large part of what many people regard as the historical heritage of their particular pieces of the territory. I have been interested for a long time in the clash between the two ethical systems that you could broadly call housing and heritage. The area is increasingly subject to housing shortages, just as it is subject to water shortages. Demographic growth has in some areas created enormous problems. In other areas, such as Greece and Italy, it has created tremendous concerns about low birth rates. But in all of these cases, what tends to happen is the emergence of a disturbingly right-wing view of what local identity should be about, and why therefore the preservation of objects such as houses of historic interest and monuments should in fact be pursued as a matter of national policy. And I think that we can see that this is likely in a not-too-distant future to lead to the kind of anger and resentment that does not justify, but does partially explain, the current attacks by some self-styled Islamic fundamentalists on monuments in Mali and in Afghanistan. In other words, I see those acts as being the result not purely of some misplaced iconoclasm, but actually as the expression of the anger and resentment that subaltern classes and other repressed populations feel against the forces that have held them back for so long.

Again, these are not particularly Mediterranean features, but I think that what happens sometimes in the Mediterranean region is that individual countries lay claims to a Mediterranean identity in order to paper over the sources of this kind of dispute. In other words, there is a desire to repress the potentially beneficial presence of conflict. I think conflict can be beneficial — it depends on what kind of conflict. Violent conflicts leading to bloodshed are hard to justify; but the conflict of ideas can allow cities to become places for the expression of a multiplicity of views. Diversity is a very hard thing to manage, because the human tendency, perhaps universally, seems to be to try to push everything into simple molds. Anthropologists, as you know, have long been interested in that process; the most famous exponent of their interest was Mary Douglas.[6] And while there may be arguments against seeing this as a universal phenomenon, it is certainly pretty common. So my concern here, given all of these elements, is to understand how urbanists and architects might plan in ways that won't trigger the emergence of a kind of supra-Mediterranean — I don't want to call it nationalism, but it might take the form of a variety of fascism — that would be reproduced in all the constituents countries and used to justify the suppression of anything that does not conform to the stereotypes. But at the same time, how do we do it in such a way that it does not result in a wholesale destruction of those elements of the past that people for various reasons want to keep? It is a delicate balancing act.

6   Mary Douglas, *Purity and Danger: An Analysis of Concepts of Pollution and Taboo* (London: Routledge & Kegan Paul, 1966).

Ben-Yehoyada: The danger of such reification is clear. The relationship between conflict, tension, spatial proximity, and the lack of cultural intimacy — perhaps the emergence of other kinds of intimacy — is exactly the kind of question that arises from the discussion of ethnic relations beyond the nostalgia toward erstwhile Mediterranean cities: supra-local urban structures that are neither aspiring to homogeneity nor reducing shared space to some abstract common human denominator. What would be an anthropologically informed regional urban landscape and city planning that would explicitly avoid these logical conclusions that you mentioned? What lessons can we draw from the history of the region, including the history of the reifications of the region?

Herzfeld: In our conference last year that Hashim mentioned, what I saw emerging was an interesting sense of how one might use the concept of the Mediterranean as seeing it as a set of ideas that were given material form and therefore were used for specific purposes. So we could talk then about how the stereotypes were used in politics. We could also talk about how these stereotypes translated into planning and architecture practices. That seems to be the way to go: taking advantage of all of the knowledge of the area that we have from the older forms of anthropology and from urbanism as you describe it, Hashim, as still somewhat addicted to these forms. But then we would link that to the idea that what we're really dealing with is not a set reality but something that has been created through various kinds of cultural flows, in which we have all participated, as people who lived in those countries or people who study them. We could then ask some very interesting questions such as, for example, why the term Mediterranean becomes important at a particular time. You yourself, Naor, ask this in your dissertation. Now that seems to be the crucial question. What is the particular political moment at which suddenly the Mediterranean takes on a new significance? How do people locally create that sense of the Mediterranean? That was how you had me persuaded that, after all, it would be worth talking about the Mediterranean!

The danger is always that people want to pull you back into a reifying discourse. Now, all three of us clearly don't accept that. But having said that, I think at the end we need to talk not just about how planners will build or plan in ways that would recognize these realities, but how we develop political movements that will oppose this closing-down tendency. Because it's not just the idea of the Mediterranean; what you see in the south of France, for example, or in northern Italy, is the very close association of heritage politics with anti-immigrant sentiments.

Sarkis: And in Turkey.

Herzfeld: Yes. It's the same in many parts of the world, but it seems to me that this is a feature that is particularly common in the circum-Mediterranean countries. And I think it's not coincidental, given that this is an area of confrontation where vast numbers of refugees and others are trying to enter the European Union and are being stopped by countries, Greece and Italy in particular, that are being forced by more powerful countries within the EU to play the role of coastguards. So how do you imagine, Hashim, a future in which there is enough popular pressure on governments against that kind of thing, especially in the countries outside the Mediterranean region that are controlling the destinies of Mediterranean countries, so as to ensure something more beneficent?

> **Sarkis:** I would like to imagine that the Mediterranean exists in some benevolent ways, particularly when countries like Lebanon are on the receiving side of a certain Mediterranean exchange. In Lebanon, we tend to receive many grants from the European Union or European Mediterranean countries because we happen to be on the Mediterranean. These projects may have little to do with Mediterraneaness, but the benevolent donors want to imagine Beirut or Tripoli as extensions of their future empires.

Herzfeld: This is the creation of a terrible form of dependence.

> **Sarkis:** Yes. I completely agree that the dangers are there. However, I would like to think about it as being a series of practices that are more conspiring, more deliberately transformative of the notion of the Mediterranean as we play along. It's always difficult to play that game.

Herzfeld: That's why I am asking you to tell us how to do it.

> **Sarkis:** Any form of subversive practice is always in danger of being too small to be even noticed, or of subverting itself. And in many ways, that is what is happening in the region. However, when we talk about the Mediterranean city, in Lebanon it actually becomes a very vibrant discussion — not one that is only oriented toward the north, the Mediterranean north, but one that is opposed to other conceptions of what we are. So, the Mediterranean identity is never cast as being either that or no identity. It is cast against the Arab city, the Levantine city, or the Phoenician city. All of a sudden, other group identities — not individual or national identities but larger regional identities — emerge to challenge and question. So I do feel that there is a certain productive dimension in that, because it does evoke the kinds of productive violence that you are talking about.
>
> But I also feel that in this exercise of region making or region formation, as you've distinguished between them (and I think it is a very productive distinction), there is another distinction that I think for me is very attractive about the Mediterranean. I fully endorse your introductory statement in relation to why we in architecture and urbanism are interested in the Mediterranean. We are going back to the Mediterranean city because it does provide us the trope, the archetype of what the global city is today. We are being told that the final manifestation of globalization is an entity called the global city. This global city is a dense cosmopolitan but still centralized city. It is a city that is assumed to resemble what happened in the Mediterranean in the Renaissance, when the first capitalist cities emerged, and then also when those eighteenth- or nineteenth-century cosmopolitan centers began to appear, one or two of them around the Mediterranean. So we're going back to the Mediterranean today, or we begin to be interested in it as an entity, because it does display a kind of prehistory of global cities. But person-

ally, I am interested in it because it displays a prehistory of the inverse of the world-city, *the city-world*, the sense that we might be in one of these cities, but we are very much aware of our belonging to a much larger entity, which embraces us all together; perhaps it is the Abulafia definition, but perhaps it's also the McNeill definition, where that embracing entity is a sense of nature or a collective risk.[7] Is that another form of nostalgia? Yes. And it has its dangers as well. I am very much aware of that. However, the kinds of transformation that are going on today around the Mediterranean, particularly in the radical reconfigurations of the boundaries of cities and their morphologies, do point in the direction of a city-world.

Herzfeld: Historically, in the last twenty years or so, we have seen an increase in segregation in many Mediterranean cities. I don't know how far you want to push the Mediterranean, but Jerusalem is the most dramatic example. And in many other cities, we see the emergence of immigrant ghettos and so on. I would love to believe that you are right. Because then one could say that as different nations or ethnic groups find themselves in conflict, we could say to them, "Yes, but look how much you share." If you just take the Arab-Israeli conflict, there is so much that is shared. And yet there is also a powerful sense of a radical difference. In some ways I also think it is also true that when peoples are very much alike, which I think is true of Jews and Arabs culturally in many respects, they also emphasize their differences. The anthropologist Anton Blok used Freud's notion of the narcissism of small differences to bring out, for example, what is going on in the post-Yugoslav conflict.[8] There you have Bosnians, Croatians, and Serbians, all of whom speak essentially the same language. It then becomes three languages by a kind of sleight of hand or at least by virtue of an arbitrary *Diktat*. And it seems to me that some of what is happening in the Mediterranean area is of this kind, that is, that the densification also of the centers of cities is producing more conflict, but it's producing conflict that is leading to a desire for separation.

Let me give you another example: class rather than ethnic separation in this case. In Rome, local people used to pride themselves on this notion of *convivenza*, of living together among several classes. Where I did my fieldwork in Rome, you had, for example, memories of a marquis who owned a huge *palazzo* alongside some of the poorest people in the city. And that convivenza continued until the neoliberal process of gentrification, which has driven out the poor — driven out not only the poor but actually, I would say, a significant part of the lower segments of the bourgeoisie in economic terms, with the result that now you have a one-class center and the people who have left for the suburbs have gone where their finances allow them to live. So actually the suburbs are now betraying strong class identities and are building differently in ways that reflect these differences, particularly because — given the Italian institutionalization of complaisance with any kind of ex post facto illegal building — often poor people build in one style, richer people build in some other style. And those illegal constructions are often then retrospectively ratified by the authorities because officials understand that it's better to do that than to face an even larger housing emergency. At that point, the sense of segregation increases. And although this is not only true in the Mediterranean, it seems to be true of many of the cities that you have mentioned. Think about Jerusalem and Rome. Athens is a little different. Athens is also, however, beginning to sprout ethnic ghettos, quite significant ones in fact. Thessaloniki is another story. It has actually gone the other way. It became more homogeneous, partly because of the way in which the Nazis killed all the Jewish population, partly because it's a part of the country that is home to some strongly nationalistic elements.

7   David Abulafia, *The Great Sea: A Human History of the Mediterranean* (London: Allen Lane, 2011); John McNeill, *The Mountains of the Mediterranean World: An Environmental History*, Studies in Environment and History (Cambridge: Cambridge University Press, 1992).

8   Anton Blok, "The Narcissism of Minor Differences," in *Honour and Violence* (Malden, MA: Polity Press, 2001), 115–135.

On the other hand, the people of the city elected a mayor who is himself a Koutsovlach by origin, so the situation in Thessaloniki really raises interesting questions about whether any kind of general characterization of a whole city is really possible. But while there are lots of differences, I want to emphasize the fact that so many of these cities actually become more fragmented as a result of demographic intensification.

Ben-Yehoyada: It might seem that the opposite of segregation and certain differences is homogeneity, whereas what you said before about the city can show us how the work of urban planners, as well as the work of maintenance of the urban environment more generally, is a delicate balance between separation, circulation, and exchange, which forgoes both utopia and nostalgia toward happy mixing. Images of class mixing as much as images of ethnic or any other kind of differ- ence-based mixings seem to have some kind of utopian basis to them, which cosmopolitan cities — whether in the Mediterranean or not — never really showed. If we are dealing with the balancing of difference rather than the imagining of elimination of the allusions to difference, then perhaps we could go back to what Hashim said earlier, which has to do with scale.

If cities can no longer imagine themselves as including only themselves; if cities can imagine themselves as elements in a shared destiny with other cities like them that are further apart in the city-world, then perhaps one of the things that a non-reifying discourse about the Mediterranean can offer is exactly the way to scale up — to the regional level? Such a regional scale does not have to be reified in itself to enable urban planners or any kind of other planners to emerge out of national, nationalistic, or supranational fascist scales. This scaling out is an open process. Last year's New Geographies Lab final projects (including Fadi Masoud's article in this issue) showed how this scaling up could work.

This scaling up is also a more accessible option in anthropology, if we examine the Mediterranean not as a reified culture area but rather as a modular-scale transnational constellation. It seems to me that there is something in common to urbanists and anthropologists. Both disci- plines are seemingly left with nonexistent or dead objects on our hands. We are trying to conceive and construct things Mediterranean, whereas historians argue that the Sea ceased to exist at the latest in the 1920s and have systematically defined the Mediterranean in contradistinction to modernity, no matter how the latter is perceived.

Herzfeld: Clearly I am not against the idea of discussing the Mediter- ranean or against trying to think what it means for us and how it is being used. I certainly think urbanists and anthropologists share a number of concerns with this question. That is why I am now interested in doing an ethnography of urbanists. Because it seems to me that the next stage in the game is actually to look at how urbanists themselves imagine the city in their everyday lives, how they calibrate their everyday lives to that space, and how they do their planning. We have a number of people, including some graduate students, recent and current here at Har- vard, who are doing research on urban planners. I have slowly begun to do some work myself on Italian urban planners, because I want to know what it is that sometimes gives us the sense of a total disconnect between what they propose and the way people live once the planners have done their work. I do not mean only the way that people live or have lived in the past. There often seems to be a disconnect between the ideology that urban planners express and the projects they produce, as well as between both of those things and their own lives. So there are empirical questions to be answered. I don't think they are peculiar to the Mediterranean. Jennifer Mack, for example, has completed a wonderful study on the way in which Swedish town planners encounter the Assyrian immigrant population, and the effects that they have on each other. We need many more such careful, nuanced studies; hers sets a fine example, and I hope it will be emulated.[9] What I think we will find is that, in the countries where people think of themselves as Mediterranean, there will be an effort to try to specify what they have in common. But that question is constantly in tension with equally strenuous efforts to emphasize differences.

9 Jennifer Mack, Producing the Public: Architecture, Urban Planning, and Immigration in a Swedish Town, 1965 to the Present, Ph.D. dissertation, Harvard University, 2011/12.

Sarkis: This narcissism of small differences, as you refer to it, prevails in many ways in sites of conflict, especially places I am familiar with, like Beirut. But I do want to make more out of your notion of scaling up, because it is very important. Scaling up does create a confrontation between urban planning and geopolitics. The spatial challenges that existed within the territorial political boundaries of a city now extend beyond. Environmental problems, demographic pressures and flows, infrastructural problems, are now transcending those boundaries. In contexts like Europe, urban planning is straddling national boundaries, and even boundaries between the sea and the land. Scaling up therefore completely opens up that model of the Mediterranean city as being the discreet harbor that sits at the edge of the water line. We saw that, for example, in Jarrad Morgan's project and contribution to this issue, which looked at the roll-on, roll-off terminal in Southeastern Italy and its connections to the Adriatic.

But scaling up does create another interesting challenge for us, which we did not see before. For one thing, we are beginning to act physically at the very large scale. We have always understood our role as designers to stop at a certain scale — that we can give form to a neighborhood, to an organizational structure of the city like its streets or its building heights. But when it came to region, we have invariably abandoned the formal and moved to the procedural. Increasingly, problems that are being put at our doorstep deal with huge highways, regional park systems, inter-regional corridors. So all of a sudden we are actually engaged, and increasingly so, in defining the region, shaping the region by design. So whereas we always took region to be the context to which we had to defer, now we are shaping it along the way. So at one level it seems to me an immodest exercise, because I am saying that we are involved in shaping regions, but also it is giving us a stronger sense that the notion of region is partly constituted, not simply expressed by formal means.

Herzfeld: Yes, that makes a lot of sense. But I think we also see the same kind of processes in the increased conflict along national borders, so that, as long as you are dealing with national borders, you are also going to be dealing with a real challenge to the idea of trying to create a sense of Mediterranean identity. The other problem with identity creation is the one that Cris Shore identified in his study of the European Union, namely that the European Union can create a sense of common bureaucratic organization; it can create a common currency, although that is now beginning to fray a bit at the edges, to say the least; it is creating all sorts of common institutions; but the sense of identity becomes more and more problematic.[10] Now, the concept of identity is in itself very problematic, because it's a psychological notion that is translated into social terms. But at least the sense of why people are interested in talking about being Mediterranean, and how this relates to the geopolitical issues that both of you have raised is, I think, an interesting avenue to pursue. Because we talk so much about the politics of identity, and because we tend to associate that particular form of politics with violent — and therefore nonproductive and destructive — conflict, I am still left

10 Cris Shore, Building Europe: The Cultural Politics of European Integration (London: Routledge, 2000).

with the conundrum of how we can pragmatically employ the notion of the common Mediterranean discourse — I prefer that term to "identity." Perhaps we should describe it as a conversation about the idea of the Mediterranean. The goal, in any case, would be to encourage precisely the sorts of new ways of thinking that you are talking about.

It seems to me that if you can encourage new ways of thinking, suddenly all the old hostilities will also start to look very shabby. Maybe I am being utopian myself here, but perhaps people would start to get tired of these hostilities. If we can't dream in the course of an hour-long interview, when can we do so?

Ben-Yehoyada: Perhaps the following example might measure up to this challenge. Several years ago, the Superintendent of Cultural Heritage in Sicily, who is also a professor of maritime archaeology, delivered a speech in which he made a similar point. By outlining the transnational spread of submarine relics across the Mediterranean, he showed how these relics — emblems of a Mediterranean heritage — extend beyond nationalist claims for national patrimony.[11] Even if this Mediterraneanist discourse might serve Sicilian claims to cultural and political autonomy from Italy and distinction within Europe, this was still an attempt to imagine a shared destiny, future, and a shared past in terms of heritage, without a nationalistic discourse.

11   Sebastiano Tusa, Mazara del Vallo, September 18, 2008.

Herzfeld: Yes that is a bit utopian, though it's a wonderful idea and I agree with you that it is worth pursuing. I have done a certain amount of work about and with various groups of archaeologists in the area. And I have some knowledge also of Israeli archaeology, and these archaeologies are all highly nationalistic entities. Nevertheless, they do sometimes share knowledge; they do sometimes interact, sometimes overtly and sometimes covertly, at conferences and so on, and it would be fascinating to see if you could bring together the *sovrintendenza per i beni culturali*, the Greek equivalent, the archaeological service in Israel and its equivalents in Lebanon and Turkey, and so on, and say "We want to create a union of Mediterranean archaeological services that are concerned with the preservation of the past but also with its relevance to the present, and that will do so in a way that is cooperative." That too is a utopian dream, and I suspect it would not be feasible, but it's something to imagine at least.

Moreover, I understand your concern with projecting into the future. But while I dislike the use of heritage for ultra-nationalist purposes, I also dislike the destruction of historical sites that sometimes comes also with new buildings simply because the economic forces behind new construction are simply not interested in the preservation of the past if it cuts even minimally into profit-making.

There's another twist to this. Both in Greece and in Italy, I have heard expressions that basically mean that there is nothing more permanent than the provisional, especially the illegally constructed provisional. In Greece there is this concept of the *afthereto*, which literally means "arbitrary" — in other words, a construction that the law treats as arbitrary because it has no legal basis; such, for example, are the *case abusive* in Italy. In both countries, people say that there is nothing more permanent than such supposedly temporary — because illegal — constructions. There is therefore an interesting discourse about the relationship between the erasure of the past and its preservation. That may actually be fairly characteristic of this region in a very generic sense. I don't recall reading anything framed in quite these terms in ethnographies of other parts of the world, but that could just be because it didn't happen to represent what was considered interesting at the time those ethnographies were written. But it is also closely connected with another Mediterranean stereotype — a notion that these countries are places where the bureaucracy is formally very strong but totally flexible on the inside, characterized by what the Italians call "the art of arranging oneself" (*l'arte dell'arrangiarsi*).

Sarkis: On the preservation part and on the mixing that you raised in terms of the Mediterranean model, architects think with formal tropes, and as many architectural historians argue, the cycles of renewed interest in the Mediterranean tend to correspond to when these formal tropes are either threatened or new ones are emerging. We have gone back to the Mediterranean to look for the classical trope and find it there; to look at certain vernacular tropes — even modernism and the modernist vocabulary finds its sources in the Mediterranean vernacular. However, I believe that certain tropes have been overlooked, not studied carefully, or even deliberately suppressed, and we might want to look at them a little bit more, precisely because they overemphasize their own hybridity. One of them is the *polikatikía*, a trope of architecture that I think exists all around the eastern Mediterranean in one form or another, and I am sure you can find it in other places. That does not make it exclusively Mediterranean, but it's sort of a materialization of this idea of the mixing.

Herzfeld: It's also a social phenomenon because most of those *polikatikíes* are built by civil engineers rather than architects, and so they tend to have very functional designs. That's certainly true of the eastern littoral of the Mediterranean and of Italy and Spain, but the Greek example is particularly dramatic.

Sarkis: In urban settings, we talk about mixing in terms of adjacencies among social groups or land uses and how they interact with each other, but the *polikatikía* type, like the apartment building type in Lebanon, and the apartment building type in Turkey, which are equally generic, have a certain mixing that takes place in section, vertically, that is worth studying. In those buildings, commercial activity takes place on the ground floor (part of which goes up to the first or second floor) in the form of workshops or offices. Then there is a kind of middle section that is usually family apartments. Finally, the top part, the penthouse or the roof, is dedicated to younger couples in some settings, to household staff in others, and to illicit activity in some others. This trope is hospitable to differences and to a loosely codified mixing. We've seen similar conditions in the *hôtel particulier* in France, it's not a new model. However, its prevalence and intensity produce very different spatial and social effects than in Paris. But I also feel that it is something that is completely threatened now, because this vertical mixing is happening less. Gated communities and the separation of commerce from residential are privileging (horizontal) adjacency.

Herzfeld: That disappearance might be related to what I have been talking about in relation to the process of gentrification in Rome, namely the impact of the neoliberal economy and its tendency to homogenize such social processes. It would be very interesting to take a completely different part of the world – China, for example, where you also have huge apartment buildings similar to the Greek *polikatikíes* – and to see to what extent the same kind of change occurs. I think that in China as in Greece such buildings are conditioned by local ideas about social identity. Of course those in China are mostly of very recent coinage, so it's not necessarily clear yet that what is actually happening is even analogous, let alone similar.

It would be interesting to compare the situation to the changes

The Sea of Scales and Segments

that Athens has undergone. It used to be a city of enclaves, little villages where most of the people belonged either to a social class or very often were from a particular part of the country.

> **Sarkis:** And settled at some point during a crisis of relocation.

Herzfeld: Yes, and this also animated much of what happened in these high-rise buildings.

> **Sarkis:** There is often a family component, a father and children, or siblings and cousins.

Herzfeld: Some of these *polikatikíes* began life as dower houses. In the countryside you sometimes see houses with hooks on top, waiting to receive the next floor for the next generation of daughters. So these are phenomena that are related not, I would argue, to generically Mediterranean social structures but to very localized social arrangements. In fact Greece is incredibly fragmented in terms of its inheritance rules. You see certain things including these buildings with the hooks, because some form of endowing with a daughter with an apartment is pretty widespread now. While many Greeks oppose the practice of the dowry (and it no longer has legal status), it is often viewed as an unavoidable evil with urban origins. Be that as it may, legislation removing the category of the dowry from formal usage has not eradicated the social practice. Again, I have to agree, these are all very interesting questions, and I think they can only be investigated ethnographically. You have to figure out what's happening on the ground, what people are doing, how they are adapting to these changing circumstances. There are huge problems now in getting good ethnography of, for example, multi-ethnic enclaves in the cities, because very few anthropologists are willing to learn five or six different languages for a project, although my view is that they should do so if that is the kind of research they want to do. What's fascinating is that many countries, including many of those in the Mediterranean area, are now faced with this problem, which arises in part from the fact that anthropology initially emerged there more or less of a spinoff of folklore studies and hence had a decidedly local focus. Now the immigrants have come in speaking languages that have no long history in those places. And while the theme of language is not in itself directly related to what we are discussing, it has a historical resonance, because we shouldn't forget that one thing that did make the Mediterranean rather more unified in the past was the *lingua franca*. Today there is nothing like that. Now the new *lingua franca* worldwide seems to be English; in fifty years it might be Chinese for all we know, but in any case it will be global rather than regional. Increasingly people are learning some of the more obviously "global" languages, and this provides some common ground. But again I wonder whether this means that people are going to become more alike and therefore more suspicious of each other, or whether instead they will find it easier to live and work together. These are strictly ethnographic questions.

> **Sarkis:** Some anthropologists have looked at the evolution of Lebanese urban life after the war. And it's interesting that during that period of very intense violence, these social entities such as the apartment building became probably the largest, safest entities to live in, and therefore what was separated sectionally became very heavily mixed, to the point where people encountered their neighbors for the first time in the basement — that all of a sudden the brothel that existed on the penthouse mixed with the families and with the concierge and with the *coiffeur*, all in the basement.

Herzfeld: Because they were hiding from the bombs.

> **Sarkis:**   Yes. And this sectional exposure created tensions but also a level of cohabitation that was extremely important during the war.

Herzfeld: But did it last? There were very similar situations in the Blitz in London and it didn't last.

> **Sarkis:**   It didn't last at all. It actually led to its own erasure at the end of the war.

Herzfeld: And that I think raises once again the question that Anton Blok raised, about people discovering similarities that somehow serve to underscore their differences. It's like Churchill's famous remark about British and American usage to the effect that there is nothing so divisive as their common language. Greeks have a saying about inheritance, that the more closely related you are to somebody, the more your blood boils when you encounter that person. So if you don't know that you are related, you have the sense of some kind of intensity in that relationship, but sometimes it's hostile and sometimes it's loving. And the question of which way it goes is the same question that one would ask about Greece and Turkey, about Israel and Palestine, about Bosnia, Serbia, and Croatia, and so on. In other words, if you think of nationalism as forms of kinship that have simply been raised to a larger level of inclusiveness, you see some of these same phenomena. In that sense, the area of the Mediterranean is a laboratory for understanding these processes and examining them, although I am not sure we are that much further along in knowing why they happen the way they do. But, as a planner, you have to think about what new forms of proximity you might be creating and what the social consequences might actually be. That is a key challenge, it seems to me, for the future.

> **Sarkis:**   In a way, not only proximity but forms of simultaneity, that we can feel more what others feel, because we are so invested in space that we allow for simultaneities to exist.
>   What I noticed at the conference last year was that many of the debates were in relation to the model of spatial organization of the Mediterranean. Is it organized around points of concentration? Is it about regions interacting with each other? Is it about networks? There were a lot of models being exchanged. And in effect, the Horden and Purcell model questions the Braudel model questions the Abulafia model. But somehow if we look spatially at the organization of many Mediterranean cities, these models could exist simultaneously. So whereas historiography seems to be very keen on the purity of its models, in space we don't see that as being a problem. To the contrary, actually, if we were to accept a certain Mediterraneaness, it is precisely about the simultaneity of these different models of organization and their possibility to coexist in the same space, in the same city.

Herzfeld: Certainly, while we would find that phenomenon in many other parts of the world, it is interesting to consider an area that does share a lot of cultural features over a long period of time, not to speak of the many natural features of the shared environment. Obviously the question has never been "Does the Mediterranean exist or not?" because that's a silly question, like asking how many angels can dance on the head of a pin. The question is much more about what uses the concept of the Mediterranean serves. Who uses it and why? What are the political implications? Why do some people emphasize the purity of their models, as you have so nicely put it, while others such as yourself are more willing to recognize this kind of simultaneity?

And I think that while you mention purity of models, it's also worth mentioning that the Mediterranean has several of the classic cases of language purity: the Turkish, the Arabic, and the Greek in particular. And then you have the exact opposite, as with the Italian situation, where you still have a huge amount of dialectal fragmentation. And so language actually is one area and one topic that might usefully allow us to map different kinds of spatiality and show how they coincide. Italians will tell you in the same moment that they have a national language, that they are very proud of it, and that it has a tremendous literary tradition, but that of course nobody speaks Italian. And they actually talk about Italian and all of the other dialects in the same breath. They may actually ask, for example, "Do you speak *italiano* or *romanesco*?" And then there are all these discourses about whether *romanesco* really exists or has vanished. Still others argue that Sardinian is not really a dialect but a language. These discourses about sameness and differences are strongly present in the politics of language, and the politics of language is incredibly spatialized, because it is always associated with regionalism and localism.

Another topic that is highly regionalized in Italy and also, in interesting ways, in Greece, which until recently was disinclined to recognize regional variations, is food. An anthropologist, Vassiliki Yiakoumaki, has written about the emergence, in a country that officially denies the existence of ethnic minorities, of ethnic foods, not of the migrants but of the local ethnic minorities.[12] Thus there are contemporaneous discourses that seem to contradict each other, and I suspect that while this, again, is true of many parts of the world, certainly the convenient shape of the Mediterranean allows for some useful comparisons.

I am only in favor of that as long as we don't go back to reifying the Mediterranean. The Mediterranean is as "the Mediterranean" is used, whether you are using it as a sailor or as a speaker. The materiality of language is an important issue here; when the people we study speak of "the Mediterranean," that is an interesting ethnographic and historical fact — it is their reification, not our analytic construct. For me, anyway — and I would like to see how both of you respond to this — the idea of the Mediterranean is useful insofar as it does get used, and very extensively. That creates a community of recognition. People understand each other as using this vague stereotype, so even when they are enemies, they recognize their commonalities. That it seems to me is what the conference was beginning to get at. It's not just that there is a stereotype of the Mediterranean that everyone appeals to, it's that there is a notion of Mediterraneaness to which people in very varied ways and through highly mutually contradictory discourses make an appeal and to which they try to remain attached in moments of great difficulty.

12   Vassiliki Yiakoumaki, "'Local,' 'Ethnic,' and 'Rural' Food: On the Emergence of 'Cultural Diversity' in Greece since its Integration in the European Union," *Journal of Modern Greek Studies* 24, no. 2 (2006): 415–445. See also Vassiliki Yiakoumaki, "The Nation as 'Acquired Taste': On Greekness, Consumption of Food Heritage, and the Making of the New Europe," Ph.D. dissertation, New School University, 2003.

Sarkis: I am delighted to see that you are recognizing the primacy of shape in defining identity.

Herzfeld: That's very interesting, yes, and I mean "shape" not only in the sense of determining the shape of the region, but also the fact that there are cultural forms that are recognized as similar and that then somehow create the impression, when they are manipulated — and that's the important point — that people have something in common. So I want always to ask who is doing the manipulating. This is the classical anthropological question: Who is doing what to whom, and why?

Sarkis: He took the word shape and made it a metaphor, and I want to take the word shape and make it as literal as possible. It is about these infinite concavities that the Mediterranean shapes itself.

Herzfeld: I am going to quote a Mediterranean thinker, if you want to call him that, Giambattista Vico, for whom even the literal was a trope. Now we are really getting to those angels dancing on the head of a pin!

Ben-Yehoyada: Beyond recognizing of the acceptance of the possibility of a Mediterranean, what Michael has just said is not only about the Mediterranean, it's a segmentary definition of the Mediterranean.

Herzfeld: Now we are speaking a common conceptual language.

Ben-Yehoyada: This segmentary concept of the Mediterranean connects directly to what Hashim has said about sections in buildings and the way they enable confluences when imagining urban form. Here, the notion of a segmentary Mediterranean is theoretically opposed to that of fragmentation.[13] In saying that neighborhoods, cities, nations, or regions are fragmented, we are actually invoking, against our better judgment, a holistic notion of that thing which was once united and is now fragmented. This building in Beirut, where not only each section holds a different kind of profession or community, but each section laterally interacts with its horizontal counterparts in other buildings in the city and beyond. The basement section perhaps resembles a Goiteinian model, the upper floors, the *Corrupting Sea*, and the middle section, Abulafia's construction. The result would be exactly the spatial version of Bakhtin's polyphony: a form built on dissonances and confluences, which is shaped by the phase-gaps and different wavelengths that are interacting with each other.

Herzfeld: The notion of segmentation, and you have used it effectively, does go a long way toward describing why you can get violence and complacence and cooperation, how people can conceive of themselves as being essentially the same but fundamentally different. That is what segmentation at some level is all about. And in your work you demonstrate that clearly. I hope that audiences to this kind of discussion will understand what we mean by segmentation. Because, for one thing, I noticed that the word segmentation is not on my spell checker. That's a fair indication that it is seen as an obscure term. And people often just think it means fragmentation, whereas you are using it in a precise Evans-Pritchardian, almost Durkheimian, sense, but without all the baggage of kinship and teleology. I think this is productive, but it does need careful explication.

Ben-Yehoyada: To add one more dimension to our discussion, once we switch from wholes and fragments to segments, we are also opening the realm of modular, changeable scale. This is the question with which we started: how do we enable an urban form, artistic form, to be modular, changeable in terms of scale, not because we want to re-fix or reify again the urban form on a regional level but exactly because we want to keep that modularity in terms of scale going.[14] Scale is invoked nowadays in anthropology of space, as in Ajantha Subramanian's work.[15] Yet segmentation — the idea that political forms are not fixed at any of their levels, but can actually rise from the level of the most basic unit to the highest significant scale — served as the foundation of political anthropology since the 1940s. The exercise that Hashim is promoting — to scale up the city or the urban upwards — actually meets an anthropological challenge, which tries to do exactly the same: from the interactional, above and beyond the national, toward the transnational. The Mediterranean offers a historical repertoire of such transnational forms on a regional scale.

13   "Any segment sees itself as an independent unit in relation to another segment of the same section, but sees both segments as a unity in relation to another section; and a section which from the point of view of its members comprises opposed segments is seen by members of other sections as an unsegmented unit." E.E. Evans-Pritchard, *The Nuer: A Description of the Modes of Livelihood and Political Institutions of a Nilotic People* (New York: Oxford University Press, 1940), 147.

14   Processes and projects of regional scale are illuminated in various ways by the contributions to the second issue of this journal; Ghosn, Rania. 2009. "Energy as a Spatial Project." *New Geographies* 2: 9–10.

15   Ajantha Subramanian, *Shorelines: Space and Rights in South India* (Stanford, CA: Stanford University Press, 2009).

Herzfeld: We have here the makings of the explanation, but what you are looking for is almost a policy, and a way of framing future action, and I think that this is important. I am no longer that much of a purist. I used to think that anthropologists should stick to analyzing things, but I actually rather like this more proactive stance, and it seems to me that you are asking us to think about how this Mediterranean identity, whatever it is, can be used in a productive way to overcome so many of the false alleyways and false starts that characterized a lot of the urbanism in the area generally — a lot of urban and social planning and other government interventions of various kinds. All three of us are critical of the notion of nationalism and therefore understand very well that a Mediterranean identity, if it does emerge, should not be allowed to lapse into the same kind of exclusion, but history shows us that every time a group has had to fight for its liberation and has emerged with some degree of independence, it has tended to become an exclusive — it has done the segmentary thing — it has hived off in ways that are defensive because it feels itself to be surrounded by potential enemies.

As we are coming to the close of our discussion, I would like to throw this out, perhaps as a challenge to anyone who might read this interview: How then will planners use this knowledge of how the Mediterranean concept operates in people's lives to start thinking about constructing cities and planning territories that actively discourage the sort of confrontational politics that throws up walls and barriers and creates enmities? The same processes can produce both conduits and barriers. That's the insight that Blok's analysis raises. Because he was in some ways a functionalist in his work at that time, I think it is often ignored, but he had a real sense that the paradox of similarities and difference — which as Naor has elegantly demonstrated has to do with segmentation — is really at the center of the problematic we are discussing. That is how I am able to say, at one and the same time, that I am critical of "Mediterranean studies" and yet give both of you the satisfaction of hearing me speak positively about the prospect of speaking about "the Mediterranean" in some critical sense. I have always been fascinated by the immense desire of a lot of people to recognize something as Mediterranean, and I think it is motivated by many different things. So the question then is: Are planners going to try to direct those motivations? So there is a challenge.

Sarkis: Obviously, a component of why we are interested in the Mediterranean within the New Geographies Lab has a lot to do with the kind of existential moment we are in, in terms of regional studies, and how we, when we are positioned as we are in a certain region disciplinary within regional boundaries, reflect on the crisis of regional studies particularly after the level of questioning that it went through. I do think that questions of cultural mobility as they begin to emerge in different fields are informing us positively about how we should take this forward. But I also feel that perhaps the idea that cosmopolitanism paradoxically has a place or has a locale, could be something that we cannot recover but uncover.

Herzfeld: Both you and I would be nothing if we couldn't have a place as cosmopolitans.

Sarkis: I am fine with the construction of the Mediterranean nostalgia, and Cafavy is one of my favorite poets.

Herzfeld: He is ironic, which makes it bearable; he plays perceptively with identities that others took at face value.

Sarkis: And I do feel that our role — because we are always about making places, we are stuck making places — is to be able to operate along those lines; how is it that we are able to construct a place that displays very clearly the possibility of displacement. That one is at once in the place and somewhere else. This is why I have become fascinated with the concept of interiority as it manifests itself in places like Beirut. People are obsessed with interiors that take you somewhere else.

Herzfeld: And that in itself is such a wonderfully paradoxical notion that it is hard to know where one would go with this conversation from there except to explore it and see what actually could be done with it.

I found this a very interesting exchange. I do think that a greater degree of conversation between planners and anthropologists, which is beginning to happen here and in other places, is crucial, because it is fairly evident to me that some of the other conversations, particularly between planners and economists, have produced some good things but they have also produced some real problems. And while I don't want to go out on a limb to the point of saying anthropology would save the world, the insights of people who actually live among those whose problems they study are very different from the (sometimes heuristically valuable) insights of those who look from above and see each case as a statistical sample. If planning is about thinking how people are going to live, then we must see how they actually are living and what they want to do, and also how the planners themselves are living. This is one produc-tive way to go.

I also feel that, having battered my head for forty years against the notion of the Mediterranean, a little gracious retreat does not do any harm, because actually knowledge is not produced by convincing one-self that one has arrived at a literal solution. On the contrary, knowledge emerges in moments when the classifications that we know break down. Planning is all about the classification of space. That's not the only way to look at it, but it's an important way to look at it. And the organization of space is a form of taxonomy. So as we look at how people reformulate their spaces and rethink the significance of the various categories of space, it seems to me that we also then understand, in that change-ability, why they hang on to certain ideas and why perhaps that should in some situations be discouraged and in others encouraged. But it is a complex discourse that we are embarking on here. And it is only a beginning.

Sarkis: In the past three years of the New Geographies seminar we have been reading Michel Serres on Rome.[16] *Rome: The Book of Foundations* has been very important for us, not because Rome is in the Mediterranean region but because Serres questions the idea of search-ing for foundations. He also questions the tropes that we tend to associ-ate with the city, and proposes Rome as another type of city than Athens or Jerusalem, a city/region/world. He is interested in the approximated character of the city, in its algorithmic flow, in the Romans' emphasis on networks and infrastructure rather than monuments. But along the same lines, you were talking about planning as being responsible for the *aménagement du territoire,* the allocation of uses. But it is important for us to recognize that we are also invested in the artistic form of the built environment at the largest scale, and therefore we are invested in identifying the tropes, the forms, the expressive dimension of this larger entity called "the Mediterranean." We are using Serres's Rome to speak about the whole region as one city, one form, one trope.

16   Michel Serres, *Rome: The Book of Foundations* (Stanford, CA: Stanford University Press, 1991).

Herzfeld: Any mention of aesthetics inevitably raises questions about the politics of taste. It's interesting, for example, that in northern

Europe Mediterranean styles are both adulated and regarded as kitsch. So there is a play of power in the choice of aesthetic media, and that's where I think the voice of the critic — whether it's an anthropologist or someone else — becomes important. And I am happy that we have this kind of interdisciplinary discourse. It's been going on for a lot longer than I have been aware of it, and I am excited to discover so much of it now, but I hope that it will also gain a public hearing, because to many people out there all of these questions that we have discussed still smack of obscurantism, technical obsession and so on, and yet what we are talking about is the very fabric of human life.

Sarkis: As a curious example of this intercontinental construction of Mediterraneaness, a developer of gated communities in Istanbul once explained to me that he was building a Mediterranean project. When I asked what made it Mediterranean, he explained that they gave their buyers a choice between an Andalusian-style house, a North African style, a Levantine style, and even an Ottoman style. And when I asked him who the architects were, he said, "We hire them from Florida because they make the best Mediterranean architecture." That this identity is not only kitsch but also branded and imported from somewhere else is something that we definitely need to examine.

Herzfeld: And it's parallel to the claim made by an American anthropologist in the early 1970s that Mexico, because it had a code of honor and shame, must be a Mediterranean country.[17]

17 Carroll Quigley, "Mexican National Character and Circum-Mediterranean Personality Structure," *American Anthropologist* 75, no. 1 (February 1, 1973): 319–322.

Ben-Yehoyada: These last two examples — one from architecture and the other from anthropology — show how reifications of transnational regions can travel globally as much as their nationalist counterparts. Chefs, writers, and architects often claim to draw from and then perfect aesthetic emblems of their national and regional (e.g., "Mediterranean") repertoires. While we have been used to diasporic productions of national taste, the production of Mediterraneanist taste outside the geographic Mediterranean seems more paradoxical. If that is so, then we might say that transnational regions have become more local than nations. Thank you both very much for this discussion.

The Mediterranean, A New Imaginary
Adrian Lahoud

"If the Mediterranean has done no more than force us out of our old habits it will already have done us a service."[1]

The distinctiveness of the Mediterranean is an issue of some dispute. Is it a single sea or many? Does the Mediterranean refer to a littoral, the plains, or hinterland? To a lifestyle or an ecology, to a moral geography or a physical one? The oft-used response refers to a shared climate and the cultivation of vines and olives, but in what way does "Mediterranean" explain a connection between Cadiz to the west and Qadisha to the east? What unique property reveals itself through the Mediterranean alens?

What then, is the Mediterranean? Every discipline will answer this question in its own way. A Mediterranean story told according to kinship structures and small communities for anthropologists; micro-regions or biotopes for environmental historians; naval technologies, charts, and sea routes for oceanographers; surveys, vernacular building types, and colonial master plans for architects and urbanists. Not to mention the significant disagreements within disciplines, or for that matter, those forms of knowledge transmitted through oral rather than written traditions, such as the migratory routes of pastoralists, the cultivation practices of farmers, or the navigation of fishing vessels. Within each frame of knowledge, a different distribution of relevant and irrelevant points will be plotted, and in each case the outline of a different Mediterranean will unfold.

If these epistemic differences were not enough, the temporal scales brought to bear in explaining the Mediterranean range from its distant and somewhat catastrophic geological formation to the bright flash of recent revolutions. Mediterranean historiography is so rich because

1   F. Braudel, *The Mediterranean and the Mediterranean World in the Age of Phillip II* (Los Angeles: University of California Press, 1995).

Adrian Lahoud is an architect, urban designer, and researcher. Currently he is Director of the Master of Architecture Urban Design Program at the Bartlett (University College London), where he is conducting a wide-ranging three-year design research project on the Mediterranean.

His doctoral dissertation, *The Problem of Scale: The City, the Territory, the Planetary*, sets out to reconceptualize the action of scale in the context of design and teaching. Prior to taking up a position at the Bartlett School of Architecture, he coordinated the MA program at the Centre for Research Architecture (Goldsmiths, University of London).

He has also taught in the Projective Cities program at the Architectural Association (Angewandte, Vienna) and at the University of Technology Sydney, where he retains a position as Adjunct Professor. In 2010 he coedited a special issue of *Architectural Design* titled *Post-traumatic Urbanism*, and presently he is working on book project and exhibition exploring the possibility of a "Fifth Geneva Convention" with colleagues from the Centre for Research Architecture.

it always invites methodological conjecture over the form and resolution of investigation, a continual oscillation between commonality and diversity, time and space. Rather than seek consensus and strive to resolve this argument once and for all, it is more interesting to simply imagine the Mediterranean as a site of endless epistemological provocation.

However, this in itself does not take things very far, and soon further questions arise. What is at stake in this contest? Any territory that invites sustained dispute across so many generations must conceal rewards for the combatants. This once took shape as an argument over origins in an attempt to assert a historical continuity between ancient Greek, Roman, and Western European civilization. Today, the Mediterranean is paradigmatic for another reason: as a circuit of leisure and a theater of violence. In fact, one might go so far as to say that if the Mediterranean depends on a material unity adequate to the unification conferred in its proper name, the very possibility of a "Mediterranean" is at risk.

Mediterranean Historiography: A Wider, Kaleidoscopic World

"The unifying feature is not the accident of a nucleated pattern... it is the intricate and often far-flung engagement with a wider, kaleidoscopic, world."[2]

It is impossible to approach the Mediterranean without first referring to two texts that have taken on exemplary status: Fernand Braudel's *The Mediterranean and the Mediterranean World in the Age of Phillip II,* and Peregrine Horden and Nicholas Purcell's *The Corrupting Sea.* One of the many remarkable things about both of these books is how inventively they choose to approach their object. In each case, the question of historical scale is made to resonate in a new way. For Braudel, the methodology of the Annales School and the *longue dure* allows an inversion of the foreground/background relation often found in historical writing. Rather than presenting a series of great characters and epoch-making events, a tragic human theater of victories and defeats taking shape against a scenography of incidental, contextual features, Braudel brings humans into contact with the inanimate — now revealed as the motor of history. For Braudel, it is only within the context of this environmental history that the subsequent scales of social history and individual history can make sense. Braudel distrusts the limited horizon of individual knowledge, and so he works to unfold the constellation of forces into which each individual is thrown, and of which they are often only dimly aware.

If the causal traffic in Braudel's model of history tended to flow from deep time to surface event, this was no doubt part of an attempt to invert a historiographical dependence on individual histories. The resulting system is arranged in three layers; a slow-speed geological and environmental history for a base, a social history for a midstructure, and an individual history for a surface, each layer holding a specific kind of content and time signature. This structure allows Braudel to make events, be they geological or human, commensurate since all of them keep rhythm to the same deep metronome.

2   N. Purcell and P. Horden, *The Corrupting Sea* (London: Wiley-Blackwell), 122.

Environmental Outlook. Decreased precipitation, desertification and dwindling fish stocks are apparent from this map. Shown is the disparity between sustainable and existing levels of finishing represented by the circles, with the areas marked on the north African coast representing the food production areas most vulnerable to changes in climate.

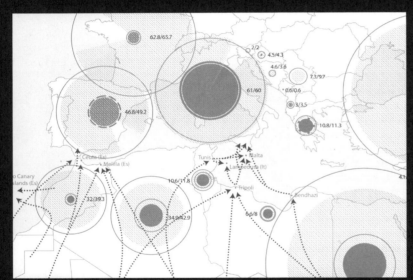

Population and Migration. Demographically North Africa and Southern Europe are experiencing opposing trends, with a consistent fall in birth rates recorded for many decades in most southern European countries and a contrary trend (shown here by the circles) in the north of Africa. The purpose of bringing together de- mographic data and vectors of migration as shown here is to raise the question of labour and to note that European border controls are opportunistically plastic in that North Africa is stil conceived as a pool of human labour power to be dipped into when the need arises.

Horden and Purcell's *The Corrupting Sea* suspends Braudel's initial pre-supposition of Mediterranean unity, beginning instead with a more fundamental question: "What is the Mediterranean?" The answer they give is as radical as the method they use to arrive at it. Rather than conceive of the Mediterranean and its distinctiveness according to a property held in common — say, the supposed sexuality of the Mediterranean male, or the use of a specific cultivar such as *Olea europaea* — they propose that what is common about the Mediterranean is not a quality but a problem. The problem that drives this Mediterranean narrative concerns risk — how to manage it and protect ones livelihood. According to the authors, the combination of erratic climate and fragmented topography produces a series of micro-ecologies whose inhabitants are forced into trade with their neighbors to diversify their energy sources and hedge against the bad years that the unreliable Mediterranean climate will inevitably bring. This drive to trade is intensified by the peculiar connectivity afforded by the sea, with its history of coastal sailing and cabotage.

This is a radical departure from Braudel. Rather than organize history in separate layers, each according to a proper category and speed, Horden and Purcell begin with a problem — say, the diversification of foodstuffs in a specific micro-ecology — using a series of case studies to track the complex network of relations that radiate out from them. The problem re-appears like a genetic element in the narrative, individuating a constellation of social, geographical, economic and technical questions around it. Like diagrammatic spiderwebs spun between Braudel's temporal strata, their threads connect heterogeneous elements and time scales. Time as chronology or periodization, and space as predefined spatial unit, are no longer presupposed and are discarded as entry points so that each problematic case can finally be posed on its own terms, individuating its own elastic spatiality and temporal rhythm.[3]

Using a problem as an entry point rather than a category of information (say topography, agriculture, or social structure), temporal scale (longue dure, moyenne dure, histoire événementielle) or spatial unit (global, regional, local) means that the definition of limits emerges from the concrete network of causes and effects in question. It is a methodology that requires the decisiveness to constitute something as problematic and then the patience to follow the lines of force that expand out, even if they lead far away from familiar territory.[4] Beginning with a problem rather than a category of information then, brings new issues into focus, allowing for unforeseen proximities between matters of concern normally separated by space, time, or simply disciplinary habit.

But what does this approach mean for today's Mediterranean?

Conflated Scales — Deep Inconsistencies

"Geological time and the chronology of human histories remained unrelated. This distance between the two calendars... has collapsed."[5]

The climate may well remain operative in writing Mediterranean history, but when that climate becomes man-made, what kinds of consequences does it hold for historical narration? Natural history and human history may have met in the pages of Braudel's books but they were never mistaken for each other. The earth set its own rhythm, humans followed. Braudel had no need to question this partition, nor did Horden and Purcell who restricted their inquiry to a specific historical problem regarding risk, a problem whose scale — though plastic — remained resolutely proximate. The problem that organizes today's Mediterranean is of a different order, an order of superimposition and conflation. It is a problem that binds together the consequences of Western industrializa-

3   "The underlying concept, rapid variation in the reaction of the producer to the surrounding world in all its complexity (variation that can take place over time as well as over distance), is fluid and inconstant. So it is unreasonable to expect that scale will not be an additional variable alongside all the others." Ibid., 79. In conversation with the author, 12 March, 2013, London: Peregrine Horden noted that the challenge with this method lay with the selection of the cases, especially since each example must in some way be able to speak through its own specificity to a larger ensemble of unnamed examples, that is, each case must become paradigmatic, an exception that reveals the intelligibility of the set to which it belongs. See also G. Agamben, "What Is a Paradigm?" Lecture at European Graduate School, 2002.

4   This might be part of the reason why *The Corrupting Sea* was twenty years in the making, and also perhaps the justification for a bibliography that takes up a quarter of the entire book.

5   D. Chakrabarty, "The Climate of History: Four Theses," *Critical Inquiry* 35 (Winter 2009): 197–222, 216.

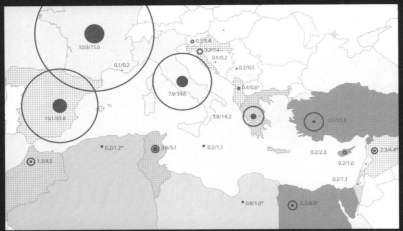

Tourism Revenue. Looking at the vast disparity of tourist receipts between the Southern European and North Afircan coast and there is no doubt that regardless of the political situation in Arabic speaking african countries, increasingly European tourist operators in an effort to open new markets will be turning to a coast line that is close by and untouched by the forms of development that have ravaged the coasts of Spain, Italy and France.

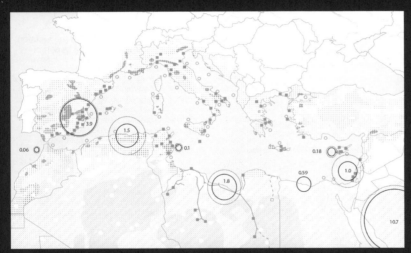

Environment and Agriculture. Project's like Libya's Great Man-Made River — one of the largest engineering projects on the planet visible here as the orange lines — form only the latest in a long series of attempts to provide additional fressh water to norht Africa cities and agricultural lands. Whether drawing water from deep aquifers north of the Sahara, diverting and daming rivers such as the Nile or more expensively — constructing desalination facilities along the coast, there is no doubt fresh water is a rare and valuable resource around the Mediterranean basin, one facing increasing pressure due to increased population growth and lower forecasts for precipitation.

tion, global carbon emissions, aerosol dispersion patterns, sea surface temperatures, monsoons, precipitation, pastoralists, herders, farmers, cultivars, migratory routes, treaties, coast guards, statistical models, satellite imagery, and detention centers. By what logic will this newly disparate historical series hold together? Where will it leave important methodological concepts like scale and limit, let alone the actual sovereignties and jurisdictions that depend on them?

The idea of the anthropocene emerges as a proposal for a new geological periodization by Paul Crutzen in a now well-known article in *Nature* published in 2002, where he proposed that with industrialization and the liberation of intensive energy sources from fossil fuels a new geological epoch had been inaugurated.[6] Humanity had begun to interact with and modify that aspect of the world once taken for an ambient backdrop: the climate. According to Crutzen, given humanity's new agency within a planetary-wide system of causes and effects, the climate — whether benign or malevolent — enters into the calculus of all those things that can be put at risk by human intervention.[7]

This era is already reorganizing the Mediterranean; one thinks not only of recent European initiatives around sustainable energy in the North of Africa, such as the Desertec project, but also the forced displacements of people toward the magnetic attractor of the European coastline. In the following essay a series of episodes chart the nascent formation of one of these problems: the nexus formed by climate, climate science, migration from the Sahel, and policing in the Mediterranean. If this is a history in the Mediterranean, rather than of the Mediterranean (to use the distinction made by Horden and Purcell), it is only insofar as the problematique that links these diverse elements — though it finds its locus in the sea — radiates out to the Sub-Sahara, to Brussels and Warsaw, Tripoli and Lampedusa.

The World Dies from the North

"... the desert is one of the faces of the Mediterranean."[8]
In his 1989 book, *Famine That Kills: Darfur, Sudan,* Alex de Waal begins by posing a question: How to define the concept of famine? Should one abide by its common English usage, famine would describe a condition of starvation leading to "widespread death."[9] For the people of Darfur, famine takes on a more nuanced sense. Most notably, African definitions of famine refer to lived experiences; they distinguish between different effects, such as a scarcity or the erosion of social bonds, but they do not refer to starvation or to mortality, nor do they appeal to metrics, statistics, or other quantifiable modes of description.

De Waal refers to Amartya Sen's well-known definition of famine as not having enough food to eat, rather than there not being enough food to eat. By making a distinction such as this, Sen lowers the threshold at which famine can be said to occur such that it begins to appear more frequently. This redefinition politicizes the concept of famine in important ways, suggesting that famine is a problem of access and not only availability. In Darfur each famine is remembered by a unique name that often refers to the lived experience produced by the event, such as the shortage of grain, the necessity of eating wild rather than cultivated foods, or conditions of destitution and hunger, reinforcing the sense of famine's historical singularity.

The names of famine often refer to conditions of social breakdown — the suspension of community and the promise of its reformulation at some point in the future. De Waal notes an important distinction in naming deadly famines that do not merit a separate name but are simply appended with the term "famine that kills" or *maja'a al gatala.*

6 P.J. Crutzen, "Geology of Mankind," *Nature* 415 (2002): 23.

7 Lest this be understood as a reinscription of man at the center of the world — a re-anthropomorphizing of the earth itself — consider how far it is from previous cosmologies such as those of microcosmic and macrocosmic reflection. After Copernicus, Darwin, and Freud, the idea of the anthropocene deals yet another blow to man's narcissistic position at the center of the universe, since what is granted agency here is no longer a subject, not even a species but rather a population. The question then is to what extent the conception of freedom as something possessed by a subject has anything to do with the kind of untethered, rampant appetite expressed by 7 billion human animals.

8 Braudel, *The Mediterranean and the Mediterranean World in the Age of Phillip II,* 24.

9 A. De Waal, *Famine That Kills: Darfur, Sudan* (New York: Oxford University Press, 2005).

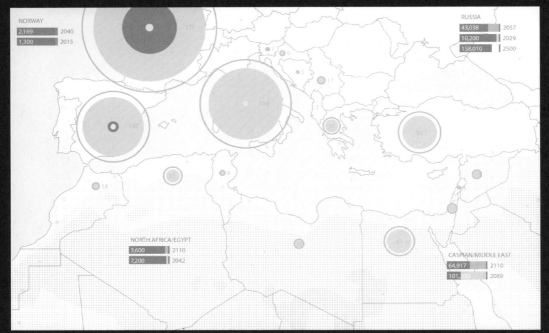

The Mediterranean, A New Imaginary

Energy resources projected. This map shows the disparity between energy demand on one hand and solar energy supply on the other. Once again North Africa beckons as a source of energy as various European initatives begin to explore the possibility of solar energy arrays that might caputre the abundant levels of insolation in the Sahara. Pilot projects like Desertec in Tunisia represent the forefront of this new drive toward clean energy soures for European countries.

He concludes that this state marks a crossing "where naming breaks down" and, more critically perhaps, that "the destitution and social breakdown it causes are more significant for the sufferers than the fact of mortality."[10] Further, he cautions against taking this practice for an implicit acknowledgment of mortality since "rural people in Darfur do not think in terms of a death *rate* at all. It is a notion that presupposes a statistical mode of thinking that is not generally found. Rural people do not think of the populace as an anonymous aggregate population, but as a moral community."[11]

The causes of famine and civil conflict are not easily disentangled. However, there is little doubt that across the Sahel a combination of weak states, poor institutions, criminal acts, and humanitarian intervention — especially the ambivalent effects of the United Nations Responsibility to Protect, or R2P initiative — have all been exacerbated by an ongoing environmental crisis. The desertification of the Sahel has been accelerating since the 1970s, and increased population growth, which puts pressure on often unsuitable land, has put more bodies at risk. Combined with lower levels of precipitation, this has caused a drying of the Sahel, leading to prolonged water stress and reduced crop yields. Periods of extreme drought in the 1980s and 1990s placed further pressure on the precarious livelihoods of its inhabitants. As the Sahara continues its expansion down into previously fertile landscapes, the deadly march is perfectly captured by the Zaghawa people of Chad and Sudan who say that "the world dies from the north."[12]

The Anthropocenic Equator

"Back then, the challenge was to stop a particular action. Now, the challenge is to inspire a particular action."[13]

As of January 2013, almost all eight situations before the International Criminal Court (ICC) involve African nations between the 20th northern and 10th southern parallel. Investigations in Uganda, Democratic Republic of Congo, Central African Republic, Darfur-Sudan, Kenya, Libya, Cote d'Ivoire, and now Mali are confined to a narrow equatorial belt on a single continent, which U.S. security experts now refer to as a "corridor of terror". Hyperbole aside, this anthropocenic equator plays a critical geopolitical role in Africa's resource security and independence, which will depend on a more autonomous management of oil and gas reserves according to a nationalized model.

Within the Western media, war crimes, crimes against humanity, and a legacy of camps, displaced persons, and famines reinforces the view of the Sahel as a space synonymous with violence and suffering. The perception of a landscape characterized by either warlords, jihadists, and child soldiers on one side, or drought- stricken adults and starving children on the other, leaves the Sahel in a bind, caught in a cliché of either hyper-aggressivity (genocide, terror, and massacre) or hyper-passivity (malnutrition and underdevelopment). While there is no doubt that serious issues are at stake and that many of them demand attention it is no less important to note that the very constitution of the crisis state forms an integral element within the neo-colonial machinery and its management of foreign territories. The south is always posed as 'not-yet' modern, 'not-yet' complete project. It is framed in terms of its underdevelopment, described in terms of stagnations and pathologies which cannot but elicit sympathetic aid programs and rescue packages from the ever vigilant North.[14]

The question that should be asked instead, is how to think the South according to its own terms, to dignify it as a subject of thought, as Franco Cassano suggests: "releasing modernity from its responsibil-

10   Ibid., 75.

11   Ibid.

12   A. De Waal, "Is Climate Change the Culprit for Darfur?" London, Royal African Society, http://africanarguments. org/2007/06/25/is-climate-change-the-culprit-for-darfur See also: "An estimated 50 to 200 km southward shift of the boundary between semi-desert and desert has occurred since rainfall and vegetation records were first held in the 1930s. This boundary is expected to continue to move southwards due to declining precipitation. i.e. remaining semi-desert and low rainfall savannah on sand, which represent some 25 percent of Sudan's agricultural land, are at considerable risk of further desertification. This is forecast to lead to a significant drop (approximately 20 percent) in food production. In addition, there is mounting evidence that the decline in precipitation due to regional climate change has been a significant stress factor on pastoralist societies — particularly in Darfur and Kordofan — and has thereby contributed to conflict." UNEP, *Sudan Post-Conflict Assessment* (Nairobi: United Nations Environmental Program, 2007), 9.

13   General Gordon R. Sullivan USA (Ret) Chairman, Military Advisory Board, Former Chief of Staff U.S Army, describing the shift from Cold War politics to Climate War preemption in G.R. Sullivan, F. Bowman, L. Farrell Jr., P.G. Gaffney Ii, P.J. Kern, J. Lopez, D. Piling, J.W. Prueher, J. Truly, C.F. Wald, and A.C. Zinni, *National Security and the Threat of Climate Change* (Virginia: Security and Climate CNA.org., 2007), 10.

14   F. Cassano, *For a Thought from the South* in *Southern Thought* (New York: Fordham University Press, 2012): 1

[30]

Niger, Tenere Desert.
There is constant traffic along the trans-saharan desert path leading to Libya from Niger — making the journey are convoys carrying hundreds of migrants stopping at various desert oasis on their way to one of the Libyan cities.

[34]

Libya, Sallum.
Migrants from Chad, and others subsaharan countries, are stranded on the Egyptian border. They are waiting for their government's official decision as to whether they are going to be taken to safety outside Libya.

[14]

Niger, Turawet Oasis.
'Every 2-3 weeks the villagers welcome between 3000 and 4000 people on their way to Dirkou. The migrants do not get off the trucks, preferring to guard their luggage from potential thieves, but some of them celebrate their success in setting off. The villagers have set up a few stands where food and water can be bought. 100 km further on the convoy will be abandoned by the soldiers, and each truck will travel onwards independently."

[43]

Mediterranean.
Migrants from Tunisia making a crossing from Libya in an inflatable Zodiac, this photo is taken in the vicinity of the Italian island Lampudesa.

ities and considering it always and only as a solution leads to two complementary mistakes that build on each other. On one hand, one relies on a therapy that often aggravates the pathologies; on the other, one suppresses from the state the possibility of reversing the relationship: not to think the South in the light of modernity, but to think modernity in the light of the South. " The paternalistic Northern episteme has concrete material effects: for decades, it was assumed that desertification in the Sahel was primarily caused by poor farming practices — that local farmers could not adapt to changing environmental conditions as quickly as they needed to, leading to overgrazing, deforestation, and erosion. Similarly, military conflict was and still is too often seen as a simple by-product of ethnic and religious differences, the manifestation of ancient hatreds and tribal rivalries. More recently, however, another factor has come to play an increasing role in this complex matrix of alleged causes. In a 2007 *Washington Post* article, U.N. Secretary-General Ban Ki-moon proposed anthropogenic climate change as a contributor:

> **Two decades ago, the rains in southern Sudan began to fail. According to U.N. statistics, average precipitation has declined some 40 percent since the early 1980s. Scientists at first considered this to be an unfortunate quirk of nature. But subsequent investigation found that it coincided with a rise in temperatures of the Indian Ocean, disrupting seasonal monsoons. This suggests that the drying of sub-Saharan Africa derives, to some degree, from man-made global warming.[15]**

15   B.K. Moon, "A Climate Culprit in Darfur," *Washington Post*, 2007.

The Sahel is marked by a high variability of annual precipitation and a long-term trend pointing to successively dryer conditions. Though it is important to avoid excessive environmental determinism, it is certain that heightened competition over shrinking plots of productive land have worked in concert with ongoing institutional and governmental failures to exacerbate conflicts. Tensions between pastoralists and farmers over dwindling resources in conditions of desertification and water stress have brought different groups and their conflicting territorial practices into intimate proximity. As with the different conceptions of famine noted above, in the case of Fur villagers and Arab pastoralists, one finds radically different understandings of, and relationships to, the earth.
The former conceive of territory according to a clear north-south striation forming a gradient of decreasing nomadism as one moves away from the desert, while in the latter spatial practices follow a fluid distribution of opportunity that knows no clear territorial demarcation.

These differences are not essentialist traits; in fact, cultural markers such as Arab or African are fixed to livelihoods more than ethnicity. What is happening in Darfur then is a conflict between different ways of existing in the world as multiple spatial and cognitive practices superimpose on the same territory. As the Sahara colonizes the Sahel, it moves this anthropocenic equator southward, dragging different spatial and cultural traditions along with it and intermixing them. In a condition of scarcity and within an ever-narrowing bandwidth of viability, the peoples of the Sahel are facing impossible pressures to coexist. In this context, the Mediterranean beckons as one horizon of escape.

The Political Management of Movement

> **"...the refugee throws into crisis the original fiction of sovereignty."[16]**

16   G. Agamben, "We Refugees," *Symposium* 49: 114–119, 119.

Refugee movements intensify during periods of drought. In Africa, drought is thought to be partially responsible for the long-term pattern of urbanization that the continent is experiencing. These movements and their environmental triggers are not exactly recent phenomena, however, nor does their renewed intensity signal a fall from some prior Edenic state of coexistence; the Sahel has always been characterized by migratory patterns that have followed resources and environmental transformation across longer and shorter terms. From the northward migrations out of the Sahara toward the Nile and Levant during the Holocene, to annual routes of herders that follow the rains and pasture, the movement of people through the Sahel and across the Sahara has a long and rich history that has — since the great drying of the Sahara thousands of years ago — been increasingly organized by the coastal area to its distant north and the cities to its south.[17]

Poor environments and social stress do not simply lead to migration, such that one term is always the precursor to the next. Disentangling the factors that lead to migration to adjudicate on migrant status, as either forced or displaced, is a fraught process through which no clear line can be drawn. Self-identification of refugee status is not enough; claims are routinely and aggressively scrutinized at any one of the many control points that extend throughout European and African territory. The veracity of testimony is one basis on which these claims will be assessed; more recently, however, in the case of dangers posed to larger populations by environmental destruction, mathematical and scientific modes of knowing have come to complement human ones. The mobilization of science and especially advanced forms of statistical analysis occupy an increasingly prominent position within the biopolitical space of environmental violation. Though they do not touch the body directly, environmental violations affect the milieu that bodies depend upon for their survival. However, because chains of cause (violation) and effect (bodies) are diffused through atmospheres, landscapes, and seas, they depend on scientific forms of knowing such as simulation to make anomalies in environmental patterning visible; these anomalies can then help point to possible causes for the violation. Within international law, evidence in the form of human testimony followed on from the aftermath of World War II, building on definitions of genocide and crimes against humanity used in trials such as that of Adolf Eichmann.[18] But what happens to the era of the witness when a crime is no longer visible to unmediated human perception? In the case of climate change, climate justice, and its future claimants around the shore of the Mediterranean, will the era of the model come to replace the era of testimony in adjudicating humanitarian claims?

The Public Use of Numbers

"Democratic power is calculated power, and numbers are intrinsic to the forms of justification that give legitimacy to political power in democracies."[19]
Within biopolitics, the problem of how to most efficiently manage problems that might beset a group of people requires the constitution of these people as population, that is, modelling them as a statistical aggregate. A certain kind of truth is constructed through the frame of an empirical project that conceives of life in terms of calculable variables, so that health, mortality, or education might be counted, secured, and made available for remedial management.[20] In cases of anthropogenic environmental destruction, the definition of a pre-violation state is difficult to ascertain — equilibrium in nature being purely relative — and so a further problem arises: How to construct a baseline or normative standard from which deviation can be measured? These reference coordinates must be produced to construct a threshold between the normal and the pathological, the acceptable and the excessive — that is, an idea of proportionality.

17 Around 5000 B.C. there is large-scale exodus from the Sahara and its primarily savannah-like conditions toward the Nile and its delta. See also R. Kuper and S. Kropelin, "Climate-Controlled Holocene Occupation in the Sahara: Motor of Africa's Evolution," *Science* 313: 803–807. It is important not to flatten this rich history of movement into simple categories since not all movements can be easily defined as either forced or voluntary, nor they can easily be fit within clear time frames, since many have evolved as adaptations to the plasticity of the climate in the Sahel. Moreover, differences both within and between terms like displacement, migration, and refugee are tactically adopted and refused, in that they form the frame through which political claims can be made. Because the political management of movement depends on these terms, the legal thresholds that distinguish between the practices and therefore the actors involved become heavily contested.

18 For a discussion on shifting ideas of testimony, see T. Keenan and E. Weizman, *Mengele's Skull: The Advent of a Forensic Aesthetics* (Frankfurt: Sterberg Press, 2012).

19 N. Rose, "Governing by Numbers: Figuring Out Democracy," *Accounting Organizations and Society* 16 (1991): 673–692, 675.

20 T. Keenan, "Publicity and Indifference: Media, Surveillance, "Humanitarian Intervention," in T.Y. Levin, U. Frohne, and P. Weibel, eds., *CTRL [SPACE]: Rhetorics of Surveillance from Bentham to Big Brother* (Cambridge, MA: MIT Press, 2002).

The location of this threshold is established through the constitution of a historical series, such that violence becomes immanent to a field of other violations. It is fixed in place, even if only temporarily, via law — say through conventions and treaties that define and set limits on acceptable levels of violence and destruction. Because this threshold works as a trigger to action, be it military, humanitarian, or media-related — the struggle over the perception of a crisis becomes an important political arena as competing actors work to make events visible in the world, convey existing suffering or its future possibility, and avert imminent threat by mobilizing some form of response.[21]

Scale is one of the terrains on which arguments for intervention are made; this disaster is more dangerous than Chernobyl, smaller than Fukushima, larger than Bhopal; these claims must always satisfy a desire for comparison according to a numeric structure of "this many killed, and this many injured" such as in the dispute over refugee deaths in the Mediterranean Sea during the recent conflict in Libya. Precisely because numbers are able to mobilize action, they are regularly abused, as if a correlation between a specific calculus of risk would directly translate into its remedy. Rony Brauman of Médecins Sans Frontières has described this as the "public use of numbers" whereby mortality figures, because they enter into a competition with other claims, suffer from continual inflation, deflation, exaggeration, and propogandisation.[22] However, as Patrick Ball, a researcher for the Human Rights Data Analysis Group, has pointed out, today what is more critical in the modelling of violations in populations is not the numbers themselves but rather their patterning, a specific distribution in time and in space that reveals information about the actions of perpetrators.[23] In this case, the mathematical model enables violations to be deduced, and although Ball's work relates specifically to genocide, the idea that statistical techniques can be used to detect the causes of climate change plays an important role in research on climate attribution and the 'finger printing' of carbon emission. The day an anomalous patterning of temperature in a climate simulation first 'testifies' in a case of environmental violation or is used to mobilize an indigenous claim within a resources dispute is drawing near. When this day arrives, access to science will emerge as a political imperative of the highest order.

Securing Freedom

"Tomorrow Europe might no longer be Europe."[24]
In 2007, soon to be French President Nicolas Sarkozy announced a new vision for the Mediterranean intended to improve on the perceived failures of the Euro-Med Partnership (EMP) and build on the unrealized potential of the Barcelona Declaration signed thirteen years prior. The proposal for the Union for the Mediterranean (UfM) arrives as the latest in a series of region-building exercises and trade agreements brokered by European, Arab, and African partners. In many ways Sarkozy's proposal for a Mediterranean union along the lines of the EU can be understood as a geopolitical stratagem, a hedge against German control of access to Eastern Europe by repositioning France in its historical role as gatekeeper to North Africa.

Despite its utopian promise, there is little doubt that what prompted this iteration of institution building across the Mediterranean was the securitization of the sea. The European agency Frontex now assumes responsibility for controlling the shared European border. Established in 2005 and working in cooperation with EU member states, it helps coordinate 500 million annual crossings at the 1,792 designated EU border crossing points. In their 2011 report *Futures of Borders: A For-*

21   For a discussion of the fluctuating claims around Darfur in the media, see M. Mamdani, "The Politics of Naming: Genocide, Civil War, Insurgency," *London Review of Books* 29 (2007): 5–8. Also see F. Weissman, "Humanitarian Dilemmas in Darfur," *CRASH Fondation Médecins Sans Frontières.*

22   In conversation with the author, London, 7–8 December 2012.

23   Col. Qaddafi as reported by N. Squires, "Gaddafi: Europe Will 'Turn Black' Unless EU Pays Libya £4bn a Year, London, *Telegraph,* 2010.

24   D. G. ad Ariely, R. Warnes, D. J. Bijak, and R. Landesman, *Futures of Borders: A Forward Study of European Border Checks* (Warsaw: Liron Systems Ltd for Frontex, 2011).

ward Study of European Border Checks, the agency proposes a series of scenarios as a way of rehearsing possible border conditions and the responses they might demand.[25] The "extreme wild card" scenario in the report describes a condition in which the Euro has collapsed, leading to the exit of member states, mass displacements of people due to climate change, and increased civil unrest in Sub-Saharan Africa, placing excessive pressure on EU border controls, which subsequently begin to collapse. The report concludes by proposing that preparations for emergency situations and mass influxes should begin in earnest, suggesting that the "Arab Spring" might have already made this wild card a reality by placing intense pressure on processing facilities such as those on the island of Lampedusa.

From about 31 B.C., Roman rule of the Mediterranean littoral was as total as its right to intervene in the sea was unquestioned. Despite this, Roman law continued to distinguish between the status of the waterway and the lands that surrounded it:

"The Romans claimed imperium — the right to command — in the Mediterranean, but they did not claim dominium — the power to own, use, enjoy, and dispose of property."[26]

Today, the European border network extends not only through the Mediterranean and around the EU territory but also deep into North and Sub-Saharan Africa, where it is conceptualized through the idea of "pre-frontiering," a kind of pre-cognition of illegality materialized through treaties and cooperative security frameworks.[27] This "'forward defense system" means that the north-south imaginary of a border must be reconceptualized. It now exists as a network of policing, surveillance, and management extending across the surface of the earth and sea, from the arctic to the equator, but also increasingly as a thick vertical depth, since it also includes electromagnetic detection systems and orbiting satellites. This infrastructure attempts to shift the burden of policing to non-EU states such as Libya, Algeria and Morocco in order to limit the legal obligations conferred to claimants within sovereign European territory.

In 1999, at a summit for the Organization of African Unity, Colonel Qadhafi initiated a policy of unrestricted movement in Libya for anyone holding an African passport. Qadhafi's decision to reorient the nation's geopolitical attention to the south can be read in two ways, first as giving a renewed impetus to the promising idea of an African Union, or more cynically as a desire to access a cheap labor pool of southern workers. Moreover, by mid-2000 Libya, at both an informal and formal level, increasingly began to operate as a staging post for African migrants wishing to enter Europe. This situation reached a climax during the NATO-backed campaign against Qadhafi in February 2011, when he strategically played on European anxieties about the creation of a "black Europe" by deliberately intensifying Sub-Saharan migrant transit to Europe and effectively weaponizing the traffic in refugees, leading to an undetermined number of deaths at sea.[28]

Desert Forensics

"On an idealized view, high-quality scientific knowledge should and will automatically command policy choices, limiting disputes by partisans to issues of implementation."[29]

There is a growing attempt to pose the question of climate change at a scale that allows for a clearer picture of impacts on specific environments and the communities that make their livelihood from them. While climate modeling has long entered into the space of politics, it has done so primarily in terms of policy disputes, and global models of average

25   P.E. Steinberg, *The Social Construction of the Ocean* (Cambridge: Cambridge University Press, 2001), 64.

26   "Cooperation between Frontex and Third Countries is carried out in the context of the overall EU security strategy. This clearly establishes that border control-related activities begin in the countries of origin or transit and continue with cooperation on both sides of the external border. These are followed by further measures implemented at the external borders, as well as inside the territory of the EU Member States." See A. Lodge, *Beyond the Frontiers. Frontex: The First Five Years* (Warsaw: Frontex, 2010).

27   See C. Heller and L. Pezzani, *Forensic Oceanography* (London, Forensic Architecture European Research Council Project, 2012), http://www.forensic-architecture.org/investigations/forensic-oceanography/. Also see C. Heler, L. Pezzani, and S. Studio, *Forensic Oceanography: Report on the 'Left-to-Die Boat'*. (London: Centre for Research Architecture, Goldsmiths), http://www.guardian.co.uk/science/interactive/2012/apr/11/left-to-die-report

28   P.N. Edwards, *A Vast Machine: Computer Models, Climate Data, and the Politics of Global Warming* (Cambridge, MA: MIT Press, 2010).

29   "Given the gaps in our understanding of the large-scale dynamics of climate that are manifest in our inability to explain the uncertainty in projections of future change, a detailed, downscaled analysis is premature. However, we anticipate that projections on regional, rather than continental, scale, and of other characteristics of rainfall besides the seasonal total (such as its intraseasonal variability, distribution of frequency and intensity of events, and monsoon onset date) will become more useful as our outlook on the future becomes less certain. Translating a climate outlook on the continental scale — say, for example, a continent-wide drying — into information useful at the regional scale — say, for example, a postponement of the West African monsoon onset, or a change in duration or frequency of dry spells within the southern African wet season — remains a challenge that will be met when scientific capacity is integrated with stakeholders' demand for climate information." A. Giannini, M. Biasutti, I.M. Held, and A.H. Sobel *A Global Perspective on African Climate* (New York: International Research Institute for Climate and Society, Earth Institute at Columbia University, 2007), .3.

temperature increase, since higher-resolution or fine-scaled models face both physical and computational challenges.[30] Yet it is precisely the resolution of the model that allows results to be mobilized within political arguments — or not. The aesthetic aspect of visualizations produced by these climate models is often derided by scientists who see them as mere illustrations of more fundamental calculations; after all, climate policy is almost always an argument over numbers rather than images. And yet the history of scientific image making continues to play an important role in understanding the behavior of complex phenomena both inside and outside the scientific domain.[31] Climate visualizations can now simulate the mixing of Sea Surface Temperatures (SST) in the Inter-tropical Convergence Zone (ITCZ), aerosol dispersion across the Mediterranean and Africa, and changes in carbon absorption in the Sahel. What these visualizations reveal, however, is more than kaleido-scopic gradients of color; they expose the dynamic and differentiated form of climate impact, the dramatic reorganization of resource avail-ability, biological viability, and human fortune — in short, they reveal a new kind of geopolitical map.

As Thomas Keenan suggests in regard to humanitarian action and its tendency toward the mobilization of shame, "No image speaks for itself, let alone… to our capacity for reason." If scientific images of climate change are to be used as the basis of political claims by groups currently marginalized from climate negotiations (like the G77 group of 120 developing nations) they will require translators, figures that can make the images speak — a qualification that might rest with all those subject to climate politics — or, today, in what amounts to the same thing, all those subject to the climate.[32] This essay is a first gesture toward this kind of translation, constructing the kind of series that might be necessary to imagine a political sphere in which the animate and inanimate intermingle, and though it began with an account of drought in the Sahel in truth it has no origin, only a relay of forces that might be entered into at any point. Foremost among these is the action of the climate itself, especially the complex physical and chemical effects that regulate precipitation in sub-Saharan Africa.

As the earth heats, it releases latent heat, usually as moisture that, if lighter than the surrounding air, rises to the troposphere. Heavier fluid precipitates to the surface in a process called deep convection. This process characterizes the earth's climate around the tropics. The density of the moist air being lifted off the surface must be low enough to achieve buoyancy, and so it depends on condensation induced by turbulence to lose some of its fluid mass. In this sense, the convection process is dependent on near-surface and higher-atmosphere tem-peratures. Also critical, especially in the tropics, is the original supply of moisture to the air column. In Africa, this process gives rise to the heavy rain-belt that "straddles the equator near the equinoxes, in April and October, and moves off into the summer hemisphere otherwise, to northern Africa in July and to southern Africa in January."[33]

The ITCZ describes an area of fertile climatic instability where northeast and southeast trade winds interact, forming powerful convec-tion currents in the atmosphere. The ITCZ plays an important role in reg-ulating the intensity of the African monsoon, which depends on the pow-erful temperature and moisture gradients that form between the West African land mass and the Atlantic Ocean. The sensitivity of this relation and the key role played by SST has been the subject of a series of landmark papers published by Alesandra Giannini at The Earth Institute at Columbia University in collaboration with colleagues in other climate research centers in the United States. This research reverses decades of orthodoxy that argued that local anthropogenic transformation (i.e., African agricultural practice) was responsible for desertification.[34] The

30   See L. Daston and P. Galison, *Objectivity* (New York: Zone Books, 2010). Daston and Galison leave out a recent though incredibly important regime of image making, namely simulation, though in many ways it could fall under the cate-gory of structural objectivity they establish. What simulation attempts to capture is something like truth to nature — but the truth of nature's deep causal structure rather than na-ture's appearance. This structure is apprehended and repro-duced mathematically. It too depends on a new relationship between the individual and the series, whereby populations of interacting agents, whether they are organisms existing within an ecosystem, carbon compounds interacting with the atmosphere, or chemicals leeching into a water system, are mathematically described so that their simulated interac-tions reproduce observations.

31   "We cannot, at least not without repeating what seems to me to be the basic strategic error here, not expect the unexpected — we cannot count on the obviousness of the image, fall for the conceit that information leads ineluctably to actions adequate to the compulsion of the image, precise-ly because images are so important. There is no compulsion, only interpretation and reinscription, and the image dictates nothing." Levin, Thomas Y., Ursula Frohne, Peter Weibel, and Zentrum feur Kunst und Medientechnologie Karlsruhe. *CTRL (SPACE) : Rhetorics of Surveillance from Bentham to Big Brother.* Karlsruhe. Cambridge, Mass.: ZKM Center for Art and Media; MIT Press, 2002.

32   Giannini, Biasutti, Held, and Sobel, *A Global Perspec-tive on African Climate.* Also see A. Giannini, *Mechanisms of Climate Change in the Semiarid African Sahel: The Local View* (New York: International Research Institute for Climate and Society, The Earth Institute at Columbia University, 2010).

33   The decades of drought that struck the Sahel in the 1970s were often blamed on local anthropogenic forces, mainly poor farming practices which, once they had led to desertification, were thought to leading to the United Nations Convention on desertification held in Nairobi in 1977. "Afri-can environmental change is often interpreted as a regional phenomenon with local anthropogenic causes and poten-tially global effects. On the one hand, the local causes are commonly ascribed to the mismanagement of limited natural resources under the ever-increasing pressure of a growing, vulnerable population, while external causes of degrada-tion such as remotely forced drought are underplayed. A perverse feedback loop in which the poorest of the poor deprive themselves by impoverishing the environment they depend on for their livelihoods is often simplistically invoked, despite much literature that expands on the complexity of the environmental degradation-poverty nexus." Giannini, *Mechanisms of Climate Change,* 19.

34   "Another Met Office study analyses how a 4C rise would differ from a 2C rise, concluding that threats to water supplies are far worse, in particular in southern Europe and north Africa, where regional temperatures would rise 6–8C. The 4C world would also see enhanced warming over most of the US, Canada and northern Asia." D. Carrington, "Climate Change Scientists Warn of 4C Global Temperature Rise," London, *The Guardian,* 2010.

work concludes by proposing that persistent drought in the Sahel is not local in origin but rather the result of an increase in SST. In other words, it is only a local manifestation of a problem that is global in scope. In a speculative coda to the research, the authors ask whether the change in SST can be attributed to the increase in greenhouse gas and aerosol emissions in the Northern Hemisphere, and though the results of this proposition are far from conclusive, early indications suggest the strong possibility of a correlation between emission in the North and drought in the South.

In the Sahel, a global average temperature increase of two degrees has been argued by some to translate into a 3.5–4 degree increase, causing widespread desertification and extreme drought, though some parts of the continent may also experience a smaller increase and more rather than less rainfall.[35] As some reports have pointed out, the impact of water stress, reduced crop yield, and new disease vectors could lead to an additional 300,000 deaths on the continent per year in the immediate term, with double that number in the coming years.[36] This does not include the exacerbation of existing conflicts and refugee movements due to war and famine.

The image of an impartial, apolitical science presenting evidence to politicians who then 'corrupt' the process of implementation is a myth. What is at stake within every scientific claim is not its objectivity — but rather its relevance, that is its imbrication within a system of meanings and actions in a larger non-scientific field. In this respect, every scientific model will propose a unique distribution of relevant and irrelevant points, make public its priorities but also harbor its own silences and elisions. The question of scale with regards to climate modelling is a paradigmatic example of this - posing an argument in global terms as an average mystifies the reorganization of temperature and its effect on real populations. What is concealed behind the scientific expertise on climate and the effort to agree on the appropriate level of global temperature increase within forums like COP is the direct dependence of first-world GDP on carbon capacity. Within each degree of average increase, billions of dollars are congealed.[37] In this regard, fossilized within every scientific model and dispute over average temperature increase is a nonscientific ethico-political paradigm. Inside every degree Celsius, a new calculus of life and death is disguised.

The Growth of Our Means Makes All Ends Equal

"The civilian, too, is an invention of recent date."[38]
Currently there are four Geneva Conventions and three Geneva Protocols; together with the Hague Conventions, these 559 articles compromise the main body of humanitarian law regulating armed combat. There are two main principles enshrined in these codes: that military action should be proportionate to strategic objectives, and that military force should discriminate between combatants and noncombatants.

In 1991, the Gulf War prompted a reconsideration of these codes in light of the unprecedented scale of damage caused by the detonation of almost 600 Kuwaiti wellheads. For every day that the fires burned, they released ten times more oil-related pollutants then the daily industrial output of the United States.[39] In this comparative fact lies an interesting equation, a certain kind of equivalence between war and peace, captured well by Michel Serres when he states: "Our peacetime economic relations, working slowly and continuously, produce the same results as would a short global conflict, as if war no longer belonged to soldiers alone now that it is prepared and waged with devices as scientific as those used by civilians in research and industry. Through a kind

35 A. C. Revkin, "Forum Says Climate Shift Brings Deaths," *New York Times,* 2009.

36 It is precisely this political background to the apparent impartiality of the scientific enterprise that is obscured by references to technical expertise, Edwards's view is typical of this conception: "So making knowledge work means getting people to trust it — to buy it on credit as it were, where the credit belongs to an authority they are willing to believe. For that you need representatives: experts from all over, whose presence provides a symbolic guarantee that the knowledge works from many local perspectives, not just from the perspectives of the centers of power. You may also need another type of representative: not an expert but a political ambassador to serve as a watchdog against the corruption of the political process by partisan interest. Second, you have to distribute the knowledge you create around the world. Here the two types of representatives can serve you well, connecting you with local experts and spreading your knowledge to a broader local public." Edwards, *A Vast Machine* Press, 397.
Idealized or not, it makes little difference, in that Edwards has already framed science in terms of its quality, that is, its veracity and credibility, when in fact these qualities are not the ones in question. In positing "good science" as a natural vector for decision-making, Edwards implies that "bad science" would be unfit for use in policy because of its unreliability. What is in question here is precisely the opposite, less the credibility of science vis-à-vis science and more the relevance of science vis-à-vis politics. In framing this debate as impartial advocates versus partisans, Edwards exemplifies the misconception of partiality as the "corrupter" of impartial science, where partiality is the realm of politics and objectivity is the realm of science. The models used by climate scientists to explicate the ambiguity of the material world can be understood in purely scientific terms, but only at the expense of unmeshing the models from the political and economic forces in which they are installed and called on to work for. By locating these models against the milieu of conflicts and negotiations that characterize the struggle over global carbon capacity, the objectivity of science can be reframed in the context of the political force field that scientific attention both enters into and forms.

37 D. Gregory, "The Death of the Civilian?" *Environment and Planning D: Society and Space* 24 (2006): 633–638, 633.

38 W. M. Arkin, D. Durrant, and M. Cherni, *On Impact: Modern Warfare and the Environment. A Case Study of the Gulf War* (London: Greenpeace, 1991).

39 M. Serres, *The Natural Contract (Le Contrat Naturel)* (Ann Arbor: University of Michigan Press (Editions Francois Bourin), 1995 [1992]), 42.

of threshold effect, the growth of our means makes all ends equal."[40]

In some sense then, for Serres what separates the state of war from the state of peace is a speed, a difference in pattern or intensity, a distribution in time and space. Five months after the conclusion of the Gulf War, the conveners of the first iteration of the Fifth Geneva Convention on the Protection of the Environment in Time of Armed Conflict proposed that the large-scale and long-term ecological effects of war demanded new laws that would strengthen the protection of the environment from the violence of future human conflict. The moment had arrived to introduce a new chapter in the body of humanitarian law dedicated to limiting the as yet unrestrained violence against nonhumans.[41]

But what is violence after nature? As Michel Serres states:"Now if there is a law, and thus a history, for subjective wars [that is war between human subjects], there is none for objective violence [violence against the material world], which is without limit or rule, and thus without history."[42]

This question might be reformulated in a number of ways: how to recognize new forms of violence in the absence of nature? If, under the anthropocene, violence takes a structural form that is difficult to recognize, what techniques might be used to make it visible, and how will law respond? Will Sub-Saharan refugees prosecute their European neighbors, even as they are prevented from crossing the Mediterranean Sea?

Currently issues of trans-boundary environmental rights exist in the absence of any authority with universal environmental jurisdiction and take place through private-law remedies such as litigation. While the 1992 Framework Convention on Climate Change can be understood in the context of the earlier 1979 Convention on Long-range Trans-boundary Air Pollution, and the Convention of the Protection of the Ozone Layer from 1985, none of these conventions is adequate to address the problem of greenhouse-gas emissions; unlike chlorofluorocarbons, carbon permeates deep into every corner of the global economy. Moreover, the conceptual difficulties posed to international law for defining something like the atmosphere are complex:

> **"The atmosphere is not a distinct category in international law. Because it consists of a fluctuating dynamic air mass, it cannot be equated with airspace, which, above land, is simply a spatial dimension subject to the sovereignty of the subjacent states. But this overlap with territorial sovereignty also means that the atmosphere cannot be treated as an area of common property beyond the jurisdiction of any state, comparable in this sense to the high seas."[43]**

Models of legal jurisdiction based on territorial sovereignty become both artificial and unworkable when used to deal with phenomena that obey no territorial limit. Because of the aforementioned disputes, the post-Kyoto period occurs outside of any binding agreements for regulating carbon emissions. In some way, the very moment at which international law discovers and begins to speak about nature, nature itself disappears. In its place, new and unfamiliar histories of anthropogenic violence are being written.

Is Darfur the first "ecological genocide"?[44] Is it possible to speak about genocide without intent, without even a direct contact between the victim and the perpetrator? The question is ambiguous to say the least, but it is an ambiguity that wholly reflects the objective ambiguity of the condition it finds itself in, what Paulo Tavares has beautifully described as the 'murkiness' of the earth.

So too with the strange complications of the contemporary Mediterranean, a space that no longer fits into neat spatial or temporal scales, or legal jurisdictions, less still into clear bodies of knowledge. The possibility that the emission of aerosols in the Northern Hemisphere

40   See P. Tavares and A. Lahoud, *Fifth Geneva Convention: Nature, Conflict and International Law in the Anthropocene* (London: Forensic Architecture European Research Council Project, 2012). Also see G. Plant, *Environmental Protection and the Law of War: A Fifth Geneva Convention on the Protection of the Environment in the Time of Armed Conflict* (London: John Wiley, 1994).

41   Serres, *The Natural Contract,* 11.

42   P. Birnie, A. Boyle, and C. Redgwell, *International Law and the Environment* (New York: Oxford University Press, 2009), 338.

43   Moon, "A Climate Culprit in Darfur."

44   For an opposing point of view on the future of the Sahara that repeats earlier arguments about the impact of local agricultural and land-use practices, see M. Claussen, *The Greening Desert* (Hamburg: Max Planck Institute for Meteorology, 2009).

changes sea-surface temperature, weakening the African monsoon and drying the Sahel, is very likely but still under conjecture.[45] That this drying exacerbates competition over resources, affecting communities undermined by poor government and abandoned by weak institutions, is not in doubt, nor is the chaos of violence and displacement that has ensued for more than three decades. As Sub-Saharan refugees enter the Mediterranean en route to Europe, they enter the most highly securitized waterway on earth, moving from south to north across an equator that divides those who are grievable from those who are not.[46]

What is the legal and ethical responsibility of the north if it is to be one day found guilty of transforming a distant southern environment? How will northerners greet the dispossessed that arrive on their shores?[47] Ethics has predominantly been understood as the domain of the proximate and the face-to-face, is it possible to imagine an ethics without this foundational encounter, beyond the proximity of the other? How would an ethics that answers to distant solicitations ground itself if not in proximate experience?

The Epoch of the Near and Far, of the Side-by-Side, of the Dispersed[48]

"The question I raise is this one: How and why were very different things in the world gathered together, characterized, analyzed, and treated?."[49]

The unconventional nature of a threat that "does not act as a single entity" in a specific point in space and time but instead manifests across a continuously shifting and multiplied set of spatio-temporal scales forces a reconceptualization of violence. In turn, a violence that is diffuse, that does not touch its object directly but is instead addressed to it through its milieu, invites a new kind of ethics and law.

The spectacular intensity of violence that took place when the Iraqi Army set Kuwaiti wellheads ablaze wreaked ecological havoc; some suggest that the intense emission of oil-related pollutants into the atmosphere delayed the onset of the Asian monsoon that year. In many ways, these kinds of environmental disasters are easy to comprehend, but what about their less visible manifestations? What about the conflict of climate negotiations concealed behind the public protocols of diplomacy or the scalar violence of a climate model used to adjudicate questions of temperature increase? What new conventions must be brought to bear upon forces that cannot distinguish between combatant or non-combatant and whose proportionality is drawn not from moral codes but instead from the laws of physics and chemical interaction?

The entangled action of climate brings near and far, small and large, weak and strong into contact in new and unforeseen ways. The action of trans-boundary impact and mitigation establishes unique difficulties for a model of law and a scale of negotiation premised either on the nation-state or principles of universality. What does the climate model mean in terms of a post-Westphalian model of the geopolitical border? Perhaps no longer the question of where to draw a line around a people — the Westphalian problem of territorial identity and sovereignty — but now the mathematical problem of climate modeling: How to simulate gradients of air columns and ocean currents? If law is to have any traction within this system, it will have to discover ways of carving out new jurisdictions and addressing the violations that take place within them?

Because the mechanics of climate form a complicated transport system, redistributing the effects of pollution according to a trans-boundary, nonlinear logic, the space of violation is separated from

45   See J. Butler, "Can One Lead a Good Life in a Bad Life?" Adorno Prize Lecture, *Radical Philosophy* 176 (2012): 9–18.

46   Though research suggests that most climate-induced displacements are short- rather than long-term, there is little doubt that the situation in the Sub-Sahara, with its complex matrix of factors, is increasingly driving trans-Saharan migration.

47   M. Foucault, "Of Other Spaces (Des Espaces Autres)," *Diacritics* 16 (1986 [1967]): 22–27.

48   M. Foucault, *Fearless Speech* (Los Angeles: Semiotext(e), 2001), 172.

49   Serres, *The Natural Contract,* 18.

the space of its repercussion. Those least responsible for carbon emission will be most susceptible to drought and rising sea levels. Locard's principle that "every contact leaves a trace' — the cornerstone of modern forensics — still applies, but with one impossible catch: the contact and the trace drift apart, carried away on ocean currents and diffused into the atmosphere. The earth's climate loosens the bond between cause and effect; it weakens the chain of custody and breaks the link between attribution, responsibility, and potentially, justice.

"The entire history of science consists of controlling and mastering this chain, of making consistent the highly improbable linkage of butterfly thought to hurricane effect. And the passage from this soft cause to these hard consequences precisely defines contemporary globalization."[50]
Reconnecting this bond through all of its complex diffusions and interweavings is a scientific, political, and legal demand. When this happens, the politics of the anthropocene can become intelligible.

A New Political Ecology of the Mediterranean

"Something in the world forces us to think." [51]
The coming epoch is characterized by two unique conditions: what appears to be action at a distance, and the conflict between incommensurable ways of knowing the world — differences between what can or should not be counted, said, described, or experienced that are not simply reconcilable. The conflation of scale and the deep inconsistency of our cognitive relation to the earth pose problems then, not just for conventional delimitations of space but also for conventional delimitations of knowledge. In a condition of multiple, sometimes incommensurate forms of knowledge production, questions of cognitive justice as described by Shiv Visvanathan and Boaventura de Sousa Santos become crucial. In the indigenous understanding of famine and territory, the medical calculus of mortality, the statistical patterning of genocide, the scale of mathematical models, the visualizations of sea-surface temperatures, the plurality of legal structures and their conflicting jurisdictions; in satellite photos registering changes in vegetation and tracking boats packed with migrants, one finds a set of epistemic frames and virtues that do not coincide to form a single world but rather superimpose like the split perspectives in a fractured mirror. So too with the various forums and spaces of discourse that this evidence enters into, and where it attempts to make itself heard; the hotel conference halls used for an ICC investigation or to host a climate summit, the press conferences, the rural councils, the courts and parliaments and academic institutions. Each ontological, epistemic, and discursive individuation — each phenomena, frame, and forum — creates its own distribution of relevant and irrelevant points, a unique order of what can be counted, what can be said, what can be made visible. Between them, like persistent dark matter, resides a space of difference. As each group assembles these distinct ways of knowing into arguments and political claims, do they make one the measure of the other forging a new hegemon in a fire of epistemic violence or instead, can they build spaces for their mutual co-existence?

Conclusion

The anthropocene marks the conjunction of human and natural history. In Braudel's Mediterranean, natural history unfolded in an almost eternal and timeless way, untroubled by human action. Now, however:

50   G. Deleuze, *Difference and Repetition (Différence et Répétition)* (New York, Paris: Columbia University Press, Gallimard, 1994 [1968])., 139.

51   Chakrabarty, "The Climate of History."

"In unwittingly destroying the artificial but time-honored distinction between natural and human histories, climate scientists posit that the human being has become something much larger than the simple biological agent that he or she always has been. Humans now wield a geological force."[52]

Today, when it comes to space, it is impossible to "carve at the natural joints," for within two or three steps, even the most isolated event will quickly lead from the Mediterranean to the Mediterranean world. If the expansion of the Sahara follows aerosol dispersion in Europe and America, the world dies from the north twice over, once with particles migrating south through the atmosphere, a second time with people fleeing north toward the sea. Where is the familiar Mediterranean in all of this, and what does it matter? More important than Mediterranean distinctiveness is the question of Mediterranean relevance?

The implications of this for design, architecture, and urbanism remain unclear, especially because they are bound to concepts of scale that emerged in response to an entirely different set of historical problems, problems that were more proximate and tangible, such as the development of anthropometry and its relation to Taylorism and later to Fordist production, or the mapping of disease and delinquency and its instrumentalization in urban reform. Nonetheless in each case, a specific problem gave birth to a form of knowledge that organised action in the world. The question that might be asked is what form of knowledge is required in a condition marked by scales that do not 'properly' belong together? To start with, the idea of the city must be situated in a far wider epistemic frame. Beyond totalizing notions of the global or the planetary, what is important on the contrary are the threads and traces that link disparate events around a problem. The question of scale then is something that should be understood as emerging from this network of linkages rather than something that pre-determines them.[53] In the Mediterranean cities of today it is less easy to find comfort in the charms of the vernacular, one finds instead the importation of Gulf development recipes to Algiers, the repeated evisceration of Lebanon's capital by petrodollars, a legacy of infrastructure around the Southern Italian coast abandoned by international labour markets. One also discovers European energy start-ups experimenting with solar plants in the Tunisian desert, heroin cartels managing international trade through ports in Marseille, black market economies of migrants on the streets of Athens salvaging steel that will be shipped around the world, in short any number of questions that might be dignified as 'a project', that might orient our collective labour, attention and intellect. In each case however, design will have to learn again how to operate between the scale of the detail and the scale of the earth.[54]

With regard to the questions of climate change, migration, and security proposed above, there are significant obstacles to be overcome since there is such a wide gap between the time signature of human experience and the time signature of the earth itself, between the scale of an individual's economic life and the endless horizon of capital and its environmental consequences.[55] Architecture and urbanism must attempt to create spaces in which these problems can be made visible and intelligible — rational spaces — but also spaces beyond any calculus and rationality, spaces able to mobilize an imaginary adequate to the age.

52   Further still, might not we dispense altogether with many of the scalar categories we use as short hands to describe the world such as the local, the urban, the regional or the global? Were they not so tied to governmental and legal structures with concrete effects the answer would surely be yes.

53   Until only recently perhaps, architectural education was still too tightly bound to a techno-optimistic vision of itself - a vestigial relic of older claims for disciplinary autonomy that must appear to us as anachronistic as medieval theological disputes about angels and pins. It was a surfeit of skill in search of a project and a problem to address. To paraphrase Heidegger, 'everyone was sharpening knives but there was nothing left to cut'.

54   Consider the vast time scales within climate science alone, periodic intervals that fall between 433,000 years and 1 nanosecond — the difference between one astronomical season and the time it takes for a wave of infrared light to complete a single oscillation. The spatial scales are no less complicated, encompassing dust particles in the atmosphere and polar jet streams.

55   Consider the vast time scales within climate science alone, periodic intervals that fall between 433,000 years and 1 nanosecond — the difference between one astronomical season and the time it takes for a wave of infrared light to complete a single oscillation. The spatial scales are no less complicated, encompassing dust particles in the atmosphere and polar jet streams.

Braudel's Donkey
Historians and the Mediterranean as a Political Project
Wouter Vanstiphout

"The wind of rebellion has swept across the Mediterranean from North Africa towards Southern Europe." So says Belgian political scientist Eric Toussaint, who writes for the left-wing blog International Viewpoint.[1] His assessment is far from unique — hundreds of similarly enthusiastic appraisals of the Arab Spring and the anti-austerity demonstrations of the past year can be found in books, magazines, blogs and Twitter accounts in Europe and the United States, by the superstars of neo-Marxism Mike Davis and David Harvey and their myriad fellow travelers.

It seems that the Mediterranean has become a zone of promise for the end of capitalism. The images of demonstrations by angry youths in Syntagma Square in Athens, Puerta del Sol in Madrid, Habib Bourguiba Avenue in Algiers, and Tahrir Square in Egypt blend into each other and become a single panorama of urban revolution. Everywhere we see the monumental squares dominated by huge bureaucratic buildings and normally congested traffic roundabouts filled with masses of flag-waving citizens, who set up camp and refuse to leave until their demands are met.

We have to ask, however, whether this blending into each other really does signify a common cause and really is the sign of a global urban revolution, or if this is not just a massive global bout of wishful thinking within the academic hives of left-wing thought and hipster activism. Both dons of the new left-wing urban theorists, the sulphurous Mike Davis and the prophet-like David Harvey, have written spirited and excited analyses of the events on both sides of the Mediterranean, identifying echoes of the revolutions of the nineteenth century.[2] Mike Davis calls the Arab Spring an Arabian 1848, Harvey the Occupy movement a twenty-first century Commune, repeating the events of Paris 1871, when the citizens seized the city from the imperial troops and declared them "Commons." Both try their utmost to link the regimes of Mubarak, Qaddafi, Ben Ali, and Assad to the same predatory capitalism that caused the financial crisis, which in turn caused the anger against Wall Street, which triggered Occupy, but which also led to the Euro crisis, which then caused the austerity measures by Southern European governments, which led to the demonstrations by the Indignados in Spain and their Greek brothers and sisters in Syntagma Square in Athens.

1 www.InternationalViewpoint.org, Eric Toussaint, Part III: From the Arab Spring to the Indignados Movement to Occupy Wall Street, The International Context of Global Outrage (in five parts), January 13, 2012, retrieved October 22, 2012.

2 Mike Davis, "Spring Confronts Winter, *New Left Review* 72, November–December 2011.

Wouter Vanstiphout is an architectural historian, founding partner of Crimson Architectural Historians in Rotterdam, and Professor of Design and Politics at the Faculty of Architecture of Delft Technical University in the Netherlands. As a practitioner with Crimson, he has directed the renewal of Hoogvliet, a Dutch industrial satellite town of Rotterdam. He has also advised municipalities, the national government, housing corporations, and project developers on matters relating to urban renewal, cultural heritage, and spatial and urban politics. In connection with this work, he has been appointed to the National Advisory Council on Infrastructure and the Environment.

Vanstiphout has curated several exhibitions including "The Banality of Good, Six Decades of New Towns, Architects, Money, and Politics" with Crimson Architectural Historians, for the 2012 Venice Architecture Biennale. During his time as Chair at Delft Technical University, he curated "Design as Politics" as part of the Fifth International Architecture Biennale of Rotterdam.

He has written and lectured extensively on postwar urbanism including urban renewal policies and projects, and more recently, on the relationship between urban riots and urban planning. He is a regular columnist for the British Architecture weekly *Building Design*, and recently edited *Design and Politics #6: Are We The World?*

While the Marxist left sees common cause in the demonstrations and riots on both sides of the sea, there is in fact an ironic contrast between the two. Occupy, the Indignados, and many of the other austerity and crisis-related demonstrations are fluid and flexible — not to say formless — in their agendas. Their one point of consensus seems to be the wholesale refutation of the politico-financial system of the World Bank, European Union, and the politically moderate coalition governments that are (mis)managing the crisis. The people on the streets in the Middle East, however, seem to ask for rights that to us have become undeniable, normal, banal even: democracy; one person, one vote; freedom of speech; good governance and the right to do business, get educated, and practice your religion. In other words, the things that they are demanding would seem utterly bourgeois to the theoreticians of the cross-Mediterranean urban revolt. To put it even more bluntly, they are demanding the benefits of free-market constitutional democracy, the very system that Occupy and many of the hard-left activists are trying to pull down.

But even if the revolts on either side of Mare Nostrum are moving in opposite directions, the idea that the two sides of the Mediterranean might be moving in each other's direction is a strong one, entertained by the hard left as well as the xenophobic and Euro-skeptical right. The political and financial crisis about the European Monetary Union has revealed a deep chasm between Northern and Southern Europe, with countries like France on the brink of belonging either to the "good" North or the "bad" South. Countries that are nearly defaulting on their debt obligations — Greece, Spain, Italy, Portugal — are lumped together pejoratively as the "garlic economies." The distrust between northern and southern countries has been fed by images of revolting youths burning cars on the streets of Athens — images easily associated and even confused with images of the Arab Spring. Xenophobic populist parties like that of Geert Wilders in the Netherlands have switched from aiming at the immigrants from North Africa to attacking the parasitical EU members Greece, Spain, and Italy. On a policy level, splitting Europe into a two-speed union is being discussed, even with two different currencies: the N-Euro and the S-Euro.

What unites the Mediterranean region at this point is that it produces most of the political, economic, and demographic issues that divide Europe, and even the world. It is the region where the European Union is breaking apart, the region the wave of immigration comes from, or passes through, fueling xenophobic populism; it is the region of the Israel-Palestine conflict, and of civil war in the Balkans and in Syria. In a purely negative way, it still is Mare Nostrum — Our Sea — that defines who we are and around which the world revolves. Only this time it does not distribute goods, knowledge, culture, and wealth, as it did in antiquity, but strife and controversy.

The divisive role of the region in the contemporary political imagination reinforces an old but controversial hypothesis that Europe and the Mediterranean are mutually exclusive as coherent regions. It was put forward from the early 1920s by the Belgian historian Henri Pirenne. In 1922 he published a legendary article called "Mahomet et Charlemagne" in which he pushed forward the beginning of the European Middle Ages from 426 AC, the year the Western Roman Empire collapsed, to 732, the battle of Tours, when Charles Martel stopped the conquering armies of the Muslim Umayyads, who in the century after Mohammed's death had conquered most of the Southern Mediterranean and large parts of Spain.[3]

For Pirenne, 732 marks the ending of a European economy that was still mostly based on the trade routes of the old Western Roman Empire, and that was until then oriented toward the south, as it had been for centuries. Cut off from the trade-based Mediterranean economy, Northern Europe went into a deep economic slump and fell back on agriculture as its main source of sustenance. The battle, however, built the foundation for the Carolingian empire that dominated Northwestern Europe for the next century. It was here, Pirenne claims, that the feudal system was developed, and the medieval civilization would grow. One of the most successful products of this originally agricultural and feudal medieval civilization was the city. Here the free burghers, capitalism, banking, insurance, democracy, philosophy, art, and most of all, a ruthless and limitless hunger for trade, were developed. It was these cities, as Pirenne stated in his seminal *Medieval Cities: Their Origins and the Revival of Trade* (1925), that would cause the comeback of Europe on the Mediterranean in the later Middle Ages. But in the end, as the "Pirenne thesis" goes, without having been cut off from the Mediterranean by the struggle with the Arab world, Europe would never have become what it is. Pirenne's version of events has been heavily criticized by historians since, but it does perfectly illustrate a conception of the Mediterranean Sea as a conflict zone, the dominion over which defines the identity and even the survival of its neigh-

3   Henri Pirenne, "Mahomet et Charlemagne," *Revue Belge de philologie et de l'histoire* 1 (1922), 77–86.

boring peoples and regions.

It is therefore of such interest and even such relief that one of Pirenne's pupils would be the one to come up with an entirely different, and much more hopeful and open, perspective on the Mediterranean. Fernand Braudel, who dominated postwar historiography just as Pirenne had dominated in the prewar period, published in 1949 *The Mediterranean and the Mediterranean World in the Age of Philip II*. The title might seem to restrict the author to a few decades in the late sixteenth century (Philip II was King of Castile, who lived from 1527 to 1598), but in fact the book exploded the whole notion of time used by historians until then. *The Mediterranean* was the book that would make the name of the Annales School of history, founded in the 1920s by Lucien Febvre. Febvre, Braudel, and like-minded colleagues such as Marc Bloch transformed history from a narrative-based science, with a strong focus on political power, warring nation-states. and strong personalities to a more scientific discipline, interested in the structural transformations on the social and economic level that underlie historical events.

In *The Mediterranean*, this approach was taken to its logical end. Braudel identifies three levels of time: the "*longue durée,*" being the "time" of geography, the "*moyenne durée,*" meaning the time of social and economic patterns and movements, and the "*courte durée*" being the time of individuals and events. This approach was defined as the radical alternative to the history of events ("*histoire evénementielle*"), which had been the rule until then. Strangely enough, this scientific, quantitative method produced one of the most absorbing epics of its time. Choosing a specific time in history, the late sixteenth century, Braudel looks deep into the geographical structure, the economic flows and social patterns, the culture and stories of the Mediterranean, nearly as ahistorical qualities, belonging much more to their space than to their time. The decades of his title are merely the way into this amazingly complex and rich singular personality that is the Mediterranean region.

Philip II was the king under whose reign the trade routes, and therefore the hub of worldwide relations, would finally shift from the Mediterranean to the Atlantic and the Indian Ocean. It was therefor somewhat of a twilight era for the Mediterranean, but a twilight pushed forward nearly a thousand years from Pirenne's thesis. In the foreword to the English edition of 1972, Braudel repeats forcefully his claim, against the analysis à la Pirenne, that the rise of Islam had early on fatally "broken"

the Mediterranean as the sea that held the surrounding regions together: "I retain the firm conviction that the Turkish Mediterranean lived and breathed with the same rhythms as the Christian, that the whole sea shared a common destiny, a heavy one indeed, with identical problems and general trends if not identical consequences."[4]

The "living and breathing" is illustrated within the first series of chapters, where Braudel describes life in the mountains, plateaus, and plains that make up the peninsulas sticking into the sea. He makes the fascinating observation that people living in the mountain areas of the region have more in common with each other, in the way they grow food, migrate, build, and trade — no matter that they might live hundreds of miles apart — than with the people who live on the plains and the plateau a few miles downhill. There is a typical section that you could make all around the sea, going from the mountains down to the seashore, that repeats the same pattern of groups of people living close by but in completely different ways, with different patterns and flows governing their lives. This sectional approach to the Mediterranean does a better job of describing the essence and coherence of the region than the often politically defined maps, with zones of influences colored into a flattened representation of geography.

Another fascinating chapter is on the boundaries that define the Mediterranean; it ironically recalls the "garlic economies" slur, as garlic consumption could have been a Braudelian definition of what holds together the Mediterranean. Braudel, however, favors the olive tree as an indicator. One of the first and most obvious boundaries identified by Braudel is the double one of the northern limit of the olive tree and that of the palm grove, with everything in between defined as "the Mediterranean." Other boundaries are defined by the endings or beginnings of the Saharan caravans, or more geologically by the great mountain ranges or the straits of Gibraltar, or politically by the edges of the zones of influence of the Northern European and Ottoman kingdoms and empires. But the chapter is mainly important not for defining the boundaries but for endlessly stretching and layering them, identifying how each border is an interface with another network of roads, passes, sea routes, etc. In offering the idea that in the sixteenth century, it was the Mediterranean that shaped the Atlantic and Asian trade routes, Braudel moved one historian, when reviewing the first edition of the book, to regret the fact that the donkey had not been given more space in the colonization of

4   Fernand Braudel, *The Mediterranean and the Mediterranean World in the Age of Philip II* (New York: University of California Press) 1976, vol. 1, 14.

the West and East Indies, because the image of a peasant riding his burro in Mexico made him realize that indeed the Mediterranean, once upon a time, stretched all the way to the Americas.[5]

Moving gradually through the book, from the long waves of geographical history, the middle waves of human settlement and economy, into the short-wave frequency of conflict and other "events," Braudel turns the normal historical description of the region on its head. He demonstrates how the conflicts of the Crusades, the struggles between the Turks and the Venetians, the Genoese and the Venetians, the Spanish, the Byzantines, the battle of Lepanto, the war of Granada, were all actually part of this one, living and breathing civilization — or history — machine called the Mediterranean. War and peace, growing and shrinking empires, could all be absorbed into the middle waves of its economy and social development. The struggles were symptomatic, short outbursts of tension, caused by the much slower movements of people and goods, just like a volcano's eruption or earthquakes are the result of the plates of the earth moving at a geological pace.

So if we bring this back to Henri Pirenne's thesis of the Mediterranean falling apart as the result of the fortunes of one empire rising over those of another, Braudel does not counter this claim directly. He absorbs it, swallows it up whole in his magnificent epic of the slow history of the Mediterranean. The temporary retreat of Europe into itself, and the development of capitalism out of the feudal Carolingian Empire, while the Arab world rules the Mediterranean, is just one wave, on the middle frequency, that serves to underline the centrality of the Mediterranean to all things human, until the colonization of the Asian and American shores made the world exponentially bigger, that is. Civilizations, economic connections and political unions, are made subservient to slower and deeper movements of people and settlement patterns, which in turn are the result of an excruciatingly incremental adaptation to landscape, climate, and geography.

Braudel does not simply absorb the conflicts between the Islamic world and the Christian world in the *longue durée* of Mediterranean history; he defines the conflict as that which keeps the regions together. To this end, he employs the term "complementary enemies," powers condemned to living together and sharing the Mediterranean Sea, with the wars and battles as the *courte durée* incidents in centuries-long periods of cohabitation. He sees conflict and competition as fundamental parts of coexistence and shows how the conflict caused by invading outsiders always results in assimilation, though not assimilation by the dominant party but assimilation in the deeper geographical and economic logic of the Mediterranean. About the role of the competing powers in Braudel's model of the region, the historian Daniel Purdy writes: "In order for either to assert a structural continuity that survives major wars, they must have an idea of the Mediterranean that exists independent of sovereign states, institutions, religions and armies."[6] Purdy also points at the relationship between the writing of *The Mediterranean* and the increasingly contentious and problematic theme of France's colonial presence on the other side of the sea, in Algeria. He, with many more contemporary historians, reads Braudel's book through the lens of the conflict between the "complementary enemies" of the Algerian liberation forces and France's army, or between the French colonist Pieds-Noirs and the Algerian natives, or between France's claim to a special role in the Mediterranean and the pressure from America for the country to let go of its colonies. In that context, Braudel's book reads like a spell, woven to absorb the conflicts, tensions, and controversies of its time, into the epic sweep of the historical annals. Braudel was certainly reformulating "the idea of the Mediterranean", and thereby indirectly redefining France's role in the region for the twentieth and twenty-first centuries.

It did not come as a total surprise then that when French President Nicolas Sarkozy unveiled his plans for a Mediterranean Union at a posh event in the Parisian Grand Palais on July 13, 2008, *Le Monde* had as headline: "The Mediterranean and the Mediterranean World in the Age of Nicolas Sarkozy," sarcastically echoing Braudel's title. In both supportive comments from the French press and critical observations from the German, North African, and even Israeli press, references were made to Braudel's nearly sixty-year-old masterpiece. Suddenly, the ideological force of the historical study of trade relations in the late sixteenth century came to the fore. *Haaretz* even accused Sarkozy of following up on the "poetic daydreams" of Fernand Braudel, and in an extensive analysis *Die Welt* connected the anti-German feelings behind Sarkozy's union with the fact that many historians of the Annales School to which Braudel belonged, including himself, had suffered at the hands of German occupiers in World War II.[7] Also, the connection was made between Braudel's work as the intellectual basis for France's Mediterranean interest and the brutal colonialism of

5 Ibid., 226.

6 Daniel Purdy, draft paper for MLA 2008, Penn State University, http://www.academia.edu/1385863/Pirenne_and_Braudel_Christian_and_Muslim_Mediterrareans, retrieved October 22, 2012.

7 Wolf Lepenies, "Fernand Braudel und die wege ans Mittelmeer," *Die Welt*, August 5, 2008 (http://www.welt.de/kultur/article2275312/Fernand-Braudel-und-die-Wege-ans-Mittelmeer.html, retrieved October 22, 2012).

the French. All the while, Sarkozy talked of a deeper bond between the civilizations of the Mediterranean, absolving France from its sins in the colonial wars and waxing romantically about a common future.

In the end, the Mediterranean Union's climax was its beginning, and soon after it was "assimilated" into the deadening bureaucratic mazes of the European Union, with all member states also belonging to the Mediterranean Union (Sweden, Lithuania, the Netherlands, etc.), and with the southern and western Mediterranean members sending third-tier representatives to the Grand Palais. Now it consists of a number of subsidy streams for depolluting the sea anddeveloping solar energy, for a Euro-Mediterranean university in Slovenia, and for some institutions, all surviving on a pittance. Sarkozy's union is a bureaucratic version of many other plans of the past hundred years that project enormous European ambitions on the Mediterranean and then flounder without any effect on the ground whatsoever. The brief moment of excitement over another doomed collective vision is added as a fourth time scale to the three scales introduced by Braudel: *longue durée, moyenne durée, courte durée,* and *non-durée.*

One of the strangest plans in this tradition of failure was Herman Sörgel's Atlantropa project for the reengineering and colonization of the entire Mediterranean region. Damming the straits of Gibraltar and lowering the sea level would create new *Lebensraum* for the European countries and land bridges between Spain and Morocco, Italy and Tunisia. Hydroelectric dams in the Sea of Marmara and a landlocked Venice would be some of the results. The aim of Atlantropa, a movement that managed to exist for three decades between 1922 and 1952 — exactly the timeframe in which Braudel developed his methods as a historian and wrote his masterpiece — and to attract enough funds to hire world-famous architects to design the engineering projects and to lobby politicians and investors, was to conjoin Europe and Africa around the *Mittelmeer* as the hub of their newfound collective prosperity.

Another, more recent example that seems ironically aware of its tradition is the "Roadmap 2050" plan by the Office for Metropolitan Architecture, for the total redesign of Europe and North Africa on a grid of renewable energy, substituting nation-states with regions specialized in one particular energy source: the Alps, the Pyrenees, and other mountain ranges become "Hydropia" because of the water energy; the North Sea becomes "The Isles of Wind;" Central Europe becomes "Enhanced Geothermalia;" and the Mediterranean coast and sea become "Solaria." Essentially the same hysterico-colonialism as Sörgel's was projected on Europe and the Mediterranean, but this time not fueled by the desire for economic power and *Lebensraum*, but by the dream of renewable energy and continental autarchy. Also interesting is the fact that just as there is a historical — or at least a chronological — resonance between Braudel's *Mediterranean* (1949) and Sörgel's Atlantropa (1928–1952), there is one too between Sarkozy's Mediterranean Union (2008) and OMA's Eneropa (2010). The plan was commissioned by the European Climate foundation and was last heard of being under consideration by the EU Council of Ministers for their possible endorsement.[8]

There is a connection between the repeated attempts by European politicians, visionary engineers, and architects to "take back" the Mediterranean and Braudel's grand historiographical vision of the wholeness of the region. Probably the connection lies not so much in the deep memory of "losing" the Mediterranean to the Muslims, as Pirenne would have it, but in the painful postwar period of decolonization in the 1950s and 1960s. Especially in France, losing Algeria and having to repatriate the hundreds of thousands of Pieds-Noirs to France, in the aftermath of a brutal war, created a national trauma. This trauma, however, was not unique; it resonated with similar feelings of resentment in the United Kingdom and the Netherlands over the loss of their East and West Indian colonies, and in Belgium and Portugal with respect to their African colonies. But the proximity and historical meaning of the Mediterranean made this particular loss all the more dramatic and prone to inspiring emotional recastings of colonial ambitions like those by Nicolas Sarkozy and OMA.

But to put it in Braudelian terms of an elastic Mediterranean: the violent decolonization not only dramatically increased the distance between Europe and the southern Mediterranean, creating a new border straight through the middle of the sea; it also collapsed distances and broke down borders between colonizer and colonized, while creating new divisions in the heart of our own territories. After losing Algeria, French cities saw the arrival of a wave of immigration from former French colonies and other North African countries. Attracted and actively sought after by the French industrial boom, they came as guest workers. During the 1970s, when the size of the immigrant population again increased, immigrants

8   For both Herman Sörgels Atlantropa and OMA's Eneropa, see Wouter Vanstiphout, "Design Is Politics," Inaugural Lecture, Chair of Design as Politics, Faculty of Architecture, Technical University Delft, June 19, 2009 (http://designaspolitics.files.wordpress.com/2010/07/wvanstiphoutinauguration_en.pdf retrieved October 22, 2012).

repopulated the enormous housing estates built in the 1950s and 1960s, now abandoned by the first generation of French middle classes who started to prefer a suburban lifestyle. The French banlieues of cities throughout the entire country became more "Mediterranean," and less French, with Spanish, Greek, and Yugoslav guest workers mixing with the immigrants from the Maghreb and eventually also from Africa. Similar processes happened in other parts of Europe as well, where the first wave of Spanish, Italian, and Greek guest workers were replaced by a second wave of Turks and Moroccans. In similar ways, they arrived in the popular prewar working-class neighborhoods of Brussels, Antwerp, Berlin, Hamburg, Rotterdam, and Amsterdam, during (or sometimes causing) the exodus of the white working classes to the new suburbs. Later, during the 1980s, they also started to move into the postwar housing estates, replacing the white working and lower-middle classes who had lived there for decades.

Similar geographies were the result, joining together cities that were otherwise completely different, with thousands of miles, borders, and languages between them. The contested space of the Mediterranean now reached the borders of the historical town centers all over Europe, from cities on the Mediterranean coast all the way to Scandinavia. We see the same basic structure of a relatively prosperous inner city surrounded by a patchwork of neighborhoods that have either been gentrified or are dominated by poor immigrant populations. Around the beltway we see the postwar housing estates, first the scene of an uneasy arrangement between the white lower-middle classes and the immigrant families, now often dominated by the latter. And further out we find the suburbs, where the middle classes and the white former inhabitants of the working-class neighborhoods and the postwar housing estates have fled. This is more or less the typical section of the European city.

Similar geographies also bring with them similar social and political shifts and controversies. The political disaffection of the white middle classes, the rise of anti-immigrant populist parties, the crackdown by the political mainstream on immigration, on radical Islam, are phenomena shared by many if not most Western European countries. What we recognize when we move from Toulouse to Antwerp to Rotterdam to Berlin, to Aarhus and back to Paris, is neighborhoods, street cultures, smells, even the same type of accentuations of the local language. Kreuzberg seems much closer to the Rotterdam Afrikaanderwijk than

it does to the adjacent center of Berlin. The 99 percent immigrant estate of Gellerup near Aarhus seems much closer to Le Mirail, the Candilis & Woods–designed satellite town of Toulouse, than to the medieval center of the Danish city. We recognize not just the mosques, the doner kebab outlets, or the headscarves; we recognize a similar hybrid culture where the immigration from the Mediterranean sphere has come together with the ruins of the welfare state from the 1950s and 1960s. This has produced an alloy between western postwar systems, either physical or socioeconomic, and cultures from far-flung reaches of the Mediterranean region and beyond. This strange combination is what nearly all Western European cities share, squeezed in between their also increasingly uniform centers and suburbs, and which distinguishes them from cities outside of Europe.

This essay started out with an observation of an observation: that certain left-wing scholars have identified the urban struggles on either side of the Mediterranean, from Syntagma Square to Tahrir Square, as signals of a new coming together between the working classes and rebellious youths of Europe, North Africa, and the Middle East. In a way this is a radical, revolutionary twin to the dreams by visionary engineers like Herman Sörgel, ironic utopians like the Office for Metropolitan Architecture, or Bonapartesque heads of state like Nicolas Sarkozy, to reunite the countries around the Middle Sea. They all share the vision of dissolving the national borders into a shared culture, whether defined by trade routes, renewable energy grids, or ideological dogma. Conversely, we have also seen how the European monetary crisis, has caused northwestern countries to assert their distance from the Mediterranean countries, and their cultures, describing them as the "garlic economies" that do not possess the fiscal rigor or political stability of northern Europe, implying that they belong more to the Mediterranean region than to Europe. Here we see very clearly the legacy of Henri Pirennes' "Mahomet et Charlemagne" being played out in the cavernous halls of European politics.

In the end, however, the real pertinence of the Mediterranean is not that of a geopolitical zone, a grouping of nation-states with clear borders around a sea, that may or may not have things in common. I think the Mediterranean shows its real presence in our cities, in an extremely condensed form, concentrating millennia of migration and conflict in urban memes that, precisely because of the copresence of so many non-European cultures, are quintessentially European — that is, Mediterranean.

To really grasp the richness and find a language to talk about it, we need something of a new Braudelian project for the twenty-first century. Not one celebrating the Mediterranean region to provide cover for empty institutionalization or technocratic visions, but one creeping into the depths of our European cities, exposing their "common destiny," "identical problems and general trends if not identical consequences," demonstrating how they also "live and breath with the same rhythms." We would use the Braudelian tool of identifying different "*durées,*" in describing how cities are not so much riding upon different economic wavelengths but are the results of how the different "durees" of politics, economics, culture, and climate sometimes violently interfere. We have to develop a similar sectional approach to urban analysis, instead of the technocratic and statist use of maps, in understanding their socio-physical makeup. We have to develop a similar literary approach, incorporating the streetwise and daily experiences in varied urban areas to demonstrate how they might be thousands of miles apart, but eerily alike.

Most of all, we could learn from Fernand Braudel his amazingly layered and complex approach to conflict, difference, and shifting boundaries. In *The Mediterranean,* the Mediterranean is not a sea with countries around it, but a dynamic process of complementary enemies, shifting boundaries, and common rhythms. This might be a very "French" structuralist, even cerebral approach to the troubles of our urban and political environment. But do not forget that for Braudel, this framework made it possible to organize the most concrete and empirical knowledge about daily lives in mountain villages, geological formations, and climate change, up to political and economic policies on the grand scale. Such a nondeterministic, even post-historical attitude could inspire a much more contextual and pragmatic approach to our urban problems. Current urban politics and planning is often determined by overly historicist thinking that sees cities as going through phases in linear development processes, sometimes cyclical, sometimes not. This creates a discourse about certain areas that are "no longer up-to-date" or a view that sometimes progress, and therefore demolition for redevelopment, is unavoidable because of the "changing times." It explains the frequent use of schematic models and diagrams that demonstrate the "ideal" positioning of services, densities, and infrastructure, such as the famous Christaller hexagons that still determine

planning. This clean, deterministic, technocratic approach makes it hard to account for the imperfections of cities. Their dark side, their opacity and idiosyncrasies, are seen as failures to conform to the plans and models, and thus a reason to intervene even harder.

Braudel can teach us to treat cities differently, without the use of metaphysical visions or technocratic models. A new Braudelian project for the city could be the analytical companion to a highly contextualist, local, and pragmatist approach to cities, which, however, does possess a certain universality, because it can constantly profit from the spiderweb of connections and resonances across the continent. Gellerup and Le Mirail share many of their problems and possible outcomes; indeed they "live and breathe with the same rhythm," one that is very different from the rhythm of central Aarhus or central Toulouse. Why then the constant attempts to force them into conforming to French or Danish standards, something that has produced nothing but failure and frustration in both cases?

If we would only learn to dissolve the rigid categories of history and geography that we now use in rationalizing our urban policies and our plans and designs, we would be able to react to the cities' real demands in a more pragmatic and exciting way. To do that, however, we need to release the "Mediterranean of the mind" that lurks inside us and inside our cities. We need to remember that Braudel chose as a key moment — from which he catapulted himself into the deep complexity of his book — a time when the Mediterranean as a central place in human geography was waning in light of the discoveries in America and Asia. This moment of waning provoked a thinking about the Mediterranean afterlife, how its former dominance over the trade routes was reincarnated in an artistic, scholarly, and philosophical dominance, with the immense creative upsurge in Venice in its powerless seventeenth and eighteenth centuries as an example.

Something similar might inspire a Braudelian project for the twenty-first century. We have a sense of the waning of the west, let alone of Europe as the dominant region of sensible politics, welfare-state services, religious tolerance, and equanimity and intelligence all around. We are also seeing our powers sapping to the south and to the east. Our former ideologies are crashing, like the neoliberal market economy, or desperately flailing about, like the neo-Marxist belief in global workers' revolution. In our cities, in the way that they seem to be ripping themselves apart alongside the boundaries of inequality and intolerance, we also seem to be losing our grip. In that sense there is a double resonance, first with the highly uncertain times when Braudel wrote his book, during and immediately after World War II, and with the time he analyzed, the late sixteenth century.

Right now is the time to stop thinking about Europe, or the Mediterranean, or our cities, as "a project." Right now is the time to start thinking about Europe, the Mediterranean, and our cities as a vast system of conflicting wavelengths, unexpectedly resonant rhythms, and a mysterious coherence that will need a radical reformulating once again. In this retelling, we must reconcile our sometimes desperate sense of being beleaguered from outside, and our fear of the future, with a longer view of history, and with a fatalistic view of conflict, as the one thing that holds us all together. Most of all, we must give a central place in our narrative of urban Europe to all of the intimate, local, and small experiences because these are the ones that truly connect us to the world, just like the donkey in Braudel's book, stretching the Mediterranean all the way to Mexico.

Mediterranean Cultural Identities Seen through the "Western" Gaze
Shifting Geographical Imaginations of Athens
Lila Leontidou

From Possessiveness to "Othering":
A Snapshot Approach

Cities that have existed for more than five millennia, as most major Mediterranean cities have, are interesting case studies into shifting identities, which are constantly negotiated within Northern and Western geographical imaginations. Their contribution to European patrimony and the concomitant possessiveness expressed by the West has been recently replaced by a peculiar, persistent Orientalism. I will attempt here a critique that shifts received geopolitical borders within the European Union vis-à-vis "the rest" of the Mediterranean through time, up to the reconstruction of a North/South divide within EU limits, within the Eurozone (Leontidou 2012a). Europe appears fragmented once again, turning into the "dark continent" (Mazower 1998), unable to stop economic aggression or possibly even warfare among its nation-states.

The Western gaze has interfered with research on the Mediterranean city, relegating it to an "exception." Mediterranean cities challenged mainstream urban development models in the nineteenth century, missing out on the industrial revolution and overt colonialism, and going through urbanization without industrialization; in the twentieth century by reversing the Burgess spatial pattern through spontaneous suburban popular and squatter settlements rather than bourgeois suburbs, and thus by spatializing popular demands for the "right to the city" (Leontidou 1990); and in the twenty-first century by initiating the crisis and spurring snowballing global upheavals of resistance to autocracies in North Africa, and for direct democracy against neoliberalism and the democratic deficit in the EU. The Mediterranean city thus challenges or even reverses recognized urban development models and has therefore been marginalized from mainstream (mainly Anglo-American) geography and urban theory. It does not figure among model cities in textbooks on urban geography. This might be because of its subversive function in overturning received wisdom about capitalist urban development. Scholars tend to define away Mediterranean particularities and ignore them in their reasoning, creating a huge gap in understanding these cities (Leontidou 1990).

Athens, the capital of Hellas (Greece), is considered as an appropriate case study in these respects, not only because of the

Lila Leontidou   (Dipl. Arch., Ethniko Metsovio Polytechnico Athens; M. Sc., London School of Economics, Ph.D., University of London) is an architect, planner, and geographer. She is a Professor of Geography and European Culture at the Hellenic Open University (2002–), as well as a Senior Fellow at the London School of Economics and Political Science (LSE Hellenic Observatory of the European Institute, 2012–). She has also been a Senior Fellow at Johns Hopkins University (Center for Metropolitan Planning and Research, now Institute for Policy Studies) since 1986.

"Hellenization of discourse"[1] during the present debt crisis but also because of its location at the crossroads. Athens stands between occident and orient, between Europe and the heart of the Mediterranean, and has followed a discontinuous itinerary over the course of six millennia. The ancient city-state has been kept within view and has time and again stirred imaginations and inspired the collective memory of Western cities (Boyer 1996, Bauman 2011). Curious European visitors since the time of Ottoman occupation have included Gustav Flaubert and Sigmund Freud, Simone de Beauvoir and Jacques Derrida. Athens is indeed a "theater of memory," combining ancient and modern, original and copy (Crang and Travlou 2001), informal as postmodern (Leontidou 1993), tourism and romantic traveling with migration and poverty, throughout its life as a capital city, which dates from merely 1834. This is where our narrative begins.

We will examine the shifting Western gaze since then, referring only to the dominant gaze of foreign governments and elites, because there are alternative geographical imaginations that cannot be taken up here. We will try to capture the discontinuity of urban history in Greek and foreign eyes by taking a snapshot approach to the beginning and the end of the modern city, by briefly examining two periods comprising three important episodes (as in Gregory 1994: 15, for another topic) during which Athens became a prototype for constructed identities: the artificial nineteenth-century neoclassical capital city, a symbol of European heritage inspiring possessiveness in Bavarians and other quasi-colonial powers;

and the twenty-first-century capital, which within a few years underwent a metamorphosis from the "Olympic" entrepreneurial city, on equal footing in global urban competition, to the present city of the debt crisis, which has become a globally renowned target of a vehement new version of Orientalism.

The Nineteenth-Century Artificial Capital City: Neoclassical Athens

The new Greek Kingdom emerged according to the 1830 London Protocol, which sealed its independence from Ottoman rule. Athens was declared the capital of Hellas in 1834, after short periods where the distinction was held by other cities, Aegina and Nafplion. Bavarian royalty arrived to implement, in collaboration with the "protective powers," one of the most successful experiments in the creation of an artificial capital on a global scale. In the course of a few decades, Athens metamorphosed from a village of only 12,000 inhabitants during the last years of Ottoman rule into a bustling city of 242,000 inhabitants at the turn of the twentieth century (Leontidou 1989, Bastea 2000). It grew to be a multi-nucleated city, surrounded by settlements called *Demoi* since antiquity, when they formed part of the city-state. The most important one was the Piraeus port to the southwest, connected with Athens through the Long Walls, built in the classical period, which metamorphosed into a railway in the late nineteenth century.

Foreigners swarmed into Athens in the 1830s: royalty, architects, and archeologists from various European power blocs. The colonization of Greek territory started in Athens through Bavarian planning sponsored by royalty, which latently colonized Athens and governed it possessively. Antiquity and its material manifestation in classical architecture provided the main source of legitimation for the new capital. Europe had rediscovered classicism in the mid-eighteenth century through the movement of neoclassicism (Boyer 1996). On its basis, Athens was built in neoclassical style and so, ironically, "neo"-classical architecture returned to the birthplace of classicism via European cities inspired from classical Hellas: via the Western gaze. Athens was built mostly by Bavarians, but the buildings were "naturalized" by the inhabitants and the modern Greek nation, so that the reception of European neoclassical design trends imported especially by Bavarians was facilitated and, even more important, colonial domination was undermined (Bastea 2000), despite the character of

1   Krugman in his LSE lecture, 2012, see http://soundcloud.com/lsepodcasts/end-this-depression-now-audio accessed in 4 September 2012.

nineteenth-century Athens as a colonial city (Leontidou 1989). Its escape from colonial domination was also ensured by the interplay of public, or royal, national-level planning with private patronage. This was a peculiar colonial penetration, instigated not only by the European Great Powers and Bavarian royalty but also by the peculiar Greek comprador bourgeoisie living abroad — in the Balkans, in Egypt, and throughout places of "unredeemed" Hellenism. These sponsored monumentalization and conspicuous buildings for culture and public amenities located in the center of the new capital (Leontidou 1989, 1990). The core of the city obtained its celebrated iconic neoclassical "Athenian trilogy" — University, Academy, Library — as well as other monumental buildings, generously funded by affluent diaspora Greeks.

As neoclassical architecture penetrated the center of Athens, urban planning and design also followed neoclassical principles, which became crucial in the process of construction of a new national Greek identity. Royal architects and planning teams adopted the "hippodameian" system of checkerboard planning, yet another classical heritage. The main reason for the legitimation of Bavarian planning on the level of the local societies, besides the echo of classical Hellas, was its departure from irregular Ottoman street layouts, with an explicit aspiration: the recovery of Hellenism through the "de-turkization" of Greek towns via regular orthogonal plans. This has a bearing on the construction of Greek identity at home and abroad through civic design, in opposition to the "Other," the Ottoman (Leontidou 1989).

The local society exhibited ambivalent attitudes to planning. About 170 plans were drafted nationwide by the mid-nineteenth century, in accordance with aspirations of citizens demanding plans for their towns. This relativizes the narratives about the anti-planning attitudes of the Greek population, although the case study of Athens reestablishes them at the stage of the implementation of plans. The Athens plan has been revised more than 3,000 times (Biris 1966), due to pressures from local landowners. Attempts to plan the capital by orthogonal grids, straight streets, and regular town squares were rarely realized. For their part, planners constructed a virtual city, the unreal landscape represented on blueprints, which has been exciting and at times menacing — as, for example, when we are reminded of the momentary risk of having the Acropolis incorporated in the royal palace as décor, in accordance with Schinkel's plan, drawn by a man who never visited Athens (Bastea 2000).

This can serve as documentation of European reliance on impression and perception — on imagination — rather than reality. As to the population, it developed different attitudes to urban renewal and speculation according to social class and culture, but also within fractions of classes, for example, the diaspora Greeks and "heterochthones" (those born abroad) versus the natives, or the elites versus the petty bourgeoisie (Leontidou 1989). In the new capital but also in other towns, some citizens objected to implementation of the plans that others, or sometimes they themselves, had asked for. This underlines the antinomies of public resistance to planning.

The clash between cosmopolitanism and neoclassicism on the one hand and anti-planning pressures and localism on the other reflected an underlying Greek dualism, seen in debates over cosmopolitanism versus tradition (Diamandouros 2000). So while "de-turkization" was a unanimous aspiration, "greekness" came under antitheses and dualisms that also cut through language, creating bilinguality. This dualism deepened from the 1870s, when rich Greeks from the diaspora repatriated (Tsoucalas 1977, Leontidou 1989), supporting the newly captured cosmopolitanism of Athens. Alternating acceptance and resistance to Westernization has been important for representations of the urban past: the clash between cosmopolitanism and provincialism was reflected in the antithesis between antiquity and Byzantium. Modernity was underplayed in urban cultural discourse. Modernism as such was not even discussed in the 1880s, when Tricoupis, the prime minister of Westernization, launched the "railway decade," starting in 1882 with 74 percent loans from abroad, especially Great Britain, which were withdrawn when the first lines were considered counterproductive and uncompetitive (Papayiannakis 1982: 165–204).

The "protective powers" were thus responsible for cultural ambiguity. They controlled different sections of the government and elites who were not resident in Greece. The peculiar comprador bourgeoisie of Greeks living abroad and colonizing Hellas, together with foreigners, stirred power plays around Greek dualism and bilinguality. In fact, the Western gaze on Athens was ambiguous and ridden with dualisms. At one extreme, some foreigners expressed their scorn for the nascent nation struggling for development, where industry was so poor that E. About (1855) exclaimed that Greece sent agricultural products to international industrial exhibitions, and that it could not even manufacture pins: "All manufactured produce consumed in the kingdom comes from abroad: in Greece they do not know how to make one of those clasp-knives sold at Paris for 5 sous!" (About 1855: 112; see also Leontidou 1989: 98).

At the other extreme, Europeans aspired to see the re-Hellenization of Athens by neoclassicism and "de-turkization" because the Greek capital was endowed with evocative symbolism, especially the sacred rock of the Acropolis and the overwhelming presence of the Parthenon as an icon of European civilization and American republicanism. This view had lasted since the Renaissance in Europe and the design of Thomas Jefferson's cities in classical and Hellenistic styles, accompanied by the discourse for democracy and equality in the United States (Loukaki 2008). The Acropolis became a contested monument of collective memory with unceasing conflicts over property and appropriation, as the Parthenon marbles — all the friezes, pediments, metopes, and much more — still remind us: these were smuggled to England in 1805 by Lord Elgin and are now standing in the British Museum, which refuses to return them to Athens even after the creation of their stands in the new Acropolis Museum. Foreigners keep intervening in several spheres, from political life to archeological excavations and the plundering of Hellas's past. The Acropolis and the archeological sites remain the object of clashing narratives and power conflicts over property and appropriation, as in the nineteenth century (Loukaki 2008).

Olympic Illusions and the Short-Lived Entrepreneurial City

Athens entered the new millennium with 3,187,734 inhabitants (Greater Athens 2001, 29.07 percent of the Greek population), or 3,761,810 if the broader Attica region is included, which is now shrinking below the level of natural increase: according to provisional data of the 2011 census, 3,122,540 people live in Greater Athens (28.94 percent of the Greek population) and 3,812,330 in the whole of Attica, which keeps growing. However many clandestine migrants the 2011 census missed, it is a fact that Greater Athens is no longer the fast-growing city as it was in the twentieth century, and the population of Greece is actually shrinking.

During the late twentieth century, Athens stepped into global urban competition, based on its advantage of classical heritage and its kaleidoscopic cityscape of antiquity, byzan-

tine elements, and modernity, constituting a postmodern collage of architectural styles. In combination with societal particularities such as informality and porosity, these belong to postmodernism long before there was such a label (Leontidou 1993). Hellenic antiquity returns to global focus regularly every four years, as the Olympic flame travels around the world. This visibility was greatly enhanced in 2004, when Athens staged the Olympic games. Place marketing and the effort to be distinguished in global urban competition started in the 1990s, with the mobilization to prepare an unsuccessful bid for the "Golden Olympics" of 1996, 100 years after their revival in Athens. Although Greece was recovering from a major slump then, it appealed to the global scene with a fresh image, based on pompous mega-events (Leontidou 1993).

Pomp and monumentalization in the midst of decline is a centuries-old counteractive strategy. In the 1890s Hermoupolis in the island of Syros spent heavily on civic design and a decorous municipal building as soon as it sensed that decay was close and depopulation toward Athens and Piraeus had set in (Leontidou 1989). This effort did not stop the decline, but it was a reassurance for the population seeking solace and dignity in changing the image of the city. Athens followed a similar strategy during the revival of the ancient Olympic Games in 1896. Greece was recovering from national bankruptcy in 1893 and probably needed this confirmation of glory. This was followed by pro-war rallies and the resurgence of the Great Idea of Greek irredentism, which led to a humiliating defeat by the Ottoman Empire in 1897.

It is debatable whether the same undercurrents of counteracting an approaching crisis were working during the turn-of-millennium Olympics. Athens did not give up after the failure of 1996 and managed to "win" the 2004 games, proudly competing on an equal footing at a global scale. International media framing stressed Greek inadequacy to complete the Olympic infrastructure in time, emphasizing delays in building the innovative constructions, especially major sports venues and transport works. Some foreign media openly branded the Greeks as inefficient. Ironically, it was all ready in time, but it may have cost Greece its subsequent crisis. Overspending for the Olympics has not been quantified, but the forecast was for 7 billion and the spending, especially for security but also for infrastructural and architectural works, as stated by various dailies based on interviews of politicians and agents involved, may have exceeded 30 billion.

[27]

The Athenian 'trilogy'
in Panepistimiou St.:
The Library

[46]

Alter-globalization
demonstration in Athens,
2006

[28]

The Athenian 'trilogy'
in Panepistimiou St.:
The Academy

[47]

French solidarity in Syntagma,
Athens 2011

The Athenian 'trilogy'
in Panepistimiou St.:
The University

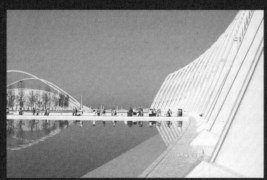

The Athens Olympic Stadium
by architect S. Calatrava

Athens staged an excellent Olympic extravaganza. International media had to admit that the mega-event was successful and kept repeating that the Olympics "returned to their birthplace" just over a century after their revival in the same city. The Greek government and elites celebrated the return of the Olympic Games to their "cradle," Greece, and "the Athenian urban majority accepted that the so-called Olympic culture can be sold to an obscure global community, whereas in fact it was this community […] that has sold it to the Athenian public" (Afouxenidis 2006: 292). Still, there were contestations. In both instances of claiming the Olympics, 1996 and 2004, certain collectivities resisted the lavishness and wastefulness, but only hesitantly, since media and public attention were so enthusiastic. The emergent Greek alter-globalization movement, however, did take up resistance to neoliberalism and the Olympics (Leontidou 2010). This was voiced in Athens and abroad, since the movement was as cosmopolitan as all new social movements are.[2] International demonstrations also shook Athens when it hosted the World Social Forum in 2006. It became the meeting place of international collectivities that, together with Greek participants, tried to emancipate the city from the hegemony of urban entrepreneurialism and mega-events — but was it too late?

The focus of the so-called glocalization of cities in neoliberal Europe is dual (Gospodini and Beriatos 2006): mega-events, references to cosmopolitan architecture and global innovative design on the one hand, and the planned revival of local heritage for visibility on the other. In the case of Athens, this combination has gravitated toward the former with respect to Olympic infrastructure built by celebrities in various locations. The major pieces of iconic architecture built for major sports events were concentrated in Santiago Calatrava's Olympic park. Later on, the Acropolis Museum was also designed by a foreigner, Bernard Tschumi, and now faces the Acropolis with the audacity of late modernism, following the much-criticized volume of the modernist Hilton, built in the 1960s (Biris 1966). Renewal promoting local built heritage and tradition with historical spatial references in the inner city was more restricted. The overrated "archeological walk" around the Acropolis was expected to be molded into everyday life and in the image of Athens as a tourist city.

Athens was also renewed massively with major transport works at the beginning of the millennium. New infrastructure now includes the international airport, the ring motorway of *Attiki odos*, the Athens metro, and an extended suburban railway system expanding from the airport to Corinth and then to Kiato. This infrastructure has been constructed in the context of neoliberal urban governance in the entrepreneurial city, through public-private partnerships and massive foreign involvement. It created a new set of urban dynamics and a new wave of urban sprawl: increasingly population and industry followed new infrastructure built in anticipation of the 2004 Olympics. Urban sprawl intensified in Athens following the Olympic infrastructural transport works, that is, the airport and the suburban train (Leontidou et al. 2007). Surface sealing swept away olive groves and vineyards in the Mesogeia plane, and the built-up area reached the coasts of Attica. Residential tourism at the seaside intensified (Leontidou et al. 2001), and second residences were turned to primary ones. Urban sprawl in the twenty-first century engulfed the whole of Attica into one major agglomeration, bustling with enterprises in mixed-use areas around the new international airport, as well as communities of cooperatives and leapfrog developments. The commodification of nature created by a growing city is well illustrated by the enormous expansion of its ecological footprint to the Evinos River in Fokida, as far as 500 kilometers to the northwest of Athens (i.e., as far as Thessaloniki on the North — see Kaika 2005, Couch et al. 2007).

The illusion of an enduring Olympic city and a prosperous entrepreneurial Athens lasted for a very short period. It began in the 1990s and the unsuccessful bid for the "Golden Olympics" in 1996 and culminated during the successful 2004 Olympics, which drained the livelihood of the nation, with only momentary improvement of Western geographical imaginations about Athens. The turn of the new millennium thus belongs to an era of urban competition where neoliberal governance, entrepreneurialism, and globalization have jeopardized the vitality of the city as they rose to hegemony internationally, reproducing place marketing. Athens has been clumsily adopting entrepreneurial city models around mega-events and postmodern iconic architecture. It did have its moment of glory in 2004, but foreign praise was momentary, between accusations of inadequacy in completing the works before the Olympics and limited valorization afterward. A little later, disaster struck.

2 Bauman 2011, Leontidou 2006, 2010, 2012. The alter-globalization new social movements escalated after the fall of the Berlin wall in 1989 and crystallized in the consumer society and digital communication, raising issues of identity, globalization, exploitation, dispossession — very different from class conflict in the industrial past. There is of course some debate about this; for a summary that includes Greece, see Kourliouros 2003 and Leontidou 2010.

Crisis and Emerging Orientalism in the EU

During the 2010s, all of this pomp and circumstance has turned into a nightmare. The debt crisis in the Eurozone hits Greece harder than other countries, with debt accumulating because of inflated interest rather than capital owed to lenders. Fictitious capital, money not existent in the market, and its accumulation into banks, squeezes the livelihoods of people and throws them into poverty in neoliberal economies of "accumulation by dispossession" (Harvey 2003). The real-estate bubble has a major role in the crisis, as anticipated by Harvey (2012). The EU has failed to put into practice its discourses for European solidarity and cohesion. It has abandoned the South to the neoliberal "markets" and still worse, it keeps accusing its people in a process of "othering."

This is not the place to unpack the reemergence of the "dark continent," Europe (Mazower 1998), not by war but by economies of "accumulation by dispossession." The present global financial crisis is reshuffling incomes and employment opportunities, but also social relations, cultural and national identities, and the sustainability of the EU itself. The roots of the problem are in the parasitic activities of banks and global usurers, which are more important in the context of neoliberal EU governance than people and their lives. The process of uneven development in the EU is an outcome of the global power of a financial system of banks and credit-rating agencies leading the system of "accumulation by dispossession" in the Eurozone and beyond. Two of these, Moody's and Standard & Poor's (with Fitz and others with a smaller share) monopolize global governance, which is no longer in the hands of national parliaments or even EU political institutions. Governance is exercised by "markets" with arbitrary rankings of the creditworthiness of whole countries, and with discursive evaluations that become self-fulfilling prophesies (Krugman 2012). Geographical imaginations for the periphery and the European South are engraved in the ongoing spectacle of these rankings.

"Othering" is actually the most important part of the story, because it makes default, or at least underdevelopment, a self-fulfilling prophesy. In EU assessments, ratings, scorn, and accusations against the periphery, we can discern a new version of Orientalism in Europe — "as a body of ideas, beliefs, *clichés*, or learning about the East" (Said 1978: 205), which, in our case, is the South of Europe and the broader periphery, too. The production of "the Orient" is not the same as in nineteenth-century Britain or France, which we find in Edward Said's postcolonial critique, but the analogy is similar and quite disturbing, too, because we are supposed to live in a unified Europe: "Orientalism is — and does not simply represent — a considerable dimension of modern politico-intellectual culture, and as such has less to do with the Orient than it does with 'our' world" (Said 1978: 12).

I will therefore use "Orientalism" metaphorically and heuristically here, to refer to the process of "othering" not of the East but of the EU periphery, which is wrongly considered responsible for the debt crisis. This is latent Orientalism, "an almost unconscious (and certainly an untouchable) positivity," which in some countries, such as Germany, is becoming manifest. Here "the various stated views about Oriental society" are not about "languages, literatures, history, sociology, and so forth" (Said 1978: 206), but about economic potential: a spectacle of hedge funds, spreads, interest rates, and inferior cultures. Other countries of northwestern Europe follow suit in seeing the Mediterranean just like "the Orient as a locale requiring Western attention, reconstruction, even redemption" (Said 1978: 206), but also punishment, in our case, because of its "untrustworthy," "immature" people. By contrast, global usury and international scandals are tolerated or hushed.

Sustainability, social cohesion, solidarity, and several similar "euro words" have now become vacant. The absence of developmental policy comes in stark contrast to the twentieth century, when aid was released to Greece in the interwar period by the League of Nations and the postwar Marshall Plan — whatever their colonial impact (Leontidou 1989). The EU achieved a wide expansion rather than integration, and the euro-currency has brought about exploitation and dispossession rather than cooperation and solidarity in the Eurozone. In this vicious circle, it is the people of the periphery who are considered responsible rather than victims. References to untrustworthiness and inferior cultures of "laziness" — biological determinism and moral-political admonishment"[3] — as well as the "delinquency" of youths rioting against the common sense of civilized nations, constitute systematic stigmatization bordering on racism. On top of this, naming, branding, and media framing has been used as the basis of austerity measures: cuts in salaries and pensions, heavy taxation across income groups, without any effort not only against tax evasion (or in effect tax indemnity) but even for the collection of unpaid certified taxes owed by entrepreneurs and smuggled abroad

3 Said 1978: 207, and 2000, where he investigates racist overtones in Orientalism.

by the rich. Greece has become a case study for "dispossession through naming" (Gregory 1994: 171)."To say simply that Orientalism was a rationalization of colonial rule is to ignore the extent to which colonial rule was justified in advance by Orientalism, rather than after the fact" (Said 1978: 166).

The new colonizers come from the Euro-zone in the guise of a troika (IMF-ECB-EC) that in early September 2012 demanded a six-day workweek and a thirteen-hour working day at almost half the salaries, returning Europe to the Middle Ages. Greece has become the test subject in the neoliberal process of annihilation of the welfare state, labor legislation, and all of the achievements of European culture over centuries. This is basically an urban rather than a rural crisis, involving the pauperization of the middle classes and the consequent urban blight, closures, and impoverishment. Athens is sinking into poverty, unemployment, despair, polarization, criminality. It is now seen as a dismal city rather than the location of European patrimony in Western eyes. The negative occidental gaze is especially noted from Germany, and the recent milder tones voiced by its government may come too late, because the damage is done. But not quite; solidarity pours in from several intellectuals and artists, who offer sympathy and acknowledge their indebtedness to classical Hellas and the Greek democratic traditions. Can this reverse the disaster in the long term?

There is a definite process of the reconstruction of the European South — or rather of the periphery, including Ireland — which echoes Gramsci's insightful analysis of "the Southern question" in Italy, no longer as a matter of development/ underdevelopment but as a question of political and financial domination in a globalized world (Leontidou 2012a). The dynamics of dependence and regional underdevelopment in interwar Italy were shaped by the restructuring of industrial production, but were also manifestly cultural rather than just economic (Gramsci 1971). Now the stigmatization of whole ethnic-national groups not only interferes with the state of the euro, suppressing national competitiveness and boosting spreads in the global markets; it also brings to the surface memories of Gramsci's Italy and fascist Germany, where different ethnic groups were stigmatized as a whole, and then destroyed with ethnic cleansing and genocides. North Europeans resurrect Gramsci's (1971: 70–71) "hegemony of the North over the Mezzogiorno in a territorial version of the town-country relationship — in other words, that the North concretely was an 'octopus'

which enriched itself at the expense of the South." Recent research has confirmed such enrichment for Germany in the context of the euro and its low cost of borrowing compared to the periphery, while at the same time the matter of a German wartime debt (Glezos 2012), as well as war reparation payments to Greece, are hushed, as if indemnity should be given. Rich countries and regions keep squeezing the poor and blaming them too in the EU today, just as in Gramsci's time, claiming that:

> **the causes of the poverty were not external, to be sought in objective economic and political conditions, but internal, innate to the population of the South — […] the organic incapacity of the inhabitants, their barbarity, their biological inferiority. These already widespread opinions (Neapolitan "vagabondry" is a legend which goes back a long way) were consolidated and actually theorised by the sociologists of positivism […], acquiring the strength of "scientific truth" in a period of superstition about science. […] Meanwhile, in the North there persisted the belief that the Mezzogiorno was a "ball and chain" for Italy, the conviction that the modern industrial civilisation of Northern Italy would have made greater progress without this "ball and chain", etc." (Gramsci 1971: 71)**

This is exactly the situation in the Eurozone today, where "the North" is mostly represented by German, but also other Northern, governments and media — and consequently by public opinion. As in the time of Gramsci, the North profits and at the same time accuses the South, adopting an arrogant colonial stance. It keeps it as a tourist destination, at the same time considering the South as a "ball and chain" holding back the development of the North. Gramsci's basic distinctions and antitheses between hegemonic and coercive power, productive and parasitic activities, and the concept of "spontaneity" return to the surface of the EU political economy, combined with geographical imaginations close to Said's Orientalism about "the lazy, unreliable, and delinquent Southerners."

Narratives of "delinquency" through media framing at home and abroad help in the negative construction of the identity of Athens, too. Media overpublicizes violent riots and underplays more massive urban social movements that assemble peacefully in the Mediterranean. They color most mobilizations as violent riots and activists as delinquents, in yet another process of "othering." Though it should not come as a surprise that destructive riots occasionally break out as impoverishment hits Athens (Vradis and Dalakoglou 2011), peaceful demonstrations are much larger. Visibility is highest for violence, unfortunately, and even for arson attacks on historic buildings in selected inner-city areas, which may well not have been random events (Leontidou 2012). Spectacles of urbicide dominate media discourses and images in Greece and abroad, and command heavy emphasis by governments, despite the fact that they are a minority phenomenon. This attention must have contributed in their recent configuration into fascist violence on the city streets and open markets (Dalakoglou 2012).

The antithesis to this was a massive peaceful movement of hundreds of thousands of people who gathered in Mediterranean piazzas in 2011 to protest and present democratic alternatives to (neo)colonialism in postcolonial Europe. Athens constitutes part of this Mediterranean mobilized space, consisting of cities of Southern Europe and North Africa. These movements were linked by political undercurrents from Tunisia and Egypt to Spain and Greece, in resistance to different kinds of autocracies (Leontidou 2012). The multi-activity and hybrid Greek urban piazzas have come to life in 2011 in the context of the South European "movement of the piazzas," which began with the "indignados" of Spain. The Athenian version was enacted in the focal public piazza, Syntagma Square. It lasted longer and spread rapidly to many other Athenian smaller piazzas, town squares in the rest of Greece, and as far as Thessaloniki. After sixty days of occupation of Syntagma by large populations and the police assault that cleared it in late July 2011, grassroots creativity reappeared less frequently in larger and smaller Athens piazzas and in other towns.

Against this process of construction of Greek identity of dignity and contention in Syntagma there emerged aggression by the dominant agents. Every mobilization after July 2011 has been met with tear gas, most often without provocation. Moreover, in direct analogy to the "de-turkization" of nineteenth-century Greece via orthogonal grids in cities, we can discern in the twenty-first century an effort for (neo)colonial de-Hellenization of Greece via neoliberal "rationality." The stereotypes are quite similar with those of Orientalism. Informality and spontaneity undergo a destructive critique in accordance with Northern stereotypes for "proper" development, and are negatively branded as tax evasion — with

the preservation of the indemnity of major tax evaders and international economic scandals such as that of Siemens. Orientalism also attacks mobilization and joie de vivre, which are negatively branded as delinquency, laziness, and untrustworthiness. "In these various ways, Mitchell observes, 'the space, the minds, and the bodies all materialized at the same moment, in a common economy of order and discipline'" (Gregory 1994: 173). For example, not only tax evasion and the shadow economy but the whole informal sector and spontaneity are under attack, and cities must be squeezed into the straightjacket of Northern neoliberal "rationality" and discipline. This analogy of Orientalism can be transferred to the whole Mediterranean, and in fact the EU periphery as a whole, where people are revolting against austerity, democratic deficit, and "othering" by the North, which have been destroying economies and cultures of the Mediterranean for over three years now.

Conclusion

The Western gaze cast on Greece, and especially Athens, passed from possessiveness with respect to European heritage and de-turkization in the nineteenth century to "othering," (neo)colonialism, and de-Hellenization in postcolonial Europe today. In West and North European eyes, Athens has been in the past the standard of civilization in the abstract sense (Boyer 1996), but mainly on the basis of antiquity. The Acropolis has remained a global symbol differentially perceived in various instances in space-time. Foreigners were possessive of the Acropolis and its treasures, and of the city hosting it (Loukaki 2008). They metamorphosed colonization into re-Hellenization by importing their neoclassical architecture to Athens during the nineteenth century. However, Athens turned against it in the postwar period: it grew by the deconstruction of its neoclassical heritage and has destroyed many layers of history. To the dismay of Westerners, Athens has been living its own history, retaining a postmodern collage in its landscape of spontaneous urbanization and informality (Leontidou 1993).

After a prolonged period of positive but colonial geographical imaginations, Europe was disillusioned with Athens and then later averted by it. The modern or perhaps postmodern city has now become the "other" city, the impoverished city, burdened with responsibilities for the collapse of the euro in an Orientalist colonial discourse bordering on racism. Today's city is not considered up to the standards of European modernity. There remains a contradiction, however, between such processes of "othering" and Western/ Northern images of Greece as the cradle of European civilization, which have been sustained globally for too long to be annihilated now, in the context of the debt crisis. It would be instructive to consider the hypothesis that the shifts discussed concern the Mediterranean as a whole, more or less, in this demanding epoch. However, the healing process has begun in the piazzas, which brought to the surface solidarity by a large community of intellectuals from the rest of Europe and the Americas. Their attitudes, perceptions, and geographical imaginations cannot ignore the contribution of Mediterranean cities to global culture.

Sources:

About, E. 1855. *Greece and the Greeks of the Present Day*. Edinburgh: Thomas Constable.

Afouxenidis A. 2006. "Urban Social Movements in Southern European Cities: Reflections on Toni Negri's 'The Mass and the Metropolis.'" *City: Analysis of Urban Trends, Culture, Theory, Policy, Action*, vol. 10, no 3: 287–294

Afouxenidis, A.,ed. 2012 (in Greek). *Inequality in the Period of the Crisis: Theoretical and Empirical Investigations*. Athens: Propobos.

Apostolopoulos Y., P. Loukissas. andL. Leontidou,eds., 2001. *Mediterranean Tourism: Facets of Socio-economic Development and Cultural Change*. London: Routledge.

Bastea, E. 2000. *The Creation of Modern Athens: Planning the Myth*. New York: Cambridge University Press.

Bauman, Z. 2011. *Collateral Damage: Social Inequalities in a Global Age*. Cambridge: Polity Press.

Biris, C. 1966 (in Greek). *Athens — From the Nineteenth to the Twentieth Century*. Athens: Foundation of Town Planning and History of Athens.

Boyer, M.C. 1996. *The City of Collective Memory: The Historical Imagery and Architectural Entertainments*. Cambridge, MA: MIT Press..

Couch, C., L. Leontidou, and G. Petschel-Held,eds. 2007. *Urban Sprawl in Europe: Landscapes, Land-use change, and Policy*. Oxford: Blackwell.

Crang, M., and P.S. Travlou. 2001. "The City and Topologies of Memory." *Society and Space* 19, 161–177.

Dalakoglou, D. 2012. "Beyond Spontaneity: Crisis, Violence, and Collective Action in Athens." *City* 16, 5: 535–545.

Diamandouros, N. 2000 (in Greek). *Cultural Dualism and Political Change in Post-authoritarian Greece*. Athens: Alexandria.

Glezos, M. 2012 (in Greek). *Even if it were one DM… German debts to Greece*. Athens: Livanis

Gospodini, A., and H. Beriatos, eds. (in Greek). 2006. *The New Urban Landscapes and the Greek City*. Athens: Kritiki.

Gramsci, A. 1971. *Selections from the Prison Notebooks*. Edited by Hoare and Smith. New York: International Publishers.

Gregory, D. 1994. *Geographical Imaginations*. Oxford: Blackwell.

Harvey, D. 2003. *The New Imperialism*. Oxford: Clarendon Press.

Harvey, D. 2012. *Rebel Cities: From the Right to the City to the Urban Revolution*. London: Verso.

Kaika, M. 2005. *City of Flows: Modernity, Nature, and the City*. New York: Routledge.

Kourliouros, E. 2003. "Reflections on the Economic-Noneconomic Debate: A Radical Geographical Perspective from the European South." *Antipode* 35: 781–789.

Krugman, P.R. 2012. *End This Depression Now!* London: Norton.

Leontidou, L. 1989 (in Greek with summary in English). *Cities of Silence: Working-Class Space in Athens and Piraeus, 1909–1940*. ETVA (Cultural Technological Foundation of the Hellenic Bank of Industrial Development) and Themelio, Athens.

Leontidou, L. 1990. *The Mediterranean City in Transition: Social Change and Urban Development*. Cambridge: Cambridge University Press.

Leontidou, L. 1993. "Postmodernism and the City: Mediterranean Versions." *Urban Studies*, vol. 30, no 6: 949–965.

Leontidou, L. 2010. "Urban Social Movements in 'Weak' Civil Societies: The Right to the City and Cosmopolitan Activism in Southern Europe." *Urban Studies* 47, 6, special issue *Cities, Justice, and Conflict*: 1179–1203.

Leontidou, L. 2012. "Athens in the Mediterranean 'Movement of the Piazzas': Spontaneity in Material and Virtual Public Spaces." *City: Analysis of Urban Trends, Culture, Theory, Policy, Action*, vol. 16, no 3: 299–312.

Leontidou, L. 2012a (in Greek). "The Reconstruction of the 'European South' in Post-Colonial Europe: From Class Conflict to Cultural Identities." In A. Afouxenidis, ed., 25–42.

Leontidou, L., and E. Marmaras. 2001. "From Tourists to Migrants: International Residential Tourism and the 'Littoralization' of Europe." In Y. Apostolopoulos et al., eds.: 257–267.

Leontidou, L., A. Afouxenidis, E. Kourliouros, and E. Marmaras. 2007. Infrastructure-Related Urban Sprawl: Mega-events and Hybrid Peri-urban Landscapes in Southern Europe." In Couch, Leontidou, and Petschel-Held, eds.: 69–101.

Loukaki, A. 2008. *Living Ruins, Value Conflicts*. Aldershot: Ashgate.

Mazower, M. 1998. *Dark Continent: Europe's Twentieth Century*. Harmondsworth: Penguin.

Papayiannakis, L. 1982 (in Greek). *The Greek Railroads (1882–1910): Geopolitical, Economic and Social Dimensions*. Educational Foundation of the National Bank, Athens.

Said, E. 1978. *Orientalism*. London: Pantheon Books.

Tsoucalas, C. 1977 (in Greek). *Dependence and Reproduction: The Social Role of Education Mechanisms in Greece (1830–1922)*. Athens: Themelio.

Vradis, A., and D. Dalakoglou, eds. 2011. *Revolt and Crisis in Greece: Between a Present Yet to Pass and a Future Still to Come*. London: AK Press & Occupied London.

A Means to Practical Ends
The Hydrometrics of Peter Fend
Timothy Ivison

The ecological theorist Wolfgang Sachs has made the observation that the image of the Earth from space — first in the hazy satellite feeds of the 1960s, and then spectacularly in Apollo 17's image from space of the "blue marble" in 1972 — eventually resulted in the formation of two ostensibly opposed logics: one, of the bounded, isolated, and fragile ecosystemic finitude of the world as it is imagined by the environmentalism movement; and the other, a validation of the vast, post-sovereign, borderless reach of global credit and capital flows. As Sachs describes:

In its detachment from the pitch-black cosmos, the terrestrial sphere stands out as a unified area whose continuous physical reality causes the frontiers between nations and polities to disappear — hence the visual message that what counts is perhaps the boundaries of the earth, but certainly not political frontiers. Only oceans, continents and islands can be seen, with no trace of nations, cultures or states.[1]

Sachs argues that ecological and transnational capitalist interpretations are constantly competing for hegemony within this semi-erased cartography, each redrawing and reinterpreting the earth through their projected desires.

In many ways, the artist Peter Fend works within this representational and conceptual tension that Sachs observes, exploiting the conceptual ambiguity and instability of the post-satellite world for his ambitious proposals. He sides with the environmentalist vision when it comes to the questions of *what is to be done*, but borrows the industrialist's borderless sense of enterprise when consulting the map, forging his own hybrid interpretation. His reasons for doing so are fairly direct: Fend believes that art can change the face of the earth.

Taking the form of modified cartography and satellite imagery, topographical sculptures, collage, patent diagrams and prototypes, models, text works, and essays, Peter Fend's work operates as a laboratory of proposals for rethinking our relationship to the earth along ecological and artistic principles. However, where Sachs sees an inherent opposition between the deterritorialization of global capital and the localized and specific territories of ecology, Fend sees an environmental art that follows the flows of

1   Wolfgang Sachs, Documentations, Papers, and Reports of the Heinrich Boell Foundation, No. 5: Globalization and Sustainability (Berlin: Heinrich-Böll-Stiftung, 2000), 4.

Timothy Ivison is an American artist and writer based in London. He has a collaborative practice with his partner, Julia Tcharfas, and they show with Hilary Crisp in London. He holds a Bachelor of Arts in Visual and Critical Studies and a Bachelor of Fine Arts in Studio Practice, both from the School of the Art Institute of Chicago. He is currently completing his Ph.D. on biopolitics in the history of British town planning at The London Consortium.

A Means to Practical Ends

the earth itself: a transnational and transcultural practice of public works responding to the shape and properties of global water-basin (that is to say, *hydrometric*) territories. Since his work began in the late 1970s, Fend has proposed to build land art installations around the world that would help remediate ancient ecologies, while introducing alternative energy technologies to transition away from fossil fuels. Working with biogas collection and fermentation technologies, Fend imagines a world after oil, where art is put to work to transform the environment. Although massive in its scale of ambition, Fend contends that the ends are necessary given the state of the world's ecosystems, and the means are plausible, supported by science and history.

Cohesive Units

In a recent show at Essex Street gallery in New York, Fend exhibited a series of collages that incorporated documentation from past projects, maps, and articles from years of work.[2] Viewing projects proposed for sites as disparate as New Zealand and the Persian Gulf, one got a keen sense of Fend's territorial practice. It was a show composed entirely of project proposals and details of their various political and practical vicissitudes, where each project began with reference to maps or satellite data, interpreted hydrometrically along the lines of the basins and coastlines rather than the conventional political boundaries. Whereas some of the projects presented significant technological experiments, such as biomass colleting mechanisms and sea rigs, others focused on mapping and comparative geographical analysis.[3]

For example, in a piece that incorporated material originally from 1981 entitled *Saltwa-ter-Basin Maps for Italy and Africa as Cohesive Units*, Fend created a tilted drawing of the African continent and its basin systems linked with the Mediterranean and Red Seas, with various smaller fragments in which the northern coast of Africa and the coastal contours of Italy form a coherent territorial formation. The image is striking in that it is drawn as an isolated mass and yet incorporates territories not commonly considered "cohesive units."

The image is sketched loosely on a large piece of archival paper — more to present the importance of the concept than to provide a decorative rendering — and it is surrounded by handwritten explanations and glued-in photocopies. Acknowledging the novelty of his diagram, Fend writes in the margins: "The NY Times and the Economist have editorialized that Africa needs post-colonial borders. I present this as a means to practical ends." One supposes that the practicality of the diagram inheres in its fidelity to the natural guidelines of the continental basins, but of course the shock lies more in its intentional disregard for existing sovereign-state territorial boundaries. The simplicity of the diagram has a compelling effect, and in front of the proposal, one quickly starts to think within its outlines. Unlike Sachs's binary reading of the earth-image, Fend suggests a logic by which it is the environmental agenda that runs freely across the globe, reorganizing society along the earth's own inherent topography. By demarcating the map along basin ridgelines — what he might call the topographic drainage systems of the globe — Fend imagines new regional economies emerging from ecologically aligned nation-states liberated from their colonial and postcolonial pasts. Within the overarching logic of water, a new reality emerges on the page that offers the Earth itself as the territorial arbiter of geopolitics.

However, more than simply reorganizing geographic thinking, Fend has concrete proposals for intervening in the hydrologic cycle, including man-made canals and lakes, hydroelectric generators, water-borne plant-harvesting devices, and biogas fermentation mechanisms. To this end, Fend has been operating under the name of his eco-engineering company, Ocean Earth Development Corporation, since its founding in 1980. Ocean Earth has been involved in a combination of satellite data analysis and research and development for renewable energy technologies, working with universities, governments, and private research organizations. Fend's maps, collages, sculptures, and text are exhibited in galleries and museums as the accretion of various ongoing proposals and contracts that

2 Peter Fend, Über Die Grenze, January 4–February 13, 2012, Essex Street, New York.

3 One piece, *After 9/11 Noticing a Parallel Between Iraq and New York*, compares the respective geography of the two regions, making note that both were first mapped by British imperialist administrations over 250 years apart. Parallel biogas energy harvesting projects are proposed.

Map of the world indicating
major hydrometric regions

Letterhead for Collaborative
Projects (Colab) circa 1978

The Offices of Fend, Fitzgibbon,
Holzer, Nadin, Prince, and
Winters, 1979

Peter Fend collecting sea plants
on the Ruhr river, Germany,
2010

[40]

Sequence of Acts to Build
A Gulf, 2011

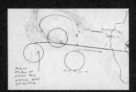

[41]

Three-Phase Excavation-
Flushing Scheme to Restore
The One Time Gulf of Triton,
2011

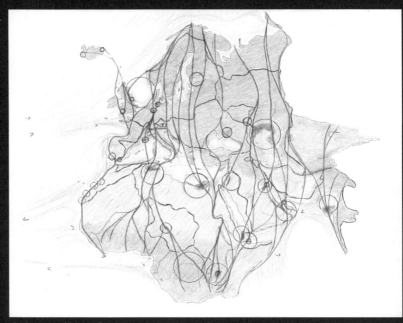

A baseline for planning of
actions: Libya/Egypt, Tunisia/
Algeria, Eritrea, Oman/UAE,
and inland Central Asia
projects, 2011

Ocean Earth pursues to develop alternative energy economies.

Ocean Earth

As one might imagine, Fend interprets his role as an artist in the broadest possible terms. He insists that it is art that will provide the means to achieve environmentalist goals, and he asserts an avant-garde model of the artist as engaged cultural catalyst rather than remote or alienated genius.[4] Instead of calling on a legacy of naturalists or climate scientists, Fend claims the work of the land art movement as his main working inspiration, especially projects by Robert Smithson, Gordon Matta-Clark, Dennis Oppenheim, Michael Heizer, and Joseph Beuys. Through the application of land art concepts to large-scale ecological projects (rather than to forms of symbolic contemplation), Fend sees an opportunity for artists to take up a legitimate and meaningful role in the contemporary political sphere. As Fend wrote in his Documenta IX essay from 1992: "Artists, if coordinated in legal ventures, can achieve — like any other profession — effective power. Art can get real."[5]

Of course the legal venture he refers to is implicitly his company, Ocean Earth Development Corporation. Part of "getting real" for Fend, is, in a sense, to secure the legitimacy of creative artistic interventions in the public sphere, and in this case, to be incorporated. But more important, the idea of an artist-run corporation is not based on the conceit of being "in business" as such, but rather on a collective model, de-emphasizing the individual artist and accrediting their practices beyond the confines of the art world. Describing the formation of Ocean Earth, Fend suggests that it "arose from efforts of artists to develop projects larger than possible for any one artist and of public rather than art-world service."[6]

This emphasis on "public rather than art-world service" and the idea that "art can get real" was a shared concern for Fend's peers in the downtown New York art scene at the end of the 1970s. Groups such as Collaborative Projects (Colab), of which Fend was an active member, made a distinct effort to engage with popular media, public spaces, and non-art audiences. For a short time he was involved in a "professional art services" group organized by the artist Jenny Holzer that exhibited as The Offices of Fend, Fitzgibbon, Holzer, Nadin, Prince, and Winters, or The Offices, for short.[7]

Ocean Earth Construction and Development (later renamed Ocean Earth Development Corporation) emerged out of these early experiments in 1980. Founding the organization against the prevailing trend in the art world to incorporate as a nonprofit, Fend took the advice of a lawyer and decided the project would be a mainstream for-profit enterprise with a number of artist shareholders, many of whom had been involved in Colab and The Offices.[8] Early collaborators included Paul Sharits, Taro Suzuki, Wolfgang Staehle, Eve Vaterlaus, Joan Waltemath, George Chaikin, Jenny Holzer, Colleen Fitzgibbon, and Dennis Oppenheim. The company was initially registered in the State of New York to "(1) provide 'media services' and (2) produce 'architectural components'" and included the production of various related technologies, under headings such as Sea Rigs, Marsh Construction, Video Monitoring, Containers, and Aqueducts.[9]

Of the many proposed ventures, it was commercially distributing and interpreting satellite-mapping data (i.e., "video monitoring") that initially became a relatively high-profile media enterprise for the group for the better part of the 1980s. Building on contacts made by Fend, Vaterlaus, and Waltemath in the course of their early exhibitions, this project entailed purchasing satellite data from organizations like the Earth Resources Observation Satellite Program in South Dakota or the European Space Agency in Rome, having the data processed at scientific imaging labs, and then selling it to global news outlets.

Although Ocean Earth often tried to pursue its environmental mandate by emphasizing the appearance of ecological anomalies in its satellite analysis, clients tended to be interested only in human geopolitical conflicts and catastrophes, which were easier to sell. Some of Ocean Earth's notable work in this field in the 1980s included providing data for major print and network news coverage of the Falklands War in 1982, the Iran-Iraq war in 1984, the Chernobyl disaster in 1986, and the Chad-Libya conflicts up through 1987.[10]

As early as 1976, Fend had been writing about the satellite view, insisting that artists must pick up where the Constructivists and the Futurists had begun in their fascination with the airplane and the aerial view. In fact, he suggests that Ocean Earth's aptitude in identifying sites and interpreting the satellite data was due not only to its critical and independent position outside the constraints of mainstream media, but also to the group's ability to think through the abstraction of satellite imagery — a distinct understanding of modern visual and spatial paradigms imparted through avant-garde art practices.[11] And although the mainstream

4   One of Fend's many manifestos on this subject, "Art Can Save Us" can be found online at http://inquest.us/art-can-save-us/

5   Peter Fend, "Paradise Built Art Gets Real?," Documenta IX, Kassel, vol. 2 (Stuttgart: Edition Cantz, 1992), 159.

6   Peter Fend, "A Post-Facto Statement Brief History of Ocean Earth Founded 1980," in Ocean Earth 1980 bis heute (Stuttgart: Oktagon Verlag, 1994), 11.

7   The artists were Peter Fend, Colleen Fitzgibbon, Jenny Holzer, Peter Nadin, Richard Prince, and Robin Winters.

8   Renamed in 1994 after years of confusion with the Paris-based Organisation for Economic Co-operation and Development (OECD).

9   For a full description, see Fend, "Founding Documents," Ocean Earth 1980 bis heute, 13.

10   A detailed account of the satellite era of Ocean Earth can be found in David Joselit and Rachel Harrison, "A Conversation with Peter Fend," October 125 (Summer 2008): 117–136.

11   "There was a very fundamental inability on the part of most media people, news-media people, to think abstractly or in twentieth-century artistic terms." Fend in Joselit and Harrison, "A Conversation with Peter Fend," 131.

Basins of Mediterranean/
Black Seas, 2012

birds, fish, b   [35]

Greece build

Iberia adapt

Gaza/Sinai b

News Room Global Milano,
Nowhere Gallery, Milan, 2011

Global Saltwater Basins
Centered on Antarctica

media rarely took an interest in the ecological purposes of their work, Fend believes that war and ecology tended to converge around the concept of territory: "who controls it, what is done with it, how it gets used."[12] This aspect of Fend's geography becomes readily apparent when one considers his land-art engineering schemes, usually sited near zones of political conflict, or historical sites of military history, or even more generally in his longstanding challenges to the fossil-fuel industry through worldwide alternative energy production — in many ways a battle over the fate of regional economies and territories.

Algeria and Libya

Fend's complex layering of science and technology, artistic intervention, and historical referencing is perhaps best reflected in a number of examples from his proposals for the Mediterranean Basin. First, I will look at two closely related sites from the south coast of the Mediterranean and then consider the wider scope for the region.

In an essay for *Ars Electronica* entitled "Art of the State," Fend writes:

In 1985, during the Iran-Iraq war, two participants in Ocean Earth visited a negotiator between Iran and Iraq, the Algerian Ambassador to France, to show him satellite photographs and war-zone analyses. There were three meetings. In the last meeting, he asked, what could we do to help the Algerian Army restore the Sahara Desert to savanna? He did not know we were artists. He just thought we could help solve their territorial problems. Since then, models and plans have been made; now, with the civil war easing, we'll respond.[13]

The models and plans that Fend and Ocean Earth developed in response to this almost mythical encounter with an Algerian ambassador bring together many of the concerns from projects already mentioned: a reassessment of regional geography, the proposal of earthworks, as well as the implementation of technologies toward a renewable resource industry. In short, Fend essentially proposes to convert a number of Algerian dry salt lakes into energy farms.

To be specific, the proposal begins with the cutting of large channels from the Mediterranean Sea on either side of the city of Gabès, in Tunisia, hundreds of kilometers west into Algeria. For this, Fend would make reference to Michael Heizer's monumental land-art piece Double Negative (1969). Double Negative is essentially two monumental 457-meter-long trenches dug into the earth on either side of a canyon in Nevada, but in Fend's version, the trenches would straddle either side of the city of Gabès. This would bring Mediterranean Sea water into a natural depression extending from the Gulf of Gabès into Algeria, where currently a series of dry salt lakes, or chotts, are all that is left of the legendary Lake Tritonis, a body of water that spanned both countries, described by Herodotus in the fifth century BC.[14]

Archeologists and colonialists of the nineteenth century studying the area revived interest in possibly flooding the site to expand trade, a project dramatized in Jules Verne's novel The Invasion of the Sea (1905), but to this day, the site remains an arid depression.[15] If completed, Fend's proposal would allow seawater to circulate continuously into the dry salt lakes, flushing out the excess salt over the course of the next few decades and eventually restoring the former gulf of Triton to a state unknown since antiquity. Rather than using it primarily as a new trading port, Fend proposes to harvest algae and to use this as the basis for a biogas hydrocarbon economy on the banks of the Triton.

Fend frames the venture not as a straightforward ecological remediation project but within a kind of symbolic monumentality more akin to a work of public art, making reference simultaneously to ancient history and twentieth-century military conquest: the chotts happen to be very near the site of the 1943 Battle of Wadi Akarit, in which Allied forces successfully pushed back the Axis powers to the city of Tunis. Fend suggests that the project could also be supported by Italian civil engineering firms, using military-grade explosives to dig the necessary channels as a commemoration of fallen soldiers. On the site of another ill-fated Italian campaign of 1942, that of El-Alamein in northern Egypt, Fend has sited another, even larger proposal that would connect the site through to Libya.[16] The work is similar in its general approach to the scheme in the Gulf of Triton, but with very different geographic and symbolic consequences. Anyone who has studied the Qattara Depression that lies just south of El-Alamein will know that, much like the Triton, there have been a number of modern proposals to flood it. At 19,605 square meters in area and 133 meters below sea level, the site has primarily been considered as a potential energy source, which would be achieved by channeling Mediterranean waters through El-Alamein down into the depression,

12   Joselit and Harrison, "A Conversation with Peter Fend," 130.

13   Peter Fend, "Art of the State," published in *Unplugged* (Linz: Ars Electronica, 2002), 307. Published in conjunction with the festival "Ars Electronica" held annually in Linz, Austria.

14   George Rawlinson, *The History of Herodotus,* vol. III (London: John Murray, 1862), 126–127.

15   See, for instance, Donald Mackenzie, *The Flooding of the Sahara: An Account of the Proposed Plan for Opening Central Africa to Commerce and Civilization from the North-west Coast, with a Description of Soudan and Western Sahara, and Notes of Ancient Manuscripts, &c.* (London: S. Low, Marston, Searle, & Rivington, 1877).

16   There were two major battles at El-Alamein in World War II. The first was in July of 1942, the second in October–November 1942

exploiting the force of gravity to generate hydroelectricity. The problem, from an ecological standpoint, is that many of the proposals have involved making the depression into a hypersaline lake — drawing water toward the depression only to allow it to evaporate in the basin, to control water levels and bring in yet more seawater. Granted, the system would be able to produce massive amounts of energy, but it would not support life, nor would it contribute to an improved regional ecosystem. Thus no local or sustainable economies would be possible — only one large-scale, export-driven hydroelectric plant.

In Fend's proposal, a solution arises from observing the larger context of the depression and considering an outlet that might provide a continuous flow of water. Instead of a salt pan created by evaporating Mediterranean waters, the depression could be connected at two points: one beginning at El-Alamein in Egypt, leading toward the right edge of the depression, and another extremely long canal that would ultimately empty out on the western coast of Libya, just south of the city of Benghazi. This crescent canal would cut directly across the northern segment of the Libyan state — the region known as Cyrenaica when it was under Italian colonial rule — turning it into an island and making the Qattara Depression into a kind of estuary serviced by a constant influx of Mediterranean water and freshwater land runoff. This process would begin to reverse hundreds of years of soil degradation and help to reinvigorate the biodiversity of the region. In 1986, in an essay called simply "Towards Libyan Development," Fend elaborated his rationale for the project:

> **For the peoples of the Mediterranean Sea, as well as of other nearby countries in Europe and Africa, the singular question is not whether Libya will be attacked by several U.S. air strikes, as perhaps a dramatic gesture, but whether Libya will become even more part of an enormous Void in the biosphere of the planet. The Sahara is expanding. It expands faster than ever in recorded history, and it expands faster throughout northern Africa, faster than it had during the Roman Empire, which is allegedly responsible for much of Libya's current emptiness. Shall we humans in modern times now outpace the destructiveness of the allegedly careless Romans?**
> **It is not just desirable to restore the Sahara to the vast, animal-rich savannah it once was; it is vital to do so.**[17]

In both projects outlined above, Fend advocates an intensive practice of algae and seaplant harvesting to produce biogas for energy production. In proposing a transition away from oil, Fend is working with regions that are both dominated by fossil-fuel economies and suffering from the ever-expanding frontiers of the desert. But rather than simply challenging the legitimacy of oil and mining companies on ecological grounds (which Fend takes as a given), he offers what seem to be fairly ambitious but feasible alternatives, using known techniques in a variety of different configurations. Instead of relying on archaic deposits of fossilized hydrocarbons, these projects attempt to realize the potential of making fuel from readily available or easily created sources of biomass. This is what Fend calls a comprehensive "biological real-time approach to oil," in which the hydrocarbon resources are harvested at the very beginning of the biomass cycle, rather than extracted from under the earth millions of years later.[18]

Mediterranean Projects

Fend often extends the logic of these projects to sites across the Mediterranean Basin, offering a series of micro-regional proposals to address points throughout the hydrometric system. In 2011, he produced a short text for an exhibition in Milan that seems to sum up the scope of his ambitions for the region, both temporally and spatially. Under the title *Middle of the World Construction Work*, Fend and the Ocean Earth Development Corporation proposed the following interventions:

1 **Ancient gulf restored, 300 km west into Algeria**
2 **New island created, separated from rest of Libya**
3 **Nile lakes cleared out, to yield local fuel and fish**
4 **Relinking with the Alps, Milan/Turin banish smog**
5 **Birds, fish, beaver, wolf all return, in migrations**
6 **Greece builds a new fuel base, and jobs, in the sea**
7 **Iberia adapts its many dams, restoring river health**
8 **Gaza/Sinai become self-reliant, using Nile runoff**
9 **Black Sea shifts to a sun-supplied gas economy**[19]

As a series of spatial overhauls, the topography of the Mediterranean mega-region is succinctly transformed between number one

17 Peter Fend, "Towards Libyan Development," in *Ocean Earth 1980 bis heute*, 91.

18 Peter Fend, in discussion with the author, August 4, 2012.

19 "News Room Global Milano," Nowhere Gallery, Milan, 2011.

and number nine. Including our two examples from Algeria and Libya, the list reads as an ecological and geopolitical manifesto — implicitly involving a number of complex economic and cultural contingencies, and potential time scales ranging from the next few decades to the next few hundred years. And yet, even out of context, no one proposal seems any less likely than another. In fact, the similarities in scale to projects already under way in places like China and Dubai make these seem strangely plausible.

The list of works in *Middle of the World Construction Work* seems to expand and complicate our sense of the Mediterranean region, but where *Middle of the World* differs from the basin mapping considered earlier is that it focuses not on the shift in geographical perception (which is implicit) but on the interrelation of a constellation of highly specific forms of intervention in regional hydrometric theaters. Much of it concerns the long-term conversion to biogas and hydroelectric economies achieved through artistic and engineering means. As with the ambitions of land art, Fend would transform the landscape of the Mediterranean Basin and its surrounding regions by carving into the earth, cultivating the waterways, and restoring wild ecosystems.

Inevitably, Fend has been criticized for the megalomania of his proposals, but he maintains that his ambitions are in line with the scale of global development and military projects. He suggests that if we are willing to spend $5 billion on defense, perhaps we are willing to spend a few million on art projects that actually intend to transform the physical environment for the better.[20]

On the other hand, the Mediterranean itself seems to attract such projects.

Long before Peter Fend turned his attention to the dry salt lakes of North Africa, geographers and military officers of the nineteenth and early twentieth centuries were surveying the territory and making plans for similar interventions, if under the auspices of quite different geopolitical motivations. Countless geographical thinkers have observed the Mediterranean and seen not an agglomeration of fragmented cultures, but a vast zone of opportunity for the choreography of economic and cultural activity. Herman Sörgel's comprehensive idea of Atlantropa from the 1930s is exemplary of the ambitions of civil engineering in the twentieth century to master the Mediterranean as a territory. Envisioned as a totally industrialized hy-

droelectric economy, Atlantropa would stretch from the damming of the Straight of Gibraltar to the settlement of a drained Adriatic Sea.[21]

As early as 1832, the Saint-Simonian engineer Michel Chevalier wrote in Le Globe an essay entitled "Système de la Méditerranée," which consisted of a visionary proposal to link up the entire region, not through ecological interventions per se but through the widespread establishment of international and intercontinental railways and canals.[22] As an engineer, free-trade advocate, and devout follower of the philosophy of Henri de Saint-Simon, Chevalier promoted the idea of universal association made possible by vast industrial systems of both government and infrastructure. As media theorist Armand Mattelart explains:

> **The confederation of peoples organized in a Mediterranean system encompassing the Black and Caspian seas was for Chevalier the first step towards a Universal Association. [...] From Sebastopol to Gibraltar, from Carthage to Smyrna, from Venice to Alexandria, from Constantinople to the Persian Gulf via Baghdad, Basra, and Mesopotamia, Chevalier projected the ramifications of this imaginary system of rail, water, and sea routes — what he called "circulating civilization" — that would "awaken slumbering countrysides from their torpor."[23]**

In many ways Fend himself reflects Chevalier's Saint-Simonian spirit, through his development entity Ocean Earth and through his belief in affecting social change through great works of civil engineering. The comparison becomes even more apt when considered alongside Fend's convictions on the role of the artist in society. It was Saint-Simon who theorized a new society led by men of science, industry, and the arts, rather than the aristocracy, constituting a "Parliament of Improvement" ruled by science and technology.[24] Although extremely influential in France in the late eighteenth and early nineteenth centuries, Saint-Simon is paradoxically not often cited in our age of global infrastructure and communications. But as Italo Calvino has commented, "If no one today reads Saint-Simon or refers to him, it is because the technocratic and productivistic 'industrial society' he prophesied has triumphed."[25]

Likewise, Fend would prefer his work to appear feasible and eminently sensible rather than radically oppositional. He constantly argues for artists' proper place alongside the highest levels of government to be regarded as seriously as the military or the oil industry.

20 Peter Fend, in discussion with the author, August 4, 2012.

21 Willey Ley, *Engineers' Dreams* (London: Phoenix House, 1955).

22 Michel Chevalier, La Système de la Méditerranée (Paris: Au Bureaux du Globe, 1832).

23 Armand Mattelart, *The Invention of Communication* (Minneapolis and London: University of Minnesota Press, 1996), 104.

24 Henri de Saint-Simon, "Extract on Social Organization," in Henri de Saint-Simon (1760–1825), *Selected Writings on Science, Industry, and Social Organisation*, edited and translated by Keith Taylor, 83 (London: Croom Helm, 1975). Originally published in Comte Henri de Saint-Simon, Lettres d'un habitant de Genève à ses contemporains (1803), réimprimées conformément à l'édition originale et suivies de deux documents inédits — Lettre aux Européens, [Essai sur l'organisation sociale], ed. Alfred Pereire, 87–93 (Paris: Libraire Felix Alcan, 1925).

25 Italo Calvino, *The Literature Machine: Essays*, translated by Patrick Creagh (London: Secker and Warburg, 1987), 223.

"We — the artists — will be your vanguard. The power of the arts is in effect the most immediate and most rapid of all powers. We have all kinds of weapons."[26] Although the words are Saint Simon's, it is as though they were ripped from a page of Fend's script.

For Saint-Simon, industrial association and civil engineering were the cornerstones of the avant-garde; man would conquer mortal life through organization and technical brilliance. But where Saint-Simon saw the need for social reconstruction through environmental projects, Fend fundamentally sees the need for ecological reconstruction via social projects. Here, Fend is not only reconceptualizing the territory but attempting to shape it for remedial and aesthetic purposes. He seems to adapt the Enlightenment idea that nature is to be improved and organized to optimize its innate potential. Even though one might say that we are now living in the fallout of the last century of attempts to improve nature — the same improvements championed by the Saint-Simonians — Fend believes we may yet improve again. North Africa, like North America and the rest of the world, must turn away from the oil economy and toward the bio-economy, away from the megastructural dams and toward the hundreds of undershot hydroelectric turbines nested in rivers and streams to produce local power.[27] Writing in response to the Three Gorges dam project in China, Fend lays out an ultimatum:

> **Either the planet continues with its self-destructive technologies of the petroleum and nuclear era, worsened with giant civil structures that destroy rivers as bloodstreams on terrain, or the planet becomes replete with technologies of renewable energy production, coupled with the harnessing and shaping of rivers which foster a "variety theater" of fish, birds and other wildlife.[28]**

This call for renewable technologies, for something like a second ecological-industrial revolution, is reminiscent of the galvanizing rhetoric of Patrick Geddes and Lewis Mumford, also diehard regionalists like Fend. As keen observers of industrial urbanization, they examined recent history as a moment mired in an environmentally and morally degrading Paleotechnic era, relying on mining and fossil fuels for a brutish industrial present. They contrasted this notion with Neotechnics, a concept that offered technological solutions for a cleaner, socially beneficial and ecologically sound future. Mumford would extend this to a notion of Biotechnics in later writing, linking his affinities with the emerging environmentalist movement.[29] The path is clear for these kinds of thinkers, and large-scale ecological and geopolitical intervention, although daunting, is, as Fend says, "a means to practical ends" in the larger scope of history.

Representation, toward Action

Thus the Mediterranean Basin awaits its transformation (or transition, as it were) toward a biotechnic future, shaped by the innovations of Peter Fend and Ocean Earth. But the catalyst for a technical and social revolution on such a scale does not seem forthcoming, and Fend keeps a long ledger of the forces that undermine his efforts. As he often points out, there has been no important land art produced since 1978, the year that Dennis Oppenheim's commission to build earthworks in Iran was cancelled by the Islamic Revolution. Within two years, Fend founded Ocean Earth and has been promoting an ecological revolution through earthworks and satellites ever since.

Although he might not endorse this interpretation, Fend has been immensely successful without ever finishing a single project. The effect of Fend's proposals are as much visual as they are conceptual, and this is perhaps why they continue to function within the art world, to his great frustration. Considering Sachs's essay on the image of the Earth from space, we realize that even simple shifts in visual perspective can precipitate considerable shifts in political consciousness. Likewise, when confronting basic continental maps, we expect to see a certain uniformity. Hydrometric visualizations essentially destabilize these assumptions. In a sense, it is the very idea of the hydrometric system that catalyzes a change in one's perception.

Fend, though, demands much more. Rachel Harrison wrote in that, "If every time you read the name Damien Hirst in the newspaper it said Peter Fend instead, we wouldn't have this BP mess in the Gulf of Mexico. If Peter Fend were as famous as Jeff Koons, there would be no toxic nightmare in our oceans."[30] Hydrometrics are merely the factual context in which interventions can be made. Art must take as a given this transformative perspective and work with it as a raw material of sorts. We need an art commensurate with the perspective that the satellite provides, but not limited to a contemplation of its frame.

26   Saint-Simon and Halévy, *Selected Writings,* 281.

27   This alludes to Fend's proposal for the Three Gorges region in China, included in the exhibition Ecologies: Mark Dion, Peter Fend, Dan Peterman, held at the Smart Museum of Art, University of Chicago, in 2000.

28   Stephanie Smith, *Ecologies: Mark Dion, Peter Fend, Dan Peterman* (Chicago: The David and Alfred Smart Museum of Art, University of Chicago, 2001), 71.

29   See Patrick Geddes, *Cities in Evolution: An Introduction to the Town Planning Movement and the Study of Civics* (London: Williams & Norgate, 1915); Lewis Mumford, *Technics and Civilization* (New York: Harcourt, Brace & Company, Inc., 1934); Lewis Mumford, *The Culture of Cities* (New York: Harcourt, Brace & Company, Inc., 1938).

30   Rachel Harrison, "Artist's Favourites," *Spike Art Quarterly* 25, Autumn 2010, 27.

Space, Memory, Rhythm, and Time
Constructing a Mediterranean Archive
Iain Chambers

Archives assemble.
— Michel-Rolph Trouillot

Time does not pass, it accumulates…
— Ian Baucom

To think of a diverse manner of reading, inhabiting, receiving, and mapping the Mediterranean is to consider how the intertwining of histories and cultures are suspended and sustained in the spatio-temporal coordinates associated with its name. I suppose the point is to seek another way of telling, a narrative style able, if not to encompass, at least to register an excess of sense that spills over and beyond reductive rationalisms and the confines imposed by existing powers. To free up the materials and materialities of the Mediterranean, and permit them to float into other accounts, is both to extend and deepen a configuration and to wrench it away from the pretense of an exhaustive telling. This is a vast argument that evokes an extended critical engagement with the disciplines, institutions, and authorities that have given rise to modern definitions of this particular space. To impose some sort of critical shape, I suggest simply to concentrate on the terms announced in the title: space, memory, rhythm, time, and the archive. We will see, however, that their separation is itself ultimately impossible: each is imbricated in the other, and the critical constellation that results is itself always in transit, an integral part of the history it seeks to pronounce.

No single definition or spatial confinement can contain what we are seeking to talk about. Looking at Philippe Rekacewicz's hand-drawn maps of present-day European borders, we note how these stretch way across the Mediterranean and deep into North Africa (Rekacewicz 2009). Not only foodstuffs destined for European markets are grown according to standards established by EU legislation, but the thousands of deaths of migrants in the Sahara and the Mediterranean Sea are also directly attributable to European law. As a commercial, political, and juridical space, the Mediterranean, and its European-dominated definition, is mobilized along invisible frontiers thousands of kilometers southward and eastward from its shorelines. Four hundred years ago, a major European and Mediterranean power — the Ottoman Empire — also exercised extensive powers on a similar scale: from Budapest to Baghdad, from the Black Sea to modern Algeria. The Mediterranean has always been sustained and suspended in wider networks. More recently, Fernand Braudel was making a similar argument, referring to a Mediterranean that rolled northward towards the Baltic and southward across the Sahara. These considerations suggest the adoption of mobile and multiple frames of reference for understanding its continual composition. If the attempt to introduce more disruptive currents into the

Iain Chambers has developed interdisciplinary and intercultural work on music and
popular and metropolitan cultures. More
recently, he has transmuted this line of
research into a series of postcolonial analyses
of the formation of the modern Mediterranean.

He is author of *Urban Rhythms: Pop
Music and Popular Culture* (1985), *The
Metropolitan Experience* (1986), *Border
Dialogues: Journeys in Postmodernity* (1990),
Migrancy, Culture, Identity (1994), *Hendrix,
Hip Hop e l'interruzione del pensiero* (with
Paul Gilroy,1995), *Culture after Humanism*
(2001), *Mediterranean Crossings: The Politics
of an Interrupted Modernity* (2008), and
*Mediterraneo Blues: Musiche, Malinconia
Postcoloniale, Pensieri marittimi* (2012).

He is also coeditor (with Lidia Curti) of
*The Post-Colonial Question: Common Skies,
Divided Horizons* (1996) and the volume
*Esercizi di Potere. Gramsci, Said e il postcolo-
niale* (2006). Several of these titles have been
translated into various languages including
Italian, Spanish, German, Japanese, and
Turkish.

consideration of the Mediterranean past — for example, Martin Bernal's *Black Athena* — have hardly dented disciplinary defenses, the insistence on the creolized cultural configuration and hybridized historical formation of the Mediterranean nevertheless persists and resists. In food, taste, language, sound, and music other cartographies are sustained, and these suggest a mixing and remixing of histories related to altogether more extensive geographies (Chambers 2012). Tomatoes from Peru and coffee from Ethiopia are a culinary cartography that travels on a far wider axis than what is assumed by largely European definitions of the composition of the present-day Mediterranean. Such geographies offer a complex and multiscalar sense of belonging. They breach those offered by the apparent stability of existing localisms, nationalisms, and their institutional definitions.

So, rather than a single space to be studied, the Mediterranean — as an area in-between Europe, Asia, and Africa — becomes an interleaved and multi-stratified constellation, a point of dispersion and dissemination rather than a single, concentrated unity. Yannis Hamilakis, referring to the exclusive pretensions of modern Western archeology, calls this "alternative engagements with materiality and temporality" (Hamilakis 2011). Responding to this perspective is to engage with multiple and diverse archeologies. This means that Egypt, Greece, and Palestine do not only exist as ancient Egypt, Greece, and Palestine. They cannot be reduced to the Pharaohs, Hellenism, and the land of the Bible, representing monumental, now superseded, moments in the subsequent development of European civilization (Ra'ad 2010). They are not merely the mirror of Europe's historical past and contemporary scientific progress, which recovers that past while measuring and ultimately setting itself against it. In this parable, the centuries in between of Arab, Ottoman, and Balkan histories and cultures can only constitute a deviation to be expunged. The eastern Mediterranean is thoroughly Europeanized, and the continuities and contemporary impact of Islam, Arab culture, and the Ottoman Empire, obliterated. To return those histories from the void carries us well beyond a structural adjustment; it offers the possibility for a radical reconfiguration of the history (and culture) that presumes it is best able to tell the tale, define the Mediterranean, manage its archive, and propose its meanings.

Memory

The materiality of memory — those sounds, flavors, and tastes sustained in linguistic, musical, and culinary arrangements, for example — suggests a Mediterranean that defies an obvious linearity. The past that survives and lives on in these languages, frequently ignored, refused and reduced to the cultural marginalia of the established historical archive, actually promotes a diverse type of historical recollection. Altogether more ragged, modest, and incomplete, this is a memory that proposes a past, which, as Nietzsche reminds us, cannot be dissolved into pure knowledge (Nietzsche 2010). Cultural and artistic proposals mark time and space, evoking localities, archives, and memories that simultaneously deepen and extend the sense of the past as a connective medium, bringing together in their differences a mobile communality and potential conviviality. Here a conventional historical and geographical map of the Mediterranean, operating along the bidimensional plane of sensorial indifference, can be torn and creased; it can be folded into other, unsuspected accountings and testimonies of time to produce a further critical space. To repeat, perhaps it is in the arts — from the musical and visual to the literary and culinary — that this critical chance is best sought.

Against the blunt impositions of institutional power, the means of memory promote a poetics that in turn leads to a very different political understanding. This other power, stemming from minor histories and subaltern cartographies, does not merely confuse and confute the existing picture, but actually sets the terms for another map and a further unplanned geography of a Mediterranean still to be acknowledged, registered, and received. Here we are constantly forced to recognize the limits of inherited narrative apparatuses. The performative power of memory promotes an archive whose coordinates may initially coincide with, but ultimately confute, the established referents.

As Chris Marker evoked so strongly in his film *Sans Soleil* (1983), memory requires a means, and is perhaps inseparable from the medium in which it is registered. Cinema as a means of memory brings us into a conversation with Michael Haneke's film *Caché* (2005). A repressed and negated presence — Algeria — irrupts in the daily fabric of modern-day Paris. Within the shared coordinates of colonialism uniting France and Algeria, the film promotes the unwinding of history under the impact of anonymous missives from a colonial past that refuses to pass. The wound remains open, unattended, and ready to infect the present. The regular beat of everyday Parisian bourgeois life is interrupted, pushed out of synch, reversed and crossed by other rhythms and voices unable to find accommodation in the accepted score. We are invited to consider who is looking at whom: the familiar gaze — under Western eyes — is challenged by objects refusing to accept the cultural and historical destiny of that ocular logic. The once colonized object insists on its rights to be a (postcolonial) subject, and the West, too, now finds itself exposed in the anonymous gaze of objectification.

Knowledge, a memory (filtered, censured, forgotten, and denied) of the place of Algeria (and colonialism) in the making of modern France (and Europe) becomes the site of an interruption. As a cut in time through which other times appear, the film insists on the ordinary, everyday textures and sentiments of this negated and unconscious dimension of modernity. Declaring he has "nothing to hide," the protagonist consistently seeks to avoid that heart of darkness that would undo his present, his presence. Time, however, like the anonymous videocassettes arriving on his doorstep, can be rapidly reversed to register the presence of the past in what is occurring today. The logic of linearity that insists on the single and homogeneous order of the present — history as the progressive passage of temporality — is cut up to encourage another montage. Here, to affront the question of time — whose, where, why, and how? — is to consider the possibility of its "normal" flow and direction being deviated and contested. To maintain this lie of time, that is, to insist that time is unique and its meaning unequivocal, is not only to negate the colonial constitution of the contemporary West seemingly consigned to the mausoleum of history. It is also to perpetuate what Hannah Arendt called the banality of evil. It is here that we encounter all the powers of a colonial present.

Rhythm

At this point, we are invited to think less in terms of the blocks of time of conventional, chronological history and geometrical space, and rather to distill such concepts into the sociality of a time-space continuum that is perceived in intervals, interruptions, and rhythm (Gérardot 2007). Rhythm is a force that pushes us into thinking the material movement of bodies and cultures in time and space. To propose a geography of rhythm is to set knowledge and its disciplines to another pulse. To consider the time and space of the Mediterranean in the manner of intervals is to witness the return of communal and conflictual elements in an unfolding composition. This is, once again, to insist on slicing up the continuum of time and space into singularities that propagate a communal discontinuity: both are disseminated in the rhythmic imperatives of diverse localities, and there folded into their immediate urgencies. If rhythm is about a regulated movement, it is clearly of an order diverse from the flat linearity announced in the ocular organization of chronology and maps. Rhythms can change both pulse and speed, pick up further accents, emphasize and fade away. Rhythm pursues a constant return that engenders difference and produces it (Lefebvre 1996). Rhythm is of the body, of the historical body, of the history that produces the body and in turn is appropriated by that body. If rhythm orders time and space into recognizable instances and intervals, it marks what Amiri Baraka and Paul Gilroy on their meditations on African-American music call a "changing same."

Listening to the intensities of historical and cultural orchestration, where multiple elements are brought into play, is not to make an argument about a perpetual state or essence of the Mediterranean. It is, rather, to insist on a radically diverse account of time and the identification of space; one that is obviously pre- and post-national in its abjuring of given geopolitical entities, but also one that insists on the heterotopic understanding of time responding to diverse rhythms that produce different versions of the apparently shared space that we call modernity. To offer a history that seeks its sources in the rhythms of the Mediterranean is not to seek a secret center that scores the narration but rather a polyrhythmic coming together that grounds, provokes, and promotes multiple and individual voicing. We are not looking for an organizing principle but a process of dissemination, not a conceptual rule but a critical rhythm. It is the latter that is potentially able to host the diversity of the unsuspected, while the former can only impose itself through refusing the interruption of elements that disturb and interrogate the premises of its taxonomies.

This, and to step into a further dimension, is to challenge the violence of the prevalent logic of "vulnerability, space and frontiers" (Ribeiro Sanches 2008), where the flattening of space and the unilateral management of time serves to confirm precise locations and limits that are the objects of surveillance, protection, policing, and the promotion of provincial political and disciplinary identities. The threat of polyvocal heterogeneity, disturbing the well-ordered picture and frame of analysis, is contested in the name of an implacable logic: the nation, the West, Christianity, Fortress Europe, together with their associated traditions and mechanisms of knowledge. Of course, we know that these traditions are all contaminated, as none of their concepts and practices have developed in isolation; they all depend on being split between their self and an other: they are all products of intercultural translations and historical transit, none are autonomous or "pure." Just as Christianity is so deeply imbricated in the genealogy of the two other monotheisms of Judaism and Islam as to be a variant, so the West without the rest collapses as a conceptual space. This is to deterritorialize an imposed understanding of the Mediterranean and the Occidental modernity that produced this picture. There exist times and spaces outside and beyond the nation and the modernity it presumes to embody. To acknowledge what Deleuze and Guattari would at this point have nominated, as "minor histories" is precisely to disseminate a discontinuity in the *grand récit* (Deleuze and Guattari 1986). It is not simply to add forgotten and repressed narratives to the historical telling. These other histories, precisely because they exceed the framing employed by the institutions telling the tale (from the national museum to the school textbook), propose another history. They virtualize a history that may well be unrecognized and largely refused, but that nevertheless exists and persists. Sustaining an alternative rhythm to our accounting of time and space, such histories expose the Mediterranean, maps of meaning sustained in a critical transit that refuses to halt in the homecoming proposed by the confines of Europe.

Folds and Sediments

A multilateral Mediterranean, irreducible to European history and geography, points to a further critical space. If the European I/eye (Pratt 1992) can clearly no longer speak for, or in the name of, its other shores, it can nevertheless take an apprenticeship in learning to speak by, in the vicinity (Djebar 1999), of an African and Asian Mediterranean. The historical narrative and European framing that seemingly sets the terms for past and present understandings, from Ferdinand Braudel to David Abulafia, can be interrupted and interrogated (Braudel 1996, Abufalia 2011). The teleology of an explanatory unfolding in time and space under the banner of "progress" (but who defines that very loaded term, even when it is part of the *longue durée*?) can be deviated and set within another set of coordinates. Space, as Henri Lefebvre insisted, is socially produced, and it can always be mapped from elsewhere (Lefebvre 1991). While engaging with European explanation, it is also possible to propose voices, bodies, and histories that such an explanation has structurally marginalized and consistently sought to rob of any significant authority. Islamic, Arab, and Turkish cultures as components of both the Mediterranean and Europe — of its cultural, religious, and political life — are reduced to culinary details and musical inflections, minor details in the epic of Occidental development. We still move within a European-derived history that remains largely oblivious to the critique of its historicism. Despite the disturbing noises that arrive from the archive — that of the contested formation of the modern Atlantic, for example — history continues to be housed in the security of continuity. Unruly bodies that refused to respect an imposed order transformed the Atlantic world into the side of the modern African diaspora and rendered acknowledging the history of racist slavery pivotal to its history. Drawing from the margins the revolt, rebellion, and revolution of slaves, runaways, convicts, sailors, and pirates produces a heterotopic space that stages the refusal of the violent rationale of capitalist organization (Gilroy 1993, Trouillot 1995, Hall 2002, Linebaugh and Rediker 2002, Baucom 2005). This is a transcultural modernity from below that most obviously challenges the imperative narrative and image of the modern Atlantic world as the untarnished site of modern democracy and its economical, cultural, political, and philosophical organization of modernity. The sea, as the Caribbean poet Derek Walcott informs us, harbors another history. This is a history sustained in an archipelago of cultures that creolize all attempts to flatten out the modern world to accommodate a unique point of view and unilateral will to power.

To abandon the prevalent historical narrative in the gardens of historicism, annotating time and registering "progress," and to lean into the margins is to catch the whiff of a counter-historiography. Surely, today it is impossible to pretend to narrate the past, to explore the archive, to mine memory, after Nietzsche and Freud, after Gramsci and Benjamin, after Derrida and Foucault, as though we are dealing with dead objects to be grasped and revealed in the seemingly neutral language of a knowledge — "history" — guaranteed by the scholarly protocols of the human and social "sciences." All of these terms — history, human, archive, memory, social, science — are critical, susceptible to interrogation, interruption, contestation, and reconfiguration. Recently the Italian philosophy Roberto Esposito has rightly suggested that the necessary contestation of this historicist reasoning should be cast further back to the initial chapters of Occidental modernity to include Nicolò Machiavelli, Giordano Bruno, and Giambattista Vico, all thinkers who based their thought on the contingent and the complexities that escape both subjective and conceptual arrest. This opposes an immunology sought in the conceptual solidity of the Cartesian subject, the Hobbesian state, and their subsequent reconfirmation by historicism and its liberal epistemology. On the contrary, we find ourselves confronting the unguaranteed and dynamic renewal of individual and collective potentialities without the protection of conservative concepts that seek to still time and control contingency (Esposito 2011).

In the light of these considerations, we might ask how is it still possible in a 600-page opus, David Abulafia's recent *The Great Sea: A Human History of the Mediterranean* (2011), which covers its history from the dawn of human records to the present, to concentrate almost exclusively on the European shore while studiously avoiding how Europe produced and managed the Mediterranean's spatiotemporal syntax (Abulafia 2011). Operating with the universalizing grammar of disciplinary "neutrality" to set the record straight and sustain a teleological narrative that ensures linear causality, an abstract idea of "human" history remains immune to such problematic concepts of modernity as colonialism, imperialism, and modern nation-state formations. The implications, despite the density and complications of empirical detail, are ultimately the reconfirmation of the status quo.

The struggle for hegemony in recent centuries in the Mediterranean (just what was Nelson doing in the Bay of Naples in 1799, or in Egyptian waters a year previously?) alerts us to the planetary coordinates that transformed the Mediterranean into a colonial theater and a European lake: from Marrakech to Damascus, the African and Asian shores and hinterlands were ruled from Paris, London, and Rome. When Shelomo Dov Goitein refers to Fustat (now incorporated into modern Cairo), the Fatimid capital of Egypt located on the Nile some 200 kilometers from the sea, as the hub of a medieval "Mediterranean society," we can better grasp the potential critical shift (Goitein 1999). There are few today who would immediately associate a Nile city with the Mediterranean. Precisely by insisting on Goitein's definition, and adding Janet Abu Lughod's analysis of the Eurasian mercantile system of the thirteenth century that orbited around such "world" cities as Cairo and Baghdad, we interrupt the pretensions of a unilateral European narrative (Abu-Lughod 1991). The presence, or coevalness, of these other knowledges — their traces, testimonies, and transmission — complicate and multiply the official Mediterranean narrative. This is not simply a case of a forgotten or repressed past returning to haunt the present. It is not simply about a richer and more nuanced picture. To reopen the archive in this manner is not only to reorder and reassemble its materials; it is also to question the manner of its construction, to interrogate the premises that disciplined its organizational will in the representation of voices, artifacts, documents, and materials. In other words, the archive is not about dead matters, but is always under construction: what it can tell us about the past (and hence the present) is frequently still to be registered and narrated. As Jacques Derrida put it, the archive imposes a responsibility for the future (Derrida 1998).

Rather than sweep the Mediterranean into a single, unified tale (ultimately that of European "progress" and civilization), it seems more instructive to consider communality sustained in differences. Let us listen once again to the scholar of the unintended Jewish archive of medieval Fustat, Shelomo Goitein. Drawing on the more than quarter of a million "documents" thrown into the "waste basket" or Geniza of the Fustat synagogue between the eleventh and thirteenth centuries, he writes:

> **The people speaking to us through our documents represent an intrinsically urban population. Their world comprised urban sites from Samarkand in central Asia and the port cities of India and Indonesia to the east, to Seville in Spain and Sijilmāsa in Morocco to the west; from Aden in the south, to Constantinople, the capital of Byzantium in the north. The maritime cities of the northern shore of the Mediterranean, such as Narbonne, Marseilles, Genoa, Pisa, and Venice, are also mentioned in the Geniza records and were indeed visited at the end of the twelfth century by Jewish traders, whose letters home are preserved in the Geniza. There are sporadic references to faraway European places, such as Rouen, the capital of Normandy in northern France, and Kiev in the present-day Ukraine. It is, however, the Islamic city of the middle ages that is most clearly reflected in our documents. (Goitein 1999, 3839)**

Within the modern Mediterranean there are countless examples of such extended, multireligious and multicultural networks characterizing both place and belonging. In his detailed historical account of the city of Salonica under the Ottomans (1430–1925) and beyond to 1950, Mark Mazower writes of the concentrated microcosm of Mediterranean monotheisms — those religions of the desert (Judaism, Christianity, and Islam) that developed in transcultural diffusion — while considering the history of Salonica in a montage of intertwined narratives that speak of discontinuities, breaks, blocks, and oblivion (Mazower 2005). The narrative concludes in the present-day Greek city of Thessalonica, and the undoing and cancellation of the cultural, historical, political, and religious composition of an Ottoman city by the violent impositions of nationalism and Fascism. If in 1925 the Muslim population was "exchanged" with the Greek one in Anatolia, in 1943–45 the Nazis then exterminated the 60,000 Sephardic Jewish population in the death camps of central Europe. The importance, however, despite such ethnic cleansing and the drive for national homogeneity, lies, as the title of Mazower's book reminds us, with

the ghosts. Here the refusal to remember is registered as being as important as the official insistence on historical precedence and preservation. These urban sites — Fustat, Salonica, as Freud realized visiting Rome — are sites of sedimentation where memories can be sought in many mediums. Brought into the present, our premises are rendered vulnerable by what is negated, repressed, and silenced.

This form of contemporaneity, the joining of past and present in a critical configuration, does not avoid the evidence of the archive, or pretend to render it transparent, but rather reworks and revitalizes it. The importance of the histories proposed by Goitein and Mazower is that they reverberate along multiple scales and dimensions. Localizing and folding time and space into unfolding and discontinuous complexities, they do not pretend that the world can be laid out as flat as a map and there conclusively catalogued. The latter style of archiving and accompanying archeology is, of course, authorized by the national drive for homogeneity accompanied by the persistent policing of identity politics (both those in dominance and those subordinated to domination in the categories of ethnic, cultural, religious, and linguistic "minorities"). The existing narrative often accommodates this dialectic of asymmetrical powers, but clearly cannot offer hospitality to the idea that its very terms and premises need to be set on altogether more transitory (that is, historical) foundations in which their being is intrinsic to an altogether wider panorama of becoming. In *The Venture of Islam,* this is precisely what Marshall Hodgson proposed to undertake in analyzing what he called Islamicist history and cultures (Hodgson 1977). He sought to unhook Western history "from Eurocentric teleologies" (Burke III 1993, xii). In other words, he applied to both the world of Islam and to the Occident the Gramscian directive to think in worldly terms.

The histories of the eastern Mediterranean under Islamic hegemony that have been swept under the carpet, relegated to the so-called dark and middle ages, are not so much recuperated to fill in the void that lies between the fall of the Roman Empire and the emergence of modern Europe. It is not about setting the record straight. What is proposed is an interrogation that epistemologically challenges the assumed superiority of the West over the rest. Set down on a wider and interleaved set of maps, respective provincialisms are exposed to questions that loosen them from secure moorings, requiring them to renegotiate the authority of their location. Islamic culture, even in its supposed heyday, was not merely Arab. Persian and Turkish were also major components in its cosmopolitan formation. And if the thirteenth century Islamic world of western Asia (and China) was overrun by pastoral nomads who then stayed (the Mongols), the then contemporary European Renaissance did not inaugurate modernity but rather brought the outer region of the Afro-Eurasian landmass to the cultural level of the other major civilizations of the *Oikoumene.* To entertain this proposal of Hodgson's is to operate a cut in the Occidental teleology of progress and to consider modernity, both past and present, as a planetary phenomenon irrespective of its presumed "origins" in Europe and the West. If paper, the compass, gunpowder, the zero, the decimal system, and algebra came from elsewhere, at a minimum we are looking at altogether wider movements of culture and technologies that require more extensive maps for their understanding. Greek thought was recovered, resurrected, and then transmitted — and in the process transformed and "modernized" — to the Occident from the Orient and the world of Islam. This is not to cancel the West but to complicate it, exposing it to a wider, less parochial series of understandings, located in altogether more extensive historical and cultural networks.

Rather than the well-known rhythms of civilization, their epic rise and tragic fall, there are the denser quotidian and improvised pulsations of an ongoing composition that is not necessarily authorized by the nation or the civilization it pretends to embody. A multitude of bodies perform histories that may not be of their own choosing but that acquire cultural form and significance in the everyday combinations of the unsuspected and unplanned that accompany historical becoming. This is a less about a theory of knowledge, and its accompanying historiography, and rather more, as Foucault would have insisted, about a knowledge still to come; not a truth (whose, where, and how?) responding to reality, but rather the power to transform thought into modalities of living. This, as Foucault points out, is not a truth that develops from the subject but rather from the world that expresses the history we have constructed and the diagnoses of who we are (Foucault 2000). Once again, time, space, memory, and rhythm conjoin in a constellation that simultaneously exceeds the empirical moment and the idealist capture of the world we presume to know and manage. Slipping beyond the ordered homogeneity of a discourse to unlearn a discipline and rationale is to enter a further, uncharted and not yet narrated spatialization of time and becoming.

Migrating Modernity

Perhaps the most acute figure of the dislocation of the time and space — that is, the history and geography — of modernity emerges from the boundary confusion and territorial complications disseminated by the modern migrant. Usually considered illegal, and hence a clandestine historical and cultural presence, the migrant both crosses and cuts up the inherited maps of modernity through the activation of other cartographies. Migrating bodies, matter out of place, challenge the places prepared for them in an existing order. The languages, institutions, and technologies that invest, identify, and catalog the migrant are themselves exposed to movement, slippage, and migration into unauthorized spaces. It is not only the migrant who has constantly to negotiate his or her passage in the world. The concepts, practices and institutions, the bio-politics that nominate and define the migrant, are themselves unstable apparatuses, prone to critical challenge, social contestation, and historical undoing. If such juridical-political practices propose the protection of so-called Occidental democracy, they simultaneously also expose the gaps, failures, and refusals of a democracy that is structurally limited to some, excluded to

others. Like the Caribbean "Black Jacobins" fighting in the late eighteenth century to throw off slavery and realize their freedom, the modern migrant rapidly discovers the limits of a discourse — democracy and human rights — that refuses to respect its own vaunted universalism and reveals a locatable assembly of power (James 2001). Article 13 of the Universal Declaration of Human Rights (1948) declares that everyone is entitled to migrate. Today there is no Western democracy that recognizes this claim.

So, to talk of migration is not to refer to a peripheral social and economic phenomenon but is rather to reference the characteristics of labor in the formation of the forces of production of Occidental modernity: slaves brought to the American shore, and into the first modern organization of mass labor in the plantation system; the rural poor of Scotland, Scandinavia, Italy, Greece, and Ireland, dispossessed of land and livelihood, sucked into the urban ghettos of the industrial city and the factory system in both the Old and New World. Today the cheap labor that is drawn, sourced, and networked from the South of the planet into the overdeveloped world's obsession with material "progress." These are different chapters in the planetary organization of labor power and the social relations of production. In this sense, migration is the story of modernity. What this history points to is both the planetary extension of modernity from its very inception five centuries ago and the institutions of legality that are unable to recognize the justice of global space: who defines it, how is it cut up, allotted, and administered?

For the interrogative presence of the migrant announces planetary processes that draw Europe and the West to the threshold of a modernity that exceeds itself and is not merely ours to manage and define. The migrant already occupies our modernity. If his body is expressly written into punitive European and North American legislation, her mobility continually exposes the instability of abstract distinctions and rigid borders. The migrant is not merely the historical symptom of a mobile modernity; rather she is the persistent and condensed interrogation of the true identity of today's political subject. At the end of the day, his or her precariousness is also ours; for it exposes the coordinates of a worldly condition in both the dramatic immediacies of everyday life and in the arbitrary violence that is sustained in the abstract reach of the polity and the law.

This is to nominate a counter-history and a counter-space: a Foucaultian heterotopia (Foucault 1991). As a blues version this telling insists on the unauthorized notes that stretch the official account until it tears and releases another narration of our time. If this has found little space in the official narratives of national histories and their explanations of modernity, it nevertheless seeds a critical and explosive link between the largely repressed historical memory of Western colonialism, and the imperial appropriation of the planet and a radical revaluation of modernity. The racializing bio-politics that mark, catalog, and define the migrant's body as an object of economical, legal, and political authority exposes the Occidental imperative to reduce the globe to its needs and reopens the colonial archive that initially established this planetary traffic in bodies, capital, and goods. The bio-political rationality displayed in the extension of the modern state to govern populations through the individuation of bodies to cure, educate, sustain, punish, and repudiate uncovers the racializing mechanism that lie at the very heart of European liberalism (Losurdo 2011). Once it is set to another rhythm, narrated according to another marking of time, another body of experience, sounded with subaltern inflections, accented in a polyvocal manner, that history turns out to be neither unique nor complete.

The historical and cultural insistence of the contemporary migrant — every night seeking to cross the Mediterranean, the English Channel, or the Mexican/U.S. border in perilous conditions — opens up a gap in the seamless pretensions of modernity. This permits another, further narration to emerge, as for example in the five-screen video installation *Western Union, Small Boats* (2007) by Isaac Julien, the Michael Winterbottom film *In This World* (2002), and the recent video installation *Traces* (2012) by Fiamma Montezemolo. Here we are invested by the altogether rougher reverberations of a world that runs on beyond the rationalizing desires of our will. The space that responds to particular powers and knowledge — ocular and unilateral — is now creased, folded and torn. It is transformed from a universal confirmation into an emerging historical constellation. This suggest other ways of knowing, other powers sustained in unsuspected bodies of resistance that reconfigure the world in a manner that does not merely mirror our own understanding. To extend critically the exemplary case of the bio-political organization of the modern metropolis outward to consider the governance of the modern world is to seek a resonance between a Fanonian and Foucaultian inheritance and the pulse of a post colonializing cartography. Working with the bodies, lives, and disciplines that populate a bio-political map is to move within a space whose temporality is neither linear nor merely the registration of chronology. That time comes undone, spirals back on itself, splits into the coeval instances of representation and repression: the past lives on, ghosting the present, setting it to a rhythm composed of continual interrogations. As Georges Didi-Huberman has argued, this is the critical imperative of the anachronism (Didi-Huberman 2000). Out of time, and out of joint with respect to an imperious linearity, such a temporality sustains the spaces of histories yet to come.

This discussion clearly impinges on a radical revaluation of the making and conceptualization of modern urban space, of the bio-political logics and languages that seek to maintain and promote confines and borders, of the associated political and cultural geographies of belonging. Today this troubled First World inheritance feels that it is under siege and invariably responds with the paranoid politics and policing of securitocracy. I personally hope that some of the perspectives laid out here might encourage another way of looking and reshaping the existing contours of sense. What is politically, culturally, and historically in play right now in the Mediterranean, particularly in its southern and eastern spheres, is by no means merely of local significance. The Mediterranean, after being a largely marginalized space in recent centuries, is now a laboratory of modernities to come.

References:

Abulafia, David. 2011. The Great Sea: A Human History of the Mediterranean. London: Penguin.
Abu-Lughod, Janet. 1991. Before European Hegemony: The World System AD 1250–1350. Oxford: Oxford University Press.
Baucom, Ian. 2005. Specters of the Atlantic… Finance Capital, Slavery, and the Philosophy of History. Durham: Duke University Press.
Braudel, Fernand. 1996. The Mediteranean and the Mediterranean World in the Age of Phillip II. Vol.1. Berkeley: University of California Press.
Burke III. Edmund. 1993. "Introduction: Marshall G. S. Hodgson and World History," in Marshall Hodgson, Rethinking World History: Essays on Europe, Islam, and World History. Cambridge: Cambridge University Press.
Chambers, Iain. 2012. Mediterraneo blues. Musiche, malinconia postcoloniale, pensieri marittimi. Turin: Bollati Boringhieri.
Deleuze, Gilles, and Félix Guattari. 1986. Kafka: Towards a Minor Literature. Minneapolis: University of Minnesota Press.
Derrida, Jacques. 1998. Archive Fever: A Freudian Impression. Chicago: University of Chicago Press.
Didi-Huberman, Georges. 2000. Devant le temps. Histoire de l'art et anachronisme des images. Paris: Les Éditions de Minuet.
Djebar, Assia. 1999. Women of Algiers in Their Apartment. Charlottesville, VA: University of Virginia Press.
Esposito, Roberto. 2011. "Fortuna e politica all'origine della filosofia italiana," California Italian Studies, 2 (1), 2011: http://escholarship.org/uc/item/5ht7n7p4. Accessed 31 July 2012.
Foucault, Michel. 1991. The Order of Things: An Archaeology of the Human Sciences. London: Routledge.
Foucault, Michel. 2000. Ethics: Subjectivity and Truth. London: Penguin.
Foucault, Michel. 2004. Society Must Be Defended. London: Penguin.
Gérardot, Maie. 2007. "Penser en rythmes," EspacesTemps.net, Textuel, 08.12.2007: http://espacestemps.net/document3803.html. Accessed 31 July 2012.
Gilroy, Paul. 1993. The Black Atlantic: Modernity and Double Consciousness. London: Verso.
Goitein, Shelomo Dov. 1999. A Mediterranean Society (abridgment in one volume). Berkeley: University of California Press.
Hall, Catherine. 2002. Civilizing Subjects: Metropole and Colony in the English Imagination 1830–1867. Oxford: Polity.
Hamilakis, Yannis. 2011. "Indigenous Archaeologies in Ottoman Greece." In Z. Bahrani, Z. Celik, and E. Eldem (editors), Scramble for the Past: A Story of Archaeology in the Ottoman Empire 1753–1914. Istanbul: Salt.
Hodgson, Marshall. 1977. The Venture of Islam (2 volumes). Chicago: University of Chicago Press.
James, C.L.R. 2001. The Black Jacobins: Touissant L'ouverture and the San Domingo Revolution. London: Penguin.
Lefebvre, Henri. 1991. The Production of Space, Oxford: Blackwell.
Lefebvre, Henri. 1996. Eléments de rythmanalyses: Introduction à la connaissance des rythmes. Paris: Éditions Syllepse.
Linebaugh, Peter, and Marcus Rediker. 2002. The Many Headed Hydra: Sailors, Slaves, Commoners, and the Hidden History of the Revolutionary Atlantic. London: Verso.
Losurdo, Domenico. 2011. Liberalism: A Counter-History. London: Verso.
Mazower, Mark. Salonica City of Ghosts: Christians, Muslims, and Jews 1430–1950. Harper Perennial: London.
Nietzsche, Friedrich. 2010. æOn the Use and Abuse of History for Life." Trans. Ian Johnston: http://records.viu.ca/~johnstoi/nietzsche/history.htm. Accessed 8 August 2012.
Pratt, Mary Louise. 1992. Imperial Eyes: Travel Writing and Transculturation. London: Routledge.
Ra'ad, Basem L. 2010. Hidden Histories: Palestine and the Eastern Mediterranean. London: Pluto.
Rekacewicz, Philippe. 2009. "Cartographier le present: Frontières, migrants et réfugiés. Études cartographiques": http://www.cartografareilpresente.org/article418.html. Accessed 31 July 2012
Ribeiro Sanches, Manuela. 2008. "Vulnerabilidade, espaços e construção de fronteiras": http://www.buala.org/pt/a-ler/vulnerabilidade-espacos-e-construcao-de-fronteiras. Accessed 31 July 2012.
Trouillot, Michel-Rolph. 1995. Silencing the Past: Power and the Production of History. Boston: Beacon Press.

Beyond "Mediterraneanism"
A View from Cultural Anthropology
Henk Driessen

From Land to Sea-Oriented Approaches

Until recently, the dominant research perspectives on the Mediterranean have been marked by a land bias and saltwater fear. The hesitant emergence of a maritime perspective and a "new thalassology," beyond the narrow specializations of maritime history and maritime anthropology, point to a need for a reinvigorated dynamics in history, anthropology, geography, and area studies (Driessen 2008: 445).[1] This need has been spurred, among other things, by the growing importance of global mobility and exchange, connectivity, and transnationalism as focal themes in the humanities and social sciences.[2] It has also been prompted by the openness of an increasing number of scholars to transregional and global approaches in history, anthropology, and geography.

In the intellectual movement toward a reconsideration of oceans and sea basins, concepts have been revisited such as seascape and its relation to land; coast, littoral, island, and shipping; the organization of power by empires and states across the water; and the nature of social relationships on board and at ports (Bentley, Bridenthal and Wigen 2007). We may see this trend as part of an attempt to revive area studies along new lines, following its crisis in the 1990s. The end of the Cold War, the disintegration of the Soviet Union and the Eastern European bloc, the acceleration of the globalization process, and the south and eastward enlargement of the European Union — all unsettled the division of the world into large regions and forced politicians, funding agencies, and scholars to redefine regions and their boundaries. In academia, pleas could be heard to abandon the rigid area-studies model and its tendency to reify cultural traits and disregard transitional zones and supra-regional processes. Moreover, it was increasingly claimed that the area-studies model hindered interregional comparisons. One of the responses to this crisis has been a maritime turn, an attempt to reframe area studies around oceans and sea basins and maritime interconnections (Lewis and Wigen 1999).

Mediterranean studies are a case in point (Driessen 2002, 2011). Seen from an anthropological point of view, the study of and in the Mediterranean over the past six or seven decades has been divided into two more-or-less separate fields of specialization roughly following the Mediterranean north-south divide, apart from linguistic and national splits, such as the

1 See, for instance, the interdisciplinary journal Maritime Studies launched by the Center for Maritime Research at the University of Amsterdam.

2 See pathbreaking publications by Lewis and Wigen (1997), the special issue "Oceans Connect" of the Geographical Review (1999), Horden and Purcell (2000), and Steinberg (2001).

Henk Driessen is a cultural anthropologist and Professor of Mediterranean Studies at the Radboud University of Nijmegen in the Netherlands. He has been conducting research in the Mediterranean, particularly in Spain and Morocco. He has written extensively on issues of migration, borders, ritual, religion, power, humor, masculinity, the body, identity, and pain.

His publications include *On the Spanish-Moroccan Frontier* (1992), the edited volume *Perplexities of Identification* (with Ton Otto, 2000), two books on the Mediterranean Sea (2002, 2008), and numerous articles in scholarly journals. He is now working on the folklorization of religious ceremony and the history of ethnography and fieldwork.

Anglo-Saxon, French, Italian, and German ones (Driessen 2001a). During the 1990s the anglophone anthropology of the Mediterranean area gradually slipped into the margins of the research agenda, though Mediterranean ethnography continues as a minor field of regional specialization, mostly devoid of comparative claims. The only major exception is France, in particular the ethnology, history, and political science sections of the *Maison Méditerranéenne de Sciences de l'Homme* in Aix-en-Provence (see Albera, Blok, and Bromberger 2001; Albera and Tozy 2005). Here, of course, France's Mediterranean vocation and its colonial past play an important role. The same is true, albeit to a lesser degree, for Italy and Spain.

Whereas interest in the Mediterranean has been on the wane as far as cultural anthropology is concerned, historiography has witnessed a striking revival of Mediterranean interest since Fernand Braudel. Recent books on the Mediterranean by historians often take into account anthropological studies and contributions (Horden and Purcell 2000, Harris 2005). At the same time, geography is going through a rediscovery of the Mediterranean (see Giaccaria and Minca 2010). Recent positions vis-à-vis Mediterranean comparison indicates much less rigid definitions of the Mediterranean. They aim at comparison not only within but also across the region's boundaries, increasingly seen as shifting ones. In this view, the Mediterranean is a region of fractures, connections, continuities, discontinuities, complementary differences, and crossings (Blok and Albera 2001, Driessen 2002, Suárez-Navaz 2004, Ribas-Mateos 2005, Bromberger 2007, Fabre and Sant Cassia 2007, Chambers 2008).

Struggling with Dichotomies

Progress in the interdisciplinary study of the Mediterranean has been hampered considerably by persistent dichotomies in the descriptive and analytical frameworks. Cases in point are sea-land, town-country, mountain-plain, and center-periphery oppositions.[3] These have a long history in the area as used by its inhabitants as well as outsiders, scholars included, which in itself is an interesting empirical fact. Many people around the Mediterranean tend to think about and classify their environments in terms of such dichotomies; in other words, they serve as models of the realities they live in. Such pairs of opposition often imply hierarchies of values. Writes Michael Herzfeld (2001: 176):

> **"Such ideas die hard: southern European peoples, for example, often accuse their northern neighbors of being 'cold' and champion their own 'warmth' as an acceptable substitute for efficiency; the moral economy of stereotypes demonstrates the ease with which such classifications of humankind take hold and endure."** Scholars have uncritically taken over local oppositions, confusing insider, local, or emic perspectives with outsider, analytical, or etic ones.

It is important to stress that the term Mediterranean is not, contrary to a widespread commonsense assumption, a neutral geographical category but rather a cultural construct. It belongs to a semantic field consisting of similar constructs such as Europe, the Balkans, the Middle East, North Africa, and Asia. The shifting meanings of "Mediterranean" emerged in the configuration of such categories, in which "Mediterranean" often held an intermediate position. These categories not only reflect power differences between North and South but also tend to perpetuate such differentials. They carry a heavy load of moral associations and (mostly implicit) political and ideological connotations and stereotypes. From time to time these come into view, for instance in the recent hardening of the political opposition between North and South within the European Union. People from the northern countries tend to make derogatory remarks about the southern "garlic countries" (Greece, Italy, Cyprus, Portugal), whom they hold responsible for the debt and euro crises. Such attributes are part of a long tradition of stereotyping.

Let me briefly discuss one example of dichotomization from my own research, taken from an article dealing with port cities and

3 For an early example of a less dichotomous, comparative town-country approach with reference to transitional zones, see Blok and Driessen (1984). Also see Paul Stoller's recent book on what he calls "the power of the between" (2009).

cosmopolitanism (Driessen 2005). With the benefit of hindsight, I would now soften and further qualify the oppositions addressed in the article, for instance, between coast and interior or town and country, by differentiating more clearly among local perceptions and analytical points of view. This means focusing more than before on transitional zones between the extremes on the shore-interior and town-country continuum, not only in the local cultural organizations of space but also in their representations.

Another concept that may be helpful in getting away from dichotomous thinking is passage. This general term refers to movement through space and time and implies connectivity, division, uncertainty, and change. It points to a variety of social and cultural practices transgressing geopolitical and cultural boundaries, such as tourism and migration, which are important in the past and present of the Mediterranean. Moreover, the notion of passage is particularly relevant to this region and field of study in view of the fact that this is a transitional zone between three old continents. In this regard, ports and port towns deserve privileged treatment, as they function as sites of transfer and exchange. Taking seriously the concepts of passage and transition thus tends to unsettle taken-for-granted dichotomies, such as the one between center and (semi-) periphery.

Center and periphery have for good reasons become a problematic conceptual pair. For one thing, they are deeply ambiguous, sometimes used in a literal or spatial-geographical sense, at other times in a metaphorical, political, or economic sense. Arguments along center-periphery lines mostly moved between the extremes of equilibrium and conflict theories. In both cases the periphery is treated as little more than a residual concept, a none-center or "an area of shadow which serves to bring out the radiance of the metropolis" (Burke 1992). This dichotomy is of course also tied to a hierarchy of political and moral values.

A more constructive approach to peripheries originated in frontier studies. A good example is Owen Lattimore's notion of the periphery as a locus of innovation (see Blok 2010). Lattimore influenced my thinking on frontiers while I was doing fieldwork and archival research in the Spanish enclave of Melilla on Morocco's Mediterranean shore, during the time of great growth in border studies (Driessen 1992). Three conclusions came out of this research.[4] First, borders are multifaceted constructions that have to be studied from both sides of the divide. Second, the human dimension that tends to disappear when borders are studied from above has to be addressed in fieldwork studies from below. And finally, borders in the Mediterranean are mobile and uncertain, "more a horizon than a cartographic projection" (Matvejevic 1999: 17; Driessen 2001b).

Stereotypes and Commonplaces

The uncritical use of dichotomies has gone hand in hand with the essentialist tradition inherent in the old area-studies model, in which anthropology was one of the leading disciplines.[5] Mediterranean studies are rooted in the older literary genre of travelogs and opera librettos in which the Mediterranean figured as both the cradle and the antipode of European civilization. Early anthropological studies were in search of what we may call the holy grail of pan-Mediterranean traits, which inevitably blended with stereotypes. Examples of such stereotyping are the *dolce far niente*, the *mañana* and *inshallah* attitudes of the *uomo mediterraneo*; his and her fatalism, clan spirit, family orientation, sensuality, spontaneity, and charming and generous hospitality as well as an explosive, violent, and corrupt nature. Such often contrasting traits are ascribed to millions of people.[5] The uncritical use of the adjective Mediterranean both in popular and scholarly representations often implies an understood regional unity for which a sound empirical basis is simply lacking.[6]

Critiques of anthropological versions of essentialism in community studies in the Mediterranean area began to appear in the 1980s (Herzfeld 1984, Llobera 1986, Pina-Cabral 1989, Giordano 1990). Such critiques frequently dovetailed with changes in cultural and social anthropology at large. The postmodern turn of the 1980s raised questions of representation, authority, and signature of ethnographic knowledge. Nagging doubts arose over such basic issues as where and what is the "field"; do "we" have the right to study "them"; when we represent "others" in our voice, do we not alienate them? The most systematic and elaborate critique came from Michael Herzfeld (1984, 2005), who coined the notion of "Mediterraneanism" as a variation on and tribute to Edward Said's Orientalism.

With the construct of Mediterraneanism, Herzfeld criticized the comparative exercise involved "because it falls between the two stools of global comparativism and ethnographic precision" (2005: 48). Considering it much more than an ideology, he also took it to

4 These conclusions are now widely shared; see Wilson and Donnan (2012).

5 In the year 2000, approximately 420 million people were living in the twenty-two countries and territories bordering the Mediterranean Sea (Benoit and Comeau (2005).

6 The sometimes intimate ties between popular representations of the Mediterranean and scholarly ones alluded to above of course deserve an extended systematic study.

imply "a programme of active political engagement with patterns of cultural hierarchy" (Herzfeld 2005: 51). In other words, this is a form of what he called "practical Mediterraneanism," including strategies of stereotyping and self-stereotyping. Herzfeld's casus belli is the honor-and-shame complex that has a long history in the anthropological study of the Mediterranean, going back to one of the founding volumes edited by John Peristiany (1965). More recently, honor (and shame) was one of the cornerstones in the most elaborate historical study of the Mediterranean since Braudel (Horden and Purcell 2000).

Herzfeld (2005: 63) concluded his essay on practical Mediterraneanism with an encouraging remark:

> **"A critical study of Mediterranean identities is not necessarily and should not be an act of 'Mediterraneanism'. It can instead be a critical response to such essentializing discourses. To become that response, however, it must entail full recognition of the extent to which it is itself enmeshed in political and ideological processes." Since Herzfeld wrote these words, several attempts have been made to define a "militant Mediterraneanism" and "a Mediterranean alternative."**

A Mediterranean Alternative?

In fact, one of the first anglophone attempts to define the contours of an alternative to Mediterraneanism is a study by Iain Chambers.[7] *Mediterranean Crossings* is promising indeed, suggesting a sense of dynamism, flexibility, and openness that is lacking in most Mediterraneanist accounts. He theorizes the Mediterranean as the "uprooted geography of a postcolonial sea" (2008: 17). Following Braudel, Matvejevic, and other scholars of the Mediterranean, Chambers aptly develops the notion of a "multiple and mutable Mediterranean." His style is associative, even somewhat poetic. The vast majority of voices in his book belong to heroes of cultural, postcolonial, and literary studies, among many others Gilles Deleuze, Homi Bhabha, Edward Said, Michel de Certeau, and indeed "Mediterranean voices" of the Jewish poet from Egypt, Edmond Jabès, the French Algerian writer Albert Camus, and Jacques Derrida, whom he considers "Mediterranean thinkers" par excellence. Following Herzfeld, one may observe that this Mediterraneanist qualification begs the question of what

it means to be Mediterranean. From an anthropological point of view, one would have hoped to 'listen' to a much wider variety of voices of people in the Mediterranean, including those of recent immigrants in Naples.

I agree with Chambers (2008: 28) that the Mediterranean Sea is a sea of "passages, cultural crossovers, contaminations, creolizations, and uneven historical memories." This claim implies a political undertone critical of the state, borders, and restrictions on immigration. As a scholar of literary theory and cultural studies he however fails to show how people on the ground deal with them. *Mediterranean Crossings* is indeed an intellectual "passage" but needs to be supplemented with passages based on fieldwork in the 'real' Mediterranean world.

In a recent critical overview of mainly French and Italian Mediterranean studies from a geographical and "postcolonial" perspective, Italian geographers Paolo Giaccaria and Claudio Minca (2010), rethink the Mediterranean Sea as a "postcolonial sea." It does not come as a surprise that they comprehensively and approvingly quote from Chambers' book, claiming that the Mediterranean "represents a fertile ground for the exploration of other spaces, capable of recovering the ambiguities and plurality of voices that make a source of inspiration for experiencing alternative modernities" (Giaccaria and Minca 2010: 345). Among numerous studies, they focus on a discussion of what they call the Mediterranean alternative of *la pensée du Midi* and *pensiero meridiano*.

Does this French and Italian criticism offer a viable alternative for "mainstream Mediterraneanism" and its tropes of unity in diversity and diversity in unity and of a fragmented space of conflicts? One may agree with the authors in this militant Mediterraneanist literature that no critical representation on and of the Mediterranean is possible without debunking the colonial and Orientalist stereotypes and clichés inherent in the category of Mediterranean itself (Fabre and Ilbert 2000). Indeed, Cassano's *pensiero meridiano* and Fabre's *pensée du midi* are deeply influenced by the final chapter of Albert Camus' *The Rebel* (1991[1953]) and his essay "The new culture of the Mediterranean" (1937, reissued 1967), as well as his plea for anti-authoritarianism and "the physical" as opposed to northern European reasoning and abstraction.

I agree with Giaccaria and Minca (2010: 357–358) that the work of Camus is fraught with Orientalist clichés and stereotypes. In their celebration of Camus, militant Mediterraneanists follow their own political agendas,

7   See Driessen (2008) for a full review of this book.

fall into the same trap of essentializing, and reproduce the old dichotomy of the cold (rational) north versus the warm (emotional, spontaneous) south. Giaccaria and Minca (2010: 358–359) try to move beyond the shortcomings of both mainstream and militant Mediterraneanism by "returning to the alternative modernities envisaged within Chambers' 'uprooted' geography of the Mediterranean." They then refer in a footnote to a number of studies that in their view are critical of essentialist discourses. Let me now go into two of these studies.

Going Beyond Mediterraneanism

The first example is a study by historian and anthropologist Jocelyne Dakhlia (2009), who grew up in Tunisia as well as in France, and is at present a member of the L'École des Hautes Études en Sciences Sociales in Paris. Her book Lingua Franca is a fascinating study of the "Frankish language" that has for centuries been the most important vehicle for communication across Mediterranean linguistic, political, and cultural divides. This language was based on words from Provençal, Italian, Greek, Spanish, Arabic, Turkish, and Armenian and was used by a wide variety of in-between people such as seamen, captives, pirates, slaves, renegades, and diplomats. It was a simple language with a minimum of syntax, maximal use of infinitives, and ample repetition. The demise of this Mediterranean transcultural language coincided with the increased pressure of European colonialism in the Mediterranean. The French soldiers who conquered Algiers in 1830 still had been taught some very basic lingua franca. In the second half of the nineteenth century, it became almost obsolete with the European domination of the southern and eastern Mediterranean shores and the rise of nationalism.

The "Frankish language" was one of the tongues spoken in Mediterranean ports, in combination with the silent language of gestures. In the domain of music are similar cases of mixture and fusion in the seaports Izmir (arabesk), Piraeus (rebetika), and Oran (rai). In fact, cultural exchange has been going on for centuries in the domains of architecture, technology, religion, commerce, music and, more recently, fashion. Examples include the migration of architectural styles and elements from ancient Egypt, Greece, and Rome, not only around the Mediterranean but also to Northern Europe and in colonial times to the New World. Cases in point are the loggia that originated in ancient Egypt and evolved around

the Mediterranean, where it reached its apex during the Renaissance, and the walled inner courtyard (atrium) and its Arab/Berber variant (hawsh). An interesting early case of architectural hybridity is the so-called Mudejar style that developed in the Iberian Peninsula. It is a mixing of Christian, Jewish, and Muslim elements, such as ornamental geometric motifs and elaborately worked tiles, wood, and plaster carvings, and brickwork.

A second exemplary study (Albera and Couroucli 2012) deals with sharing sacred space, past and present, in ten countries bordering the Mediterranean Sea and is based on a combination of ethnographic fieldwork and archival research.[8] A fieldwork focus on religion as practiced challenges received views of "the three religions of the book" (based on the scripturalist view of religion as prescribed) and brings out both historical and contemporary similarities in religious practice and organization around the Mediterranean. Essentialist views, widespread among religious scholars and politicians, conversely tend to emphasize differences in religious doctrine and practice.

It is refreshing to read the contributions to Sharing Sacred Spaces in the Mediterranean, as they undermine too simplistic views of religion on the spectrum between liberalism and fundamentalism, particularly the commonplace that religious identities in the Mediterranean are divided by the fault line between the West and Islam. The volume is the first comparative study of mixed religious practices that also makes it clear that, unlike contemporary Western European migration policies, age-old practices of sharing sacra are not informed by any top-down multicultural policy or ideology. The case studies deal with the historical heritage of societies where the coexistence of several religious groups within one territory, under one authority, represents a legacy of mostly Byzantine and Ottoman systems (Couroucli 2012: 5).

Mixed shrines are often to be found in rural areas, part of a sacred topography that transcends religious diversity. In several cases, the devotional gestures performed by Muslims in Christian (or Jewish) spaces derive from a shared repertoire of tactile piety (Albera 2012: 235). The case studies in the Albera and Couroucli volume also demonstrate the polyphonic nature of religious mixing, not unlike the lingua franca example.[9] Such instances may well serve as a model for global tolerance.

8   The English translation of the Albera and Couroucli volume appeared in 2012.

9   Also see the comprehensive overview of the geography of religion in the Mediterranean by Horden and Purcell (2000: 401–461).

Sources:

Albera, Dionigi, Anton Blok, and Christian Bromberger, eds. 2001. *L'Anthropologie de la Méditerranée*. Paris: Éditions de la Maison des Sciences de l'Homme.

Albera, Dionigi, and Mohammed Tozy, eds. 2005. *La Méditerranée des anthropologues : Fractures, filiations, contiguities*. Paris: Maissonneuve & Larose.

Albera, Dionigi, and Maria Couroucli, eds. 2012. *Sharing Sacred Spaces in the Mediterranean: Christians, Muslims, and Jews at Shrines and Sanctuaries*. Bloomington and Indianapolis: Indiana University Press.

Albera, Dionigi. 2012. "Conclusion: Crossing the Frontiers between the Monotheistic Religions, an Anthropological Approach." In *Sharing Sacred Spaces in the Mediterranean*, ed. Alberaand Couroucli, 219–245.

Benoît, Guillaume, and Aline Comeau, eds. 2005. *A Sustainable Future for the Mediterranean*. London: Earthscan.

Bentley, Jerry H., Renate Bridenthal, and Kären Wigen, eds. 2007. *Seascapes: Maritime Histories, Littoral Cultures, and Transoceanic Exchanges*. Honolulu: University of Hawaii Press.

Blok, Anton. 2010. "Behavior Codes in Sicily: Bypassing the Law." *Behemoth* 3 (2): 56–71.

Blok, Anton, and Henk Driessen. 1984. "Mediterranean Agro-Towns as a Form of Cultural Dominance. With Special Reference to Sicily and Andalusia." *Ethnologia Europaea* 14: 111–125.

Bromberger, Christian. 2007. "Bridge, Wall, Mirror: Coexistence and Confrontation in the Mediterranean World." *History and Anthropology* 18: 201–307.

Burke, Peter. 1992. *History & Social Theory*. Cambridge: Polity Press.

Camus, Albert. 1991[1953]. *The Rebel. An Essay on Man in Revolt*. New York: Vintage.

Camus, Albert. 1967 [1937]. "The New Culture of the Mediterranean." In Albert Camus, *Lyrical and Critical Essays*. London: Hamish Hamilton, 188–195.

Chambers, Iain. 2008. *Mediterranean Crossings: The Politics of an Interrupted Modernity*. Durham, N.C. and London: Duke University Press.

Couroucli, Maria. 2012. "Introduction: Sharing Sacred Places: A Mediterranean Tradition." In *Sharing Sacred Spaces in the Mediterranean*. ed. Albera and Couroucli, 1–10.

Dahlia, Jocelyne. 2009. *Lingua franca. Histoire d'une langue métisse en Méditerranée*. Arles: Acted Sud.

Driessen, Henk. 1992. *On the Spanish-Moroccan Frontier: A Study in Ritual, Power, and Ethnicity*. Oxford: Berg.

Driessen, Henk. 2001a. "Divisions in Mediterranean Ethnography: A View from Both Shores." In *L'anthropologie de la Méditerranée*, ed. Albera, Blok, and Bromberger, 625–644.

Driessen, Henk. 2001b. "The Connecting Sea: History, Anthropology, and the Mediterranean." *American Anthropologist* 103 (1): 528–541.

Driessen, Henk. 2002. *Mediterrane passages*. Amsterdam: Wereldbibliotheek.

Driessen, Henk. 2005. "Mediterranean Port Cities: Cosmopolitanism Reconsidered." *History and Anthropology* 16 (1): 129–141.

Driessen, Henk. 2008. "Seascapes and Mediterranean Crossings. Review Article." *Journal of Global History* 3: 445–450.

Driessen, Henk. 2011. "Shifting Boundaries: Ethnography, Community, and Area in the Mediterranean." In *Epistemische Orte. Gemeinde und Region als Forschungsformate*, ed. Gisela Welz, Antonia Davidovic, and Anke S. Weber. Frankfurt: Institut für Kulturanthropologie uns Europäische Ethnologie der Johann Wolfgang Goethe Universität, 45–55.

Fabre, Thierry, and Robert Ilbert, eds. 2000. *Les representations de la Méditerranée*. Paris: Maissonneuve & Larose.

Fabre, Thierry, and Paul Sant Cassia. 2007. *Between Europe and the Mediterranean: The Challenges and the Fears*. Basingstoke: Palgrave Macmillan.

Giaccaria, Paolo, and Claudio Minca. 2010. "The Mediterranean Alternative." *Progress in Human Geography* 35 (3): 345–365.

Giordano, Christian. 1990. "Is There a Mediterranean Anthropology? The Point of View of an Outsider." *Anthropological Journal on European Cultures* 1: 109–121.

Harris, William, ed. 2005. *Rethinking the Mediterranean*. Oxford: Oxford University Press.

Herzfeld, Michael. 1984. "The Horns of the Mediterraneanist Dilemma." *American Ethnologist* 11: 439–454.

Herzfeld, Michael. 2001. *Anthropology: Theoretical Practice in Culture and Society*. Malden, MA: Blackwell, Unesco.

Herzfeld, Michael. 2005. "Practical Mediterraneanism: Excuses for Everything, from Epistemology to Eating." In *Rethinking the Mediterranean*, ed. William Harris. Oxford: Oxford University Press, 45–64.

Horden, Peregrine, and Nicholas Purcell. 2000. *The Corrupting Sea: A Study of Mediterranean History*. Oxford: Blackwell.

Lewis, Martin, and Kären Wigen. 1997. *The Myth of Continents: A Critique of Metageography*. Berkeley: University of California Press.

Lewis, Martin, and Kären Wigen. 1999. "A Maritime Response to the Crisis in Area Studies." *The Geographical Review* 89: 161–168.

Llobera, Josep R. 1986. "Fieldwork in Southwestern Europe: Anthropological Panacea or Epistemological Straitjacket." *Critique of Anthropology* 6: 25–33.

Matvejevic, Predrag. 1999. *Mediterranean: A Cultural Landscape*. Berkeley: University of California Press.

Peristiany, John. G. ed. 1965. *Honor and Shame: The Values of Mediterranean Society*. London: Weidenfeld and Nicholson.

Pina-Cabral, Joao de. 1989. "The Mediterranean as a Category of Regional Comparison: A Critical View." *Current Anthropology* 30: 399–406.

Ribas-Mateos, Natalia. 2005. *The Mediterranean in the Age of Globalization: Migration, Welfare, and Borders*. New Brunswick, N.J.: Transaction.

Steinberg, Philip E. 2001. *The Social Construction of the Ocean*. Cambridge: Cambridge University Press.

Stoller, Paul. 2009. *The Power of the Between: An Anthropological Odyssey*. Chicago, London: University of Chicago Press.

Suárez-Navaz, Liliana. 2004. *Rebordering the Mediterranean: Boundaries and Citizenship in Southern Europe*. New York, Oxford: Berghahn Books.

Wilson, Thomas, and Hastings Donnan, eds. 2012. *A Companion to Border Studies*. Malden, MA, Oxford: Wiley-Blackwell, 2012.

Beyond "Mediterraneanism"

The Maghreb
A Laboratory of New Migrations
Michel Peraldi

Powerful and enduring events have a tendency to be transformed into myths, or the icons of myths. When it comes to migration, any migratory movement perceived as massive[1] is portrayed by, or at least assimilated with, a threat of invasion, a fear that often originates in the symbolic image of a wall being torn down. Indeed, in 1989, once the general euphoria that met the end of the Socialist empire had receded, the sight of long lines of Trabants crossing over to the other side of the collapsed wall gave rise, in Western Europe, to a fear of invasion. According to observers, scientists and experts included, flows of this sort could signal only one thing: mass migration. And yet, something in this process, albeit elusive at the time, had altered. Visitors were not necessarily migrating. Instead, they were adopting a split form of mobility, both maintaining a life in the East and occupying economic niches of the West. It is thus clear today that although migration fluxes did occur, they were mere visits. In 1989, this fear of invasion concealed an ongoing process, a process in which migration was no longer a form of exile but a form of mobility.

In the 2000s, the phenomenon repeated itself with the continuous influx, on the European shores, of new "boat people" coming this time from Sub-Saharan Africa, via the Maghreb. The media coverage of the September 2005 Ceuta events[2] — when hundreds of prospective migrants attempted to cross what has now become one of the many fortresses through which Western states hope to fend off flows of "undesirables" migrants (Agier 2008) — became the symbol of this new fear of invasion. As is often the case with media reporting, the intense focus on one reality and a few symbolic events overshadowed the rest of the process. For a majority of Europeans today, the bulk of migratory dynamics and flows bound for Europe can be reduced to the strain that this massive influx — continuously fueled by Africa's political turmoil, fragile economies, and the migrants' illogical and economically unsound "longing for Europe" — puts on Europe. Although there are numerous critiques of this vision today, there is still a need to insist

1 Although the power of migration flows may appear indisputable, such a representation is prone to "ideological formatting" and should therefore be approached with caution. The so-called massiveness of refugees or "illegal migrants" ("*clandestins,*" in French) that regularly "flood" Europe consist in fact of a few thousand people, who land for a few days in areas that are strictly circumscribed, thus producing high yet temporary visibility. Over a year, this hardly amounts to an "invasion." In 2007, Frontex, a European agency, reports 163,000 arrests on the European borders, most of those occurring on what we could call the "Eastern Front," that is, the border with Greece, which accounts for 73,000 arrests in 2007. Figures for Spain and Italy revolve around 20,000 to 25,000 arrests, mostly in Lampedusa and the Canary Islands. But these figures are significantly decreasing: a 2011 UNHCR (United Nations High Commission for Refugees) report speaks of a 50 to 90 percent decrease in the number of arrests, varying depending on the location; for instance, it mentions 8,700 arrests in Lampedusa in 2010, compared to 22,000 in 2006 (*Le Monde,* June 6, 2010).

2 On September 29, 2005, the usual attempt by migrants to cross the borders of the Spanish enclave of Ceuta turned into a tragic event when the Spanish and Moroccan police coordinated their repressive response against the migrants, killing approximately fifteen and injuring a hundred. This spectacular attack, widely broadcasted by the media and the European press, underscores the symbolical character of the North African states' collaboration with "Fortress Europe." See Migreurop 2006.

Michel Peraldi is an anthropologist and Director of Research at the Centre National de la Recherche Scientifique (CNRS) in France. From 2005 to 2010, he directed the Centre Jacques Berque for the Development of Human and Social Sciences in Rabat, Morocco. He has been affiliated with the Centre d'Analyse et d'Intervention Sociologiques (CADIS) at the cole des Hautes Études en Sciences Sociales (EHESS) in Paris since September 2010. For over ten years, Peraldi has worked on issues related to the dynamics of migration flows in the Mediterranean Basin and informal trade networks between Europe and North Africa, combining the socio-economy of gray economies with the urban anthropology of metropolises that are directly animated by such flows and the markets that organize them: Marseille, Istanbul, Naples, and Tangiers.

on the semantic changes induced by such a portrayal and its symbolic "usefulness" in trying to understand states' or institutions' behavioral change toward the migratory phenomenon. The political fiction of a "migratory push," from Africa to Europe, obfuscates the existing variegation of migratory dynamics and of their actual territorial distribution. Furthermore, portraying the migratory act as a desperate, irrational gesture only serves to justify policies that have since shifted toward a "obsession with borders" (Fassin 2010); while also benefiting nation-states that seem to focus all their efforts and activities on surveillance and enforcements of "rights-of-entry" (Fassin 2010, Andreas 2001, Torpey 2000, Rodier 2012).

When seen from a North African perspective, however, and beyond the political fiction described above — including its politically motivated forms — contemporary migration dynamics prove to be complex equations. It can be argued, simply, that the five North African countries, each in their own particular way, now receive migration flows as much as they generate them. Moreover, these countries are opening up new geographic and professional destinations, which are attracting migrants from an increasingly wide range of social categories. Europe's security policies, in turn, have not only resulted in blocking borders and filtering the undesirables. They have also generated, in criminalizing the irregular migrants (Palidda 2008), instances of segmentation and discrimination that favor the inversion of the social direction of migration itself, even within local societies: indeed, the "upwardly mobile" migrations, highly valued and engendering cosmopolitan and transnational elites, now oppose the "slandered" migrations, which confine to a stigmatized and alienating instability those who attempt the journey. I shall only address here one aspect of these mutations, by describing the migratory dynamics that take place in the Maghreb today, as well as the socio-economic changes that they signal.

The Maghreb, a New Migratory Destination

In Algeria, it is estimated that 40,000 Chinese have settled in two of the country's main cities, Oran and Algiers, where they form the labor armies that are building new infrastructures and large housing developments.[3] Initially confined to construction sites out of which they never ventured, Chinese are now opening businesses and enterprises (Souiah 2010), in a way both intriguing to the Algerian population and inspiring its distrust. In Algeria still, there is also an established Sub-Saharan presence — one that is not only located in the South, where the redevelopment of sleepy towns such as Agades or Tamanrasset was made possible by migrants' transits, passage, and settlement, and by the commercial life that migration generates. Indeed, Sub-Saharan migrants have settled in the North as well; more discreet and discredited, they live in the Algeria-Morocco border region, often awaiting transit toward Morocco and Europe. As supported by the biographical accounts that we were able to gather in Morocco (Edogué Ntang and Peraldi 2011), Cameroonian and Malian youths find insecure livelihood opportunities in the businesses of Algiers, Oran, and Tlemcen, working as street vendors or waiters.

In Mauritania, the new entrepreneurs that are industrializing the fisheries and dried fish trades are Nigerian and Senegalese, although they must form partnerships with Mauritanian nationals to carry out their activities. This industry is mobilizing a Senegalese, Malian, and Cameroonian workforce (Poutignat and Streiff Fenart 2006). Although hard to capture numerically, these migration flows have played a key

3 Widely contradictory estimates are given, depending on the source: 35,000 according to the Chinese authorities, 40,000 according to the Algerian authorities, while the press goes as far as 100,000 to capture the Chinese presence in Algeria. See Souiah 2010.

role in the recent urban development of Nouakchott (Choplin 2008). Certainly more than in other countries of the Maghreb, Sub-Saharan migration in Mauritania has been the longest established and the most involved at the very origins of modernity. Indeed, because the local population is predominantly pastoral,[4] it was very early in Mauritanian history that Senegalese, Malian, Guinean, Cameroonian, and Beninese migrants came to occupy a range of "sedentary" trades and sectors of the economy. Since the 1950s, their numbers have been steadily growing. According to Amelie Choplin (2008), 60,000 to 80,000 Sub-Saharan Africans live today in Nouakchott, representing approximately 10 percent of the urban population; a little over 20,000 live in Nouadhibou, representing approximately 20 percent of the urban population. To be sure, starting from the 2000s, Mauritania became one of the key hubs where African migration toward the Canary Islands was organized, and where Mauritanian and Senegalese fishermen, those established in Nouadhibou in particular, came to play the roles of savvy smugglers. 2005 and 2006 are especially important years for these movements[5]: on one hand, monitoring of migration flows' frequency begin; on the other hand, their reporting increasingly supports the implementation of policy-related partnerships, through which Europe becomes directly involved in systems of maritime control off the African coasts. The goal here is certainly not to deny the existence of the Europe-bound Sub-Saharan migratory flows that occur via the Maghreb, in this case, via Mauritania or Morocco; we will come back to those later. Rather, the goal is to distance ourselves from the political fiction of "transit migrations" and, by way of shifting the focus from Europe to Africa, from the euro-focused interests that this fiction serves. In this regard, Mauritania is a well-studied example and offers a case of a country that combines, in space and time, three distinct types of migratory flows. The first one is ancient and historically inscribed in the slow journeys across the Sahara; it relates to the interlacing of migratory and trade routes, woven around the Saharan hub. The second, more recent one (although it dates to the period of the independence wars), relates to the migrations of tradesmen and labor toward the "new countries" — countries that were claiming or reclaiming their economies at the end of the colonial cycle, such as Mauritania. If the predominance of "European elites" in Mauritania's post-colonial period is indeed better known, the role played by its Sub-Saharan neighbors is as consistent and equally important. Finally, since the 2000s, a third type of migratory flow has emerged, as a consequence of the political and military upheavals that have rocked the prosperous parts of Central Africa, namely Ivory Coast and Nigeria. It covers the "upward shift" of migration streams that were otherwise bound for more prosperous parts of Africa. Europe-bound transits account for part of these migration flows, but by no means must they be overemphasized, by presupposing that every Sub-Saharan migrant is pursuing the "European dream," nor must they be substantiated, by assuming that all departures are final. Precisely a key characteristic of these flows resides in their mobility, their liquidity — to borrow Zygmunt Bauman's term (2006). Traveling through a space crisscrossed with the diasporic networks that tie Senegal with the European shores, which now incidentally include those of the Atlantic Maghreb, the same migrant may alternatively act as a long-distance trader, a "trailblazer" on his way to Europe, and a locally employed casual laborer.

In Libya, prior to the revolution, Sub-Saharan, but also Moroccan and Egyptian, labor, occupied nearly all jobs in both the industrial and services sectors. Rare observers reported that over 2 million migrants were living in the country (Pliez 2005). As was the case in Algeria from the 1990s onward, Sub-Saharan migrants to Libya had diverted from their usual course because of political instability, especially in Ivory Coast, and were largely contributing to the revival of sleepy Saharan towns, particularly Sahba and Kafra (Pliez 2003). One must not underestimate Libya's historical ties with bordering Saharan countries, similar to those between Mauritania and Morocco, which are predominantly the result of a long-established tradition of cross-border trade, still alive today (Bennafla 2002). In Libya, however, the ways in which migrants are treated have always fluctuated in accordance with the political relations that the Qaddafi regime imposed on its African and European neighbors (Bredeloup and Pliez 2011). As a result, following the Western-imposed embargo starting in 1990, the Libyan borders opened to migrants. This openness culminated

4   Indeed it is estimated that at the time of the independence, toward the late 1950s, 70 percent of the Mauritanian population was nomadic. See Choplin 2008. On Mauritanian pastoralism, see also Antil 1999 and Bonte 2008.

5   In January 2006, no fewer than 3,500 landings coming from Mauritania are reported in the Canary Islands, with a frequency of approximately 100 arrivals every day, according to the Mauritanian Red Crescent (Choplin and Lombard 2007). The opening of a paved road between Nouakchott and Nouadhibou in 2005 probably had something to do with these transits (Antil and Choplin 2003), since it facilitated transfers toward the fishing port closest to the Canary Islands, where long-standing practices and navigational experience enabled shuttling. The existence and the reporting of these flows, including in the media, precedes the 2006 police treaties, signed by the European Union and the Mauritanian Government, allowing the Spanish Guardia Civil to patrol and control the waters off the Mauritanian shores (Valluy 2010).

with the creation of a "free-trade community," set-up between the Sahel and the Sahara countries and presided by Colonel Qaddafi, which widely opened Libya to Sub-Saharan migration stemming from the Sahel belt (Niger, Guinea, Cameroon, Senegal). Aside from the fact that they formed the bulk of an informal and insecure workforce employed by small business owners closely connected to the regime, little was known about the social and professional conditions of migrants in Libya. From 2000 onward, in the aftermath of violent events in which some Sub-Saharan workers were killed and other prosecuted, a form of stigmatizing prosecution starts to unfold. It results in numerous deportations, and a gradual realignment with European countries' policies, culminating with the ratification, by the Libyan regime and Europe, of close cooperation agreements on the monitoring of Libyan shores, the principal point of departure toward Italy.[6] Finally, in Tunisia, although the presence of migrant labor is not all that visible (Boubakri and Mazzella 2009), the transit of Europe-bound "trailblazers"[7] is very real, especially those heading for Italian shores. Also, Sub-Saharan students are now enrolled in universities, both public and private (Mazzella 2009).

Undoubtedly, each of the examples related here deserves to be addressed more thoroughly, and further research is required to assess these migration flows and settlement patterns (De Hass 2007). It must nonetheless be acknowledged that migration in the Maghreb is neither an anecdotal phenomenon nor a remnant of pre-colonial relations; nor is the Maghreb merely a zone of transit or passage, as the eurocentric views of these dynamics would contend. As asked very simply by most observers, if a journey from West Africa to the Mediterranean lasts an average of two years (De Hass 2007, Withol de Wenden 2012), whether or not the final destination is Europe, how then does one define "transit"? It is clear today that the societies of Southern Mediterranean countries are opening up, in locally specific ways, to migration; this signals, in turn, a genuine transformation of their economies, which makes the integration of migrants[8] possible in the first place.

The Morocco Case

Indisputedly, Morocco is the country where, on the one hand, the migrants' participation in the local economy is the most noticeable and diffuse, and on the other hand, where the phenomenon is currently being assessed and analyzed (Pian 2009, Timera 2011, Alioua 2005). This is hardly surprising, because after all, Morocco is where ties with francophone Sub-Saharan Africa have been the longest established, and are the most constant, to the point of being the most institutionalized. The Tidjaniya Sufi Order, founded in Fez, its holy city, and later expanded to Sub-Saharan Africa, provides a significant example of these ties. Thus far, it has permitted regular contacts and exchanges between Senegal and Morocco (Timera 2011, Triaud and Robinson 2000), as well as the establishment, in Fes and other cities, of the order's Senegalese members married to Moroccan women (Therrien 2009). Besides, thanks to agreements that date back to Independence, Senegalese are allowed to travel to, set up businesses, and pursue studies in Morocco without visas. Today they are unquestionably the largest Sub-Saharan group to have lastingly settled in Morocco (Pian 2009, Timera 2011). Similar agreements exist with other countries such as Guinea, or even Congo, whose deposed leader sought refuge in Rabat, along with his extended family and entourage. It is this very event that many observers have linked to the increasing presence of Sub-Saharan peoples in the working-class neighborhoods of the Moroccan capital (Edogué Ntang and Peraldi 2011). Finally, Moroccan migrants who have been living in Senegal, Mali, or Ivory Coast for a long time, are, to this day, taking part in initiating the transit of domestic staff employed by Moroccan households. Although these communities are neither responsible for, nor the organizers of, new Sub-Saharan migration to Morocco, they have the specific capacity to create contacts or bridges.

Observers unanimously point to a second migratory movement that started in the late 1990s, when migration routes leading to Nigeria or Ivory Coast closed (Marfaing and Wippel 2004). Following a lengthy journey through Niger and the Algerian south, and then temporarily gathering in Northern Morocco (Tanjer, Oujda), thus

6 While the number of illegal landings on Lampedusa island reached a record figure of almost 40,000 in 2006, during Agence Frontex's first year of operation, the figures steadily decreased following the softening of the relations between Europe and the Qaddafi regime. In 2010, when the Berlusconi administration ratified a symbolic treaty with Libya, targeting the financial settlements for damages caused during colonization, the number of reported landings on the island was close to zero (Palidda 2011).

7 The term "aventurier" in French is now frequently used in Sub-Saharan Africa to convey the nature of today's new migratory experience. This experience has indeed become a personal, individual, and individualizing experience, due to the challenges of the journey and the fact that the migrant is neither "expected" nor "sent" (Bredeloup 2008 and Pian 2009).

8 Thanks to the work of M. Piore (1979), we now know that migrants may embed themselves into economic activities only if they promote, by their mere presence, an organizational transformation of key sectors, particularly through the fragmentation of careers and vocational pathways. This may very well be what the presence of a migrant workforce reveals today in some of the Maghreb's industrial sectors (Kettani and Peraldi 2011).

giving the impression of planning a passage to Europe, these Sub-Saharan migrants finally "settled" in Rabat, Casablanca, and Marrakesh — the use of the term "settle" here aims to convey the powerful meaning it possesses in anthropology (Elias 1997). It must be noted that a large portion of Sub-Saharan Africans living in Morocco are students, originating mostly from French-speaking countries in Africa; today they are estimated to be a little under 10,000 (Infantino 2011, Berriane 2009). The erratic nature of their studies, as well as the students' precarious economic conditions, especially in the case of those receiving financial support from bankrupt states, often blurs the difference between them and the other migrants, whose living conditions are similar. Many students choose to stay in Morocco after graduating. They find, with relative ease, employment in a wide range of activities, from call centers to medical and paramedical careers, from jobs in media and IT, to teaching positions in private institutions. Their perfect command of French and their technical skills are, more often than not, what makes them competitive on the local job market. Although the Sub-Saharan students that graduate from Moroccan universities have a slight advantage over migrants, most of those who have investigated Sub-Saharan migration in the Maghreb (De Hass 2007) and in Morocco more specifically (Khachani 2009, Peraldi 2011, Pian 2009) note that Sub-Saharan migrants are usually young graduates themselves. Over a third of the individuals investigated by AMERM[9] in 2009, for instance, had postgraduate degrees.

Therein lies the paradox of the new North African migratory dynamics; and this is even more acute in Morocco, due to the diversity and the fragmentation of the sectors to which migrants attach themselves. As is well known, Algeria, Morocco, and Tunisia all have high rates of structural unemployment — particularly among young graduates. In 2012, the unemployment rates among youths (16–25 years old) was 22 percent in Morocco 22 percent in Algeria — although this figure is highly contested because it is deemed to be an underestimation — and 35.6 percent in Tunisia.[10] It would thus seem inconceivable that young Sub-Saharan graduates would be able to secure jobs, even if only a few of them, especially given the powerful political mobilization of national graduates, also young and unemployed (Emperador Badimon 2011). These Sub-Saharan graduates are hired by the French-speaking press as freelancers or journalists, or by call centers, which value their professional ability to speak French without any accent. Some also work informally, acting as classrooms assistants for primary school pupils, while others are recruited as teachers in the private school system, which is currently expanding in Morocco.

The question therefore is to understand why Moroccan graduates, French speakers themselves, do not access such employment opportunities. The answer is both predictable and obvious: most of the time, Moroccans reject these working conditions, because they find them too precarious or too poorly remunerated. Migrants, to the contrary, accept them. For if a Moroccan graduate may be able to "cope" with unemployment thanks to family backing, a migrant is, more often than not, alone and lacking support. It is clear that, insofar as the government regularly carries out targeted hiring campaigns, unemployed Moroccan graduates have a lot to gain by waiting for such recruiting opportunities. Today, as a result, this divide tends to widen the gap between the public sector and the private sector, which tends not to meet the national applicants' requirements and expectations, precisely because it can resort to hiring migrant workers.

American sociologists have described this phenomenon well, in the context of the competition between African-American youth and the recent migrants (Waldinger 2007). A hypothesis must therefore be put forward, one that could be supported only by thorough sectorial investigations. This hypothesis posits that turning to migration is not an inconsequential event; rather, it is one, if not the sole, condition that facilitates the emergence of an entrepreneurial and independent private sector, in industries that are new and uncertain (communication, media, tourism). Strategic as they may be, such industries are not the only ones hiring Sub-Saharan migrants. Sub-Saharan migrants also find jobs, even more precarious, as vendors in small-scale informal businesses, or as daily workers in the crafts industry or semi-industrial sectors such as construction material factories. Sub-Saharan prostitution, both male and female (Senegalese and Malians for males; Senegalese, Ghanaian, and

9   Association Marocaine d'Étude et de Recherche sur les Migrations.

10   Knowing that this figure comes after the change of regime, it is possible to infer a comparison on the basis of the 2009 figure that placed rates of unemployment at 21.6 percent, which is closer to that of the other North African states.

Nigerians for females), exists in Rabat, Casablanca, and Marrakech, where, for instance, internet networks offer the sexual services of young Cameroonians or Malians. Additionally, Sub-Saharan workers are also largely present in the construction trades; I shall return to this later.

If their numbers cannot be adequately assessed, Sub-Saharan migrants still manifest their presence by the diversity of their functions in Moroccan society, the diversity of their professional status, and by the increasing prevalence of distinct spatial markings, which stem from that very diversity and from the long-term establishment of their communities. In Rabat, the neighborhood of Douar Hajja, which is part of the large working-class district called Takkadoum, is now labeled the city's "black neighborhood" (Edogué Ntang and Peraldi 2011). There, single Sub-Saharans live in "communal homes," together with isolated families and single mothers; there are also cafés, cyber cafés, and associations, all catering to Sub-Saharans. More recently, and despite eviction threats, customary places of worship (mostly Pentecostal churches) have also begun emerging; this adds to an increase in Sub-Saharan religious practices in the official places of worship, either Catholic or Protestant, that already exist in Rabat, Casablanca, Marrakesh, Fez, and Tangiers. The durable settlement of a Sub-Saharan "society," rather than of individuals, is revealed by these urban markings, much more so than by uncertain headcounts of a community whose largely informal and relatively mobile nature hinders surveys. To be sure, although one can observe typical high turnovers and constant movements, mobility does not prevent the occurrence of an enduring appropriation of certain places, nor the inscription of a distinct "Africanity" in Morocco's urban space. And this occurs through public spaces, cafés, places of worship, the informal sights of labor exchanges or of urban figures (the street vendors, the local shoemakers, the prostitutes); and especially, although less frequently, through shared places such as the nightclubs of Rabat, Casablanca, and Marrakesh, who feature Ivoirian, Senegalese, and Malians owners, performers, and musicians. In Marrakesh, furthermore, the presence of African arts and crafts, ranging from bronze decorations to pottery and masks, discreet at first and then more visible, confirms the presence of vendors and supply chains.

Today, the issue of defining migration and its socioeconomic status is sparking debates across North African societies. At an earlier stage, it appeared as though Sub-Saharan migrants would be using the Maghreb as a transit space (Lahlou 2005, Alioua 2005, Brachet 2009), offloading zone, or "boosting station" on their migratory journeys toward Europe. And it is on this very idea, accepted as a fact and not actually proven, that North African and European states have based their migration control and deportation treaties (Valluy 2010). It is now clear that this migration can be described differently. Obviously, a significant portion of Sub-Saharan migrants living in the Maghreb still pursue the "European dream," just as Armenians traveling through Marseille in the 1920s were pursuing the "American dream" (Temime 1990); this cannot, however, be taken as a rational migratory narrative.

It is true that diasporic ties between France and French-speaking Africa still result in some prospective migrants continuing to set their target on Europe, and thus choosing to journey across the Maghreb merely because official procedures — both lengthy and costly — deny them direct access.[11] And yet, it is hard to question the fact that migration — Chinese migration in the case of Algeria, Sub-Saharan migration in that of Morocco and Mauritania — is indeed having an effect on these countries' economies. Debates and controversies merely revolve around the nature of the arguments. If the intention is to establish the resilience of migration through an assessment of the migrants' projects and the "trailblazers'" objectives, then one may still believe that migrants' stays in the Maghreb are mere layovers. But if one examines the space that migrants occupy when they settle, one may easily see that this space is structural; and although mobility prevails and high turnover rates in the migrant workforce do exist, one may easily notice that the economic benefit, or to use an economist's term, the "structural profitability" that migrants have is real.

Let us use one last example to illustrate this fact: in both Algeria and Morocco, the construction industry has been the first to resort to foreign labor. In Algeria, massive reliance on Chinese workers unfolded under the aegis of political agreements (Souiah 2010) granting Chinese firms contracts to carry out large-scale infrastructure

11 Let us look at the telling example of R, a young Cameroonian shoemaker, met in Rabat's Takadoum District. A professional football player, holding a degree in economics, he is blocked in Morocco, waiting to travel to France where his mother and his siblings live. R was raised by his grandparents. Ironically, his brothers, who have the French nationality, regularly travel to Morocco, on tourist visas, to visit him.

works, such as the Algiers Airport or the Algiers-Oran freeway; and it continued to evolve following other massive housing development plans on the outskirts of Oran and Algiers. Inversely, in Morocco, Sub-Saharan migrants make their appearance in the construction market via small-scale enterprises. Actually, in the early 2000s, the Moroccan government launched a series of large-scale projects: first, "Plan Azur," which included large touristic developments (for instance, 6,000 beds for a touristic area near Oujda, on the Mediterranean coast; then, plans for "New Towns" adjacent to major urban poles (two near Marrakesh, one near Rabat, whose first phase included, for instance, 10,000 to 20,000 housing units); finally, vast housing and infrastructure projects to develop the banks of the Bouregreg, linking Rabat and Salé.

By absorbing all of the national labor available, these massive developments, carried out by Spanish, French, and Moroccan consortiums, created a genuine shortage of workers; it particularly affected the small and medium-sized enterprises, which were unable to offer competitive packages comparable to those provided by larger firms. These smaller businesses thus turned to Sub-Saharan migrant workers, whom they hired on a daily, casual, basis (Kettani and Peraldi 2011). This resulted in a process of sectorial fragmentation, similar to what was previously analyzed in the context of the French construction industry (Anselme and Weisz 1985). As discussed earlier with regard to specific types of services, it is precisely, yet again, the availability of migrant workers that enables small and medium-sized businesses to strive. This sector can be characterized as modern (no moral connotations intended) in the sense that it neither pertains to a small-scale, more traditional, cottage industry (Buob 2010), nor does relates to the world of large-scale international or national firms that are dependent, for the most part, on political partnerships between governments.

I realize that the reading of North African migration flows proposed here might be surprising, in that it distinguishes itself from the mainstream perspectives that prevail today. To put it simply, and without insisting too much, most of the existing work on the topic has thus far combined a view of the political dynamics and their role in determining and directing migration fluxes (Streiff Fenart 2012) with a focus on the migratory projects and life stories of migrants. That combination has the benefit of breaking away from economic determinism, as it is applied to migration. A schism of this sort succeeds in highlighting the complexity of migratory flows; above all, it frames these flows in a biographical temporality and puts the emphasis on the fluid (Bauman 2006), mobile nature of contemporary migrations. Prolonged exiles have become uncommon today (Portes and DeWind 2007). And yet, these lucid accounts at times slightly overlook the local architecture and economic dynamics within which migration unfolds, within which it embeds itself (verbalized this way to avoid using the negative term "insert").

However rare, a few studies (Poutignat and Streiff Fenart 2006) have shown that North African migrations unravel in a context of overall rearrangement of African circulations, and the reconfiguration of individual destinies and career paths. They are, in fact, agents of the transformation of local economies, particularly through the emergence of a middle class in North African economic architecture. An additional type of migration could exemplify this phenomenon, one that is even more masked than the Sub-Saharan migration, essentially composed of Europeans.

There is no doubt that Europeans represent the densest segment of all foreigners living in both Morocco and Tunisia today. Conservative estimates from the Moroccan census place the number of Europeans residing in Morocco slightly above 32,000, of which 21,000 are French nationals. The French consulate places these figures slightly higher, indicating a total of 34,000 Europeans surveyed, including 6,000 to 7,000 Spanish nationals and 4,500 Italians. Conventionally, most of these Europeans would be labeled "expatriates," a term that refers either to public servants sent out by their own government on temporary assignments (usually ranging from three to five years for the French), or to private-sector employees mandated for equally variable durations. The "expat" status refers here both to the assignments' duration, fixed beforehand, and to the "protected" status enjoyed by these professionals, in the sense that governments or companies sending out expatriates are responsible for any administrative challenges their employees may face, which often requires bilateral agreements between foreign countries and the host states. In the past decade, however, a large number of Europeans based in the Maghreb have escaped this protective narrative. We cannot provide the figures, but it is obvious that Europeans have now taken root in the emergent economies of North African countries. What is more, they have done so in a manner that is closer to the classic modes of migration than to the expatriate model defined above. The tourism industry is a case in point, with Tunisia and Morocco being high-ranking international tourist destinations.

Admittedly, European migrants enjoy the same freedom that is accorded to European tourists, since they are entitled to long-term, easily renewable visits. The obligation to regularly return to their country of origins to "reset the (administrative) clock" is their sole constraint. As part of an ongoing study,[12] we have begun to meet them and have initiated a description of their activities in Marrakesh. In this city, North Africa's first tourism destination, European migrants are promoting a tourism industry that could be labeled mid-sized. In spite of the fact that large hotel chains do employ European expats, it is the European migrants who have captured the niche within the small-scale hotel industry (the famous *riads*), catering businesses, cafés, and bars; they also operate in the neo-craftsmanship and semi-industrial markets, reinventing local arts and crafts traditions, in response to tourists' wishes and the tourism industry's needs (furniture, decoration, design).

Small and medium-sized businesses, developed by Europeans migrants and the local workforce they employ, make up the fabric that is at the origins of both the industrial and commercial district of Sidi Ghanem and part of the Medina's touristic infrastructure.[13] Furthermore, these same entrepreneurs are also creating, in a more diffuse manner, Morocco's internationally renowned arts and crafts products, ranging from argan oil, cosmetics, ceramics, and textiles. Parts of these Europeans migrants, although not all, are in fact descendants of migrants who chose to come back to their country of origin. However, as far as our research indicates, most of the European migration stems from the European middle classes, which have suffered from the crisis and stalemates induced by the public sector's hiring freeze. Italians, Spaniards, Belgians, and French, the last forming the bulk of the European migrants, are by no means seasoned businessmen or wealthy offspring. Most of them have left jobs with the aim of opening their own business, which they usually create ex nihilo.

12   This CADIS/EHESS initiative is chaired by Alexandre Poli, Giulia Fabbiano, Lizza Terrazzoni, and Michel Peraldi and addresses the question of European migration to the Mediterranean's North African shores, as well as the role that these migrations play in the economic and social restructuring that occurs in Morocco, Algeria, and Tunisia.

13   Obviously, the bulk of this "intermediate economy" is informal, hence the vague data. In Marrakesh's Medina, the number of riads is estimated at 900, all linked to hotels or restaurants. Two-thirds of these riads are run by Europeans, while one-third are run by Moroccans or Franco-Moroccans. See Sebti, Courbage, Festy, and Kursak Souali 2011.

Conclusion

A fair amount of work remains to be done on the study of the Southern Mediterranean shores if we are to better understand the mechanisms of migratory flows that are occurring in the crucially important spatiotemporal hubs of North Africa. This work is critical because, by describing these phenomena, it readily challenges the political fictions that European media employ to represent them. We may nevertheless draw one general characteristic from our brief investigation: whether accessing it "from the top," as entrepreneurs do, or "from below," as the precarious workers do, migrants who enter North African society are locating themselves in a new median economic realm. Cohorts of mobile traders, who roam the trans-Mediterranean routes and revive the local markets of North Africa, are joining the ranks of the Senegalese dry-fishery owners of Mauritania, the Chinese tradesmen of Algeria, and the European craftsmen of Marrakesh. Such variegated cases have one thing in common: they introduce a novel socioeconomic level in the local economic architecture — a level that did not exist before, or if it did, was weak and inactive. New migrants are inventing an intermediate level, a distinct middle ground of some sort, that distances itself both economically and socially from the small-sized informal industries that occupy the bulk of the economic realm, as well as from the large-scale industries that are tied up to governments and bureaucracies. The very purpose of this account is to show that the local middle classes are not disadvantaged by this situation; indeed when they situate themselves in this intermediate economic level, they regularly benefit from an abundant migrant labor force.

Translated by Marianne Potvin

References:

Agier, M., 2008. Gérer les indésirables. Des camps de réfugiés au gouvernement humanitaire. Paris: Flammarion.

Alioua, M. 2005. La migration transnationale des africains subsahariens au Maghreb : l'exemple de l'étape marocaine. In Maghreb-Machrek 185: 37–57.

Andreas, P. 2001. Border Games: Policing the U.S.-Mexico Divide. Ithaca: Cornell University Press.

Anselme, M., and R. Weisz. 1985. "Good and Bad Jobs: A Differentiated Structuring of the Labor Market." In Acta Sociologica 28/1: 137–145.

Antil, A. 1999. "Le territoire d'Etat en Mauritanie, genèse, héritage et representation." Doctoral thesis, Université de Rouen.

Antil, A., and A. Choplin. 2003. "Le chaînon manquant: la route Nouakchott-Nouadhibou, dernier tronçon de la transharienne Tanger-Dakar." In Afrique Contemporaine 208: 115_126.

Bauman, Z. 2006. La vie liquide,. Rodez: Editions du Rouergue.

Bennafla, K. 2002. Le commerce transfrontalier en Afrique Centrale. Paris: Karthala.

Berriane, J., 2009. "Les étudiants subsahariens au maroc : des migrants parmi d'autres?," in Méditerranée 113.

Bensaad, A., 2005. "Les migrations transsahariennes, une mondialisation par la marge." In Maghreb-Machrek 185: 13–36.

Bonte, P. 2008. L'émirat de l'Adrar mauritanien. Paris: Karthala.

Boubakri, H., and S. Mazzella. 2005. "La Tunisie entre transit et immigration: politiques migratoires et condition d'accueil des migrants africains en Tunisie." In Autrepart 36: 149–165.

Brachet, J. 2009. Migrations transsahariennes. Vers un desert cosmopolite et morcelé. Paris: Editions du Croquant.

Bredeloup, S. 2008. "L'aventurier, une figure de la migration africaine." In Cahiers Internationaux de Sociologie 2/125: 281–306.

Bredeloup, S., and O. Pliez. 2011. The Libyan Migration Corridor. Research Report EU/US Immigration Systems, 2011/3, Robert Schuman Center for Advanced Studies, San Domenico di Fiesole, European University Institute.

Buob, B. 2009. La dinanderie de Fès. Un artisanat traditionnel dans les temps modernes. Paris: Ibis Press/Editions de la MSH.

Choplin, A. 2008. "L'immigré, le migrant, l'allochtone : circulations migratoires et figures de l'étranger en Mauritanie." In Politiques Africaines 109: 73–90.

Choplin, A., and J. Lombard. 2007. "Nouadhibou: destination Canaries pour les migrants africains." In Mappemonde 88/4.

De Haas, H. 2007. The Myth of Invasion: Irregular Migration from West Africa to the Maghreb and the European Union. Oxford: International Migration Institute, IMI Research Report.

Edogué Ntang J.L., and M. Peraldi. 2011. Un ancrage discret. L'établissement des migrations subsahariennes dans la capitale marocaine. In M. Peraldi, ed., D'une Afrique à l'autre. Migrations subsahariennes au Maroc. Paris: Karthala.

Elias, N. 1997. Logique de l'exclusion. Paris: Fayart.

Emperador Badimon, M. 2011. "Les mobilisations des diplômés chômeurs au Maroc. Organisation et avatars d'une cause revendicatrice." Doctoral thesis, IEP Aix en Provence.

Fassin, D., ed. 2010. Les nouvelles frontières de la société française. Paris: La Découverte.

Infantino, F. 2011. "Les mondes des étudiants subsahariens au Maroc." In Peraldi, ed., D'une Afrique à l'autre.

Khachani, M. 2006. Lé migration subsaharienne. Le Maroc comme espace de transit. Rabat: Amerm.

Kettani, M., and M. Peraldi. 2011. "Les mondes du travail. Segmentations et informalities." In Peraldi, ed., D'une Afrique à l'autre.

Lahlou, M. 2005. "Le Maroc et les migrations des africains du sud du Sahara. Evolutions récentes et possibilités d'action." In Critique Economique 16.

Marfaing, L., and S. Wippel. 2004. Les relations transsahariennes à l'époque contemporaine. Paris: Karthala, ZMO.

Migreurop. 2006. Le livre noir de Ceuta et Melilla, disponible sur le site http://www.migreurop.org/rubrique177.html

Mazzella, S., ed. 2009. La mondialisation étudiante. Le Maghreb entre nord et sud. Paris: Karthala/IRMC.

Palidda, S. 2008. Mobilità umane. Introduzione alla sociologia delle migrazioni. Milan: Raffaelo Cortino editore.

Palidda, S., ed. 2011. Migrations critiques : repenser les mobilités humainesen Méditerranée. Paris: Karthala.

Peraldi, M., ed. 2011. D'une Afrique à l'autre. Migrations subsahariennes au Maroc. Paris: Karthala.

Pian, A. 2009. Aux nouvelles frontières de l'Europe. L'aventure incertaine des sénégalais au Maroc. Paris: Editions La Dispute.

Piore, M. 1979. Birds of Passage: Migrant Labour and Industrial Society. Cambridge: Cambridge University Press.

Pliez, O. 2005. "Le Sahara libyen dans les nouvelles configurations migratoires." In Revue Européenne des Migrations Internationales 16/3: 165–182.

Portes, A., and J. DeWind, eds. 2007. Rethinking Migration: New Theoretical and Empirical Perspectives. New York: Berghahn Books.

Poutignat, P., and J. Streiff Fenart. 2006. De l'aventurier au commerçant transnational, trajectoires croisées et lieux intermédiaires à Nouadhibou. In Cahiers de la méditerranée 73, December: 129–149.

Rodier, C. 2012. Xénophobie business. A quoi servent les contrôles migratoires? Paris: La Découverte.

Sebti, M., and Y. Courbage, P. Festy, and A.C. Kursak Souali. 2009. "Gens de Marrakech. Géo-démographie de la ville rouge." In Cahiers de l'INED 164.

Streiff Fenart, J., and A. Segatti, eds. 2012. The Challenge of the Threshold, Border Closures, and Migration Movements in Africa. Lanham, MD: Lexington Books.

Souiah, F. 2010. La société algérienne au miroir des migrations chinoises. Mémoire Master 2, IEP Paris.

Spiga, S. 2005. "Aménageurs et migrants dans les villes du grand sud algérien." Autrepart 36: 81–103.

Tarrius, A. 2002. La mondialisation par le bas. Les nouveaux nomades de l'économie souterraine. Paris: Balland.

Temime, E. 1990. Migrance. Histoire des migrations à Marseille T.3. Aix en Provence: Edisud.

Timera, M. 2011. "La religion en partage, la couleur et l'origine comme frontière. Les migrants sénégalais au Maroc." In Cahiers d'Etudes Africaines 201.

Torpey, J. 2000. *The Invention of the Passport: Surveillance, Citizenship, and the State.* Cambridge, Cambridge University Press.

Triaud, J.L., and D. Robinson, eds. *La Tijaniyya. Une confrérie musulmane à la conquête de l'Afrique.* Paris: Karthala.

Valluy, J. 2010. L'exportation de la xénophobie de gouvernement. De la politique européenne des frontières à la répression dans les pays limitrophes. In D. Fassin, ed., *Les nouvelles frontières de la société française.*

Waldinger, R. 2007. "Bad Jobs, Good Jobs, No Job? The Employment Experience of the Mexican-American Second Generation." In *Journal of Ethnic and Migration Studies* 33/1: 1–35.

Wihtol de Wenden, C. 2012. *Atlas des migrations. Un équilibre mondial à inventer.* Paris: Editions Autrement.

A Laboratory of New Migrations

The Mediterranean as Expansionist Theater
The Case of Atlantropa
Peter Christensen

It would be difficult to conjure up an architectural vision more utopian, more technologically audacious, more polemical than Herman Sörgel's Atlantropa. Sörgel, a Bavarian architect, developed the scheme in the interwar years and tenaciously propagated it until his death in 1952. The opus schematizes a tightly linked Europe-Africa formed by the damming of the Strait of Gibraltar and the Dardanelles, the lowering of the Mediterranean's sea level, and the subsequent emergence of new arable land. At its core is the design of several trans-Mediterranean arteries supporting the flow of people and natural resources between the civilizations inhabiting the Eurasian peninsula west of the Ural Mountains and Persia, including the Arabian Peninsula and the entire continent of Africa. Sörgel conceived the connection as a two-way "geopolitical valve" that would harness European technological and engineering know-how as a means of securing the vast natural resources of the African continent, which in turn would ensure the prosperity and development of Europe and Africa and the Middle East within a larger global geopolitical order.

A survey of the literature on the project highlights some of the open issues. For one, Atlantropa is largely ignored outside of German historical circles.[1] German scholarship on the project has focused on Atlantropa's visionary qualities, its technological feasibility, and its relationship to European and German intellectual traditions, including mega-scale environmental design, anti-ecological theory, and environmental determinism.[2]

What remains suspended is a consideration of the deeply geographical and political earth in which the project is planted, particularly as it relates to the voiceless populations of the Middle East and Africa who were, nonetheless, to be its lynchpin. Alexander Gall analyzes some of the racial and geopolitical implications found in the project's archive. In his book *Das Atlantropa-Projekt — Die Geschichte einer gescheiterten Vision: Herman Sörgel und die Absenkung des Mittelmeers*, Gall points out the deep-seated racism of Sörgel's plans for the African and

1   Important secondary sources on Atlantropa include: Alexander Gall, *Das Atlantropa-Projekt: die Geschichte einer gescheiterten Vision: Herman Sörgel und die Absenkung des Mittelmeeres* (Frankfurt: Campus, 1998); Anne Sophie Günzel, *Das "Atlantropa" — Projekt — Erschließung Europas und Afrikas* (Norderstedt: GRIN Verlag, 2003); Wolfgang Voigt, *Atlantropa: Weltbauen am Mittelmeer. Ein Architektentraum der Moderne* (Hamburg: Dölling und Gallitz, 1998). Also see relevant articles: Eva Dockal, „J.J.P. Oud als Architekt des 'neuen München'? Eine verpaßte Chance," *Zeitschrift für Kunstgeschichte* 64 Bd., H. 1 (2001): 103–15; Dirk van Laak, „Planung, Geschichte und Gegenwart des Vorgriffs auf die Zukunft," *Geschichte und Gesellschaft,* vol. 34, issue 3 (July–Sept. 2008): 305–326.

2   Here I refer primarily to Voigt, which was the companion publication to the Deutsches Architektur Museum's 1997 exhibition on Atlantropa. The exhibition included a one-hour DVD that expanded on the apolitical qualities of the projects through impressive computer animations illustrating the complexity and sophistication of many of the port, dam, bridge, and highway designs Sörgel articulated.

Peter H. Christensen is a Ph.D. Candidate in Architecture at Harvard University. His research centers on the practice and historiography of geopolitics (as a discrete field of inquiry since the nineteenth century) and its implications on spatial practices, with particular interest in the borders of Islamic and Judeo-Christian civilizations. He also researches the museology of architecture and the critical practices of connoisseurship. His current doctoral research considers cultural, infrastructural, and architectural exchanges between the German, Austro-Hungarian, and Ottoman Empires. Prior to his graduate studies, he served as Curatorial Assistant in the Department of Architecture and Design at the Museum of Modern Art (2005–2008).

Christensen holds a professional Bachelor of Architecture from Cornell University, a Master of Design Studies in the History and Theory of Architecture (with Distinction), and a Master of Arts, both from Harvard University. He is the recipient of the Philip Johnson Book Award from the Society of Architectural Historians (2010), as well as grants from the Fulbright Foundation, the Deutsche Akademischer Austauschdienst (DAAD), the Society of Architectural Historians, and the Society of Historians of Islamic Art and Architecture, among others.

Asian populations of the to-be continent, noting how the massive relocation and repopulation schemes for these people were essentially the opposite of the additive strategy for settlement north of the Mediterranean and therefore representative of the scheme's Eurocentric function.

Gall and several others vest considerable effort in situating Atlantropa relationally with National Socialist ideology, and it is easy to see why. A grand geopolitical scheme in the interwar years that was to change the way Europe (and Germany in particular) related to its neighbors, bears the burden of inevitable historical hindsight. To be sure, the complicated connection between Atlantropa and National Socialism is relevant, but the project's intellectual and architectural origins have less to do with Nazism than with the way in which the enfeeblement of Germany after World War I shaped its highly physicalized sense of self, drawing on a rich home-grown tradition of geopolitical thought and technological optimism.[3] Atlantropa's racial undertones were, however, just that — undertones. They were also hardly anachronistic. The argument that has been made is that Atlantropa demonstrates a new type of imperialism contradistinctive to the more familiar narratives of Nazism and colonialism, and presents a new modus operandi for imperialism in the post-imperial portion of the twentieth century. This places a primacy on the project's ideology and sublimates its architectonic ambitions as part and parcel of its written record. Here I look closely at the way in which Atlantropa implicated a complex Muslim Mediterranean, with its diverse populations stretching from Tangier to Istanbul. It is argued that this space was not simply about subordination but that Sörgel's project indeed envisioned that space in uneven ways that can hardly be encapsulated by Gall's claims of "racism," but must be unfolded rather on their own terms. In this discussion, visual material — plans, pictorial images, and films — plays a primary role in displacing the dominance of textual analyses in understanding this project, while also relying upon new and previously uncited archival material.

The Geopolitical Architect

Sörgel's education at the Technische Universität München, where he trained until 1908, was primarily technical and eschewed Beaux-Arts artistic idioms in favor of a strong emphasis on civil engineering and the development of the expansive German Empire's newly unified and swiftly developing economy.[4] His early architectural works were limited mostly to multifamily residences and small-scale industrial buildings in and around Munich. Nonetheless, Sörgel, as early as the late 1910s, executed designs for large infrastructural entities, including dams and power plants, independent of commissions. Sörgel cultivated these imaginary grand projects on his own time in a professional double life that pursued polemical modernist projects in private and humble traditionalist projects in public.

Sörgel was also a consummate student of geography, a field he believed to be integral rather than collateral to architecture.[5] Geographical theory, particularly that of Friedrich Ratzel, the director of the Geographic Institute at the Universität Leipzig, was elemental to the German Empire's understanding of self and offered up positivist rationales to expansionist impulses beginning in the 1870s. One pervasive theory was that of *der Staat als Organismus* (the state as organism), which likened states to organic entities. Ratzel analogized dams, autobahns, railways, and bridges to the digestive and circulatory systems found in natural organisms. The more extensively and qualitatively they were built, the more likely the organism or the state would thrive. This way of conceiving civil infrastructure takes on supranational and supra-imperial theoretical qualities as well, formulating the idea of *Lebensraum* (living space), which meant the amount of actual land needed by a nation or peoples to sustain their maximum agricultural productivity as it relates to their calorific needs. This term, appropriated by Hitler and National Socialist geographers to rationalize the invasion of Poland in 1939, had a less political implication when first conceived

3   See Axel Goodbody, *Nature, Technology, and Cultural Change in Twentieth-Century German Literature: The Challenge of Ecocriticism* (Hampshire, UK: Palgrave MacMillan, 2007).

4   Kathleen James-Chakraborty explains the political and sociological popularization of modernist design ideals in interwar Germany and the Weimar Republic in particular, demonstrating how the Beaux-Arts tradition had a steadier currency in practice than in theory, a condition that sheds some light on Sörgel's instrumental compartmentalization of architectural style and doctrine within and outside of Atlantropa. See James-Chakraborty, *German Architecture for a Mass Audience* (London: Routledge, 2000).

5   Voigt, *Alantropa,* 101.

[4]

The actor Walter Holten depicts a Sörgel-like figure in the 1936 Nazi film "ein Meer versinkt"

European archers demonstrating the triadic connection between Europe and Africa, 1938

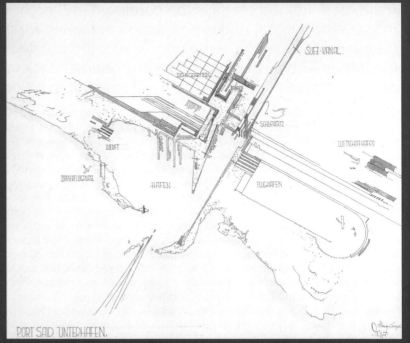

Hans Döllgast and Herman Sörgel's design for the new Port Said, 1931

in the late nineteenth century. Part philosophical and part hegemonic construction, Sörgel's geopolitical chimera spoke dialectically to both utopian visions of human prosperity and happiness and the disheartening abuse of power and the environment.

A handful of remarkable projects employing German civil engineering know-how abroad situate Atlantropa historically. The last several Ottoman sultans, building on a mandate of aggressive infrastructural development enshrined in the Tanzimat reforms of 1832, personally oversaw the selection of architects for several important infrastructural transformations of Istanbul. German expertise was preferred with increasing frequency over that of the British and French over the course of the nineteenth and early twentieth centuries. This included the completion of the German planner Helmuth von Möltke's extensive plan to normalize the urban street fabric and build gutters and raised sidewalks in the wake of a devastating fire that levelled a large swath of the city in 1839. Sultan Abdulhamid II commissioned a colleague of Sörgel, architect Baron Moritz von Hirsch, to design a daring suspension bridge for automobiles and trains across the Bosphorus in a high Orientalist (or "neo-Islamic") posture in 1900, a design that was ultimately never realized.

The Bosphorus proved its importance yet again as a site for German geopolitical yearnings in the most ambitious of all German penetrations in the Near East — the *Bagdadbahn*, or Berlin-Baghdad Railway.[6] The railway, a complex amalgamation of the private economic speculation of German industrialists and the realpolitik of Kaiser Wilhelm, was to interlock the port of Hamburg with the port of Basra, effectively connecting the Atlantic to the Indian Ocean and allowing German trade to bypass its reliance on the British-controlled Suez Canal. The project fostered a delicate and tendentious linkage between German expertise and finance and a bankrupt but eagerly "Westernizing" Ottoman Empire.

Politics and Grand Plans in the Mediterranean

In his writing, Sörgel makes scant reference to a handful of important paradigmatic mega-engineering projects in North America. For example, Sörgel's 1938 publication *Die drei Grossen "A"/ The Three Big "A's,"* the most vivid written description of Atlantropa, fails to mention the establishment of the Tennessee Valley Authority (TVA) charter in the United States five years prior, which ushered in an era of extensive civic infrastructure building in the form of dams, reservoirs, bridges, roads, etc.[7] This is surprising given the commensurability of such large-scale projects in both Europe and North America, as has been described by Diane Ghirardo, who has drawn important connections between Roosevelt's New Deal infrastructure ambitions and their architectural ramifications and those of Fascist Italy, demonstrating how the scale of the ambition of interwar civil engineering programs had nothing necessarily to do with political or geopolitical ideology.[8]

It is curious that Sörgel does not explore these precedents more carefully, as they could have furnished leitmotifs instructive in grasping the actual technological feasibility of Atlantropa's staggering ambition. In severing links to the Atlantic Ocean and the Black Sea, Atlantropa was to lower the Mediterranean by 500 meters. For the most part, the grand scale at which the dams were rendered, in a lively, diagrammatic and quasi-constructivist style, indicates little about any particular architectural party line. Vast new swaths of land along the Mediterranean littoral added arable land, while artificial lakes created in the Belgian Congo and the Sahara created greater irrigation capacity in arid regions. Together, this aggregate new land, the size of France and Spain combined, was to serve as a vast new breadbasket and source of hydroelectric power for Europe and in turn bolster the productivity and economic health of the myriad European colonial holdings from Tunis to Cape Town.

Evocative imagery using anthropomorphic and animal figures was used to capture the essence of the project. These images reveal the liminal role that the anonymous people who inhabited these soon to be transformed areas played in Sörgel's ambitious scheme. One 1932 depiction produced for a promotional pamphlet depicts a scantily dressed African woman lifting aloft a basket of *Rohstoffe* (raw

6   See Jonathan McMurray, *Distant Ties: Germany, the Ottoman Empire, and the Construction of the Berlin-Baghdad Railway* (Westport, CT: Praeger, 2001); Gregor Schöllgen, *Imperialismus und Gleichgewicht. Deutschland, England, und die orientalische Frage 1871–1914* (Munich: Oldenbourg, 1984); Kevin D. Stubbs, *Race to the Front: The Material Foundations of Coalition Strategy in the Great War* (Santa Barbara, CA: Greenwood Press, 2002); and Sean McMeekin, *The Berlin-Baghdad Express: The Ottoman Empire and Germany's Bid for World Power* (Cambridge, MA: Belknap Press of Harvard University Press, 2010).

7   Herman Sörgel, *Die drei grossen „A"; gross Deutschland und Italienisches Imperium, die Pfeiler Atlantropas* (Munich: Piloty and Loehle, 1938).

8   See Diane Ghirardo, *Building New Communities: New Deal America and Fascist Italy* (New York: Princeton University Press, 1989). Regarding later ideas of American nuclear development, with a relevant back story, see Scott L. Kirsch, *Proving Grounds: Project Plowshare and the Unrealized Dream of Nuclear Earthmoving* (Piscataway, NJ: Rutgers University Press, 2005).

goods), in exchange for the *Fertigwaren* (finished goods) supplied by a European man.[9] The basket she is lifting toward the Mediterranean appears to contain an elephant tusk and wheat. The well-heeled European accepts the basket, and while we understand from the caption that he is providing her, in return, with finished goods, we do not see what they are. Despite the fact that this encounter is depicted as an "exchange" (*Austausch*), the image highlights the process of acquisition as opposed to production. The gendering of the two halves of the supra-continent reinforces this portrayal of a power dynamic — the fertile African woman providing for the modernized European man. It is notable that the Mediterranean region is entirely obscured in this image.

Another similar depiction takes on a very different anthropomorphic tone. Africa assumes the form of an elephant that lifts aloft a nude Lady Europe, the elephant replacing the mythical bull. Together, they are protected from the rest of the world by a wreath of barbed wire.[10] The elephant dons traditional "oriental" regalia. Despite their obvious mythological as well as allegorical connection, Lady Europe is in fact not actually sitting on the elephant. The entirety of her body remains fully within the continental boundaries, her feet (ending somewhere in Andalusia) come closest to touching the elephant's head without actually doing so. The Mediterranean, it would appear, remains something of a buffer zone between the beautiful nude Lady Europe and the beastly "oriental" animal. The barbed wire does something entirely different in alluding to the rest of the world and employing no visual subtlety as to the isolationist nature of the project.

Another diagram shows Europe as triad archers, "shooting" their power in three north-south axes: Cairo to Cape Town (reminiscent of the unrealized train line of the same name); trans-Sahara; and a shorter segment ending in Dakar. Here the power mechanisms of the project (signified by the arrow) are rendered as something that is projected axiomatically from Europe as opposed to mediated in or by the Mediterranean basin.

Administrative plans for Atlantropa were equally diagrammatic. The closest Sörgel comes to outlining a political structure for an Atlantropa is found in a diagram entitled "Politisches Struktur Europas," which draws a symbolic set of magnets around a north-south axis running from Germany through Italy into Africa (a preliminary sketch coloring both Germany and Italy in yellow), making the particular importance of Italo-German collaboration evident in the tacit political strategy while also indicating the central place of the Muslim Mediterranean in the scheme, even if only as a place and space passed over for access to the South.[11]

It is worth considering these administrative models in comparison to those of German colonies in Togo, Ghana, and South West Africa, colonies founded initially through the acquisitive interests of private individuals. Once formalized politically, administrative styles in German colonies remained fairly focused on the development of economic infrastructure (as opposed to the "civilizing mission" of culture and religion enforced by French and British colonial authorities).[12] The historical tradition of individual autonomy in German colonialism (Karl Peters, Georg von Siemens) may have also given a bit more conceptual currency to Sörgel's idiosyncratic imperial ambition than it may have had elsewhere. The new Europe-Africa was destined, in Sörgel's worldview, to be positioned as *the* world superpower. Atlantropa would be a bulwark of Europeanity so long as it was willing to bring the diverse climes, peoples, and natural resources of Africa into its collective geopolitical order. Atlantropa could buttress the cradle of civilization from the "yellow peril" to the right and American ascendancy to the left. The term "yellow peril" (*gelbe Gefahr*) is often attributed to none other than Kaiser Wilhelm II, who used the moniker in a public statement made in September 1895. He insisted on having a plaque of this term, depicting the Archangel Michael and an allegorical Germany leading a charge against the threat of an expanding Asiatic power, represented by a golden Buddha, hung in all of the ships of the Hamburg America Line.[13]

A pamphlet produced to solicit popular and financial support for the scheme postulates three continents all beginning with the letter "A" — the Americas, Asia, and Atlantropa — that formulate a tripartite shorthand of world order. The promotional imagery depicts an ideology in motion.[14] At first, Atlantropa was to be a harmo-

9   See Vogt, *Alantropa,* 103. Deutsches museum reference number: Bild Nr. 35834, 35835 (s-w), Ordner Nr. 341/1.

10   See Vogt, *Alantropa,* 104. This image is contained in Sörgel, *Die Drei Grossen „A".* Deutsches Museum reference number: Bild Nr. 35834, 35835 (s-w), Ergänz Nr. 35835a, Ordner Nr. 341/1.

11   Deutsches Museum reference number: Bild Nr. 35822.

12   See, for example, L.H. Gann and Peter Duignan, *The Rulers of German Africa, 1884–1914* (Palo Alto, CA: Stanford University Press), 22–45. Here the role of acquisitive private individual "metropole" capitalists is highlighted as a singular feature of German dominion in Africa that had a significant bearing on administrative style and ideological (or non-ideological) relationship to questions of African civilization and culture.

13   See Daniel C. Kane, introduction to A.B. de Guerville, *Au Japon, Memoirs of a Foreign Correspondent in Japan, Korea, and China, 1892–1894* (West Lafayette, IN: Parlor Press, 2009), xxix. In America the term was popularized in the newspapers owned by William Randolph Hearst. See, for example, "Foreign News: Again, Yellow Peril," *Time,* September 11, 1933. For a general consideration of German fears of American ascendancy, see Michael H. Hunt, *American Ascendancy: How the United States Gained and Wielded Global Dominance* (Raleigh, N.C.: University of North Carolina Press, 2008), 88–91.

14   Sörgel, *Die drei grossen „A".*. Also illustrated in much of the visual materials held in the Archiv der Technischen, Zeichnungen, Deutschen Museum Munich, Boxes 04682–04685.

nious and bilateral geopolitical construction that conflated the notions of a Concert of Europe with the colonial economic interests in Africa and the Middle East. By the dawn of World War II, it would become something quite different, a geopolitical order bound by sheer necessity and fear of the ascendant powers typified by the United States and Japan. Sörgel's scheme testifies to a tacit and optimistic assumption that Europe, rife with international problems and unsettled scores of its own, had the ability to coalesce.

Mediterranean Europe too had plenty of reason not to look fondly upon Sörgel's scheme. Italy, perhaps aware of the German desire for having it coerced into a political axis, reacted with particular vehemence against it, with the *Corriere della Sera* deriding the scheme in an article describing the project as a "bizarre German dream" in 1928.[15] With the Strait of Messina clogged, a 66-kilometer bridge connecting Sicily to Tunisia was to be the most important artery of Atlantropa, bringing both the potential for economic betterment and cultural dilution to swollen Italian soil. Sörgel's plans for the historic port cities of Genoa and Venice demonstrated two vastly different approaches to dealing with the geo-historical ramifications of the scheme. The old port of Genoa, on the one hand, would be definitively landlocked, connected to a futuristic new port by monolithic architecture and urban arteries.[16] Venice, on the other, was to be protected by UNESCO as a world heritage site, and thus its waterfront would be dammed so that it could remain Venice, if only in form, not function.[17] Italy, understandably, watched the proposal with more concern than any other nation.

These port city redesigns illustrate how Sörgel and the team of architects with whom he collaborated, including Peter Behrens, Erich Mendelsohn, and Fritz Höger, had a sensitivity to the importance of cities in maintaining European culture and history writ large. The port cities of the eastern and southern Mediterranean were perceived to be inconsequential historically and, to a lesser extent, commercially, and were in turn treated in much different terms. The fates of Istanbul, Haifa, Alexandria, Tripoli, and Algiers, all slated to be dramatically recast with harbors of salty shrub, were ostensibly not worthy of redesign or historic preservation in the vein of either Genoa or Venice. Port Said, Tunis, and Tangier, on the other hand, did receive architectural and urban treatments.

Atlantropa, Zionism, and the Vicissitudes of City Building in the Muslim Mediterranean

Published as well as previously unpublished drawings from Sörgel's archive reveal a bit more about the new landscape of North Africa, the "Near East," and the "caps" of the Mediterranean at Gibraltar and the Dardanelles. As the fulcrums of two continents as well as religious spheres, their architectural and/or infrastructural schematization bear directly on the renovation of Islamic port cities and landscapes in the image of a German-sponsored Eurafrican superbody.

The Strait of Gibraltar is the most complex of all of the engineering proposals in Atlantropa. In a bird's-eye illustration, we see a vast dam gradually emerging out of the Andalusian hinterland, southwest of Algeciras, curving across the strait to Morocco and receding back into the land gradually somewhere between Ceuta and Tangier. Both landward sides of the dam have ports, designated as "north" and "south" ports (marked "Items A") as well as canals for the securing of ships ("Items B"). On the Spanish embankment stands a massive Futurist hydroelectric plant rendered at a height comparable to the Rock of Gibraltar ("Item C"). On the Moroccan side there is no plant but rather a cascaded gap for the overflow of water from the Atlantic ("Item D"), making the environs of Tangier the location the most susceptible to flooding within Atlantropa.

At the Dardanelles, Sörgel imagines a valve-like structure to connect the Mediterranean with the Sea of Marmara and the Black Sea. The dam capping this end of the Mediterranean is far shorter than that at Gibraltar, abutting the coast of Çanakkale and the coast north of it abruptly, without architectural intervention. At the narrowest point on the Dardanelles peninsula, just east of Gallipoli, Sörgel imagines

15 Voigt, *Alantropa,* 50.

16 Archiv der Technischen Zeichnungen, Deutsches Museum Munich, Box 04843.

17 Ibid., Box 04871.

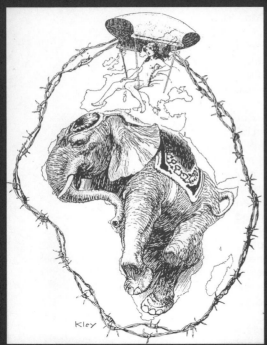

Lady Europe atop the African
elephant, motif for Atlantropa,
1938

Illustration of extension of
Suez Canal, 1931

View of the Strait of Gibraltar,
1932

a single two-way thoroughfare for ship traffic in and out of the Mediterranean. On the north end, another hydroelectric plant fans out from the overflow passageway ("Item A"), while a sheltered port sits on the southern end of the peninsula ("Item B"). Sörgel constructed a model of the hydroelectric plant on the northern edge, demonstrating its radial strategy, not dissimilar to that of Gibraltar. At the center is a large tower that houses the energy storage mechanisms ("Item A"). At ground level, adjacent to the various cascades fueling the power station, are a series of smaller structures that are to function as smaller individual stations to regulate the flow and processing of water as it makes the dramatic elevational shift from the Sea of Marmara to the eastern Mediterranean ("Item B").

At the Straits of Messina and Tunis, the triadic geopolitical structure of Atlantropa is made most evident through design. A road, snaking its way over Italy (and then to London, as marked on the map, and then across Sicily) functions doubly as a dam as it passes the island of Pantelleria. The Mediterranean, here divided effectively into east and west segments, stands 100 meters higher on its western edge than on its eastern, which permits the coastal changes to Western Europe (specifically western Italy, France, and Spain) and the western edge of North Africa to be far less dramatic than that of Eastern Europe (specifically the Adriatic, Greece, Turkey, Lebanon, Palestine, Egypt, and Libya). Malta is lowered to be merely an extension of Sicily, while the port of Tunis is reduced to sandy brush. After crossing a maritime separation only 66 kilometers long, the road makes landfall and quickly arrives at "New Tunis," a city Sörgel implicates as a tabula rasa coastal settlement. From there, the road forks in three directions, echoing the directions of the archers. Westward is a road to Morocco, which is then to bend around the whole western coast of Africa, ending at Dakar. Heading directly south from Tunis is a new train line known as the *Saharabahn*, which would be the most important infrastructural part of the new Tunisian port, connecting the raw goods of the entire continent to Italy and subsequently Europe at unprecedented speed. Eastward is the road to Cairo and then onward south to Cape Town.

No power station is indicated in the larger-scale drawing of New Tunis, but a later drawing produced in 1932 by an illustrator identifying him or herself simply as "H. Dübell" details the modernist grandiloquence Sörgel imagined for the hydroelectric plants across the Mediterranean. Flanking the city's new port, the drawing beautifully shows the conflagration of road and dam as well as the dramatic elevational shift between the western and eastern Mediterranean. Directly attached to the land is the plant itself whose two-stepped structure echoes the stepping, rather than sloping, of all the dams in the basin. Adjunct to the building's southern edge is a near-Brutalist three-story train depot and terminus for the *Saharabahn*, creating a nodal point on the nexus of energy, a rail and maritime shipping junction at the center of Sörgel's economic plan for Atlantropa.

Due east of Tunis, the Suez Canal, unlike the city of Tunis, was renovated to maintain that thoroughfare's critical importance.[18] One illustration shows this in an uncharacteristic Orientalist illustrative mode, replete with out-of-scale and incongruous depictions of Mamluk mosques, the Pyramids, the Sphinx, a feluca boat, and a Bedouin with a camel. Up close, the port of Suez's new design recalls the soaring and optimistic aesthetic posture of Futurism and has uncanny visual connections to the projects constructed by the TVA in the United States. Again, with both passenger and industrial train stations, an elaborate port, an airport, a shipyard, and even dedicated living quarters for on-site workers, Sörgel, along with the architect Hans Döllgast, illustrate the North African ports at the critical architectural nexuses of Atlantropa's economic objectives.

Where Sörgel appears to have been more politically and less economically concerned is on the issue of Palestine. Sörgel's myriad communications demonstrate a wide-eyed reverence for his collaborators, most of whom had won more renown nationally and internationally for their work. Top among them was Erich Mendelsohn, a Jewish-German architect known for his innovation of expressionism in the 1920s, who, after much correspondence, never submitted a completed design. He did, however, express vehement concern over the issue of Palestine. In a 1933

18 Ibid., Box 04677.

letter to Kurt Blumenfeld, a Zionist politician, Mendelsohn described his architectural and Zionist ambitions with zeal:

> **You know of all of the attempts to make our country. All of them have failed. Every year I have seen Palestine designed by my hands, its spiritual structure flowing naturally from my deepest abilities. But Palestine has not yet summoned me.**[19]

These ideas were immediately relevant to Atlantropa because Mendelsohn understood that the scheme could increase the area of Palestine by 50 percent, which made Jewish resettlement all the more plausible. It was to be a grand solution that could placate European Jews and possibly Palestinian Arab nationalists alike. Sörgel's wife, Irina, was Jewish as well, and it appears that this, and his professional connections with Mendelsohn, made Atlantropa appear like a project that sought to undercut the nationalist conception of architecture as *Kultur*.[20]

With theosophical grandiloquence, Sörgel explains that culture has a "system" and a "method." The system connotes what we are capable of as humans (Philosophy, Religion, and Art) and the method of how we are capable of it (Understanding, Spirit, Mind). Rather than being tied to geography, ethnicity, or race, *Kultur* is transcendent and connective, affording geographic unity simply through shared aspirations as opposed to conflicting ones.[21]

Atlantropa and the Public Eye

Sörgel's public campaigns for Atlantropa did not bother the Nazi authorities until he began earning both publicity and, to some extent, interest within architectural circles elsewhere in Europe in the mid-to-late 1930s. Hitler's propaganda arm went so far as to produce a film committed to discrediting Sörgel and Atlantropa.[22] The half-hour film, entitled *Ein Meer Versinkt /A Sea Sinks* ominously portrays the leaders of every state of the Mediterranean littoral sitting around a gigantic model of Sörgel's scheme.[23] Arab heads of state are conspicuous in their *thiyaab* and seem to hold equanimity in the proceedings with their northerly neighbors. A metaphorical expert explains the project to the leaders and, in a flash of truly formidable drama, illustrates how a tiny bomb detonated on the Gibraltar Dam would unleash havoc on each nation. Water suddenly floods the model and we see various close-ups of port cities crushed under the tsunami that is the product of Sörgel's architectural zeal. The film's message was clear: Sörgel's pan-national, pan-continental scheme, even with its inherent mechanisms of power and subordination, was not consonant with the expansionist vision of National Socialism. The film is an unprecedented attack on an individual architect, intended to win over the hearts and minds of German citizens and to convince them of the peril of Sörgel's degenerate cultural scheme.

Recent scholarship, most prominently historian Jeffrey Herf's *Nazi Propaganda for the Arab World*, has cast a sharper light on the close ties that the Nazis tried to develop with the Muslim populations of Turkey, the Levant, and North Africa. Nazi strategists translated Muslim antipathy to the Allied Forces as the support needed to buttress their ambitions in Europe, a task accomplished through propagandist efforts like *Ein Meer Versinkt*.[24] The analysis of this relationship focuses on the encouragement of anti-Zionist sentiment, but there are other ways in which the Nazis sought a meeting of minds with the Muslim Mediterranean world. The National Socialists make a spatial argument directly to the Muslim Mediterranean in *Ein Meer Versinkt* that gives contours to the chthonic reality awaiting them if they were to vest their trust and support in an alternative form of know-how.

The vast destruction that could be found across Europe in the wake of World War II, the weight of the human misery endured and the absence of a staunch nemesis — all were factors that offered Sörgel another chance to curry international support for Atlantropa. A popular 1939 book by the Swiss novelist John Knittel entitled *Amadeus* had taken publicity of the project in a yet further creative direction, casting Sörgel and Atlantropa as the fictional hero. The fictive Sörgel explains the "opening up" of Africa in polemical and combative prose to a group of awestruck students:

19   Letter from Erich Mendelsohn to Kurt Blumenfeld, dated July 11, 1933 as cited by Ita Heinze-Mühleib, *Erich Mendelsohn: Bauten und Projekte in Palästina, 1934–1941 (Beiträge zur Kunstwissenschaft*, Bd. 7, Munich, 1986), 21–22. For other documentation of Mendelsohn's Zionist ambitions, see also Gilbert Herbert, "The Divided Heart: Erich Mendelsohn and the Zionist Dream," in *Erich Mendelsohn in Palestine* (Exhibition Catalogue, Haifa: 1994), 11–15. Original form in German reads: „Du kennst alle Versuche […] für unser Land zu arbeiten. Alle sind gescheitert […]. Alle Jahre sah ich Palästina von meiner Hand aufgebaut, sein ganzes Bauwesen von meiner Hand in einheitliche Form gebracht, seine geistige Struktur von meiner Organisationfähigkeit geordnet und einem Ziel zustrebend. Aber Palästina hat mich nicht gerufen."

20   The biographical information on Irina Sörgel is gleaned from the DVD accompanying Voigt, time code 24:10.

21   It is obligatory here to mention the fundamental differences between *Kultur* and its English translation "culture," In addition to connoting the material, sociological, and anthropological qualities of place, *Kultur* emphasizes practical efficiency and the acquiescence of the individual in a greater population group (*volk*) to the state. Underneath both Hohenzollern and Nazi leadership, the term codified the grounds on which Germanness was superior to other civilizations. To this end, material culture can be said to have had a much more direct line to the machinations of the state, a theme that has been explored time and again by both philosophers and historians. Among the most important exegeses on *Kultur* for this article are Terry Eagleton, *Was ist Kultur?* (Oxford: Blackwell, 2000); Jürgen Habermas, *Knowledge and Human Interests* (Boston: Beacon, 1972); Suzanne Marchand, *German Orientalism in the Age of Empire* (Cambridge: Cambridge University Press, 2009).

22   Voigt, *Alantropa,* 106–107.

23   *Ein Meer Versinkt* was produced in 1936, written and directed by Anton Kunner and produced by Bavaria-Filmkunst. The film can be found in the Bundesarchov-Filmarchiv Abteilung in Berlin. Kunner too had somewhat megalomaniacal inclinations, developing highly complex devices for viewing the solar system, which he built out of his own house.

24   See Jeffrey Herf, *Nazi Propaganda for the Arab World* (New Haven: Yale University Press, 2010), 1–34.

The future of our continent is so brilliant with the prospect opened up by Atlantropa that I am amazed when I see people doubting it. African colonization has been going on hitherto from the coast toward the interior. That means that colonists have hardly touched the possibilities of Africa, and is also one reason why the colonial nations are so jealous of each other. The slightest tickle on their boundaries makes them itch to fight [...]. The Atlantropa project [...] attacks Africa from the inside. Africa can only be thoroughly opened up from within. Immense engineering jobs will have to be carried out to make the climate suitable for the white race to live and thrive in. Such jobs can only be carried through by the combined energies of all the European nations. It would really mean a European working community.[25]

Atlantropa reached a large popular audience through Knittel's novel and raised the stakes for a viable debate on its feasibility in the real world until 1945. Knittel's depiction of Atlantropa accords closely with Gall's interpretation, overlooking the important place that the Muslim Mediterranean played in this scheme and instead regarding the uneven relations between Europe and Africa as the key point. Knittel's rendering has quietly yet considerably affected understandings of Atlantropa that followed it, largely due to its popular nature.

But World War II also took its toll on Atlantropa, its economic viability incongruent with a battered postwar economy and a totalizing geopolitical ideology that ran counter to the diplomacy-based foreign policy of Konrad Adenauer. The war had also proven the vast potential of atomic power, a source of energy exponentially more powerful than hydroelectric power production, even at the scale of Atlantropa.[26]

Any potential for the realization of Atlantropa in the postwar period ended suddenly and violently. On the morning of December 23, 1952, an unidentified driver ran over Sörgel while he rode his bicycle on a road, described by one local as "straight as an arrow," while en route to a lecture in Munich.[27]

Atlantropa and a New "Middle East"

In the second printing of The Mathematics of the Ideal Villa, Colin Rowe revised his language to strengthen a previous denouncement of utopian architectural thinking.[28] Rowe was reacting not only to the lockstep milieu of modernists of architecture but also to the perceived sociological and political hubris that came with the thinking behind the designs. As Joan Ockman has put it, Rowe condemned utopian thought "as implying a planned and hermetically sealed society, leading to stasis in the guise of change, intolerance, suppression of diversity and ultimately violence,"[29] Rowe's thinking is derived from the philosophy of Karl Popper, who insisted on the dialectical interchange of freedom and order. To be sure, Atlantropa was the ultimate exercise in order, but what it said about the issue of freedom is far less clear. This examination of Atlantopa, which focuses on the non-European component of this to-be continent, is neither recuperative nor activist. It functions rather as a heuristic thought exercise on German notions and defintions of the Middle East, revealing a particularist and geopolitical imagination. The question is to what extent Atlantropa envisioned these populations to be entitled to freedom and to what degree was that freedom — economic, political, social — dependent on the vision of Atlantropa and the architecture that made it possible. As this is no garden-variety colonial scheme, the answers remain in the historiography.

The project's historiography speaks little to the project's geopolitical content, a problem exacerbated by the primacy of text-only records. The designs, however, read perhaps more articulately than Sörgel himself is able to express in writing, and the overall architectural and planning program is worthy of an analysis that is neither exclusively art historical nor political. In other words, the drawings and diagrams read as primary sources. Sörgel's racialist ideology is not as ardent or as developed as that of some of his contemporaries. To develop a proper analytical strategy for Atlantropa means both pointing out what was not considered and stitching together

25   See John Knittel, Power for Sale (New York: Fredrick A. Stokes, 1939).

26   The rise of pan-European thinking, which first took hold in transnational institutions like the European Coal and Steel Community, of which Germany was a part, and developed into the European Union as we know it today, is also an important ideological development to consider in relation to Atlantropa. Pan-Europeanism posited a very different model for economic development predicated on ideologies and models of mutual support, not economic exploitation. See, for example, a discussion of this in Michael Heffernan, The Meaning of Europe: Geography and Geopolitics (London: A. Hodder Arnold, 1995). Heffernan's analysis notes the contrapuntal relationship that pan-European ideology had to colonial ideology in Europe and makes the general argument that the ascent of the former was predicated on the decline of the latter.

27   Voigt, Alantropa, 122. Description of road gleaned from Atlantropa DVD, time code 52:05.

28   See Colin Rowe, The Mathematics of the Ideal Villa (Cambridge, MA: MIT Press, 1976), 213–216.

29   Joan Ockman, "Form without Utopia: Contextualizing Colin Rowe," Journal of the Society of Architectural Historians 57, no. 4 (December 1998): 452.

the visual and textual material to explore what Sörgel's latent vision for Atlantropa's subaltern population served to articulate.

The irrigation of the Sahara and the creation of dams and artificial lakes in Congo and Chad are the most obvious geophysical changes. But the incorporation of the Arabian Peninsula and Mesopotamia into a Eurafrican network holds in it the goal of developing a pan-continental design template that had just begun to move beyond schematic articulation before being abandoned. What I hope to have offered here is a consideration of what this template may have meant on the eve of decolonization and the opportunity to ponder how infrastructure, found in Atlantropa's visual output, sought to codify a Christian-Islamic-Pagan Pangaea within a last-gasp imperialist impulse. In other words, once one moves beyond the project's theatrics, it is possible to find a sublime marriage of general utopian polemics with the specifics of race, culture, and geography, a union wholly new to modernism if not incongruent to it. The deployment of modernist architectural tenets here and there thus reinforces Atlantropa's uneasy tension with its own ideology. Sörgel's deep reliance on non-architectural graphics only reinforces his failure to make an architectural treatise that was as strong as the geopolitical imperatives that it was to serve.

In its design, Atlantropa contains the tacit supposition that the "Middle East" has always been a fundamentally amorphous space of the subjective "Western" imagination. The degree to which Sörgel eliminated, rearranged, and fabricated a host of new geographic terms beyond that of Atlantropa is largely underestimated. The terms "Near East" and "Middle East," both prevalent in German literature at the time (and most certainly earlier if one considers, for example, the role that these terms played in Goethe's *Westöstlicher Diwan*), were rendered obsolete. Sörgel organizes his geographic terminology around the Mediterranean itself, now a vast inland lake that could no longer be dubbed "*Mittelmeer*," the German word for Mediterranean and literally translatable as "Middle Sea." Echoing the tripartite division of the world, Atlantropa has three constituent zones: the Mediterranean lake's littoral and the areas to the north and south of it. The "middle zone," a historically familiar geographic trope, recalls older European geographic terminology for and cartography of Islamic, Semitic, and Persian lands. With Atlantropa, Sörgel recalibrates the orientation of the "middle" and places it on a cardinal north–south axis. The middle zone's boundaries were thus defined as patently geophysical, and it was to be the religiously, linguistically, and ethnically diverse cultures of the Mediterranean that constituted the imaginary "space between." It is ever the Braudelian conception of Mediterraneanity — a melting pot of cultural exchange, of economic transaction and political intrigue. But it recalibrates the axis in which these exchanges, transactions, and intrigues are staged, turning this Europe's relationship to the "other" ninety degrees clockwise.

What Sörgel left behind was a life work of bewildering ambition — ambition at once frightening in its lack of technical complexity, sense of justice, and political reason; and simultaneously vivifying in its will to deliver a better baseline human condition for the peoples of Europe, Africa, and the Near East. Though its image never became actual and barely architectural, the call to arms for a unified visual infrastructure between the disparate and diverse Islamic, Christian, and Pagan shores of this vast region at the very least speaks to a late-stage imperial vision of architecture and aesthetics in the service of statecraft that recalibrated the strategies and scale of the imperialist or colonial design programs that preceded it. Here the Mediterranean becomes not just the design site of a new world order but also the fulcrum between the geopolitical and architectural imaginations.

This article is an adapted version of an article appearing in the *International Journal of Islamic Architecture* in the Fall of 2012: Christensen, P. (2012). 'Dam nation: imaging and imagining the space of the 'Middle East' in Herman Sörgel's Atlantropa'. International Journal of Islamic Architecture 1: 2, pp. 325–346, doi: 10.1386/ijia.1.2.325_1

A Mediterranean Photodossier
Bas Princen

180

Bas Princen is an artist who lives and works in Rotterdam. He studied Design for Public Space at the Design Academy in Eindhoven and Architecture at the Postgraduate Berlage Institute in Rotterdam. A publication entitled *Reservoir* (2011) was done on the occasion of his solo show at deSingel in Antwerp. He was awarded the Charlotte Köhler Prize (2004) and the Silver Lion (together with Office KGDVS) at the Venice Biennale 2010.

A Geography of Lines
Breaching the Walls of the Mediterranean Port City
Jarrad Morgan

To cover the world, to cross it in every direction, will only
ever be to know a few square metres of it, a few acres [...]
out beyond the railway stations and the roads, and the
gleaming runways of airports...[1]

— Georges Perec, *Species of Spaces*

1   Georges Perec, *Species of Spaces and Other Pieces* (New York: Penguin Books, 1997), 78.

A change is under way to the geography of Europe and the
Mediterranean that confirms Perec's observation. We have
increasingly come to know and inhabit the world through a
geography of lines — complex paths of commerce and trade, leisure
and evasion through which we can begin to piece together the
picture of a territory. This in turn is introducing a radical change to
the morphology of the Mediterranean, or at least the Mediterranean
as we have inherited it. The Mediterranean port city — once fully
orchestrated around the moment of arrival and departure by sea
— is having its finality challenged. The emergence of intermodal
networks combining land and sea routes at a trans-European scale
has begun to breach its monumental formation. No longer simply
viewed as a terminus and moment of completion, Mediterranean
port cities are increasingly brief pauses along much longer
itineraries, and where once their horizons were strictly maritime, we
are now witnessing the opening to the horizons of the hinterland.

Mediterranean Meshworks
On the planet of the angels, the old walls have crumbled. But bad
angels also fly and follow in the wake of the good ones. Therefore
what is urgent is not finding out how to save the disappearing
order, but how to face the questions posed by the emergence of the
cosmopolis of the networks.[2]

    Michel Serres provides us with a paradigm for thinking
of the contemporary city, for assessing its relationship with the
works of its engineers, its infrastructures, and for understanding
the links between the local and the global.[3] There is, however, a
temptation when thinking within this model of the network to view its
geometry as a succession of points, moments of completion rather
than tension, in a static constellation of connectors. When viewed
in relation to the multiple trajectories of the emergent intermodal
networks today transforming the morphology of the Mediterranean
port city, it is more useful to think of what Marcel Hénaff calls

2   Marcel Hénaff, "Of Stones, Angels, and Humans: Michel Serres and the Global City," *SubStance* 26, no. 2 (1997): 187.

3   For Serres, the network of imperial Rome represents the geometry of multiple "transitions" from local to global. See Hénaff, "Of Stones, Angels, and Humans," 180–183.

Jarrad Morgan received his Master of Architecture (with Distinction) from Harvard University Graduate School of Design (GSD), where his research in the New Geographies Lab focused on the recalibration of maritime and terrestrial relationships in the Mediterranean port cities in response to emergent conditions of infrastructural continuity and simultaneity. Through a fellowship, this research expanded at the GSD to form a broader and ongoing investigation into architecture's ability to effectively engage scales that transcend the traditionally perceived limits of the profession, seeking a better understanding of the continuities between modes of representation, modes of seeing, and modes of experience. Prior to attending the GSD, Morgan lived and practiced in Melbourne, Australia, and holds a Bachelor of Planning and Design and a Bachelor of Architecture (with Honors) from the University of Melbourne.

"centerless networks" or what Henri Lefebvre and Timothy Ingold identify as "meshworks."[4]

Constituted through the entanglement of lines rather than the connection of points, the concept of "meshworks" may help to free us from exhausted inherited conceptions of the Mediterranean that overemphasize the naturalization of place and posit a nostalgic relationship between settlement and geography. Rather than place being tied to a specific location and oriented to specific destinations, it becomes defined instead as "a knot tied from multiple and interlaced strands of movement and growth."[5] The Mediterranean port becomes a space of commonality through which local, regional, and global networks flow, with the actors of each momentarily brought into proximity. The port becomes a zone of abutment — of scales, social groups, and economies — and a space of flexibility, defined not by qualities of under determination but rather as a space whereby multiple possibilities of inhabitation exist simultaneously. It is in this space of abutment that great architectural potentials emerge, and here that opportunity exists for architecture to reclaim its voice in relation to issues of territory and urbanization.

The Thickness of the Line

While the lines of these "meshworks" are usually traced on maps and charts as thin threads, viewed up close and in light of the cultural diversity they represent, they develop a certain thickness. In his recent historiographies of the Mediterranean, David Abulafia brings a human thickness to the line.[6] His "Mediterraneans" conjure up histories of coexistence, of vigorous interaction between diverse groups on distant yet accessible shores, and of port cities where the intersections of numerous cultural lines occur.[7] In a model where movement rather than settlement is the pattern, the spatial implications of the "meshwork" and its imbedded cultural cross-section enable us to critically examine and challenge the formation of fixed identities and to rethink the orientation of cities in relation to a much broader set of phenomena.

In the Mediterranean ports of today, the trajectories of holiday makers, truck drivers, freight transporters, and commuters run parallel. In attempts to capitalize on the lucrative Mediterranean cruise market, the sea is now frequently crossed by huge "cruise ferries":

ships combining the features of a cruise ship with that of a roll-on/roll-off (Ro-Ro) freight ferry, easily reaching over 200 meters in length and accommodating more than 2,000 lane meters of freight, 3,000 passengers, and up to 1,000 vehicles. This latest breed of Ro-Ro ships accommodate the full range and cultural diversity of the networks they serve: bars, restaurants, shops, pools, arcades, casinos, and nightclubs entertain the passengers. While on the common space of the ship's deck, one may find a Syrian truck driver chatting with a retired German couple, an English woman and her young family watching as a busload of Greek students pose for a group photo, and a dutiful GSD student standing by and documenting the scene, explaining to an inquisitive Turkish businessman the workings of his camera.[8]

Over 450 Ro-Ro ships are currently deployed in the Mediterranean, a total of approximately 170,000 lane meters of freight/passenger capacity — enough to span the Mediterranean between North Africa and the south of Spain, or between Sicily and Tunisia.[9] Through concepts such as the "Motorways of the Sea" (MoS), the European Commission's Trans-European Transportation Network (TEN-T) has provided funding frameworks and advocated for the expansion of this network, encouraging a substantial modal shift from congested European roads to key combined land-maritime routes.[10] In the process, a number of ports have undergone significant transformation and recalibration. As the emergence of the combined maritime/terrestrial network has challenged the notion of the city as a well-circumscribed monumental formation, and the new dimension, direction, and velocities the new network introduced has created the necessity to review the use and quality of space where the city meets the sea.[11] Today's ports are neither a public space integrated into the life of the city nor an active site of commerce and trade — none of the old models of the port city seem to apply. The meshwork of lines crossing the sea increasingly extends through and beyond the ports of the Mediterranean, necessitating the reexamination of the role of the city in relation to much broader urban formations and infrastructures that are weakening geopolitical boundaries and actively reshaping strategic port cities along the edges of the sea.

At various historical junctures, moments of clarity in the relationship between land and sea, between city and world, have crystalized into specific architectural forms — forms in which these issues of the city and its relation-

4 See Hénaff, "Of Stones, Angels, and Humans," 184. See also Timothy Ingold, Lines: A Brief History (New York: Routledge, 2007), 80–84, where Ingold borrows the term from Lefebvre.

5 Ingold, Lines: A Brief History, 75.

6 See David Abulafia, The Great Sea: A Human History of the Mediterranean, (New York: Oxford University Press, 2011).

7 Abulafia applies the model of the Mediterranean not only to the waters connecting Europe, North Africa, and the East but also to other seas: the North Sea and the Baltic, the Atlantic and Indian Oceans, the waters between Japan and the Asian mainland, as well as to the Sahara, and eventually the world. See David Abulafia, "Mediterraneans," in W. V. Harris, ed., Rethinking the Mediterranean (New York: Oxford University Press, 2004), 64–93.

8 A personal account by the author of a ferry trip from Ancona, Italy, to Igoumenitsa, Greece, on the March 12, 2012.

9 Michael Garrant, "Market Prospects for the Ro-Ro Sector," presentation delivered at the RoRo Exhibition and Conference in Gothenburg, May 2012.

10 European Commission, Elaboration of the East Mediterranean Motorways of the Sea Master Plan: Report on Policy Initiatives, December 2009.

11 For example, the redevelopment of the port of Igoumenitsa, Greece, in combination with the development of the Egnatia Odos highway from Greece's westernmost port to the eastern border with Turkey as part of the trans-European road, E-90.

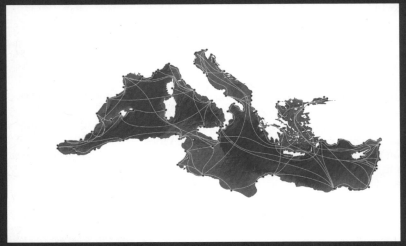

Maritime Mediterranean.
The Lines of Mare Nostrum

[23]

Igoumenitsa, Greece. City
Morphology and Intermodal
Connectivity

[45]

Ancona, Italy. City Morphology
and Intermodal Connectivity

ship to the world coalesce and elevate the form to the status of an archetype. The columns and steps of Brindisi, located where Rome's Via Appia met the sea on its way to the capital in Byzantium, embodying the scale of the empire and giving the world a presence in the city; the Terrazzo di Marmo in Genoa, an expansive public boulevard built on the roof of the entrepôt, uniting city and port by means of an "urban balcony";[12] and in the ancient Adriatic port of Ancona, the Arches of Trajan and Clementine, sitting at the threshold between the worlds of the city and the sea and presenting alternate façades to each. Each of these architectural forms acts as catalytic pieces addressing the transitions between local and global, evidence that thinking at the scale of the world doesn't necessarily mean a shift in scale.

So how may we recalibrate these archetypes to address the new questions posed by the "meshworks" of the Mediterranean? We can remind ourselves of Bernard Rudofsky's allegorical use of the Mediterranean and repeated deployment of the archetypal courtyard house, not relating to geographic or locational specificities, but rather to an idealized culture of living associated with conditions of mobility and uprootedness. It demonstrates the potential for a mode of production based on global circulations yet not merely circulatory, one based on mobility yet not without anchorage in local predicaments. The spatialization of this mode thus becomes one of simultaneities and adjacencies. Applied to the site of the contemporary Mediterranean port city, it begins to develop a repertoire of forms that deal with the common set of confrontations at play — forms that unfold into the scenery of the city while relating to a set of geographically dispersed yet highly connected locations. Through the excavation of the diverse lines that together weave the environment of the port, and their thickening through the modes of habitation and occupation of territory that they encourage — through giving them a more figurative presence — a geographic condition emerges. The two-dimensional line is rendered thick and extended along trajectories momentarily allied. The columns of Brindisi become a colonnade, the arches of Ancona an arcade, exploded and infiltrated by movement from every direction. The city is created through the bringing together of lines prior to their release, and in so doing a space of commonality emerges — a balcony to the world and a moment of its comprehension.

12   Han Meyer, *City and Port: Urban Planning as a Cultural Venture in London, Barcelona, New York, and Rotterdam: Changing Relations between Public Urban Space and Large-Scale Infrastructure* (Utrecht: International Books, 1999), 121.

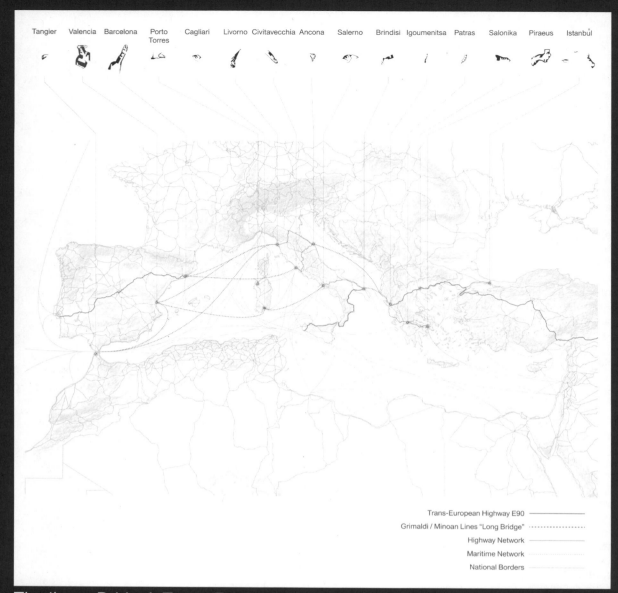

Tangier Valencia Barcelona Porto Cagliari Livorno Civitavecchia Ancona Salerno Brindisi Igoumenitsa Patras Salonika Piraeus Istanbul
Torres

Trans-European Highway E90 ————————
Grimaldi / Minoan Lines "Long Bridge" ·····················
Highway Network ————————
Maritime Network ————————
National Borders ————————

The 'Long Bridge'. Trans-European Intermodal Networks Spanning
Land and Sea

Topographic Potentials
Revisiting the Valley Cross-Section
Fadi Masoud

Topo-urban Relations

Critical sectional relationships emerge when mountains, valleys, and plains are seen in relation to their regional extraction economies, infrastructure routes, irrigation systems, urban centers, and ports of exchange. Over the centuries it has been proven that in the absence of a continued anthropogenic manipulation, management, and maintenance of such a "section," substantial environmental and ecological fallouts ensue. This essay uses the case of the Mediterranean mountains to reveal the historical role that the "section" played in the development of the basin. It then makes the case for its reappropriation, as a design and planning tool, to recalibrate our understanding of regionalism and employ it as a substantial device in developing a contemporary attitude towards urbanism.

The region as a unit offers valuable potentials for the imagining of new urban morphologies at the local project scale. During the second half of the twentieth century, many regions around the world, and the Mediterranean especially, transformed their nineteenth-century industrial waterfronts to accommodate post-industrial economic activities — mostly related to tourism and real-estate development. Designers were called upon to unlock and transform thousands of square kilometers of derelict and contaminated shoreline to accommodate an expanding service sector. Modern monofunctional technology, such as motorway infrastructure, glass-steel construction, air-conditioning, and desalinization created a regional urbanization ribbon of consumption around the Mediterranean that decontextualized its somatic fabric from its physiographic region. While this process is irreversible, the regeneration of a metabolic relationship between coastal urbanization and the topographic hinterland, using an expanded and redefined unit of the "section," is plausible.

Vertical Niles: The Sierra Nevada

The mountains of the Mediterranean have played a fundamental infrastructural role for the last four millennia. Like the High Atlas, the Caucasus, the Elburz, the Tian Shan, the Southern Rockies, and the Andes, the Mediterranean mountains provided year-round water to areas that otherwise would be too dry for agriculture. Where Egypt is the gift of the Nile, in the rest of the Mediterranean it is the verticality of mountains and their snow-melt streams that made possible the rich plains of Marrakesh, Granada, and Damascus (McNeil 1992). The Sierra Nevada in Spain represents the best-case example of this anthro-topo-urban relation. Historically, the geologic form of narrow ravines cut by cascading streams provoked the development of unique regional urban conditions. Since these ranges have no accommodating glaciated U-shaped valleys (like the Alps or Pyrenees), they have no interior population and are consequently ringed by villages at the terminus of each ravine (McNeil 1992). The crystalline slate,

Fadi Masoud holds a Bachelor of Environmental Studies from the School of Planning at the University of Waterloo, with a concentration in Urban Design and Land Development. He holds a certificate in Town Planning in the United Kingdom from Oxford Brookes University. He completed his Master of Landscape Architecture at the University of Toronto (2010) and a post-professional Master of Landscape Architecture (with Distinction) from Harvard University Graduate School of Design (2012).

Masoud has received numerous awards including a Fulbright Fellowship, the Jacob Weidenman Prize, the Heather M. Reisman Gold Medal in Design, and the American Society of Landscape Architects Certificate of Honor. He has practiced as a planner and a landscape architect in several leading firms and has been selected as a finalist in numerous international design competitions. His work has also been published in Topos, Landscape World, MASS Context, and Design for Flooding.

Masoud's work is heavily exhibited internationally. He is currently a Research Associate and Visiting Fellow at the Harvard University GSD, where he is continuing his design and research on large-scale landscape projects and planning frameworks in contexts of extreme hydrological regimes and trans-boundary conditions.

gneisses, and schist slopes are the highest of the Mediterranean ranges, Trevélez at 1,460 meters has considerable snow cover for about 125 days of the year (McNeil 1992).

Along the southern slopes of the Sierra Nevada are about forty villages in the Alpujarra range that were settled and built with the first Arab migrations. The cascades of whitewashed buildings, mostly sheltered from the weather and located to get maximum sunlight, are nestled a short distance from a stream and near a lifeblood of transportation networks. Their strategic elevation allowed them to exploit agricultural possibilities from 500 to 2,000 meters, giving them access to ecological zones from subtropical to subarctic and permitting the cultivation of year-round food (McNeil 1992). Their positioning was also ideal for exploiting the irrigation potential of the Sierra. Starting at 1,000 meters, the water is diffused in a capillary fashion through thousands of tiny tentacle channels that are connected to a larger grid network downstream. This grid arranged plots of land along the topographic ridge and into the valley according to a logic of crop type and settlement density, ultimately providing running water to the cities and palaces of Andalusia. This was a regional urban system that functioned in a clearly scalable sectional manner. The mountains acted as a water tank, an energy generator, a climate-control mechanism, and a nutrient resource depot. Regional urbanization emerged in relation to this topographic infrastructure. McNeil (1992) claims that "The Sierra Nevada, and specifically the Alpujjars, are the finest example of an anthropic understanding of a landscape painstakingly arranged to exploit its particular geography." This thirteenth-century form of urbanization, which unequivocally emerged from a multi-scalar sectional understanding of physical geography, was only abandoned in the 1950s when the implementation of carbon-based modern infrastructural technologies and a global service economy irreversibly transformed the region's spatial configuration (McNeil 1992).

Globalization simply expanded this sectional relation as it began to transcend the local. Over the centuries the Sierra Nevada, like many other mountains, were exploited for mining, mostly lead to accommodate the need for sewer pipes in Northern European cities. Clearly, market booms and busts are inextricably intertwined with global financial flows, and these cycles have had serious consequences on the macro economy, resource availability, and the resultant environmental degradation (Harvey 2012). For example, the exhaustion of firewood for mineshaft construction led to an increase in food and fuel prices, to the point where such operations were no longer profitable and population outmigration became imminent. In that same context, severe soil erosion transpired with the cessation of mining activities and the abandonment of wheat terraces for grain cultivation in the Americas. In these cases, the Mediterranean mountains clearly represented a dialectic by which an anthropogenic presence, within a certain threshold and density, created a level of ecological integrity that floundered in the absence of human manipulation and intervention.

If the nineteenth century was defined by its industrial legacy and the twentieth by its consumption, one could claim that the beginning of the twenty-first century has been an attempt at resuscitation and reassertion based on principles of sustainability. Just as the post-industrial urban waterfront was the opportunity through which cities reached a globalized state, the hinterland is where the systemic, metabolic, and operative potentials might lie in the twenty-first century. Urbanism can begin to imagine new morphologies in relation to its geographic parameters, beyond what is traditionally defined as the "city." By revisiting tools associated with planning, landscape, and geography, we reveal the inherent potential of recapitalizing on the regional landscape to function as contemporary infrastructure, form maker, and a resource.

The Unit of the Valley (Cross) Section

As it once merged the cultural with the geologic, the valley section emphasized a physical unit larger than that described by existing administrative municipal boundaries. The diagram, first published in 1909 by Patrick Geddes, is a longitudinal section that follows a river from its source in the mountains to its entrance to the sea. It combined physical conditions, represented by plants and geology, and the so-called basic occupations, represented by tools, as an anthropogenic and opportunistic understanding of the region (Welter 2002). Settlements along the section are the consequence of the social organizations arising from these natural occupations, and as such best adapted to their environments.

The construction of the city planometrically is typically addressed by fragmented building and dated land-use measures. What is needed is a renewed concept for gauging urbanism that fuses infrastructure and ecology to the urban field using overlooked tools, such as the section. British planner Patrick Abercrombie, when commissioned to deal with London's postwar reconstruction efforts, said:

> **Civic survey, in actuality is a sinister and complicated business, the more so since it must widen to embrace the region and finally the world... Geddes constantly argued that planner's ordinary maps were useless: you must ideally start with the great globe, which Reculs proposed but never got built; failing that you must draw cross-sections "of that general slope from mountains to sea which we can readily adapt to any scale, and to any proportions, of our particular and characteristic range, of hills, and slopes and plain..." (Welter 2002)**

Essential to the reappropriation of the "valley section" today is the understanding that global economic forces are no longer dictated by "natural occupations," nor geology, and as a result subsequent urban patterns can no longer be seen in a static and fixed stricture. The cross section becomes a fundamental relational diagram between project

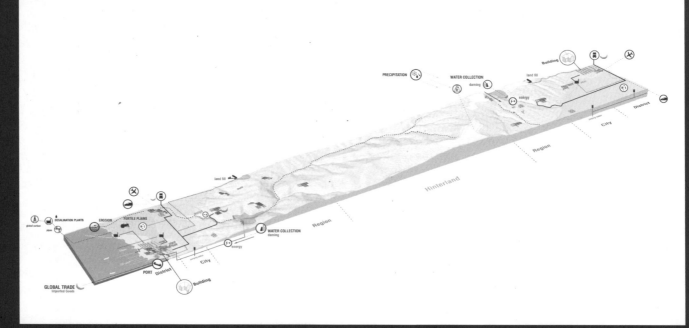

Today buildings and infrastructure as markers of urbanization are rendered as rigid, sterile, and fragmented because of a clear detachment from the geographic and ecological processes that surround them.

The cross section becomes a fundamental relational diagram between project and geography. By revisiting the valley section, an ecological dimension to this relationship capable of reducing the scale of urban operations can be envisioned. Combining formal precision with a re-tooled sectional zoning approach, one can imagine territories that could become half urban and half productive, giving rise to new types of settlements conditions. The cross section becomes a fundamental relational diagram between project and geography.

and geography. The new valley section must be scalable and adapted to make vivid the range of physiographic and cultural conditions shaping urban patterns. It provides us the ability to connect to the world using the human as its medium, qualities that a plan by itself it is not capable of achieving. Inherent to its agency is that it creates metabolic relations between systems and forms. It combines operative dynamics through flows, strata, and hierarchy, as well as spatial and formal conceptions through the precision of foundations, operation, and intervention.

Mediterranean Mountains — A Twenty-first Century Sectional Urbanism

Since these mountains are no longer the raison d'être for the continued urbanization of the basin, they provide the grounds for the study of a new potential twenty-first-century cross-sectional urban expansion. Recognizing that the Eastern and Southern Mediterranean are in a different economic and developmental state than the Western and Northern Mediterranean, a gradient of these sectional relations exists. The amelioration of environmental conditions around the basin means that there needs to be a constant presence of human activity along such a section. This activity could be strategically introduced, refined, protected, or eliminated. Connection to physical geography in design discourse is a continuously reemerging theme. In 1933, section 3 of CIAM IV's Athens Charter emphasized the importance of mountains and geography in the edifice of cities:

> **In the first place they are influenced by the geographical and topographical condition; the constitution of the elements, land and water, nature, soil, climate […] Geography and topography play a considerable role in the destiny of men. Plains, hills, and mountains likewise intermediate to shape a sensibility and to give rise to a mentality. It is the crestlines of the mountain ranges that have delimited the "gathering zones" in which, little by little men have gathered…**

Today however, buildings and infrastructure as markers of urbanization are rendered as rigid, sterile, and fragmented because of a clear detachment from the geographic and ecological processes that surround them. For example, in Southern Spain's Costa del Sol, not too far from Sierra Nevada's Moorish irrigation channels, is the highest concentration of desalinization plants in the Mediterranean — a monofunctional infrastructure with an expensive energy bill required to support service-based tourist towns.

Dialectally, these plants embroider the Mediterranean's most profitable coastal agricultural plains that have resulted from decades of mountain erosion. Elsewhere in the Mediterranean, the shift of cities from centers of production to centers of consumption continues to provoke massive environmental degradation in the urban hinterlands.

By revisiting the valley section, an ecological dimension to this relationship capable of reducing the scale of urban operations can be envisioned. Combining formal precision with a re-tooled sectional zoning approach, one can imagine territories that could become half urban and half productive, agricultural or energetic, giving rise to new types of settlements conditions (Waldheim 2010). This can be done by introducing urban externalities (such as waste, energy, food, and water) to utilize the physiographic potentials of the Mediterranean mountains in constructing urban form. In doing so, the region's geological condition is redefined neither as resource nor as commodity, but an extension of urbanization.

By recapitalizing on the topographic edge, or the "crestlines," for the collection and treatment of water, landfill composting for soil cultivation, climate-responsive agriculture, the generation of energy, and the unlocking of new real estate, a new regional dynamic and resilient front emerges. One can imagine the process of designing erosion, turning waste into soil, and harnessing gravity and wastewater to generate energy. Architecture arises from the synergies of ground operations to physically connect it to the regional geographies beyond. Analysis and design seen through such a lens allows for the development of robust forms of urbanization that are ecologically liable because they stem from an understanding of the particularities of the physical landscape.

Conclusion

Recognition of a substantial association between patterns of urbanization and the topographic hinterlands does not imply a nostalgic attitude toward conservation or restoration, but simply a reiteration of a relationship between urban processes and their geographic contexts. Looking at the Moorish Sierra Nevada in contrast to twentieth-century Costa del Sol reveals cyclical patterns and exposes a retroactive analysis to understand possible futures. Contrary to the current view that associates modernity with non-places, physical geography remains a fundamental dimension of modernity and of our incipient global civilization (Scalbert 2010). This recognition allows us to envisage urban forms that are more adaptable and resilient to processes of global change by situating them in the geographic.

In that regard, contemporary design discourse is once again renewing its understanding of geography and ecology by intensively reexamining its devices for representing and intervening upon the territorial scale. Units that operate between landscape architecture and planning have the potential to become the responsive and effectual mediators to present-day urban ecological pressures. The reappropriation of tools such as cartographic precision, as well as geo-spatial-cultural explorations such as Geddes's valley section, can serve as effective measures for design at the geographic scale.

[33]

Urban development in the Alpujarra range positioned itself to exploit the irrigation potential of the Sierra. Starting at 1,000 meters, the water is diffused in a capillary fashion through thousands of tiny tentacle channels that are connected to a larger grid network downstream.

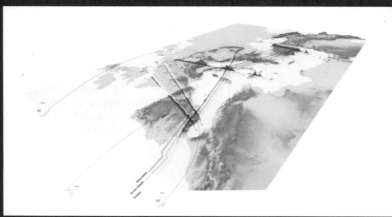

Globalization expanded the sectional relation as it began to transcend the local. The transfer of grain cultivation and mining from the Mediterranean mountains to the Americas resulted in the abandonment of extraction infrastructure and terrace collapse; resulting in deforestation and massive erosion.

[22]

The Sierra Nevada in Spain represents the best-case example anthro-topo-urban relation. Historically, the geologic form of narrow ravines cut by cascading streams provoked the development of unique regional urban conditions. Since these ranges have no accommodating glaciated U-shaped valleys they have no interior population and are consequently ringed by villages at the terminus of each ravine that exploited the climatic and hydrological potential of the topography.

References:

Allen, Stan.2001. "Mat Urbanism: The Thick 2-D," in Hashim Sarkis, ed.,
    CASE: Le Corbusier´s Venice Hospital. Munich: Prestel.
Allen, Stan, and Marc McQuade, eds. 2011. *Landform Building:*
    Architecture's New Terrain. Baden, Switzerland: Lars Müller.
Brenner, N., D. Madden, and D. Wachsmuth.2011. "Assemblage Urbanism
    and the Challenges of Critical Urban Theory." *City* 15(2).
Corner, James. 2004. "Not Unlike Life Itself: Landscape Strategy Now."
    Harvard Design Magazine 21 (Fall/Winter): 32–34.
Harvey, David. 1996. "The Dialectics of Social and Environmental Change."
    In *Justice, Nature, and the Geography of Difference.* Cambridge, MA :
    Blackwell Publishers, p.468
Ibañez, Daniel. 2012. *"Metabolic Assemblage," Flexible Urbanism.*
    *Retroactive Assemblage for the Contemporary City*master's thesis,
    Harvard University Graduate School of Design.
Jakob, Michael. 2011. "On Mountains, Scalable and Unscalable." in Allen
    and McQuade, eds., *Landform Building.*
Le Corbusier. 1973. *The Athens Charter.* New York: Grossman Publishers.
McNeil, J. R. 1992. *The Mountains of the Mediterranean World.* Cambridge:
    Cambridge University Press.
Moore, Jason W. 2011. "Transcending the Metabolic Rift: A Theory of Crises
    in the Capitalist World Ecology."*Journal of Peasant Studies* 38: 1, 1–46.
Scalbert, Irénée. 2010. *"The Perfect Worlds of Ecology." Field*
    Journal,"Ecology," vol. 4, issue 1, December 2010.
Shearer, A. W., D. A. Mouat, S. D. Bassett, M. W. Binford, C. W. Johnson, and
    J. A. Saarinen. 2009. *Land Use Scenarios: Environmental Consequences*
    of Development. Taylor & Francis Ltd, Boca Raton, FL: CRC Press. 1–15
Waldheim, Charles. 2010. "Weak Work: Andrea Branzi´s 'Weak Metropolis'
    and the Projective Potential of an 'Ecological Urbanism.'" In Mohsen
    Mostafavi, ed., *Ecological Urbanism.* Cambridge, MA,Baden,
    Switzerland: Harvard University Graduate School of Design, Lars Müller
    Publishers.
Welter, Volker. 2002. *Biopolis: Patrick Geddes and the City of Life.*
    Cambridge, MA: MIT Press.

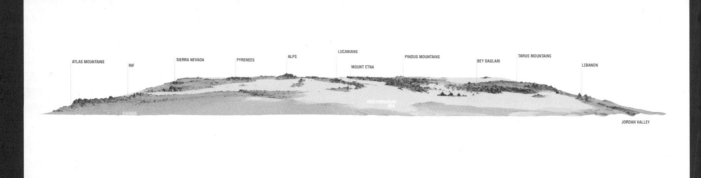

Mediterranean Mountains as geologic entities could be seen as a type of urban infrastructure. They provided year-round water to areas that otherwise would be too dry for agriculture. Where Egypt is the gift of the Nile, in the rest of the Mediterranean it is the verticality of mountains and their snow-melt streams that made possible the rich plains of Mediterranean civilizations.

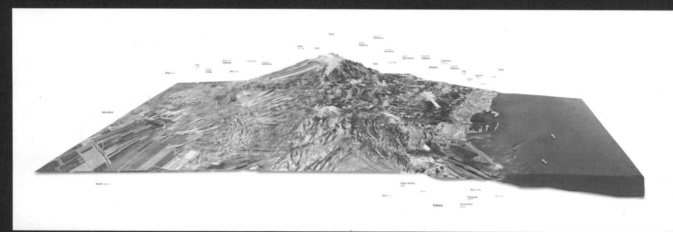

A Mediterranean cross-section, and its resultant urbanization, is a transferable and scalable generic unit that remains relevant in a globalized condition. Global economic forces are no longer dictated by "natural occupations," nor geology, and as a result subsequent urban patterns can no longer be seen in a static and fixed stricture, yet physical geography could still be designed to shape regional urbanization patterns.

The New Colossus
Of Islands and Origins
Andrew McGee

In mid-July 1831, following reports of smoke, bubbling water, and scores of dead fish rising to the surface of the sea off the coast of Sicily, an island burst from beneath the waves. Small at first, a series of subterranean volcanic eruptions bolstered the island's mass until it grew several thousand feet in circumference and over 200 feet high. Known alternatively as Ferdinandea, Graham Island, and *Île Julia* by the myriad nations attempting to claim it as their own, concerns began to arise that the island was a harbinger of more eruptions, possibly creating a chain of new mountains that would connect Tunisia with Sicily, forever upsetting the delicate balance between the north and south shores of the Mediterranean.[1] But no sooner had the island appeared than it began to sink. By December 1831, the island had disintegrated back beneath the water, putting the related territorial and geopolitical disputes on hold.

Islands have long played a pivotal role in the complicated choreography of exchange and control between the Mediterranean Sea and its shores. The Greeks referred to areas of land that lie opposite a coastal island as *peraiai*,[2] defining such mainland tracts as extensions of the island, rather than vice versa — a striking reflection of "the conceptual primacy of [this] maritime world," and a key to the unique power the Mediterranean island exerts onshore and off.[3]

Extreme proximity to the mainland as well as to important maritime trade routes has primed the Mediterranean island for a double life, acting both on the fringe and at the center of the daily machinations of the sea. This doubleness allows the island to operate simultaneously as an invisible outpost and a highly visible marker of distance and scale; as an isolated experimental utopia and a focused node in a massive maritime mobility infrastructure. The Mediterranean island has hosted an array of programs over the centuries that require this paradoxical balance of isolation and interconnectivity, from pirate hideouts to sites of exile and imprisonment.

In a densely packed region where twenty-one nations across three continents share the coastline of the sea, the islands represent an opportunity for satellite territorial expansion, cross pollination, and in some instances, escape.[4] The islands positioned in the straights and gaps between major coastlines have for millennia served as waypoints in otherwise intractable stretches of

1 Maryann Bird, "Fire from the Sea," *Time*, 20 March 2000 (accessed online 20 December 2012).

2 Oswald Ashton Wentworth Dilke, *Greek and Roman Maps* (Ithaca, NY: Cornell University Press, 1985), 74–75.

3 Peregrine Horden and Nicholas Purcell, *The Corrupting Sea: A Study of Mediterranean History* (Oxford, U.K.: Blackwell, 2000), 135.

4 Ibid.

Andrew McGee is an architectural designer at Deborah Berke Partners in New York City. Interested in how smallness influences mega-scales, his projects have ranged from a branding strategy that raises awareness about national debt to artificial island creation as new recreational infrastructure in New York City. His design work has been exhibited at the Berlage Institute in Rotterdam, Harvard University, and the University of Michigan, among others, and published in *Volume* and *Platform*. Previously, McGee worked as a researcher and designer for Somatic Collaborative in Cambridge, Massachusetts, and Quito, Ecuador. In 2007, he studied in Zurich, where his design pursuits focused on subversive retrofit strategies in dense urban environments.

Recently he cofounded DIN Studio, an informal design collective that focuses on small-scale architectural insertions into existing large-scale urban infrastructures. He earned a Master of Architecture (with Distinction) from the Harvard University Graduate School of Design, where his work focused on symbiotic relationships between architectural details and infrastructural networks. He also holds a Bachelor of Arts in Literature and a Bachelor of Science in Architecture from the University of Michigan.

dangerous water for travelers fleeing political and social unrest.[5] Even the smallest landfall proves invaluable in these situations; and every Mediterranean island falls under the territorial jurisdiction of one nation or another, according to current Laws of the Sea.[6] It is no wonder then that on that fateful night in 1831, the violent emergence of a new island was met with such contestation.

The addition of new land to the region is far from revolutionary. Artificial augmentation of coastlines and islands has existed in the Mediterranean for thousands of years. Some of the earliest reports of artificial island creation stem from the Romans, who in 47 AD began bolstering their northernmost territorial expansions with offshore earthen mounds to help mitigate the effects of high tides and storm surges on local settlements.[7] But an unexpected island is a disconcerting notion, as it forces a direct confrontation with systems often thought of as timeless and unchanging.

Where does the island come from? In a world accustomed to understanding location through flattened projections on a map, and in a realm, the sea, that is often conceptualized in the age of globalization as a smooth surface, the island comes from beneath, a reminder of depth, the tip of the iceberg.[8]

How is the island made? Like man-made infrastructure that is visible only when it fails, the island is the result of a sudden, massive shift in the stability of the geological infrastructure, the exclamation point on a series of processes and variables that are so slow acting as to be almost imperceptible.[9]

To whom does the island belong? Aside from its natural spectacle, the far more alarming element in the case of Ferdinandea was its status as a territory unclaimed and uncontrolled by a single entity. This was not a man-made augmentation to an already existing frontier, but the sudden eruption of an entirely new one, beyond the reach of existing jurisdictions.

The case of Ferdinandea remained unique in its scalar and geopolitical implications in the region until recently. In 2006, the ENEA (National Agency for New Technologies, Energy, and Sustainable Economic Develop-

ment), a research and development agency sponsored by the Italian government, presented a proposal for a massive subterranean rail tunnel that would connect Cape Bon, Tunisia, with Pizzolato, Sicily, effectively bridging the historically separated north and south shores of the Mediterranean with a permanent physical infrastructure. At 150 kilometers in length, the project would be almost three times longer than any submarine tunnel in existence.[10]

To bridge this expansive distance, the tunnel would be broken up at four points along its length to allow for exhaust release and for emergency and monitoring services to access it. These services would be housed on four artificial islands, created from the excavated material of the tunnel. Though the proposal has never been realized, the project presents an opportunity to speculate on the form and influence of these potential new Mediterranean islands and their role in helping to recalibrate modern conceptions of agency, territory, and infrastructure in the region.

If the addition of one new island in 1831 caused such an upheaval, the introduction almost 200 years later of a series of four could destabilize the entire territorial system of the Mediterranean. In his essay entitled *Desert Islands*, Gilles Deleuze muses on the power that islands play as serial elements, and the potential these series hold to reinvigorate the cultural and spatial imaginary, leading to new scales of thought:

> **The second origin [...] gives us the law of repetition, the law of the series, whose first origin gave us only moments [...] Here we see original creation caught in a re-creation, which is concentrated in a holy land in the middle of the ocean. This second origin of the world is more important than the first: it is a sacred island.**[11]

For Deleuze, the island is an origin in itself, capable of framing reality within the context of a clear boundary, condensing the immensity of the world to a scale that allows the global to register in a local, contained environment. But the island is also a reminder that there exists a larger network of connectivity beyond the liminal edge of its shoreline. There are other islands, other worlds, simultaneously closed and open to the outside. There are multiple origins, with unique geographies and atmospheres, which relate to one another at scales sometimes beyond immediate perception.

In a region of such extreme overlap and constant exchange, this originary mindset has imbued the Mediterranean island with an immense and mysterious power to magnify

5   Gilles Deleuze, David Lapoujade, and Michael Taormina, *Desert Islands and Other Texts: 1953-1974* (Los Angeles: Semiotext(e), 2004), 13.

6   Horden and Purcell, *The Corrupting Sea*.

7   Maurice L. Schwartz, *Encyclopedia of Coastal Science* (Dordrecht: Springer, 2005), 55.

8   Mark Bonta and John Protevi, *Deleuze and Geophilosophy: A Guide and Glossary* (Edinburgh University Press, 2004), 151.

9   Bruce Mau and Jennifer Leonard, *Massive Change* (London: Phaidon, 2005), 1–10.

10   Nino Galloni, "The Sicily-Tunisia Tunnel and the Extension of the Eurasian Land-Bridge into Africa," proceedings of Schiller Institute Conference, Kiedrich, Germany, 15–16 September 2007.

11   Deleuze, Lapoujade, and Taormina, *Desert Islands*.

An experiential site section of the tunnel and its island exhaust points, as they might interface with the water, the seafloor, the stars and seasons, and shipping traffic on the water's surface.

certain monumental scales of production and experimentation. The Colossus of Rhodes is an emblematic example of this unique power. A wonder of the ancient world, the massive statue was constructed with the debris from a failed invasion of the small island, only to be toppled fifty years after its construction by a massive earthquake.[12] The island acts as a crucible, allowing specific and separate elements — political, territorial, and architectural — to galvanize and reconstitute into a fleeting registration of scale outside of expected boundaries.

The Mediterranean island to this point in history has represented a unique site upon which the production of a new Colossus can occur, accelerated and magnified. But what if the island itself became the Colossus? The ENEA's tunnel proposal would create this very situation. This artificial series of islands would represent a new manifestation of Colossus, one that hybridizes the site and the object, and creates an often overlooked frame of reference for the massive scale of infrastructure that exists in globalized society.

This island series would connect elements outside of the region through the specific thread of a new understanding of mobility, underscoring the territorial and geopolitical weight attached to endeavors and constructions increasingly in the realm of the man-made. The soft infrastructure of globalization, often represented by the sea itself, has created an abstraction of scale that has become difficult to process and understand at a local level. The hard infrastructure that these new islands connect would allow for a reinsertion of this scalar awareness and the establishment of a new type of territory, one not bound by the control of a single nation or power but supranational in origin and practice.

The new geographies of the Mediterranean, acting as a gateway for existing flows of global shipping as well as a connector across historically separated political boundaries, would reframe and recalibrate often misunderstood and overlooked elements in an increasingly networked society. Within every network lies an enterprise of public works that cut across nations and boundaries, tying ideas of infrastructure to a series of origins that lie far beyond the scales they are generally associated with. As monumental nodes of this new public works infrastructure, the island Colossus would, both symbolically and functionally, create awareness of these nested scales outside of the expected frame of reference.

12   For a sculptor's speculations on the Colossus of Rhodes, see Herbert Maryon, "The Colossus of Rhodes," *Journal of Hellenic Studies* 76 (1956), 68–86.

Two musings on what the architectonics of the series and its construction might become, as it relates to the a co-opted "geology" of the new island, as well as the infrastructural, political, and symbolic pressures exerted on it from outside and in.

Is the Mediterranean Urban?
Neil Brenner, Nikos Katsikis

1

Where do the boundaries of the urban begin, and where do they end? This question has long preoccupied urban scholars, and it continues to stimulate debate in the early twenty-first century as urbanization processes intensify and accelerate across the world.

Despite major disagreements regarding basic questions of method, conceptualization, and ontology, most twentieth-century urban theorists conceived the urban (or: the city) as a distinctive type of settlement space that could be delineated in contradistinction to suburban or rural spaces. The nature of this space, and the appropriate demarcation of its boundaries, have generated considerable disagreement.[1] However, all major twentieth-century traditions of urban theory have presupposed an underlying vision of the urban as a densely concentrated territorial zone that is both analytically and geographically distinct from the putatively non-urban areas situated "outside" or "beyond" its boundaries.[2]

Such conceptualizations are embodied paradigmatically in Chicago urban sociologist Ernest Burgess's 1925 "dartboard" model of the city, in which diverse population groups are clustered densely together in concentric rings radiating progressively outward from a dominant central point until the map abruptly ends (Figure 1). Beyond the single-family dwellings of the suburbs begins a void, a realm disconnected from the urban territory and thus representationally empty.[3]

Jean Gottmann's equally famous 1961 vision of the BosWash megalopolis complicated the clean, mono-centric geometries of Burgess's model and considerably expanded its territorial scale (Figure 2).[4] Yet Gottmann's otherwise pioneering approach continued to embrace a notion of the urban as a type of settlement, now upscaled from city to megalopolis, and a vision of settlement space as being divided, fundamentally, among urban and non-urban territorial zones. In Gottmann's provocative map, the territory of megalopolis is vast and its boundaries are jagged, but the zones beyond it are, as in Burgess's visualization of the city, depicted simply as empty spaces.

1 Manuel Castells, *The Urban Question: A Marxist Approach* (Cambridge, MA: MIT Press, 1977); Peter Saunders, *Social Theory and the Urban Question*, second edition (London: Routledge, 1985); Andy Merrifield, *Metromarxism* (New York: Routledge, 2007).

2 Neil Brenner, "Theses on Urbanization," *Public Culture*, 25, 1, (2013): 85–114.

3 Ernest Burgess, "The Growth of the City: An Introduction to a Research Project," in Robert Park and Ernest Burgess, *The City* (Chicago: University of Chicago Press, 1967 [1925]): 55.

4 Jean Gottmann, *Megalopolis: The Urbanized Northeastern Seaboard of the United States* (Cambridge, MA: MIT Press, 1961): 20.

Neil Brenner is a Professor of Urban
Theory at the Harvard University Graduate
School of Design and the coordinator of the
newly founded Urban Theory Lab-GSD. His
writing and teaching focus on the theoretical,
conceptual, and methodological dimensions
of urban questions in relation to the developmental dynamics of modern capitalism,
state strategies, and sociopolitical struggles.
He is currently working on a new book with
Christian Schmid of the ETH-Zurich, *Planetary
Urbanization.* Brenner's previous books
include *New State Spaces: Urban Governance
and the Rescaling of Statehood* (2004), *Cities
for People, Not for Profit: Critical Urban Theory
and the Right to the City* (coedited with Peter
Marcuse and Margit Mayer, 2011), and *Spaces
of Neoliberalism: Urban Restructuring in North
America and Western Europe* (coedited with
Nik Theodore, 2003).

Nikos Katsikis is an architect, urbanist,
and Doctor of Design Candidate (Harvard
University Graduate School of Design,
2009–). He holds a professional degree in
Architecture–Architectural Engineering (with
highest Distinction,2006) and a Master of
Science in Architecture and Spatial Planning
(2009) from the National Technical University
Athens (NTUA). He is a registered architect
in Greece (2006) and has practiced architecture and urban design both individually and
as an associate architect. He has worked as
a Teaching Fellow and Research Associate
(NTUA, 2007–2008; GSD, 2009–) and has
taught studios in the NTUA, GSD, and the
Amsterdam Academy of Architecture.

His research focuses on theoretical,
conceptual, and methodological models from
urban and economic geography, and their
connection to questions of regional morphology and design. His work seeks to contribute to
an expanded understanding of "urban fabric"
as an intersection of material and sociotech-
nical territorial structures. His research in the
DDes program at the GSD is supported by
grants and scholarships from the Fulbright
Foundation, A.S. Onassis Foundation, and the
A.G. Leventis Foundation.

In contemporary debates on global city formation, the urban/non-urban opposition is reinscribed onto a still larger scale, but the basic geographical imaginary developed in earlier twentieth- century traditions of urban theory is perpetuated. Thus in John Friedmann's foundational speculations on the emergent world-city network, the urban is understood not as a bordered territory but as a concentrated node for trans-national investment and corporate control embedded within a worldwide network of capital flows (Figure 3).[5] Yet here too, the non-urban zones surrounding the world cities are depicted simply as a void — as a vast empty that is both functionally and geographically disconnected from the urban condition. Indeed, in the models devel-oped by world-city theorists, the space of flows produced under global capitalism appears to have further separated urban zones from their erstwhile territorial hinter-lands. Enhanced global connectivity and urban concentration are thus accompanied by new forms of macro-territorial fragmentation that render the non-urban even more distant — socially, economically, institutionally, and geographically — from the trans-national urban networks that crosscut its unevenly developed landscape.[6]

Urbanization processes are intensifying and accelerating, creating new, multi-scalar geographies of urban transformation around the world that are difficult, if not impossible, to decipher on the basis of inherited, settlement-based notions of urbanism and their associated assumption that most of the world's territory can be viewed as a "non-urban" void. Edward Soja and Miguel Kanai describe emergent formations of urbanization as follows:

> [...] urbanism as a way of life, once confined to the historical central city, has been spreading outwards, creating urban densities and new 'outer' and 'edge' cities in what were formerly suburban fringes and green field or rural sites. In some areas, urbanization has expanded on even larger regional scales, creating giant urban galaxies with population sizes and degrees of polycentricity far beyond anything imagined only a few decades ago [...] [I]n some cases city regions are coalescing into even larger agglomerations in a process that can be called 'extended regional urbanization'.[7]

Can the urban/non-urban distinction be maintained under these conditions? Already in the early 1970s, French sociospatial theorist Henri Lefebvre suggested otherwise. In his classic text, *La révolution urbaine*, Lefebvre proposed a provocative hypothesis that exploded the urban/non-urban binarism on which investigations and visualiza-tions of urban transformations had long been based: "Society has been completely urbanized," he declared, and on this basis he proceeded to develop a radically new understanding of urbanization as a worldwide process of sociospatial reorganiza-tion encompassing diverse places, territories, and scales, including those situated far beyond the traditional centers of agglomeration, urbanism, and metropolitan life.[8] Rather than conceiving the urban as a distinctive type of settlement space, to be contrasted to suburban, rural, and other putatively non-urban zones, Lefebvre argued that capitalist urbanization had formed an uneven "mesh" of "varying density, thickness and activity" that was now being stretched across the entire surface of the world.[9]

This situation of complete urbanization, Lefebvre proposed, was creating new, territorially variegated urban landscapes, embodied in huge, polycentric concentra-tions of infrastructure, investment, and population that radically superseded the local and metropolitan formations of cityness inherited from earlier rounds of capitalist industrialization. Additionally, in Lefebvre's conceptualization, the contemporary urban revolution entailed the "prodigious extension of the urban to the entire planet" through a process of "explosion-implosion" in which inherited models of centrality, territorial organization, and scalar hierarchy were being blurred and tendentially su-perseded.[10] Somewhat polemically, Lefebvre presented this situation using a starkly linear diagram in which urbanization was measured on a 0–to–100 percent axis; his claim was that a "critical point" would soon be reached in which "the *urban problem-atic* becomes a global phenomenon" (Figure 4).[11] Under these circumstances, Le-febvre proposed, the urban condition would soon become synonymous with that of planetary capitalism as a whole. Urban transformations would impact all zones of the planet, from the oceans to the earth's atmosphere, and planetary processes, both

5   John Friedmann, "The World City Hypothesis," *Development and Change*, 17, (1986): 69–84.

6   Versions of this argument are developed explicitly by Saskia Sassen, *The Global City* second edition (Princeton, N.J.: Princeton University Press, 2000); and Stephen Graham and Simon Marvin, *Splintering Urbanism* (New York: Routledge, 2005).

7   Edward Soja and Miguel Kanai, "The Urbanization of the World," in Ricky Burdett and Deyan Sudjic, eds., *The Endless City* (London: Phaidon, 2006): 59.

8   Henri Lefebvre, *The Urban Revolution*. Translated by Robert Bononno (Minneapolis, MN: University of Minnesota Press, 2003 [1970]): 1.

9   Ibid., 4.

10   Ibid., 169.

11   Ibid., 15; italics in original.

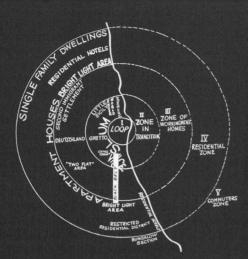

1   Burgess' dartboard (1925): the urban as bounded, concentrated settlement space

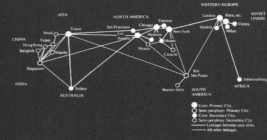

3   World city network (1986): urban nodal points in a world-wide system of flows

4   Lefebvre's critical point of generalized urbanization

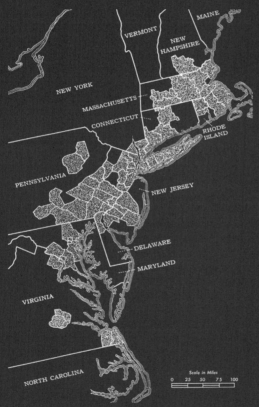

2   Megalopolis (1961): the explosion of urban boundaries

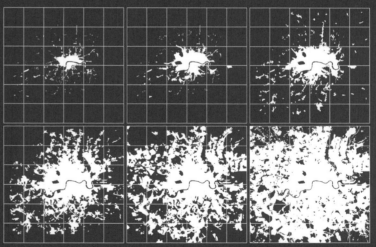

5   A window into concentrated urbanization: the expanding scale of agglomeration (Urban expansion of London 1800, 1840, 1880, 1920, 1960, 1980).

Sources:

1   Ernest Burgess, "The growth of the city: an introduction to a research project," in Robert Park and Ernest Burgess, *The City*. Chicago: University of Chicago Press, 1967 [1925], p. 55

2   Jean Gottmann, *Megalopolis: the Urbanized Northeastern Seaboard of the United States*. Cambridge, Mass.: The MIT Press, 1961, p. 20

3   John Friedmann, "The world city hypothesis." *Development and change* 17, no. 1, 1986, p 74

4   Henri Lefebvre, *La révolution urbaine*. Paris: Gallimard, 1970, p. 26

5   Based on historical datasets from Angel Shlomo, Jason Parent, Daniel L. Civco, and Alejandro M. Blei. *The atlas of urban expansion*, Cambridge, Mass.: Lincoln Institute of Land Policy, 2010, accessible at http://www.lincolninst. edu/subcenters/atlas-urban-expansion

social and ecological, would in turn shape all dimensions of the urban landscape, at once within and beyond inherited centers of dense agglomeration.

Lefebvre's hypothesis has often been misinterpreted as a vision of planet-wide densification akin to the dystopian science-fiction fantasies of writers such as H.G. Wells, J.G. Ballard, or Isaac Asimov, in which the entire world is envisioned as a single, seamless skein of built-up, metallic or concrete infrastructure. More recently, however, Lefebvre's notion of an urban revolution has been productively reappropriated by critical urban theorists concerned to decipher some of the patterns and pathways associated with early twenty-first-century urbanization processes.[12] For example, building upon several ideas from Lefebvre, geographer Andy Merrifield has interpreted planetary urbanization as a simultaneous instrumentalization and transformation of the erstwhile countryside within an unevenly integrated, thickly urbanized mesh:

> **The urbanization of the world is a kind of exteriorization of the inside as well as interiorization of the outside: the urban *unfolds* into the countryside just as the countryside *folds* back into the city [...] Yet the fault-lines between these two worlds aren't defined by any simple urban-rural divide, nor by anything North-South; instead, centers and peripheries are *immanent* within the accumulation of capital itself [...] Therein centrality creates its own periphery, crisis-ridden on both flanks. The two worlds — center and periphery — exist side-by-side everywhere, cordoned off from one another, everywhere [...] Absorbed and obliterated by vaster units, rural places have become an integral part of post-industrial production and financial speculation, swallowed up by an 'urban fabric' continually extending its borders, ceaselessly corroding the residue of agrarian life, gobbling up everything and everywhere in order to increase surplus value and accumulate capital.[13]**

Within the unevenly woven skein of the planetary-urban condition, the infrastructures of urbanization are no longer localized within dense agglomerations or polycentric metropolitan regions, where they can be counterposed to the "outside" realm of rural existence. Instead, urbanization increasingly crosscuts and supersedes the erstwhile urban/rural divide, stretching across and around the earth's entire surface, as well as into both subterranean and atmospheric zones, which provide "liminal landscapes" for resource extraction, agro-industrial production, energy and information circulation, waste management, and diverse geopolitical strategies.[14] Thus understood, planetary urbanization intensifies interdependence, differentiation, *and* polarization across and among places, territories, and scales rather than creating the "borderless world" envisioned by globalization boosterists or, for that matter, the globally consolidated "endless city" predicted by some contemporary urban intellectuals.

Such developments pose huge challenges for urbanists and all other scholars concerned to decipher emergent urbanization processes and sociospatial conditions. Insofar as the conceptual grammar of urban theory is inherited from a period of capitalist development and territorial organization that has now been largely superseded, it is essential to experiment with alternative "cognitive maps" that can more effectively grasp the rapidly changing geographies of our planetary-urban existence.[15] In collaboration with Christian Schmid, our own efforts to confront this challenge hinge upon the conceptual distinction between concentrated and extended urbanization, which we consider an essential foundation for theorizing and investigating the geographies of urbanization processes during the last two centuries of world capitalist development.[16]

The concept of *concentrated urbanization* refers to the perpetual formation and crisis-induced restructuring of densely concentrated agglomerations (cities, city-regions, megalopolises, mega-city regions, and the like). The geographies of concentrated urbanization broadly approximate those of cities, agglomerations, urban regions, and metropolitan areas, as traditionally understood and visualized by urban geographers with reference to successive historical formations of urban territorial organization (Figure 5).

By contrast, *extended urbanization* denotes the consolidation and continued

12   See, among other works, Christian Schmid, "Theory," in Roger Diener, Jacques Herzog, Marcel Meili, Pierre de Meuron, and Christian Schmid, *Switzerland: An Urban Portrait*, vol. 1, ETH Studio Basel (Zürich: Birkhäuser, *2003); Andy Merrifield, "The Right to the City and Beyond: Notes on a Lefebvrian Conceptualization," *City*, 15, 3–4, (2011): 468–476; Edward Soja, "Regional Urbanization and the End of the Metropolis Era," in G. Bridge and S. Watson, eds., *The new Blackwell companion to the city* (Blackwell: Cambridge MA, 2011); David Madden, "City Becoming world: Nancy, Lefebvre, and the Global-Urban Imagination," *Environment and Planning D: Society and Space*, forthcoming (2013); R. L. M. Monte-Mór, "What Is the Urban in the Contemporary World? *Cadernos de Saúde Pública*, 21, 3, (2005): 942–948; and David Wachsmuth, "City as Ideology," *Environment and Planning D: Society and Space*, forthcoming (2013).

13   Andy Merrifield, "The Right to the City and Beyond," 468, 469.

14   The phrase "liminal landscapes" is drawn from Alan Berger, *Drosscape: Wasting Land in Urban America* (Princeton, N.J.: Princeton Architectural Press, 2006): 29.

15   The concept of cognitive mapping is developed in Fredric Jameson, "Cognitive Mapping," in Lawrence Grossberg and Cary Nelson, eds., *Marxism and the Interpretation of Culture* (Chicago: University of Illinois Press, 1992): 347–357.

16   This distinction and its implications are developed at length in Neil Brenner and Christian Schmid, *Planetary Urbanization*, book manuscript in progress. See also Neil Brenner and Christian Schmid, "The Urban Age in Question," *Urban Theory Lab-GSD + Urban Theory Lab-ETH, Working Paper* (2012); Neil Brenner and Christian Schmid, "Planetary Urbanization," in Matthew Gandy, ed., *Urban Constellations* (Berlin: Jovis, 2001): 10–13; and Neil Brenner, "Theses on Urbanization." We are grateful to Christian Schmid for permission to deploy this conceptual dyad in a preliminary way here.

Sources:

6   Road and rail networks are based on the Vector Map Level 0 (VMap0) dataset released by the National Imagery and Mapping Agency (NIMA) in 1997. Marine routes are based on the global commercial activity (shipping) dataset compiled by The National Center for Ecological Analysis and Synthesis (NCEAS). http://www.nceas.ucsb.edu/globalmarine

7   Fernand Braudel, *The Mediterranean and The Mediterranean World in the Age of Philip II*, Volume I. Translated by Siân Reynolds. Berkeley and Los Angeles: University of California Press, 1995, p. 367

6   A window into extended urbanization: the operational landscape of global transportation. Compilation of road, rail and marine transportation networks

[17]

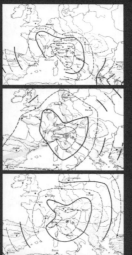

7   News travelling to Venice (5 days intervals) 1733–1765 AD

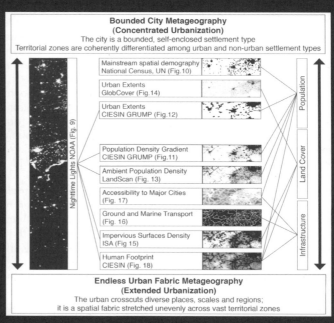

8   Geospatial data and the metageographies of urbanization

reorganization of broader operational landscapes — including infrastructures for transportation and communication, food, water and energy production, resource extraction, waste disposal, and environmental management — that at once facilitate and result from the dynamics of urban agglomeration. Although it has largely been ignored or "black-boxed" by urban theorists, this realm of drosscapes, *terrains vagues*, in-between cities (*Zwischenstädte*), horizontal urbanization, holey planes, quiet zones, fallow lands, and liminal landscapes has long been integral to the urban process under capitalism, and during the last few decades it has become increasingly strategic in both economic and ecological terms.[17] The visualization of extended urbanization, with its intensely variegated morphologies, its vast territorial scales, its dispersed networks, and its apparently all-pervasive voids, poses complex analytical and cartographic challenges. How to understand, and on this basis to represent, the various ways in which agglomerations hinge upon, and continually transform, the operational landscapes associated with such diverse, multi-scalar processes as transportation, communication, resource extraction, energy circulation, and waste management? A recent visualization of worldwide transportation infrastructures offers one among many possible strategies for interpreting such connections and their systemic importance to the dynamics of planetary urbanization (Figure 6).[18]

    We believe that this distinction can provide a powerful analytical and cartographic tool for exploring the question of urban boundaries posed above. It can also offer a basis on which to explore Lefebvre's famous hypothesis of an urban revolution. From the point of view of concentrated urbanization, the urban revolution involves the spatial expansion and increasing strategic centrality of major metropolitan regions, as postulated by global city theorists and other more recent commentators on the role of cities in economic life.[19] However, consideration of the *problematique* of extended urbanization introduces a more complex, fluid, diffuse, and spatially variegated conceptualization of the Lefebvrian notion of an urban revolution, one that we consider essential for investigating and visualizing early twenty-first-century forms of planetary urbanization. From this perspective, the urban revolution entails the consolidation of a new relationship between urban agglomerations and their operational landscapes. The latter no longer serve simply as hinterlands, resource extraction zones, supply depots, and waste dumps for city growth — the realms of "un-building" (*Abbau*) and planetary ecological degradation that Lewis Mumford observed with considerable alarm in the early 1960s.[20] Instead, the operational landscapes of extended urbanization are today increasingly designed, comprehensively managed, logistically coordinated, and "creatively destroyed" to serve specific purposes within the broader political-economic and ecological infrastructures of a planetary-urban system. This ongoing instrumentalization, operationalization, and logistical coordination of erstwhile hinterlands — their tendential transformation into zones of customized infrastructure designed and managed to fulfill specific production, reproduction, and circulatory functions within a worldwide spatial division of labor — represents one of the distinctive tendencies within emergent formations of planetary urbanization.

2

The preceding considerations point toward an ambitious, far-reaching, and long-term theoretical, historical, and cartographic agenda that we are pursuing with other researchers in the Urban Theory Lab-GSD, as well as with Christian Schmid and his team of collaborators at the ETH-Zürich. In the remainder of this essay, taking the contemporary Mediterranean region as a "test site" for our approach to planetary urbanization, we explore one specific challenge within this massive *problematique* — namely, that of visualizing the contemporary urban condition. As Denis Cosgrove has noted, "Urban space and cartographic space are intimately related."[21] For this reason, visualizations of the Mediterranean urban fabric may offer some potentially fruitful clues for deciphering the transformed forms, patterns, and pathways of urbanization both within and beyond this important global region and in relation to some of the conceptual and epistemological challenges demarcated above.

17 These terms are discussed and elaborated in Diener et al., *Switzerland: An Urban Portrait*, *as well as* by Alan Berger in *Drosscapes*.

18 Berger's *Drosscapes* represents a particularly sophisticated effort to confront this challenge through a brilliant combination of theoretical analysis, photographic documentation, and creative visualization.

19 See, for example, Edward Glaeser, *Triumph of the City* (New York: Trantor, 2011); for a critique, see Brendan Gleeson, "The Urban Age: Paradox and Prospect," *Urban Studies*, 49, 5, (2012): 931–943.

20 Lewis Mumford, "Mechanization and Abbau," in *The City in History* (New York: Harcourt, Brace, Jovanovich, 1961): 450–452.

21 Denis Cosgrove, "Carto-city," in *Geography & Vision* (London: I.B. Tauris, 2008): 169.

9   Nighttime lights around the Mediterranean region

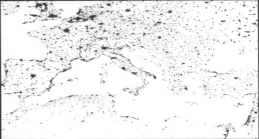

12   Urban extents around the Mediterranean

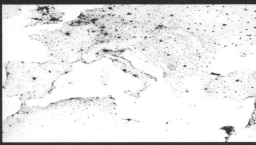

10   Cities containing populations of larger than 10,000 around the Mediterranean

13   Ambient population density around the Mediterranean

11   Population density gradients around the Mediterranean

[38]

14   Urban land cover around the Mediterranean. The black outline corresponds to urban areas defined as more than 50% artificial areas. The background of light gray areas depicts all cultivated areas.

Sources:

9   Based on the 2003 Nighttime Lights of the World dataset; National Geophysical Data Center (NGDC) of the National Oceanic and Atmospheric Administration (NOAA). http://sabr.ngdc.noaa.gov.

10   Based on the Global Urban-Rural mapping project (GRUMP) settlement points dataset (NASA Socioeconomic Data and Applications Center (SEDAC): http://sedac.ciesin. columbia.edu).

11   Based on the Global Urban Rural mapping project (GRUMP) population density dataset. Center for International Earth Science Information Network (CIESIN)/Columbia University, International Food Policy Research Institute (IFPRI), The World Bank, and Centro Internacional de Agricultura Tropical (CIAT). 2011. Global Rural-Urban Mapping Project, Version 1 (GRUMPv1): Population Density Grid. Palisades, NY: NASA Socioeconomic Data and Applications Center (SEDAC). http:// sedac.ciesin.columbia.edu/ data/set/grump-v1-population-density

12   Based on the Global Urban Rural mapping project (GRUMP) urban extents dataset. Columbia University Center for International Earth Science Information Network (CIESIN) http:// ciesin.columbia.edu

13   This product was made utilizing the LandScan (2009)™ High Resolution global Population Data Set copyrighted by UT-Battelle, LLC, operator of Oak Ridge National Laboratory under Contract No. DEAC05-00OR22725 with the United States Department of Energy. The United States Government has certain rights in this Data Set Neither ut-battelle, llc nor the united states department of energy, nor any of their employees, makes any warranty, express or implied, or assumes any legal liability or responsibility for the accuracy, completeness, or usefulness of the data set. http://www.ornl.gov/sci/ landscan

14   GlobCover Land Cover v2 2008 database. European Space Agency, European Space Agency GlobCover Project, led by MEDIAS-France. 2008. http://ionia1.esrin.esa.int/ index.asp

Since Braudel's classic investigations of the Mediterranean economy and ecology during early modern capitalism, the distinctively urban dimensions of this zone have been widely appreciated.[22] In Braudel's conceptualization, Mediterranean cities represented sites of intense commercial activity within a steadily expanding mercantile capitalist economy. With several major centers, including the city-states of Venice and Genoa, the Mediterranean urban system was visualized primarily with reference to levels of connectivity — especially for communication flows and trade networks — among nodes dispersed within a vast terrestrial and coastal zone (Figure 7).

Even though many of the cities examined by Braudel remain vibrant economic centers, the urban fabric of the Mediterranean has of course been transformed dramatically over the last four centuries of capitalist industrial growth, logistical intensification, socio-ecological reorganization, and political-territorial restructuring. Yet the Mediterranean remains a densely urbanized zone, permeated by thick transportation and communications networks; processes of urbanization and capital accumulation remain as tightly intertwined as they were during the period of Braudel's investigation.

For present purposes, the urban geographies of the contemporary Mediterranean are explored on the basis of an extensive assemblage of recent geo-referenced information that have been derived from some of the world's major laboratories for spatial data procurement and analysis.[23] Since the 1970s, the proliferation of new representational techniques associated with geographical information systems (GIS) and other recently established forms of spatial data has radically transformed the cartographic toolkit available to practitioners, policymakers, and scholars for mapping the urban landscape. Although many new mapping techniques continue to rely, at least in part, on data collected by state census agencies, most have significantly loosened the hold of state-centric, methodologically territorialist methods in contemporary geospatial analysis. In a methodological maneuver that seriously challenges the hegemonic embrace of "state-istics" within the social sciences, the development of increasingly sophisticated, remotely sensed imaging techniques has permitted the reaggregation of administratively derived data with reference to coordinates, contours, morphologies, and gradients that more directly approximate de facto terrestrial conditions across the earth's landscape than has ever previously been possible.[24] The availability of such fine-grained, readily customizable data on diverse spatial conditions presents urban theorists with a unique opportunity to interrogate inherited assumptions regarding urban boundaries, and on this basis, to develop new conceptualizations and visualizations.[25]

We confront this challenge using contemporary geo-referenced data sets on three key indicators that have been commonly invoked to represent urban territories: (1) population distribution, (2) land cover, and (3) transportation networks.[26] In exploring the visualizations associated with such spatial data, we devote particular attention to their metageographical assumptions and implications — that is, to the underlying conceptions of sociospatial order they presuppose or that flow from their technical operations — with specific reference to the analytical and cartographic status of the urban. According to historians Martin Lewis and Kären Wigen, "Every global construction of knowledge deploys a metageography, whether acknowledged or not."[27] This proposition certainly applies to the construction of global knowledge on urbanization, including at the smaller scale of the Mediterranean explored here. Figure 8 offers a stylized contrast between the two opposing metageographical frameworks — labeled, respectively, the *bounded city* and the *endless urban fabric* — that emerge from the visualizations under discussion here and that broadly correspond to our own distinction between concentrated and extended urbanization. It is the bounded city metageography that is presupposed in each of the three models from twentieth-century urban theory discussed above (Figures 1, 2 and 3), although Jean Gottmann's concept of megalopolis begins to overturn this vision of territorial organization by extending and interweaving urban borders deeply into the erstwhile hinterlands. The bounded city metageography is still widely taken for granted in much of contemporary urban social science, and it is also evident in several of the geospatial models of population and land cover discussed below. However, since the

22 See Fernand Braudel, *The Mediterranean and the Mediterranean World in the Age of Philip II*, volumes I and II, translated by Siân Reynolds (Berkeley and Los Angeles: University of California Press, 1995).

23 These include the Columbia University Center for International Earth Science Information Network, the Oak Ridge National Laboratory, the European Environmental Agency, the European Space Agency, the National Geophysical Data Center), the National Imagery and Mapping Agency, the National Center for Ecological Analysis and Synthesis, and the Joint Research Centre of the European Commission.

24 On the relation between statistics and "state-istics," see Peter J. Taylor, "A Brief Guide to Quantitative Data Collection at GaWC, 1997–2001," Globalization and World Cities Research Network, Loughborough University [WWW document]. URL http://www.lboro.ac.uk/gawc/guide.html (accessed 30 May 2012).

25 Unfortunately, however, this opportunity has yet to be exploited effectively. To date, the dominant approach to the use of spatial data and analytical technologies in urban research has privileged description over theorization or conceptualization. This is a highly problematic tendency, in our view, because the descriptive sophistication and aesthetic complexity of geo-referenced data visualizations can easily mask underlying conceptual confusions and a lack of theoretical coherence — in particular, a lack of definitional agreement on basic concepts, such as the "urban." For present purposes, our goal is to appropriate contemporary geo-referenced data sets to explore visualizations of the conceptual distinctions introduced above. We shall elsewhere consider the theoretical and epistemological blind spots of GIS and other new georeferencing technologies in relation to the investigation of planetary urbanization (see Neil Brenner and Nikos Katsikis, *Visualizing an Urban World: A Metageographical Analysis*, Urban Theory Lab-GSD research project, Harvard University).

26 There are other socio-ecological indicators relevant to this inquiry that cannot be considered here — including, among others, agricultural land-use intensity, artificial irrigation infrastructures, and human footprints, all of which figure crucially in the operational landscapes of extended urbanization. For present purposes, we have chosen three main indicators and associated forms of spatial data that most readily illustrate the challenges of visualizing the landscapes of extended urbanization.

27 Marin Lewis and Kären Wigen, *The Myth of Continents: A Critique of Metageography* (Berkeley and Los Angeles: University of California Press, 1997): ix.

15   Density and distribution of impervious surfaces around the Mediterranean. Visualization of the distribution and density of constructed impervious surfaces. Based on the Global Distribution and Density of Constructed Impervious Surfaces dataset.

17   Map of accessibility around the Mediterranean. Visualization of an accessibility gradient estimating theoretical travel time to major cities with population over 50000 in the year 2000.

16   Major ground and marine transportation routes around the Mediterranean. Compilation of road, rail and marine transportation networks.

18   The human footprint around the Mediterranean. The Human Footprint is a quantitative analysis of human influence. In this map, human impact is rated on a scale of 0 (minimum) to 100 (maximum).

Sources:

15   National Geophysical Data Center (NGDC) of the National Oceanic and Atmospheric Administration (NOAA). http://sabr. ngdc.noaa.gov and http:// ionia1.esrin.esa.int

16   Road and rail networks are based on the Vector Map Level 0 (VMap0) dataset released by the National Imagery and Mapping Agency (NIMA) in 1997. Marine routes are based on the global commercial activity (shipping) dataset compiled by The National Center for Ecological Analysis and Synthesis (NCEAS). http:// www.nceas.ucsb.edu/ globalmarine

17   Nelson, A. (2008) Estimated travel time to the nearest city of 50,000 or more people in year 2000. Global Environment Monitoring Unit - Joint Research Centre of the European Commission, Ispra Italy. http://bioval.jrc.ec.europa. eu/products/gam

18   Based on the Global Human Footprint dataset, developed by the Wildlife Conservation Society (WCS), and Center for International Earth Science Information Network (CIESIN)/ Columbia University. 2005. Last of the Wild Project, Version 2, 2005 (LWP-2): Global Human Footprint Dataset (Geographic). Palisades, NY: NASA Socioeconomic Data and Applications Center (SEDAC). http:// sedac.ciesin.columbia.edu/ data/set/wildareas-v2-human-footprint-geographic

introduction of geospatial data on nighttime lights in the late 1990s, several major approaches to geospatial visualization have begun to advance a more radical, quasi-Lefebvrian vision of an endless urban fabric stretched and woven across place, territory, and scale.

In Figure 8, the various approaches under discussion in this essay are positioned along an analytical continuum in relation to the two opposed metageographies of urbanization. Those positioned closest to the top of the figure are most tightly connected to a bounded city metageography, whereas those closest to the bottom are most directly oriented toward an endless urban fabric metageography. The figure also differentiates the representations according to which indicator (population, land cover, and infrastructure) they attempt to visualize. Finally, the figure shows how several of the approaches build upon the influential nighttime lights data set, which has been connected to a rather broad spectrum of metageographical assumptions. By excavating such metageographies, this analysis is intended to highlight the basic theoretical assumptions that invariably underpin efforts to visualize spatial data on urban questions. In the absence of critical reflexivity regarding such metageographical assumptions, even the most exhaustive, fine-grained forms of spatial data cannot be appropriated effectively to illuminate the urban condition and its restlessly changing geographies.

3

Few images have had a greater impact on contemporary metanarratives of global urbanization than the "nighttime lights of the world" series, one of the oldest and most basic sources of remote-sensed information about urbanization. Although this approach was under development as of the early 1970s, it was only in 1997 that the data set produced by the National Geophysical Data Center (NGDC) in Boulder, Colorado, was first used to create an integrated global image showing light sources, including human settlements, thus producing a visually striking, intuitively plausible representation of world urbanization patterns.[28]

According to one prominent team of urban geographers, this paradigmatic image of world urbanization has effectively superseded earlier state-centric, territorialist, and Eurocentric models of modernity in favor of a globalized, city-centric model that highlights "flows, linkages, connections and relations; an alternative metageography of networks rather than the mosaic of states."[29] Moreover, as the representation of the Mediterranean in Figure 9 strikingly indicates, such images have also entailed a radical shift in the visualization of urban spaces themselves.

Earlier mappings of an urban landscape configured among distinct, bordered, neatly separated places are here replaced by that of an urbanized continuum based upon varying density gradients of settlement and infrastructure ranging from massive, bright metropolitan agglomerations at one extreme to zones of apparent emptiness, darkness, and wilderness at the other. Beyond this metageographical influence, the nighttime lights data sets have been among the most ubiquitous sources of spatial information regarding contemporary urban systems; they play an important role in many of the visualizations of spatial data presented below

The haphazardly intermixed patterns of light depicted in this overview visualization of the Mediterranean lend some initial plausibility to the conceptual distinction between concentrated and extended urbanization. Traditional zones of urban concentration in the Mediterranean region are readily discernible in the map — for example, Barcelona, Rome, Naples, Athens, Istanbul, Izmir, Beirut, Tel Aviv, Cairo, Tripoli, Tunis, Algiers, and Casablanca. But so too are some much larger-scale territories of urbanization whose contours extend well beyond established urban cores, often in uninterrupted bands of high-intensity light emissions stretched along coastal edges. Such large-scale territorial configurations include the lengthy urbanized corridor along the Iberian coastline, the French Riviera conurbation, the Rome-Naples corridor, a northern Adriatic urbanized zone articulated unevenly between Venice and Trieste, and an eastern Mediterranean urban corridor stretching almost continuously from Beirut to Gaza. Significant bands of this coastal zone were highlighted

28 Until recently, the only satellite sensor collecting global nighttime lights data was the Operational Linescan System (OLS) developed by the US Air Force Defense Meteorological Satellite Program(DMSP). The program was designed in the 1960s for the observation of clouds illuminated by moonlight for meteorological purposes. However, it was soon realized that the instrument could also detect light sources present at the earth's surface, including human settlements and transportation networks. Nighttime lights data sets produced by the OLS have been widely used ever since, but they have until recently been dependent upon somewhat outdated technologies that generate a relatively low image resolution. In late 2011, NASA launched the improved National Polar-orbiting Operational Environmental Satellite System Preparatory Project (or Suomi — NPP). Suomi is considerably more accurate than the earlier OLS system — it uses a much higher resolution for its images and it is more sensitive to dim lights. For details on the initial DMSP program, see Christopher D. Elvidge, Kimberly E. Baugh, Eric A. Kihn, Herbert W. Kroehl, and Ethan R. Davis, "Mapping City Lights with Nighttime Data from the DMSP Operational Linescan System," *Photogrammetric Engineering and Remote Sensing,* 63, no. 6 (1997): 727–734; for a comparison of the two, see Steven D. Miller, Stephen P. Mills, Christopher D. Elvidge, Daniel T. Lindsey, Thomas F. Lee, and Jeffrey D. Hawkins. "Suomi Satellite Brings to Light a Unique Frontier of Nighttime Environmental Sensing Capabilities," *Proceedings of the National Academy of Sciences*, 109, no. 39 (2012): 15706–15711.

29 Jon Beaverstock, R.G. Smith, and P.J. Taylor, "World City Network: A New Metageography?", *Annals of the Association of American Geographers*, 90, 1, (2000): 123.

for their megalopolitan potentials by Jean Gottmann in the 1970s, and in more recent years scholars have described it variously as the Mediterranean Arc (extending from Barcelona to Marseilles and Genoa), the Mediterranean Sunbelt, or the Latin Arc (including the latter corridor but encompassing a still larger zone stretching from Andalusia to Rome and Naples); others have suggested it also juts inland along Alpine extensions toward Lyon and Milan, among other large cities.[30] Along the North African rim of the Mediterranean, the map reveals impressive complexes of activity bursting westward along the coastlines of both Tripoli and Algiers, as well as, most strikingly, the thin but intense concentration of light emissions threaded southward from the Nile River Delta along a tightly circumscribed, fluvial band down to the Aswan Dam.[31]

Most crucially for our purposes, the nighttime lights map depicts an intricate, transnational complex of settlement patterns and infrastructural grids that crosscut and interpenetrate the major metropolitan zones across the entire Mediterranean region. In stark contrast to the concentric circles of Chicago School urban sociology, the jagged territorial borders of Gottmann's megalopolis or the networked nodal points of world-city theory, these urban geographies more closely resemble an uneven latticework woven around and among the major conurbations, metropolitan regions, cities, and towns, across an unevenly organized but densely settled transnational territory. This aspect of the nighttime lights image thus provides an initial, impressionistic visualization of the vast, variegated, and unevenly developed terrain of extended urbanization in the Mediterranean region as well as across much of Northern, Central, and Eastern Europe. Can other visualizations be produced that add more precise analytical content to the metageography of endless urbanization suggested by the nighttime lights image?

4

One obvious indicator for such an endeavor is population, the spatial distribution of which was a focal point for visualizations of urban conditions well before the development of remote-sensed, geo-referenced data sources. Contemporary geo-referenced spatial data permit the visualization of population distribution in several distinct ways corresponding in various gradations to the bounded city or endless urban metageographies.

In the standard demographic approach, whose roots lie in the pioneering research efforts of Kingsley Davis in the post–World War II period, population distribution is represented with reference to extant municipal units; a numerical threshold is used to delineate urban from non-urban settlement units.[32] Although debates have raged for over five decades regarding the appropriate threshold on which to delineate urban from non-urban populations (100,000? 20,000? 10,000?), this approach still figures crucially in the data classification systems used by the United Nations Population Division. For instance, it underpins the widely repeated but hugely problematic proclamation that a global "urban age" has dawned due to the purported fact that over 50 percent of the world's population now lives within urban areas.[33]

Using a population threshold of 10,000, Figure 10 illustrates the implications of this approach for the visualization of Mediterranean urbanization. Here cities are considered to be dimensionless points, positioned according to the terrestrial coordinates of their abstractly defined centers, and weighted according to their population size. Aside from the persistent problem of justifying an appropriate numerical threshold on which to base such visualizations, the resulting representational landscape suggests a purely locational conception of the urban: it is simply a point on the earth's surface, lacking areal articulation or morphological specificity. The operational landscapes of extended urbanization thereby disappear completely from view; cities appear as relatively self-sufficient islands within a vast territorial void. This model thus paradigmatically embodies the bounded city metageography.

Although this approach is still a popular way of representing urban population levels, whether at a world scale or nationally, its core data are not connected to de facto settlement patterns but are derived from extant administrative units. The limits

30   Jean Gottmann, "Megalopolitan Systems Around the World," Ekistics, 41, 243, 1976, 109–113. For a contemporary discussion of the development of large-scale agglomerations across Europe, see Gert-Jan Hospers, "Beyond the Blue Banana? Structural Change in Europe's Geo-Economy", 42nd European Congress of the Regional Science Association (2002).

31   For a recent discussion of urbanization around the Mediterranean, see Claude Chaline, "Urbanisation and Town Management in the Mediterranean Countries," Assessment and Perspectives for Sustainable Urban Development (Barcelona: Mediterranean Commission on Sustainable Development, 2001).

32   Kingsley Davis, "The Origins and Growth of Urbanization in the World," American Journal of Sociology 60, 5, (1955): 429–437; and Kingsley Davis, "The Urbanization of the Human Population," Scientific American, 213, 3, (1965): 40–53.

33   For an analysis and critique of this proposition — and of the use of urban population thresholds (UPTs) in the study of urbanization — see Neil Brenner and Christian Schmid, "The Urban Age in Question." Already in the 1930s, the Chicago School sociologist Louis Wirth critiqued the use of UPTs, even though his own theory of urbanism emphasized the importance of population size as an important dimension of urban life. Wirth's critique was echoed in the early 1970s by his neo-Marxist theoretical antagonist Manuel Castells, who likewise emphasized the arbitrariness of the UPTs used in mainstream demography and the persistent need for a theoretical demarcation of "the urban question." See Castells, The Urban Question.

of such procedures are recognized but not resolved through the establishment of larger units for statistical aggregation — agglomerations, standard metropolitan areas, metropolitan regions, and the like — by the United Nations and many national census bureaus. For as Louis Wirth, Jean Gottmann, Lewis Mumford, and other major twentieth-century urbanists recognized, the complex demographic patterns associated with modern urbanization processes persistently leapfrog beyond the boundaries of such administrative units; data derived from them are therefore an extremely imprecise basis on which to interpret the geographies of urban processes. Moreover, population settlement patterns are being still further reshuffled in profound ways that undermine even the most reflexive efforts to develop an appropriate statistical/spatial unit for calculating urban population levels. As Edward Soja notes:

> Once-steep density gradients from the center have begun to level off as peripheral agglomerations multiply and the dominance of the singular central city weakens. What were formerly relatively clear boundaries between city and suburb, the urban and the non-urban, urbanism and suburbanism as ways of life are becoming increasingly blurred as new networks of interaction emerge and the city and the suburb flow into one another in what can best be described as a regional urbanization process.[34]

A second approach to spatial demography, the Global Rural-Urban Mapping Project (GRUMP) developed by a research team at Columbia University's Earth Institute, has attempted to grapple with such issues by plotting population density gradients across broad territorial landscapes around the world. Using a multi-parameter algorithm, the GRUMP approach synthesizes three basic types of data to estimate and visually distribute population densities: (1) population levels within official administrative zones, (2) the locations of settlement boundaries, and (3) the presence of nighttime lights. Figures 11 and 12 build upon various types of GRUMP spatial data to illustrate some of its implications for the visualization of urban population geographies in the Mediterranean.

At first glance, Figure 11 appears to transcend the bounded city metageography of urbanization, offering more nuanced visualizations of population geographies than those associated with standard demographic approaches. This figure illustrates not only the concentrations of high population density in all of the major Mediterranean cities and urban regions mentioned above but also the outward spread of population clusters across and among the extended metropolitan corridors that are on display in the nighttime lights map in Figure 9. This map of population density gradients appears to reinforce the image of extended urbanization produced through the nighttime lights images and thus to advance the endless urban fabric metageographical model. Intense light emissions appear to equate seamlessly with high levels of population density, which now occur through the broad networks of interaction mentioned by Soja rather than being confined to traditional city cores.

However, as its acronym suggests, an uninterrogated, methodologically territorialist distinction between urban and non-urban zones fundamentally underpins the statistical procedures used in the GRUMP approach to visualizing density gradients. Indeed, despite its capacity to map population density gradients across the entire territorial landscape, a key element of the GRUMP approach is to delineate a clear, continuous territorial border around the most densely populated zones. To this end, GRUMP researchers construct what they term an "urban mask" by combining data on the locations of settlements whose populations exceed 5,000 with information on the distribution of continuous-intensity nighttime lights.[35] On this basis, urban areas are represented as clearly bounded territories; other areas are classified as rural, and thus as empty, blank spaces on the map. Whereas Figure 11 uses GRUMP data to plot the population density gradient across the entire Mediterranean territory, Figure 12 illustrates the bounded city metageography that underpins the GRUMP's urban mask technique. As illustrated starkly by the vast, empty spaces scattered across the map, the GRUMP urban mask algorithm generates a visualization of territorial differentiation that, despite its expanded mapping of the urban, is still as untenably binary as the mainstream approach to spatial demography discussed with reference to Figure 10.

34   Edward Soja, "Reflections on the Concept of Global City Regions." Originally published in Spanish translation in *Ekonomiaz* (Basque Journal of Economics), edited English version in *Glocalogue*, online magazine *Artefact: Strategies of Resistance* (Belgrade), http://artefact.mi2.hr/_/_a04/lang_en/theory_soja_en.htm (accessed on 3 December 2012).

35   The details of this approach are explained in Deborah Balk, Francesca Pozzi, Gregory Yetman, Uwe Deichmann, and Andy Nelson, "The Distribution of People and the Dimension of Place: Methodologies to Improve the Global Estimation of Urban Extents," *Proceedings of the Urban Remote Sensing Conference* (Tempe, Arizona, 2006).

One further, still more far-reaching approach to spatial demography has been associated with the LandScan data set, which was originally introduced in 1988 at the Oak Ridge National Laboratories. While its initial purpose was to serve emergency workers responding to disasters, it has subsequently been used to inform investigations of large-scale population distributions. In contrast to the static residential or nighttime population data used by national census bureaus, the LandScan approach uses a complex probability coefficient to capture the fluid movement of populations over a twenty-four-hour period.[36] This "ambient" population is intended more closely to approximate the actual daily distribution of people in space (Figure 13).

Although LandScan takes urban agglomerations into account, the database does not impose boundaries on urban areas, nor does it formally distinguish urban and rural populations. Consequently, even though it does reveal the broad contours of diverse settlement areas, the LandScan approach offers a particularly striking visualization of the vast commuter sheds that undergird and crisscross large territorial zones. Thus, looking more closely, major transportation corridors appear highly urbanized. This reveals the intensive daily use of social space, not only road infrastructures, far beyond the core zones of metropolitan areas. In effect, the LandScan database provides a geo-referenced foundation for the classic concepts of megalopolis, daily urban systems, and commuter sheds developed in the 1960s and 1970s by innovative urbanists such as Jean Gottmann, Constantinos Doxiadis, and Brian Berry.[37] Much like the LandScan scientists, but lacking such precise geospatial data, each of these theorists was centrally concerned to underscore the fluid movement of populations within and across a large-scale regional or national territory. Mapping this fluidity, the imprint of human mobility within and across territory, is a key contribution of the LandScan approach.

Among major geospatial visualizations of population distribution, then, it is the LandScan approach that pushes most forcefully toward an endless urban fabric metageography. Due to its expansive mapping of urban morphologies beyond traditional city cores and its fluid depiction of urban boundaries, the LandScan approach provides a powerful visualization of how population flows produce a landscape of extended urbanization in the Mediterranean.

5

All population-based attempts to bound urban areas in cartographic space, and thus to examine processes of concentrated urbanization, require the specification of some threshold — usually either population size or population density — in terms of which to separate the urban from the non-urban. Mainstream approaches to spatial demography and the GRUMP effort to define the urban mask specify this threshold in different ways, but both undertake a basic statistical operation to visualize the presumed areal bounding of urban units from a surrounding non-urban realm. A second approach to the problem of specifying such boundaries focuses not on population distribution or density gradients but on land cover indicators, with particular reference to the spatial patterns of artificially constructed or built-up areas. Here, too, the delineation of a statistical threshold for the unit of data collection has massive implications for visualization outcomes.

A powerful contemporary method for investigating land cover types is through remote sensing. This technique entails the regular use of satellite sensors to scan the earth's surface, producing gridded data sets in which dominant land cover types are classified and then visualized with reference to quite fine-grained spatial units, ranging in size from 1 square kilometer to, most recently, 300 square meters. Since the major task of these satellites is environmental monitoring, most of their land cover classifications pertain to types of vegetation or hydrological conditions rather than to human settlement types or infrastructural arrangements. Despite this, however, any number of metageographical assumptions regarding the nature of urban space emerge from geo-referenced studies and visualizations of urban land cover. As with the major approaches to geospatial data on population discussed above, contemporary approaches to urban land cover oscillate between metageographies that

36   The data used in LandScan are produced as follows: "[P]robability coefficients are assigned to every value of each input variable, and a composite probability coefficient is calculated for each LandScan cell. [...] The coefficients for all regions are based on the following factors: roads, weighted by distance from major roads; elevation, weighted by favorability of slope categories; and land cover, weighted by type with exclusions for certain types; nighttime lights of the world, weighted by frequency. The resulting coefficients are weighted values, independent of census data, which can then be used to apportion shares of actual population counts within any particular area of interest." See Jerome E. Dobson, Edward A. Bright, Phillip R. Coleman, Richard C. Durfee, and Brian A. Worley, "LandScan: a Global Population Database for Estimating Populations at Risk," *Remotely Sensed Cities,* V. Mesev, ed. (London: Taylor & Francis, 2003): 277.

37   Jean Gottmann, *Megalopolis*; Brian J. L. Berry and Quentin Gillard, *The Changing Shape of Metropolitan America: Commuting Patterns, Urban Fields and Decentralization Processes, 1960–1970* (Cambridge, MA: Ballinger, 1977); Constantinos Doxiadis, *Ekistics: An Introduction to the Science of Human Settlements* (New York: Oxford University Press, 1968).

attempt to circumscribe urban zones and those that emphasize their explosion and differentiation across a vast territorial landscape.

Two of the major approaches to global land cover have been developed by the European Space Agency (the GlobCover data set) and NASA (the MODIS data set).[38] In the case of GlobCover, the MERIS sensor has been used to scan and classify every gridded cell on the earth's surface among twenty-two classes, only one of which is used to define urban areas. As in almost all land cover data sets, GlobCover defines the urban condition as a physical feature of the earth's surface, formally analogous to the different types of vegetation or hydrological conditions to which the other twenty-one land cover categories apply (examples of the latter include: cultivated and managed terrestrial areas, bare areas, and artificial water bodies). Within this classificatory scheme, urban areas are those in which built, artificial, or non-vegetative surfaces predominate over other land-use arrangements. Under the rubric of the technical term "impervious surfaces," such delineations of the urban generally include not only buildings but also roads, pavements, driveways, sidewalks, parking lots, and any other surfaces in which artificial forms of land coverage predominate.[39] Crucially, within this database, the threshold for the predominance of any feature within the landscape unit being studied is 50 percent of total land cover. The implications of this approach for visualizing the urban Mediterranean are presented in Figure 14, which is derived from the 2008 GlobCover data set.

As Figure 14 indicates, the GlobCover data set produces a bounded city metageography in which urban zones are relatively circumscribed and separated representationally from a diversity of other landscape features, which occupy the bulk of the territory. This metageographical orientation stems, first, from the GlobCover's use of a 50 percent threshold as the basis for classifying each landscape unit. Even when a very fine grain of data collection is used, this typological approach to visualization automatically erases all features of land cover that fall beneath the 50 percent threshold within the unit in question. This means, for example, that densely forested or vegetated zones containing moderately dense built environments or populations cannot register on the map as having any urban features. Second, this approach to land cover analysis replaces the urban/rural dualism used in mainstream spatial demography with an equally binary urban/nature divide. Because the GlobCover approach is oriented toward classifying the diversity of ecological landscapes, it envisions the natural environment as extending across the entire earth, thus enabling its features to be investigated systematically and then visually differentiated. This in turn consigns the urban to tightly delineated "bins," in which the 50 percent threshold for artificial surfaces has been crossed. The possibility that putatively "natural" spaces, or those with dense concentrations of particular ecological features (grasslands, water, ice, and so forth), may be permeated, crosscut, and/or transformed through urbanization processes is thereby excluded from consideration by classificatory fiat.

The Global Impervious Surface (ISA) data set, developed in the early 2000s by the Earth Observation Group in Boulder, Colorado, offers an alternative approach to the *problematique* of urban land cover that begins to map infrastructural geographies beyond city cores and metropolitan regions, and thus to explore the land cover features of extended urbanization. Unlike GlobCover and MODIS, the ISA does not draw upon remotely sensed land cover data; instead it combines nighttime lights data from NOAA and ambient population information from LandScan (see Figures 9 and 13). Most crucially, because the ISA is focused on only one general landscape feature, artificially covered or impervious surfaces, it need not deploy a classificatory threshold, 50 percent or otherwise. Instead the ISA creates a 0 to 100 percent density gradient for artificial surfaces, leading to a differentiated visualization of built land cover densities across vast territorial zones.[40] The visual consequences of this approach are readily evident in Figure 15, which reveals a thick mosaic of built-up areas and connective infrastructure corridors stretched and threaded unevenly across the Mediterranean zone. The comparison of Figure 15 with the GlobCover urban extents (Figure 14 offers a striking contrast between an approach to urban land cover oriented toward a bounded city metageography and one that produces an endless urban fabric metageography.

38   On GlobCover, see Pierre Defourny, Patrice Bicheron, Carsten Brockmann, and Marc Leroy, "GLOBCOVER: A 300 m Global Land Cover Product for 2005 Using Envisat MERIS Time Series," in *Proceedings of the ISPRS Commission VII Mid-term Symposium, Remote Sensing: From Pixels to Processes* (Enschede, the Netherlands, 2006): 8–11; on MODIS, see Christopher O. Justice "An Overview of MODIS Land Data Processing and Product Status," *Remote Sensing of Environment* 83, 1, (2002): 3–15.

39   See David Potere, Annemarie Schneider, Shlomo Angel, and Daniel L. Civco, "Mapping Urban Areas on a Global Scale: Which of the Eight Maps Now Available Is More Accurate?," *International Journal of Remote Sensing*, 30, 24, (2009): 6531–6558.

40   See Christopher Elvidge, Benjamin T. Tuttle, Paul C. Sutton, Kimberly E. Baugh, Ara T. Howard, Cristina Milesi, Budhendra Bhaduri, and Ramakrishna Neman, "Global Distribution and Density of Constructed Impervious Surfaces," *Sensors* 7, 9 (2007): 1962–1979.

While the theoretical significance of impervious surface distribution requires further investigation and clarification, the ISA visualizations underscore the massive extent and variegated distribution of built structures and surfaces across the Mediterranean. According to one team of geospatial scientists, the construction of impervious surfaces is "a universal phenomenon — akin to clothing — and represents one of the primary anthropogenic modifications of the environment."[41] However, rather than viewing the contemporary production and transformation of built surfaces as a universal feature of anthropogenic activity, we emphasize the historically and geographically specific frameworks of capitalist urbanization within which such processes have been occurring, both in the Mediterranean and beyond, since the period of mercantile expansion investigated in Braudel's classic studies. But the metaphor of clothing — or, better, a skein — covering major zones of the earth seems appropriate. In John Friedmann's recent formulation, "as the skein of the urban steadily advances across the earth, its vertical dimensions are layered to produce a new global topography of the urban."[42] The ISA visualization usefully illuminates one strategically important layer of this emergent global-urban topography. While such visualizations do not in themselves reveal much regarding the institutions, strategies, and struggles through which this skein is produced and transformed, they do offer a more plausible representation of their geographies, than the bounded city model associated with the GlobCover and MODIS approaches.

41   Elvidge et al., "Global Distribution and Density of Constructed Impervious Surfaces," 1963.

42   John Friedmann, *The Prospect of Cities* (Minneapolis: University of Minnesota Press, 2002): 6.

6

At a very large scale, visualizations of impervious surface gradients reveal the material imprints of infrastructural networks, including those of transportation systems, which extend well beyond city cores and metropolitan centers. These transportation networks — road, rail, marine, and air — are obviously essential to both historical and contemporary forms of capitalist urbanization, facilitating the circulation of capital, labor, and commodities across large-scale territories and, as David Harvey has famously argued, continuously accelerating both the turnover time of capital accumulation and the "annihilation of space by time."[43] The role of such infrastructures of circulation in the urbanization process has long been recognized. For instance, as discussed above, Braudel's analysis of the urban Mediterranean devoted some attention to the vectors of interconnectivity, for both information and commerce, linking the major ports and economic centers (Figure 7). Likewise, despite his territorialist conception of the urban, Jean Gottmann's investigation of megalopolis included a detailed analysis of internal and external transportation linkages, and presented national-scale visualizations of rail, highway, and airplane networks as part of his investigation of commuter flows.[44] In most such approaches, however, the geographies of transportation connectivity are understood as being extrinsic to an urban process that is animated internally, through the powerful socioeconomic and cultural forces unleashed by agglomeration.

43   David Harvey, *The Limits to Capital* (Chicago: University of Chicago Press, 1982), ch. 12.

44   Gottmann, *Megalopolis*, ch. 12.

Following from the analytical and cartographic explosion of the urban that we have been tracking in this discussion, it is no longer plausible to reduce the *problematique* of transport geographies to an adjunct spatial formation, subordinate to the nodal points and bounded urban territories upon which twentieth-century urban theory was focused. Consideration of transportation connectivity offers a powerful basis on which to visualize the thickening landscapes of extended urbanization. Of course, such a perspective requires continued attention to concentrated urbanization, and to the diverse processes through which centers of socioeconomic activity and population are constructed, reproduced, and interconnected. Just as important, such an investigation requires an interpretation of transportation networks and their sociomaterial infrastructures as essential elements within an extended fabric of urbanization, regardless of their locational geometries or morphological configurations.[45]

45   Christian Schmid, "Theory," in Roger Diener et al., eds., *Switzerland: An Urban Portrait*, 170–171.

Drawing upon a data set produced by the National Imagery and Mapping Agency of the U.S. Geological Survey, Figure 16 presents such a visualization with reference to the major terrestrial and marine transportation networks around the

Mediterranean. This visualization reveals a generalized geography of interconnectivity that stretches across the entire region, from the hyper-dense webs along the coastlines and around the major agglomerations, to the latticework of corridors stretched across both marine and terrestrial zones and the sparsely equipped North African desert and mountain hinterlands. It illustrates not only connections among major centers but also the density and scope of the transportation networks themselves, which are woven thickly across regions, territories, and scales, and thus represent important spatial infrastructures for extended urbanization.

A complementary visualization of the operational geographies associated with these transportation infrastructures is presented in Figure 17, which is based upon the Global Accessibility Map, a data set that was commissioned in conjunction with the World Bank's *World Development Report* of 2009. Whereas Figure 16 depicts the positionality, shape, and density of the various routes, Figure 17 uses a cost-distance algorithm to compute the projected travel time to major settlement areas. The resultant "friction surface" is represented spatially using a gray-scale coding system in which brightness denotes high accessibility and darkness indicates low accessibility. The friction surface used to color-code the map is calculated with reference to estimated travel times associated with different types of transport infrastructures, while also taking into account intervening factors such as land cover, slope, and political borders.[46] In effect, this approach generalizes Braudel's earlier diagrams of Venetian accessibility (Figure 7) to every major destination within the entire Mediterranean territory. Each portion of the zone is assigned a projected travel time to the nearest major city, but as in Braudel's maps, the changing gradient (here, a gray-scale coding scheme) represents not a spatial attribute but a time-distance vector. In this way, urbanization is revealed as a relation of access to a broader terrain through networks that link cities, yet expand beyond them via long-distance transport corridors that cumulatively become important landscape attributes.

In different ways, Figures 16 and 17 provide evidence for the continued centrality of agglomerations as nodal points within medium and long-distance transport networks. In Figure 16, this is due to the obvious presence of cities as endpoints and way stations within the networks. In the case of Figure 17, the calculations that generate the gray-scale gradient are tied to the locations of cities containing more than 50,000 people as of the year 2000. Despite this, however, both maps also serve to destabilize the bounded city metageography by illuminating the impressive density and territorial coverage of crisscrossing transportation networks within and around the Mediterranean. For this reason, both maps have been aligned with the endless urban fabric metageography in Figure 8. Even if they are not as expansive in their estimation of urban boundaries as the impervious surfaces density (ISA) data set, they do extend them well beyond those associated with GRUMP population density gradients and the LandScan account of ambient population density. More generally, insofar as these maps transpose the territorialist concern with urban boundaries into a more fluid *problematique* of networked infrastructures, interdependencies, and connectivities, they offer particularly vivid illustrations of John Friedmann's metaphor of the "skein of the urban."[47]

46   Hirotsugu Uchida and Andrew Nelson, "Agglomeration Index: Towards a New Measure of Urban Concentration," *Background Paper for the World Bank World Development Report 2009* (2008).

47   Friedmann, *The Prospect of Cities*, 6.

7

How far can this extended model of Mediterranean urban geographies be stretched? Are there not additional traces, layers, and vectors of the urban radiating beyond population density gradients or ambient population densities, the "hardscapes" associated with impervious surfaces and the variegated geographies of transportation accessibility? A particularly expansive visualization of urbanization processes, which almost completely explodes the urban/non-urban distinction, is engendered through the Human Footprint data sets produced by the Wildlife Conservation Society and Columbia's Earth Institute. These approaches are grounded in a synthetic combination of population, land cover, land use, transportation, and energy data, and they attempt to grasp the cumulative effects of human transformations on the landscape through a gray-scale color-coding system (with darkness signifying high impact, lightness signifying low impact). In Figure 18, these putative human impacts on the Mediterranean landscape — arguably a proxy measure for the diverse, historically specific social processes associated with modern capitalist urbanization — are depicted as being nearly coextensive with the entire region.[48] The non-urban "outside" presupposed in earlier approaches has now been almost totally annihilated; urbanization is represented as an encompassing continuum expressed through a vast assemblage of landscape conditions across the entire territory. This and the previously discussed visualizations of the Mediterranean thus clearly underscore the futility of attempts to demarcate fixed urban boundaries within a territorial landscape that, as Lefebvre recognized over four decades ago, is simultaneously exploding and imploding around, across, among, and through inherited city centers.[49]

However, despite their usefulness in illustrating the large-scale areal continuity of the urban fabric and the densely networked interconnections among places and regions across the Mediterranean, one of the most serious limitations of the visualizations discussed here is their static character — their depiction of synchronic conditions and cross-sectional distributions rather than restructuring processes and sociospatial transformations. In the case of geospatial data on population, the visualizations discussed above are purely descriptive; they do not effectively illuminate the unevenly articulated, crisis-prone urbanization processes, with associated moments of explosion and implosion, that underlie and continually transform the variegated patterns of population distribution, growth, and decline around the Mediterranean.[50] Similarly, geospatial data on land cover serve mainly to describe the material and morphological configuration of built space around the contemporary Mediterranean, but they explain almost nothing regarding the cyclical, often speculative processes of creative destruction that constantly reshape the region. Even visualizations that explore the density of impervious surfaces do not effectively illuminate the ways in which such differentiated geographies are mediated through common, large-scale forces of restructuring, such as state planning strategies, tourist infrastructural investment, or real-estate speculation. Finally, the abstract visualizations of transportation networks presented above are no more than a generic starting point for investigating the interplay between connectivity infrastructures and strategies of urban and regional development at various scales.[51] Indeed, this relationship is left completely indeterminate in Figures 16 and 17, which do little more than represent real or hypothesized connections among already established population centers.

Such visualizations may also contain profoundly ideological assumptions, which are naturalized through their technoscientific representation as self-evident spatial conditions. For instance, the vision of the bounded city presented in mainstream spatial demography as well as in the GRUMP data on population density is symptomatic of a broader, increasingly hegemonic discourse on the "urban age" that is often used to justify the continued concentration of infrastructure, investment, and population within the most economically prosperous cities and metropolitan regions. Such visualizations are thus deeply implicated in the proliferation of urban locational policies that effectively naturalize the shrinkage of redistributive spatial policies and the ongoing state-mediated, publicly funded proliferation of territorial inequalities at all spatial scales, across Europe and beyond.[52] Similarly, the recent rollout of large-scale, trans-European motorway and sea infrastructures is intended to promote the forms of large-scale spatial integration envisioned in Figure 17. However, this visualization is blind to ways in which such initiatives fragment and marginalize some zones precisely as they more tightly interconnect others, thus contributing to a wide-ranging "splintering" of territory.[53] Many other examples of the naturalization of spatial ideology could be excavated from these and other forms of geospatial visualization, not least in relation to the representation of urbanization processes. As powerful and provocative as such representational techniques may appear, therefore, urban scholars must treat them with extreme caution, recognizing their politically inflected, ideologically strategic character, especially in their most technically sophisticated forms.

A fundamental challenge for any attempt to visualize twenty-first century urbanization is to specify, in substantive theoretical terms, the essential properties

48   For further details on the Human Footprint dataset, see Eric Sanderson, Malanding Jaiteh, Marc A. Levy, Kent H. Redford, Antoinette V. Wannebo, and Gillian Woolmer, "The Human Footprint and the Last of the Wild," *BioScience*, 52, 10 (2002): 891–904.49 Lefebvre, *The Urban Revolution*, 14

49   Lefebvre, *The Urban Revolution*, 14

50   For a discussion of demographic growth along the Mediterranean rim since the 1950s, see UN Habitat, *State of the World Cities 2008/2009: Harmonious Cities* (Nairobi: UN Habitat, 2008); and for a general recent discussion on contemporary urbanization, Claude Chaline, "Urbanisation and Town Management in the Mediterranean Countries."

51   See, for example, Debra Johnson and Colin Turner, *Trans-European Networks: The Political Economy of Integrating Europe's Infrastructure* (London: Macmillan, 1997); and Andreas Faludi, *Making the European Spatial Development Perspective*, vol. 2 (London: Routledge, 2002).

52   Neil Brenner, *New State Spaces: Urban Governance and the Rescaling of Statehood* (Oxford: Oxford University Press, 2004).

53   Stephen Graham and Simon Marvin, *Splintering Urbanism* (New York: Routledge, 2003).

and dynamics of this process, at any spatial scale, such that its geographical imprint and effects can be investigated and subjected to representational ordering. Visualization strategies, including those based on geospatial data, can serve as powerful aids in the effort to build such a theorization, but they cannot substitute for the basic analytical work required to invent, refine, and operationalize concepts. Indeed, the sources of geospatial data analyzed here deploy relatively simple, mostly descriptive understandings of the urban that may prove useful for information processing and visualization, but do little to clarify the metageographical questions explored above or, for that matter, to illuminate the transformative dynamics that shape and reshape urban landscapes. From our point of view, a new theory of urbanization is today required for deciphering sociospatial transformations, but its key conceptual elements have yet to be consolidated. This exercise in the visualization of urban boundaries and spaces within the Mediterranean is therefore intended to facilitate reflection and debate regarding the "transformed form" of contemporary urbanization, and thereby to stimulate further reflection on the "urban question" under twenty-first-century conditions. This is a task to which we and our colleagues in the Urban Theory Lab-GSD are now dedicating considerable energies.

Meanwhile, urban ideologies and associated visualizations persist.[54] The vision of a bounded city, the notion of a worldwide "urban age," the assumption of an urban/non-urban divide, and the fantasy of total connectivity continue to pervade scholarly writing, administrative discourse, planning practice, and public culture. The production of such ideologies is an important dimension of the urbanization process itself, especially during a conjuncture in which inherited spatial formations are being exploded and reconstituted anew. The visualization of urban space (as bounded or unbounded, for example) and of territorial order (as unified, divided, or variegated, for example) may figure crucially in the production and entrenchment of such spatial ideologies. For this reason, even though they are often derived from seemingly technical decisions regarding numerical threshold percentages, measurement instruments, classificatory schemes, or unit boundaries, the metageographies associated with geospatial data are never neutral. Such apparently trivial statistical or cartographic manipulations may serve to naturalize, or to unsettle, established assumptions regarding territorial organization, sociospatial interdependence, and geopolitical identity. In this sense, our metageographical explorations may be articulated to some of the broader questions about historical and contemporary Mediterranean urbanisms that are explored in this issue of *New Geographies*.

54 David Wachsmuth, "City as Ideology," *Environment and Planning D: Society and Space*.

Challenges to Urbanity in Contemporary Mediterranean Metropolises
New Urban Forms, Dynamics, Boundaries and Tensions
Denis Bocquet

Many things have changed over the last three decades in Mediterranean metropolises, and globalization and its local declensions have had profound effects not only on their spatial structure but also on their social functioning and on the institutional practices of their planning and governance. Such new spatial regimes have transformed metropolises of the Mediterranean region and invite a revision of the general perception of such cities. The changes reflected in these cities suggest addressing cities in other regions of the world with new research perspectives, as what is happening might have echoes in other geographical contexts. Globalization has been accompanied by the emergence of challenges to what was typically perceived as the traditional form of Mediterranean urbanity — a historically, culturally, and anthropologically constructed combination of urban form, urban governance, and urban lifestyle, and to its values. This process has sometimes been violent, inducing rapid transformation not only of urban morphology but also of the general organization of urban life at various scales, from the neighborhood to the street and the family. It has also been accompanied by the invention of new architectural and urban forms that have challenged the very Mediterranean nature of such cities.

But urban growth in previous periods, such as the 1950s and 1960s, had surely already shaken tradition, with urban sprawl, illegal urbanism, large social housing projects, and low-quality concrete peripheries or the traumatic consequences for urbanity of the intrusion of motorized mobility into historical cities: the Mediterranean did not enter the current phase of globalization in an unaltered, sleepy urban form (which, moreover, is perfectly mythical). Mediterranean cities are the result of previous globalizations, from Neolithic times to the era of industrialization, and are not merely the product of the simple application of ancient and medieval urban ideals on space. Mediterranean cities, in their diversity, are complex entities and can't be reduced to a static category or type. With globalization, boundaries between Mediterranean city regions and their hinterlands, or even the world, as well as internal boundaries within cities, have been redefined once again, a phenomenon that invites reflection on the possible value of the Mediterranean as a spatial model for the understanding of contemporary global interactions.

As they tend to challenge conventional boundaries, forms, and social configurations, recent trends in the development of Mediterranean metropolises do indeed deserve specific attention. They also illustrate the necessity of deconstructing dichotomies pertaining to North/South and East/West shifts: Mediterranean metropolises are "in between" in many regards, and their understanding might help refine categories. Just as historians have illustrated how the history of Mediterranean cities between the nineteenth and twentieth centuries has been more complex than that of a modernity exported from West and North to East and South (Lafi 2005), Mediterranean urban geography today has to integrate new

Denis Bocquet   is a researcher with Ecole des Ponts (ParisTech/LATTS). He studied history and town planning (Ecole normale supérieure de Fontenay/Saint-Cloud and Paris I Sorbonne University). He graduated in 2002 from Aix-Marseille I University (Mediterranean Urban Studies) with a work on Rome (*Rome Ville Technique*, 2007). He has worked on the urban history of several Mediterranean cities, as well as contemporary urban trends in the region. He guest-edited, with Filippo De Pieri, a special issue of the journal *Storia Urbana* (2005) on the roots of illegal urbanism in Mediterranean cities. He taught Urban Studies, Urban History, and Mediterranean Studies in Aix-en-Provence (Aix-Marseille I), Dresden (TU), and now Paris (Ecole des Ponts).

With Nora Lafi, he founded H-Mediterranean (H-Net, Michigan State University) in 2001 and still serves as editor of this list. Bocquet is a member of the advisory board of the Urban and Regional Policy Program of the German Marshall Fund of the United States, the SITI Research Centre (Politecnico di Torino/Compagnia di San Paolo), and the UrbanGrad Program (Technische Universität Darmstadt). At Ecole des Ponts in Paris, he manages the program on Mediterranean metropolises of the "Chaire Ville."

methods and perspectives. In other words, metropolitanization in the age of globalization constitutes a kind of new frontier for Mediterranean urban geography (Courtot 2001). But this process of reintroducing the Mediterranean on the global urban scene must not itself create unexamined categories, among which the Mediterranean metropolis itself might be the most delicate. This reintroduction of the Mediterranean must indeed be built on local micro-geographies and on a reflection on the articulation between this local dimension and the global one in different contexts, and in no way on new ontological visions on the Mediterranean nature of cities of the Mediterranean region. Even if the cities of the region do share many common historical, morphological, social, and anthropological features, they cannot be the object of the construction of a single category.

But they can be the subjects instead of a focused analysis based on a variety of questions. Not all cities of the region are affected in the same way by all questions posed to contemporary metropolises, but on the basis of a certain number of features they have in common, a Mediterranean entry might have a relative pertinence. The myth of Mediterranean unity having long been deconstructed, and warnings about a homogenizing Mediterranean approach heard (Herzfeld 2005: Horden 2005), it might be the time to come back to Mediterranean cities with the aim of addressing contemporary stakes. As for a possible Mediterranean unity, which anthropologists have long been seeking in common rural traditions (Albera 2006, Albera and Tozy 2005), it has never had more relevance, outside of colonial ideological elaborations, for the question of cities. The history of the Mediterranean since Braudel is more one of blocs of civilizations than of convergences. The geographical invention of the Mediterranean itself has, since Braudel, been critically discussed (Deprest 2002). So the question today is not of a possible Mediterranean ontology but rather of a pragmatic approach to a region that shares common characteristics — among which the high value given to urbanity is central — and is subjected to some common global transformations that constitute real challenges to the very nature of this urbanity. It is also the pertinent approach to cities in terms of social sciences (Sant Cassia and Schäfer 2005), at a time when the relationship to culture has been reconceptualized (Gupta and Ferguson 1992) and common narratives on the East/West relationship are being revisited (Mallette 2010).

Metropolises have been the object, during the last fifteen years, of growing interest among the scholarly community. Their fast transformation constitutes, for researchers, both a materialization of globalization and a symbol of changing equilibria in the world order. Metropolises are also seen as places where the stakes of the relationship between global trends, space, and society are most legible and their effects, both physical and social, for better or worse, most spectacular. Logically, cities of the emerging world, those experiencing the fastest transformations, have been at the center of this focus, and from Shanghai to Mumbai, or Dubai to Rio, new paradigms about metropolitan growth, dynamism, and governance have been fashioned (Lorrain 2011). The emergence of such new research objects was also an opportunity to answer calls for an address of the persisting Eurocentrism affecting academia, and indeed, studies of urban issues became more international and truly multicultural, with a critically engaged examination of the roots of globalization and the new forms of urban life that result.

Big cities of the emerging world, characterized by growing social and spatial injustices (Brenner 1997, Harvey 2006), have been read in light of the relationship between urbanization, urbanity, globalization, and local governance (Eade and Mele 2011). They have become objects of debate about the social nature of cities and the capacity of global capitalism to produce harmonious forms of urban development. Here again, the main focus has been placed on cities like Lagos, Mexico City, or Jakarta. The result, for cities of the Mediterranean region, has been a certain marginalization in research. Of course there was a reason for that: our generation is witnessing the development of what was once called the Third World, and scholarly interest in the analysis of the effects of this huge phenomenon on urban spaces and societies is more than legitimate. And no one doubts that the relative position of Mediterranean cities in this new world has decreased: the world economy now has other cores: skyscrapers are higher in Kuala Lumpur than in Cairo, gated-communities are more gated in Capetown than in Istanbul, and the condition of slums is probably worse in Delhi than in Naples.

Mediterranean cities had already experienced such economic, cultural (and academic) shifts in history, from the development of the Atlantic world to the industrialization of Europe, while retaining a central position in reflections on the nature of urbanity. When Lisbon and then Paris, London, Berlin, New York, Los Angeles, and Tokyo became world metropolises, cities of the Mediterranean region, for their historical richness, retained a central position in judgments on what is a city and for understanding how such social and spatial constructions work. Urbanity as a value has always been marked by a certain Mediterranean nostalgia, and historians have illustrated how Mediterranean metropolises have constituted central paradigms in the evaluation of what makes a city urban in different periods (Ilbert et al. 2000). It is still the case in many respects, even if today cities of the region can seem marginal compared to Hong Kong or Singapore and are sometimes known more for their traces of the past than for the innovations they bring to the international urban scene. I argue in this chapter that in present Mediterranean metropolises, many important phenomena remain to be read, and that their study might contribute to the understanding of the stakes of urbanity at a much larger scale.

The Complex Heritage of Illegal Urbanism

One of the first common features of Mediterranean cities that comes to mind in the context of a general trend toward urbanization, which has been particularly spectacular on the eastern and southern shores of the Mediterranean, is that of littoralization (Côte and Joannon 1999). In Mediterranean countries, an always growing share of the population tends to live not only in cities but also in larger cities of the coast or within coastal regions. This phenomenon has roots in the history of the Mediterranean (and probably of humankind in general) since ancient times, but more specifically in the rural exodus leading to massive urbanization in the nineteenth century. But since the 1970s, the trend toward littoralization has increased, with the result of the creation of large coastal urban regions, which have changed the nature of metropolises. There is in France the example of the Nice-Toulon-Marseilles-Montpellier-Perpignan conurbation (Ferrier 1993), but this reality is even more spectacular on the southern shore of the Mediterranean, whose (mostly) coastal cities have been deeply transformed by a mass rural-urban migration of which international migrations are only a partial echo. Urban growth since the middle of the twentieth century has created a series of Mediterranean metropolises with multimillion populations, from Athens (Leontidou 1990) to Cairo (Abu-Lughod 2004), and from Beirut (Verdeil 2010) to Istanbul (Pérouse 2000), Algiers, and Tripoli. Metropolises of the northern shore, except maybe Barcelona, Rome, and Athens, have long been overshadowed in terms of inhabitants, and cities like Marseilles, Genoa, Naples, Palermo, and Thessaloniki have become more regional than global metropolises. A city like Istanbul grew from 1 million in 1950 to 14 million in 2012, and Cairo expanded from 700,000 circa 1920 to about 17 million in 2010.

What most of these cities share is a heritage of architecture and planning from the 1950s to the 1980s, a mix of urban sprawl, urbanization of former rural surroundings, more or less articulated informal settlements, neighborhoods of social housing, and low-quality forms of housing for the middle classes. They also share the fact of having been massively subjected to the invasion of cars into the historical urban fabric, a traumatic process that has deeply affected not only the general functioning of cities but also the form of Mediterranean urbanity that they materialized. And indeed, reclaiming urban space from cars has been one of the stakes of the rediscovery of urbanity in many

Mediterranean cities during the last few decades. Metropolises of the Mediterranean also share (except maybe for France) a long heritage of "illegal" or "informal" architecture and urbanism. We are entering an era in which the consideration given to such urban forms is changing, both in the scholarly community and in governance and planning practices. The Mediterranean might be a kind of laboratory of urban change in addressing the heritage of illegal planning — which we now know had little to do with the informal dimension and often occurred just outside of the official planning system. Scholarly criticism of perceptions of the phenomenon based on a legalistic reading is now widespread; illegal urbanism can no longer be assessed in terms of simple dichotomies between the formal and the informal, or the planned and the spontaneous (Bocquet and De Pieri 2005).

That the illegal dimension has always been part of a more complex social and spatial system is now recognized, as part of an evolution of ideas in which studies about Mediterranean metropolises have been instrumental. Illegal urbanism, which has long been the object of a scholarly blindness (Destro 2010), is now being subjected to a truly critical approach. In the case of Italy, for example, urban planning has long been seen by scholars as a way of controlling speculation and the grip of landowners on the city. For ideological reasons, and the belief in the political virtues of the master plan, this Marxist vision of planning has delayed a more comprehensive approach to urban realities. But changed perspectives are now clearly at work (Zanfi 2008). In Rome since the 2000s, official planning does take into account the urban reality as it is, and not as it should be (without the dimension of illegal urbanism — entire blocks in some cases), and the new master plan has been designed in a more dynamic negotiation with landowners and investors (Cellamare 2010), at the cost sometimes of ambiguous compromises, but at least from a more realistic vision of the city and its dynamics of transformation. Even in Naples, where conventional attitudes of planners and municipal rulers toward the illegal city have lasted longer, things are changing, as in Palermo (Maccaglia 2009).

In this Italian context, the practice of amnesties (*condoni edilizi*) by the various Berlusconi governments since the 1990s has also obliged municipalities to take this newly legal reality into account (and has helped the ruling party expand its political clientele). On the academic scene, studies about Italy have also contributed to illustrate how illegal and formerly illegal neighborhoods also have a soul (De Pieri 2010). Studies about Athens and Istanbul, two metropolises in which urban growth has long largely happened outside of the framework of the master plan, also illustrate how these processes were highly socialized, and how spontaneity was inserted into a strong network of social control. Studies about the *Gecekondu* neighborhoods of Istanbul emphasize the role of small entrepreneurs within the real-estate sector, as well as the insertion of the population into networks of local political patronage (Pérouse 2004, Esen and Lang 2007). This change of perception, as in Italy or Greece, is accompanied by the invention of new planning methods within municipal offices (Içduygu

2004). As in Rome, new processes of negotiation, both with inhabitants and entrepreneurs or investors, are progressively inserted into planning procedures (Gülöksüz 2002). In Beirut, studies have shown how illegal urbanism was in fact always part of a very socialized process, with informal negotiations between authorities and investors or inhabitants, or even the informal intervention of professional planners for the planning of what has long been considered unplanned (Fawaz 2005). In the Mediterranean, beyond the great typological differences between metropolises affected by the heritage of illegal urbanism, new planning methods seem to be at work, or at least there appears to be a new perspective on the relationship between planning and the actual evolution of the built environment — fewer norms, rules, and illusions about their implementation, but also more strategic planning and big projects, sometimes seen as partial substitutes for planning (Carrière 2002). But these new solutions, just like the complex urban growth of the previous period, also constitute new challenges to the Mediterranean form of urbanity: they produce a new urban morphology, which doesn't necessarily relate either to the existing city or to the spirit it managed to continue embodying despite previous traumatic urban changes.

New Morphological Challenges to Mediterranean Urbanity

Urban sprawl is not new in Mediterranean metropolises, but the phenomenon recently acquired a new face (Munoz 2003, De Rossi 1999). During the last two decades, a Mediterranean form of urban decentralization emerged, with the birth of new peripheries, whose relationship with the urban center proves difficult. Of course, the extension of peripheries of the 1980s type continued, with the urbanization of former rural areas around most cities. In a city like Barcelona, this extension even flourished during the real-estate boom of the 1990s, which only ended with the present crisis (Dura-Guimera 2003). But, because they are increasingly further from the city center, these peripheries articulate differently with it, and their existence modifies the Mediterranean metropolitan lifestyle. There are even more cars and long hours in networks of public transportation that always arrive too late to follow the peripheral extensions of the city. The very landscape of Mediterranean cities is also modified by such trends, the transition between city and hinterland being now made of motorways, commercial zones, and endless suburbs. In Rome, the *Agro Romano* is progressively transformed into a vast suburb (Salvaggiulio et al. 2010). In Athens too, sprawling peripheries have completely altered the historical relationship between the city and its hinterland (Chorianopoulos 2010). The same happened in Istanbul (Cakir 2008, Terzi and Bolen 2010). Studies on land-cover indicators suggest that sprawling peripheries are consuming the historical landscape surrounding Mediterranean cities (Salvati 2012). This is true for Rome, but also for Tunis (Weber and Puissant 2003). In most Mediterranean metropolises, more people now live in the peripheries than downtown — major cultural shifts whose consequences for the idea of urbanity and the daily practices of urban living still have to be understood. In contexts where the pattern of the compact city was of century-long historical importance, having metropolises develop along motorways and orbital ring roads — with resulting land acquisition and major challenges to existing transportation schemes, as in Rome (Munafo 2010) — also has huge consequences for the idea of the city, on its image, practices, and representations. Sprawled cities are truly a challenge to Mediterranean urbanity (Monclus 1998).

The form of the new peripheries also presents a challenge. In many Mediterranean cities, gated communities were built since the 1990s and are now part of the new metropolitan landscape as well as of the social practices of urban space. This new form of Mediterranean enclosed living is of course in contradiction with many of the anthropological features that defined the essence of cities and urbanity in the region (Munoz 2003). From New Cairo (Abu-Lughod 2004) to the enclaves of villas surrounded by golf courses in many cities of the southern and eastern shores of the Mediterranean (Denis 2006), but also from the numerous gated communities of Istanbul and even Rome or Montpelier, such islands of prosperity separated from the rest of the urban landscape and society have deeply altered, with the adaptation of a model developed for other regions, the traditional proximity between rich and poor in Mediterranean cities and the patterns of communication that formed the very essence of urbanity. Of course segregation has always existed, and one shouldn't have a mythical vision of class coexistence in Mediterranean cities of the past, but now a new form of segregation tends to be materialized by walls and fences, as well as by distance, and people have less chance to meet in the street. This growing uniformity of urban landscapes in the Mediterranean could also lead to what Francesc Munoz calls "urbanalization" (Munoz 2008): a loss of character that would have tremendous effects on the idea of the Mediterranean city and the values it carries.

Such recent trends in Mediterranean metropolises have been accompanied on the other hand by a spectacular downtown renaissance, which saw degraded city centers being renovated, changing the whole image of such neighborhoods and boosting tourism. The model for this form of urban renovation is of course Barcelona, a city that on the occasion of the 1992 Olympic Games both reclaimed its own waterfront and initiated the renovation of its medieval city center (Marshall 2004, Bocquet, De Pieri, Infusino 2006). This initiative had a strong echo in many cities of the Mediterranean, from the renaissance of the medinas of North Africa (Balbo 2012) to the rebuilding of downtown Beirut (Kassab 1997), or from the rebirth of Valencia and Genoa. Urban policies have largely focused on boosting the dynamism of such historical city parts, and a new model was definitely invented in the Mediterranean. The success of such initiatives in terms of urban revitalization (if not necessarily social justice) derived from the conjunction between greater pedestrian access around many major downtown arteries, the rebirth of the downtown prestige retail sector, and the Mediterranean passion for urban promenade. This practice was reinvented in the last two decades, and seeing Istiklal Avenue in Istanbul with hundreds of thousands of pedestrians dedicating themselves to promenade, from morning to night, is a sign of this rebirth after decades of decay. Such avenues are definitely part of a renewed Mediterranean urbanity (Sema Kubat 2001), and Istiklal Avenue's equivalents in other cities of the Mediterranean, from Athens to Thessaloniki or Florence to Marseilles, are the sign of the positive interaction between one of the few truly Mediterranean anthropological constants, urban promenade, and a practice of urban renovation. In general, in Mediterranean metropolises, policies have tended during the last two decades toward a transformation of public space in which the values of such spaces are emphasized and in which the space given to cars, their circulation, and their parking has been reduced, with the result of resurrecting some characters of Mediterranean urbanity.

Recent trends in urban renovation and renewal in Mediterranean cities have also led to a genuine rediscovery of waterfronts. Paradoxically indeed, many Mediterranean cities had been cut off from their contact with the sea by the constitution of harbors as spatial enclaves between the nineteenth and the end of the twentieth centuries. With the decline of port industrial zones, many cities had the occasion to reclaim their seaside. Here again, Barcelona has been an example, with the invention of a Mediterranean version of waterfront urbanism. This reopening of Mediterranean cities toward the sea has spread throughout the region and has become a central feature in planning (Cattedra 2011). Waterfronts have even become tools of metropolitan image and Mediterraneanism (Rodrigues-Malta 2004). But if they facilitate the rebirth of urbanity, as they open downtowns toward the maritime horizon and landscape, they also pose new challenges to this urbanity, as they sometimes were given urban forms in contradiction with the Mediterranean heritage. Condo living, for example, is not necessarily a Mediterranean tradition. Debates about the seafront in Beirut illustrate the risk of a morphological juxtaposition whose effect on the urban landscape could be devastating (Fawaz and Krijnen 2010).

This also poses the question of mega-urban projects in contemporary Mediterranean metropolises and of their relation to a possible Dubai paradigm. Of course, many such projects were partially designed before the arrival of investors from the Gulf. In Algiers, the most prominent projects in this regard date back to the *Grand Projet Urbain* of 1988 (Zitoun 2010) and the Berges du Lac project in Tunis also answers to logics more complex than just the importation of a new model (Barthel 2006). The Dubai paradigm, however, constitutes a true challenge to the urban form as previously conceived in the Mediterranean (Stanley 2003). Even if the extent of the Dubai effect is to be relativized (Barthel 2010), projects responding to a such logic constitute exceptions to the usual urban regime and fabric of the region, with a leading role for holdings based in Gulf capitals and a new conception of the urban soil and of its link to the historical dimension of urbanism and urbanity (Barthel 2008). The Dubai model also brought to the Mediterranean new professional practices, with a new role for architects, a new conception of planning, and a new relationship between investors, planners, and policymakers (Souami and Verdeil 2006). Of course, the global crisis partially stopped the spread of the model (Bloch 2010; Barthel 2010), and true duplicates are rare and often affected by redimensionings and delays (sometimes even cancellations) which deeply altered initial ideas: Tunis Sport-City, by Bukhatir Group, modeled on Dubai Sport-City, and Cairo Festival-City, modeled on Dubai's Festival-City (Barthel 2010). Things are more complex in Mediterranean cities, as studies on Beirut's Haret Hreik (Fawaz and Krijnen 2010) and Algiers (Zitoun 2010) illustrated.

But the fact remains that the conjunction of waterfront renewal and of a Dubai-style urbanism poses a strong challenge to the Mediterranean urban form. Even if target clients in the Mediterranean do not wish to live in towers, what is most potentially damaging for Mediterranean urbanity is surely the scale of the projects and the weak relationship between such conceptions of architecture and urbanism and the existing historical urban landscape. Ornamentalism can't be a satisfactory substitute. Many Mediterranean metropolises have also been affected recently by the new paradigm of shopping-mall commerce. In Istanbul, every new development has been accompanied by the opening of huge commercial malls, whose relationship to Mediterranean urbanity is also very weak (Takatli and Boyaci 1999). With this privatization of retail space — private malls being substitutes for streets and squares — there is a risk of loss of public space and of a reinforcement of tendencies toward social fragmentation. Such a risk is also present in many other trends in Mediterranean urbanism.

Social Challenges to Mediterranean Urbanity

The impact of globalization on Mediterranean cities is of course not limited to transformations in the morphology of the built environment. It has strong effects on the population and challenges existing social and governance schemes (Ribas-Mateos 2005). As far as cities are concerned, however, each of the new forms that globalization has promoted has also brought new social configurations that constitute a challenge to what was perceived as a kind of Mediterranean model of social coexistence. Of course this model is largely mythical, and patterns of segregation and planning practices aimed at separation have always existed, but the simple fact that contemporary challenges do affect the idea of this coexistence is already very telling. Research has now illustrated how the development of gated communities, of four- and five-star hotel enclaves, of office towers and condos, is a threat to coexistence, and often happens at the expense of preexisting more or less formalized urban structures whose inhabitants are subject to eviction. In Istanbul, such global urban forms have contributed to the expulsion of urban dwellers of the popular classes toward more distant peripheries and sometimes even more precarious living conditions (Keyder 2005). The same has happened, with diverse intensities, in many Mediterranean cities. Contested claims on land by international firms, or firms connected to the international sphere, and local inhabitants have become a common feature of urban conflict (Keivani and Mattingly 2007).

This logic is also true for downtowns, as studies about the Solidere operation in Beirut have documented. Neoliberal downtowns are also, beyond the glitter of their rebirth, a threat to Mediterranean urbanity and to its essence related to a shared urban space (Summer 2006). Globalization has brought heavy fragmenting dynamics into Mediterranean cities, and trends toward social and spatial exclusion. Even the Barcelona model has been denounced for such devastating side effects (Capel 2005, Borja 2009). Gentrification, eviction, and greater segregation are cited as common characteristics in urban renovation processes, and for such reasons, the Barcelona model has been called an impostor more than once (Delgado 2007). In extreme cases — the Mediterranean region is unfortunately rich in such configurations — recent years have also seen reinforcement of the prevalence of violent urban frontiers, giving credence to the condemnation of splintering trends in urbanism (Graham and Marvin 2001) or to fears of a new urban great divide (Elsheshtawy 2011). Landscapes marked by fences are more common (Gold and Revill 2000), and many cities of the Mediterranean are more or less literally living under siege (Graham 2010) or are divided by communal barriers (Silver 2010). In a city like Jerusalem, one of the most extreme examples of loss of Mediterranean urbanity, the planning of segregation, annexation, and eviction at the scale of the metropolitan region has been denounced by many activists and researchers (Yiftachel 1997), as well as the effects of the new wall on what was left of shared urbanity (Chiodelli 2012). Many cities of the region are affected by a tendency toward urban polarization. But even in less extreme cases, gentrification seems to be one of the most common results of recent urban policies, with its share of evictions and social homogenization. Research about Mediterranean cities has, however, also highlighted the existence of innovative forms of protest that relate to the civic dynamism of the Mediterranean. From the Roma neighborhood of Sulukulu in Istanbul (Uysal 2012) to different forms of protest against megaprojects in Arab cities (Barthel 2010, Navez-Bouchanine 2012) or gentrification in downtown Naples and Barcelona, mobilization in the Mediterranean has followed a path that, beyond the differences between those contexts, only the strength of urbanity make possible.

Urban growth and globalization also have represented a challenge to urban and metropolitan governance in Mediterranean cities. Research has illustrated how municipal patronage and urban growth by speculation were intimately related. Naples and Marseilles are the most studied examples (Mattina 2007, Morel 1999), but such urban regimes are found in many other cities of the region. With urban growth, the relationship between inhabitants and the sphere of governance has changed in both nature and scale. What research has documented for the last few decades is a renewal in the relationship between local party politics, urban society, and space, the urban integration of the old and new peripheries having happened through networks of patronage. This process is not of course an exclusively Mediterranean characteristic: community and factional patronage is also at the root of American local democracy (Erie 1990). In Mediterranean cities since the Middle Ages, local governance was conducted through patronage relationships between urban factions and notables. In more recent times, such a pact knew many variations, but always with the result of confirming the importance of municipal patronage, as studies about Palermo (Maccaglia 2009) and Naples have illustrated. Big cities of the regions seem to be the theater for the development of new trends in political patronage in which Islamic conservatism plays a key role, from Cairo or the Greater Istanbul municipality and local municipal districts in the Turkish metropolis (Heper 1989) to the case of Beirut (Harb 2010). The task is to understand whether such trends illustrate a risk in the rise of a kind of fundamentalist city (Alsayyad and Massoumi 2011) or just represent new forms of a traditional relationship between governance and society in the Mediterranean.

Conclusion

In the age of globalization, and specifically the present global crisis, metropolises of the Mediterranean are the object of various influxes in urban change that challenge the very urbanity that they materialized. Yet paradoxically, we are also witnessing a kind of Mediterranean revival, with Mediterraneanism used as a branding tool by cities to reinforce their images on the global scene. The example of Marseilles, with the Mediterraneanization of cultural projects for the city, has been extensively studied (Bullen 2012). Mediterraneanism is also used as a tool of place marketing outside of the Mediterranean region (in the Gulf, for example) as a sign of its vitality. However, the complex extension of the Mediterranean place marketing has reached the limits of the top-down vision of identity making within the frameworks of networked branding (Muniz Martinez 2012). They invite the insertion of judgments about what is happening in the Mediterranean in the context of tensions between global influxes and local practices or accommodations — the only real stake for researchers being that of unpacking discourses and shedding light on actual transformations, their causes, and their consequences.

If studies on Mediterranean cities do make the region a laboratory for understanding the impact of new trends on old cities, there is also the question whether the Mediterranean of today has retained something of its historically proven capacity to be innovative in urbanity. Is the sustainable city of tomorrow going to be invented in the Mediterranean (McDonogh 2011)? Will Mediterranean urbanity and the strength of the civic sphere help counter trends toward segregation? In his 2010 essay on what makes great city, Savitch listed currency, cosmopolitanism, concentration, and charisma as the four most necessary features (Savitch 2010). Currency might be lacking in present Mediterranean metropolises; cosmopolitanism might be more past than present; concentration might be challenged by urban sprawl; and charisma might be reduced to advertising flyers for tourists. But there are other signs, less tangible maybe, which could invite one to still have faith in the strength of Mediterranean urbanity. Let me cite just one, totally anecdotal, but so telling. The Warner Village in the surroundings of Rome is a totally fake cityscape built along the motorway to the airport, the result of the conjunction of international capital, local speculation, and the consequences on urban leisure of the closure of downtown to cars for inhabitants of the periphery. On the fake Mediterranean piazza at the center of the resort, however, urban life is as real as on Campo de' Fiori, a sign that people can carry urbanity and its values with them.

References:

Abu-Lughod, Janet. 2004. "Cairo: Too Many People, Not Enough Land, Too Few Resources." In *Word Cities Beyond the West,* edited by Joseph Gugler. Cambridge: Cambridge University Press. 119–150.

Albera, Dionigi. 2006. "Anthropology of the Mediterranean: Between Crisis and Renewal." *History and Anthropology* 17-2: 109–133.

Albera, Dionigi, and Mohammed Tozy. 2005. *La Méditerranée des anthropologues: fractures, filiations, continuités.* Paris: Maisonneuve et Larose. 385.

Alsayyad, Nezar, and Mejgan Massoumi, eds. 2011. *The Fundamentalist City? Religiosity and the Remaking of Urban Space.* London: Routledge. 313.

Balbo, Marcello, ed. 2012. *The Medina: Restoration and Conservation of Historic Islamic Cities.* London: Tauris. 272.

Barthel, Pierre-Arnaud. 2010. "Arab Mega-Projects Between the Dubai-Effect, Global Crisis, Social Mobilization, and a Sustainable Shift." *Built Environment* 36-2: 133–145.

Barthel, Pierre-Arnaud. 2006. *Tunis en projet(s): la fabrique d'une métropole au bord de l'eau.* Rennes: PUR. 208.

Barthel, Pierre-Arnaud. 2008. "Faire du 'grand-projet' au Maghreb: l'exemple des fronts d'eau (Casablanca et Tunis). *Géocarrefour* 83-1: 25–34.

Bloch, Robin. 2010. "Dubai's Long Goodbye. *International Journal of Urban and Regional Research* 34-4: 943–951.

Bocquet, Denis, and Filippo De Pieri. 2005. "Tra Regola e Trasgressione: Percorsi di Ricerca. *Storia Urbana.* 1–10.

Bocquet, Denis, Filippo De Pieri, and Silvia Infusino. 2006. "Le trasformazioni urbane di Berlino e Barcellona (1970–2000). In Francesca Filippi, Luca Gibello, and Manfredo Robilant, eds. *1970–2000: Episodi e Temi di Storia dell'Architettura.* Turin: Celid-Politecnico di Torino. 115–124.

Borja, Jordi. 2009. *Luces y Sombras del Urbanismo de Barcelona.* Barcelona: UOC. 306.

Boumaza, Nadir, ed. 2006. *Villes réelles, villes projetées: fabrication de la ville au Maghreb.* Paris: Maisonneuve et Larose. 691.

Brenner, Neil. 1997. "Global, Fragmented, Hierarchical: Henri Lefebvre's Geographies of Globalization." *Public Culture* 10: 135–167.

Bullen, Claire. 2012. "Marseille, ville méditerranéennes? Des enjeux d'espace, d'échelle et d'identité dans une ville en transformation." *Rives méditerranéennes* 42: 157–171.

G. Cakir, C. Un, E.Z. Baskent, S. Kose, F. Sivrikaya, and S. Keles. 2008. "Evaluating Urbanization, Fragmentation, and Land Use/Cover Change Pattern in Istanbul City, Turkey, from 1971 to 2002." 19: 663–675.

Capel, Horacio. 2005. . Barcelona: Serbal. 119.

Carrière, Jean-Paul. 2003. . Tours: Presses Universitaires. 135.

Cattedra, Raffaele. 2011. "Projet urbain et interface ville-port en Méditerranée: Perspectives pour une recherche comparative." *Rives Méditerranéennes* 30-2: 81–102.

Cellamare, Carlo. 2010. "Politiche e processi dell'abitare nella città abusiva/informale romana." 97-98: 145–168.

Chiodelli, Francesco. 2012. "Re-shaping Jerusalem: The Transformation of Jerusalem's Metropolitan Area by the Israeli Barrier." *Cities.*

Chorianopoulos, I., et al. 2010. "Planning, Competitiveness, and Sprawl in the Mediterranean City: The Case of Athens." *Cities* 27-4: 428–259.

Côte, Marc, and Michèle Joannon. 1999. "La littoralisation en Méditerranée." *Méditerranée* 91: 112–116.

Courtot, Roland. 2001. "Méditerranée et les villes de la Méditerranée." *Méditerranée* 97: 33–38.

Delgado, Manuel. 2007. *La ciudad mentirosa: fraude e miseria del 'modelo Barcelona.* Barcelona: Catarata. 242.

Denis, Eric. 2006. "From the Walled City to the Walled Community: Spectres of Risk, Enclaves of Affluence in Neo-liberal Cairo." In P. Amar and D. Singerman, eds. *Cosmopolitan Cairo.* Cairo: AUC Press. 41–71.

Deprest, Florence. 2002. "L'invention géographique de la Méditerranée: éléments de réflexion." *L'espace géographique* 31: 73–92.

De Pieri, Filippo. 2010. "Searching for Memories in the Suburbs of Rome." *Modern Italy* 15-3: 371–379.

De Rossi, A., ed. 1999. *Sprawlscape: il paesaggio come redenzione.* Turin: UTET.

Destro, Nicola. 2010. "Perchè i geografi non si occupano di abusivismo edilizio? Il difficile rapporto tra e costruire illegale in Italia." Università degli Studi di Padova, *Quaderni del Dottorato della Scuola Superiore di Studi Storici, Geografici e Antropoligici.* 11.

Di Mario, Marco. 2011. *Abusivismo e recupero urbanistico nel PRG di Roma Capitale.* Masters thesis, LUISS. 93.

Dura-Guimera, Antoni. 2003. "Population Deconcentration and Social Restructuring in Barcelona, a European Mediterranean City." *Cities* 20-6: 387–394.

Eade, John, and Christopher Mele, eds. 2011. *Understanding the City: Contemporary and Future Perspectives.* London: Wiley. 448.

Elsheshtawy, Yasser, ed. 2011. *The Evolving Arab City: Tradition, Modernity, and Urban Development.* London, Routledge. 314.

Erie, Steven. 1990. *Rainbow's End: Irish Americans and the Dilemmas of Urban Machines (1840–1985).* Berkeley: University of California Press. 359.

Esen, Orhan, and Stephan Lang, eds. 2007. *Self-Service City: Istanbul.* Berlin: B-Books. 420.

Fawaz, Mona. 2005. "La costruzione di un sobborgo informale: imprenditori e stato a Hayy el Sellom, Beirut, 1950–2000." 28-3: 123–138.

Fawaz, Mona, and Marieke Krijnen. 2010. "Exception as the Rule: High-End Developments in Neo-Liberal Beirut." *Built Environment* 36-4: 245–259.

Ferrier, Jean-Paul. 1993. "La métropole méditerranéenne: modèle de la métropole de la modernité?" *Méditerranée* 1-2: 91–94.

Gold, John Robert, and George Revill, eds. 2000. *Landscapes of Defence.* London: Pearson. 297.

Graham, Stephen. 2010. *Cities under Siege: The New Military Urbanism.* London: Verso. 432.

Graham, Stephen, and Steven Marvin. 2001. *Splintering Urbanism: Networked Infrastructures, Technological Mobilities, and the Urban Condition.* London: Routledge.

Gülöksüz, Elwan. 2002. "Negotiation of Property Rights in Urban Land Istanbul." *International Journal of Urban and Regional Research* 26-2: 462–476.

Gupta, Anita, and James Ferguson. 1992. "Beyond 'Culture': Space, Identity, and the Politics of Difference." *Cultural Anthropology* 1-7: 6–23.

Harb, Mona. 2010. *Le Hezbollah à Beyrouth (1985–2005). De la banlieue à la ville.* Paris: Karthala. 300.

Harvey, David. 2006. *Spaces of Global Capitalism: Towards a Theory of Uneven Geographical Development.* London: Verso. 155,

Heper, Metin, ed. 1989. *Local Government in Turkey: Governing Greater Istanbul.* London: Routledge. 103.

Herzfeld, Michael. 2005. "Practical Mediterraneanisms: Excuses for Everything, from Epistemology to Eating." In W.V. Harris, ed., *Rethinking the Mediterranean.* Oxford: OUP. 414.

Horden, Peregrine. 2005. "Mediterranean Excuses: Historical Writing on the Mediterranean since Braudel." *History and Anthropology* 1-16, 25–30.

İçduygu, Ahmet. 2004. "From Nation-Building to Globalization: An Account of the Past and Present in Recent Urban Studies in Turkey." *International Journal of Urban and Regional Research* 28-4: 941–951.

Ilbert, Robert, Jean-Charles Depaule, and Claude Nicolet, eds. 2000. *Mégapoles méditerranéennes: géographie urbaine rétrospective.* Paris: Maisonneuve et Larose. 1071.

Kassab, S. 1997. "On Two Conceptions of Globalization: The Debate around the Reconstruction of Beirut." In A. Oncu and P. Weyland, eds., *Space, Culture, and Power: New Identities in Globalizing Cities.* London and New Jersey: Zed Books. 42–55.

Keivani, Ramin, and Michael Mattingly. 2007. "The Interface of Globalization and Peripheral Land in the Cities of the South." *International Journal of Urban and Regional Research* 31-2: 459–474.

Keyder, Caglar. 2005. "Globalization and Social Exclusion in Istanbul." *International Journal of Urban and Regional Research* 29-1: 125–134.

Lafi, Nora, ed. 2005. *Municipalités méditerranéennes: les réformes urbaines ottomanes au miroir d'une histoire comparée.* Berlin: Schwarz. 305.

Leontidou, Lila. 1990. *The Mediterranean City in Transition: Social Change and Urban Development.* Cambridge: Cambridge University Press. 296.

Lorrain, Dominique, ed. 2011. *Métropoles XXL en pays émergents.* Paris: Presses de Sciences Po. 410.

Maccaglia, Fabrizio. 2009. *Palerme, illégalismes et gouvernement urbain d'exception.* Lyon: ENS. 260.

Mallette, Karla. 2010. *European Modernity and the Arab Mediterranean: Toward a New Philology and a Counter-Orientalism*. Philadelphia: University of Pennsylvania Press. 311.

Marshall, Tim. 2004. *Transforming Barcelona: The Renewal of a European Metropolis*. London: Routledge. 288.

Mattina, Cesare. 2007. "Changes in Clientelism and Urban Government: A Comparative Case Study of Naples and Marseilles." *International Journal of Urban and Regional Research* 31-1: 73–90.

McDonogh, Gary. 2011. "Learning from Barcelona: Discourse, Power, and Practice in the Sustainable City." *City & Society* 23-2: 135–153.

Monclus, F.J. 1998. *La Ciudad Dispersa*. Barcelona: CCCB.

Morel, Bernard. *Marseille, naissance d'une métropole*. Paris: L'Harmattan. 221.

M. Munafò, C. Norero, A. Sabbi, and L. Salvati. 2010. "Soil Consumption in the Growing City: A Survey in Rome." 126: 153–161.

Muniz Martinez, Norberto. 2012. "City Marketing and Place Branding: A Critical Review of Practice and Academic Research." *Journal of Town and City Management* 2-4: 369–394.

Munoz, Francesc. 2003. "Lock Living: Urban Sprawl in Mediterranean Cities." *Cities* 20-6: 381–385.

Munoz, Francesc. 2008. *Urbanalizacion*. Barcelona: Gili. 216.

Navez-Bouchanine, Françoise, ed. 2012. *Les effets sociaux des politiques urbaines*. Paris: Karthala. 349.

Pérouse, Jean-François. 2000. *La mégapole d'Istanbul (1960–2000): Guide bibliographique*. Istanbul: IFEA. 19.

Pérouse, Jean-François. 2004. "Les tribulations du terme (1947–2004): une lente perte de substance. Pour une clarification terminologique." *European Journal of Turkish Studies* 1.

Ribas-Mateos, Natalia. 2005. *The Mediterranean in the Age of Globalization: Migration, Welfare, and Borders*. New Brunswick, N.J.: Transaction. 389.

Rodrigues-Malta, R. 2004. "Une vitrine métropolitaine sur les quais. Villes portuaires au sud de l'Europe," 97: 93-101.

Salvaggiulio, Giuseppe, Antonio Massari, Ferruccio Sansa, Marco Preve, and Andrea Garibaldi. 2010. *La colata: Il partito del cemento che sta cancellando l'Italia e il suo futuro*. Rome: Chiarelettere. 540.

Salvati, Luca, et al. 2012. "To Grow or to Sprawl? Land Cover Relationships in a Mediterranean City Region and Implications for Land-Use Management." *Cities*.

Sant Cassia, Paul, and Isabel Schäfer. 2005. "Mediterranean Conundrums: Pluridisciplinary Perspectives for Research in the Social Sciences." *History and Anthropology* 16-1: 1–23.

Savitch, H.V. 2010. "What Makes a Great City Great? An American Perspective." *Cities* 27-1: 42–49.

Sema Kubat, Ayse. 2001. "Istanbul: A Configurational Model for a Metropolis." *Proceedings of the Third International Space Syntax Symposium*, Atlanta, paper no. 62, 7.

Silver, Hilary. 2010. "Divided Cities in the Middle East." *City & Community* 9-4: 345–357.

Souami, Taoufik, and Eric Verdeil. 2006. Economica, Anthropos, collection "Villes." 230.

Stanley, Bruce. 2003. "Going Global: Wannabe World Cities in the Middle East." In Wilma Dunaway, ed., *Emerging Issues in the Twenty-first-Century World System*. Westport: Greenwood. 151–170; 288.

Summer, Doris. 2006. "The Neoliberalization of Urban Space." *Villes et Territoires du Moyen-Orient* 2: 9.

Terzi, F., and F. Bolen. 2009. "Urban Sprawl Measurement of Istanbul." *European Planning Studies* 17: 1559–1570.

Tokatli, Nebahat, and Yonka Boyaci. 1999, "The Changing Morphology of Commercial Activity in Istanbul." 16-3: 181–193.

Uysal, Ülke Evrim. 2012. "An Urban Social Movement Challenging Social Regeneration: The Case of Sulukulu, Istanbul." *Cities* 29-1: 12–22.

Verdeil, Eric. 2010. *Beyrouth et ses urbanistes: une ville en plans (1946–1975)*, Beyrouth, IFPO. 397.

Weber, C., and A. Puissant. 2003. "Urbanisation Pressure and Modeling of Urban Growth: Example of the Tunis Metropolitan Area." 86: 341–352.

Yiftachel, Oren. 1997. "Israel: Metropolitan Integration or 'Fractured Regions'? An Alternative Perspective." 14-6: 371–380.

Zanfi, Federico. 2008. . Milan: Mondadori. 287.

Zitoun, Madani Safar. 2010. "The Development of the Bay of Algiers: Rethinking the City through Contemporary Paradigms." *Built Environment* 36-2: 206–215.

Middle Sea City
The Med Net Atlas Project
Mosè Ricci

Context

Let's think of the Mediterranean as a city, in the physical sense of the term, even though obviously not as a traditional urban figure. Not a void filled with water between continents, but a city with an imposing central landscape. A real borderless city organized around its empty center, as is already the case elsewhere. Tokyo, for example, rotates like a vortex around the Imperial Gardens, while Washington is designed along the borders of the esplanade, and Manhattan encompasses Central Park. Let's try and think of it as Plato did in Phaedo: "We are all like frogs around a drinking pond."[1] Of course the spatial dimensions are another matter, but they are not the only things that count. The attraction capacity of social, touristic, and residential amenities, the intensity of internal relations (both material and non), the population identifying itself and recognizing the landscape as a single anthropological and cultural mark, but also acknowledging the conflicts and impetuosity of change — all of this generates the internal cohesion toward a single living environment that we all consciously call the Mediterranean.

In short, if through an abstraction we try to think of it as a city — not only in the sense given by Baumann[2] or Ilardi,[3] but above all as a living space with its own particular settlement and life characteristics — the Mediterranean is the only occidental city in continuous growth.

In this Middle Sea City, nothing works well. In contrast to Northern Europe, administrative efficiency does not exist. The possibility of managing change processes or even carrying out the normal procedures of urban life is often conditioned by the ability to maintain a system of interpersonal relations. Behavior often prevails over rules, and regulations establish new automatisms in the inhabitants' lifestyles. The decay in the city is physiological. It leaves a sense of the unfinished in the urban spaces that clashes with the magnificence of the landscape and augments its charm. Yet the attractiveness of the Middle Sea City is irresistible. Studying the data provided by Espon or the European Environment Agency (EEA) on migration in the last twenty years, one can observe growth in both the population and number of residences on the Mediterranean coastline greater than that in the rest of Europe. Over the past ten years, the population of the twenty-one countries bordering the Mediterranean Sea has undergone a rapid increase due to both

1   Plato, *Phaedo*, *Plato in Twelve Volumes*, vol. 1, translated by Harold North Fowler; introduction by W.R.M. Lamb (Cambridge, MA:Harvard University Press, 1971; London: William Heinemann Ltd., 1966).

2   See Zygmund Bauman, *Liquid Modernity* (Cambridge: Polity Press, 2000).

3   See Massimo Ilardi and Alessandra Castellani, *La Città senza Luoghi* (Rome: Costa and Nolan, 1990).

Mosè Ricci is a Full Professor of Urbanism at the School of Architecture of the University of Genoa and Emeritus of Italian Art and Culture. He is a member of the scientific committee and was curator of the urbanism and landscape section *Recycle, Strategies for Architecture, Cities and Planet, International Exhibition MAXXI* (2010–12). He has also been a member of the Italian Society of Urban Planners Steering Committee (2007–11), the Mies Foundation Mediterranean Program Board (Barcelona, 2010–), and the Scientific Board of the International Doctorate Villard de Honnecourt (2004–).

Academic appointments include Visiting Professor of Sustainable Urbanism at Technische Universitat of Munich (2008–09) and Universitad Moderna de Lisboa (2006–07). In 2011, he was ranked among the top-100 world educators by the Cambridge Institute. In 2003, he was appointed Emeritus of Italian Art and Culture with a Silver Medal of the Republic.

From 1996 to1997, he was a Fulbright Recipient and Visiting Scholar at the Harvard University Graduate School of Design.

Ricci's projects with the firm RICCISPAINI have received several prizes in international competitions and have been exhibited in the Venice Biennale in 1996 and again in 2012. He has edited the series *BABEL* (2000–12) and authored several books including *New Paradigms* (2012), *UniverCity* (2010), *iSpace* (2008), and *RISCHIOPAESAGGIO* (2003).

tourist and migratory flows. The population of those countries is expected to grow to over 31 million people by 2025; more than one-third of the increase will occur in coastal areas.[4] Since 2000, along the northern arc of the Mediterranean Basin, a positive demographic trend, related to North-South and South-North migrations, is recorded.[5] The high growth in the coastal urban regions (3.10 percent in the period 1990–2006)[6] confirms that trend.

We are dealing in most cases with population moving from Central European areas or immigrants from Middle Eastern and African countries, although these immigrants, after a temporary stay, tend to continue moving toward the big cities of Northern Europe or the United States. Therefore it is those coming from the northern metropolitan areas, from the European "never-ending city"[7], who transfer to the coasts of the Mediterranean, such as the Ligurian coast of Italy, where everything works worse but costs less, making it seem for many a better place to live. This new inhabiting behavior that stably occupies the existing tourist residences or builds new ones is called *Rapallizzation* (from the city of Rapallo near Genoa).[8] The same thing happened in Majorca, Spain, where we can observe at least three German influxes that have completely changed the life and landscape of the island.[9]

This phenomenon is even more striking on the Ionian coast of Turkey, where recent urbanization is blotting out natural characteristics.[10] It is sufficient to go to Kuşadasi or Bodrum to understand what is happening; official data attest to the destruction of the natural landscape of the Greek coast and the raging transformation into a continuous city. The Mediterranean is therefore an immense aquatic space around which a complex settlement system is disposing itself. It has diverse intensities of internal relations, and the landscape represents the main urban catalyzer.

If this is a city, we must begin to deal with it through disciplinary research. What is happening? Why are people moving to live in the Mediterranean? How is life there lived? What are the values that we cannot renounce and

that must be conserved? What are the risks of this growth for society and landscape? Which are the areas that can or must be transformed? Which are the economic motors of its development? What are the qualities that make it irresistible to live there? How can we valorize this city in change? What are the future scenarios?

These questions produce the necessity to put together a map, or an atlas, of the most significant research projects regarding urbanism and landscape in the Mediterranean, to see if it is possible to find a common understanding for preserving and transforming this Middle Sea City. For this reason, with the aim of interpreting changes in the most rapidly growing city of the European area, with Manuel Gausa and other young scholars we created the Med Net Atlas project laboratory in the School of Architecture at the University of Genoa. We are working with a double scientific methodology, as if using a microscope to understand the present and a computer to simulate the future. We work in depth by using as case studies the areas that emerge from existing scientific investigations, to then recompose a sort of contemporary collage with the different urban figures that the research identifies. Moreover, we are discovering possible analogies, inventing (in both the etymological sense of recovering and the modern sense of discovering) exchanges and simulating possible futures. In short, we are using the project as an interpretive device, and also a tool to further understanding.

Visions

The originality of this research lies in the gaze and in the point of view. The figure of the Mediterranean as a possible form of the contemporary city is not frequently used in scientific studies. The Mediterranean is hardly ever described, or designed, as a single urban body. But at least two past interesting and "extreme" visions, two ways of interpreting the Mediterranean as a city, can be used as an introduction to the method and the sense of the scientific research developed by Med Net. One is a project and one is a text.

The first experience worth remembering is the visionary project of Atlantropa, possibly the only idea of the twentieth century that sees the Mediterranean as a landscape (or an infrastructure?) to be redesigned and made inhabitable. Atlantropa was the name of the immense territorial plan conceived in the 1920s by the German architect Herman Sörgel for the colonization of the Mediterranean and

4   UNEP/MAP/Blue Plan: *Demography in the Mediterranean Region: Situation and Projections*, UNEP/MAP, Sophia Antipolis, 2004.

5   Considerations based on the ESPON DEMIFER, *Demographic and Migratory Flows Affecting European Regions and Cities*, Applied Research Project, 3 January 2013.

6   European Environment Agency 2007, final report, *Urban Morphological Zones* version F2v0, *Definition and Procedural Steps*. Prepared by Alejandro Simon, Jaume Fons, and Roger Milego, 28 December 2010, project manager Birgit Georgi, data elaborated by Stefania Staniscia (Trento University).

7   The "Europe by night" satellite image reveals the new form of the European landscape, showing a continuous urban cloud that fills the nightscape. A myriad of sources of light are clustered around large infrastructural lines, which abate only when they meet the mountains and the sea. Historic centers, industrial areas, arterial roads, suburbs: everything becomes homologous. Over the past twenty years in Europe, urban lifestyles have changed radically, creating a different territorial form, a new landscape. The image of Europe offered by traditional geographic maps (those shown in weather forecasts, political programs, and territorial projects), where cities are represented as dots or concentric circles, separated one from the other and each gathered around its nucleus, is outdated and does not match reality. This new condition of urban settlements in Europe has the shape of a city with no borders, able to continue to invade any possible territory — infinite, "never-ending".

8   Rapallo is a small Italian town facing the sea on the east coast of Genoa in the Liguria region. Here the process of occupation of the former tourist houses by inhabitants moving from Northern European cities is particularly relevant, now representing 60 percent of the urban population. *Rapallizzazione* is the word that describes this phenomenon of influx.

the African continent. (See Peter Christensen's essay in this volume for a detailed account.) The key figure of this project is represented by a series of dams for the production of hydro-electric energy, to be realized with the closure of the Strait of Gibraltar. This system, which would have lowered the sea level by around 200 meters, would have dried up the lower sea-beds, generating terrain for urban and agricultural use, and created new isthmuses between the continents for the construction of vehicular connections between Europe and Africa. The enormous production of electric energy would have guaranteed industrial development. The availability of vast new agricultural terrain would have included a Sahara irrigated with the water of three new artificial lakes in Africa. The construction work of Atlantropa would have been imposing and would have lasted more than a century, guaranteeing jobs and profit even for the lowest classes. The publication and diffusion of the material regarding this project was very detailed from a technical point of view. A 300-meter tower, designed by Peter Behrens, was to have been realized at Gibraltar. There were even considerations of the environmental impact of the project and of the benefits obtainable through climate change. The project was well regarded through the 1920s and 1930s, and even through the 1940s and 1950s, until the death of Sörgel.[11]

Despite the efforts of the German architect and his supporters, the visionary program of Atlantropa was never really taken into consideration by the political authorities due to its gigantism and Eurocentric stance. The visionary power of this project has, however, left many traces in the film industry and virtual reality. From *Star Trek: The Motion Picture* (1979) to the videogame *Railroad Tycoon II: The Next Millennium* (1999), and in between through tales such as *Under the Yoke* by S. M. Stirling (1989) or in *The Man in the High Castle* by Philip Dick (1962), the Mediterranean is seen as either closed by dams at the Strait of Gibraltar or dried up. In these cases, the idea of Atlantropa is revived through imagination, transforming the Mediterranean via an extraordinary territorial device.

The second and most recent vision regards the description of urban phenomena initiated through the observation of what is happening in the Mediterranean islands, taken as samples of the Western contemporary city under stress. This is the perspective of *Islands* by Stefania Staniscia.[12] The author deals with "islandness," a word that does not exist in the English language — or rather, did not exist. Staniscia invented it some years ago when

writing her doctoral dissertation; the title of her research became *Islands* when published. It is a word that gathers meaning as one reads the text and is led to think about transformation phenomena in precisely defined landscapes where these are accentuated and can be seen more clearly. Isolation is the most favorable condition to identify and quantify change.

Staniscia uses "islandness" — the characteristics and importance of being an island — as a device capable of allowing us to understand the profound nature of the urban mutations that are affecting the European territory. She explains, with the help of three organic metaphors, how islands can be critical points of control for the European city, useful to evaluate the risks of change and anticipate the future.

The first metaphor is the fragment. *Frammento* in Italian means a small piece, detached by rupture from a given body. It expresses hope rather than the sense of being one bit from among a multitude of broken things. In this conception, the body of the city of the future could be broken if things don't change and disorder is accepted and the future unmediated. I also believe in the city of the future as the place where the fragments of something broken from the beginning will recompose themselves.[13] We can read each of the three islands of the Mediterranean that Staniscia describes as fragments of Europe. Each of these both reveals a catastrophe and brings hope.

The second metaphor is that of the sample. The islands are like samples of a biochemical analysis. The same processes of mutation that are changing the nature and form of the urban settlements on the continent are manifested. That is, the growth of accessibility and the development of transport and communication networks are causing an unexpected acceleration in the mutation process of the urban scene. The new dimensions of physical, economic, and social landscapes generate a crisis regarding the concept of the territory as a measurable space and also the vision of landscape as a framework or entity. Cities tend to lose a precise physical connotation and increasingly become fields of relations. There arises a relative indifference toward the territory with respect to moving and communicating, producing a growing need to preserve landscapes in which to recognize and identify oneself. These are the questions that decisively change the way of thinking about the future and its forms. They are driven by transformations that can be found both in the islands and on the mainland, though in the islands it is different: all of the tensions are heightened

9   Stefania Staniscia, *Islands: Hot Spots of Change* (Barcelona-Trento: List Lab, 2011).

10   Moira Valeri (Department Faculty of Engineering and Architecture, Yeditepe University, Istanbul, Turkey) International Villard de Honnecourt PhD Thesis: "*Low Coast. The inter-city bus network in the south west Turkish coast as a device of urban transformation*", 2011.

11   Hanns Günther [Walter de Haas], *In hundert Jahren* (Stuttgart: Kosmos, 1931); "Atlantropa: A Plan to Dam the Mediterranean Sea," 16 March 2005. Archive. Xefer. Retrieved 4 August 2007; "Atlantropa," Cabinet Magazine, issue 10, Spring 2003.. Retrieved 4 August 2007.

12   Staniscia, *Islands*.

13   Aldo Rossi, "Frammenti," in *Architetture 1959–1987*, ed. Alberto Ferlenga (Milan: Electa, 1987). Quote translated from Italian for this essay by Mathilde Marengo.

by anthropic pressure and delimited by the sea, and we can measure the change inside a defined border.

The third metaphor is the Darwinian one of the factory of the future. The three islands are incubators of the European city's future. In each of these it is possible to recognize the various means that determine the evolution of urban structure. Staniscia identifies the three principle forces behind this change, as demonstrated on an island: touristic pressure (Majorca), abandonment (Susak), and ethnic conflict (Lampedusa). (See Staniscia's essay in this volume for a more detailed presentation of these concepts.)

We are dealing with a narrative approach to a reading of territorial processes that is geographic, landscape, and socially based. The islands in Staniscia's tale provide a fantastic pretext for speaking about ourselves, our way of living, and how we tend to destroy primary landscape resources on which we have founded the paradigms of urban, economic, and social development. No other scholar of inhabited spaces has used a similar methodology. In Staniscia's book, as in the *Atlas of Remote Islands* by Judith Schalansky,[14] we travel to both familiar and exotic places with a strong narrative structure that describes a precise map of the aporias and actual crises of Western cities. Finally, it is a book that tells us about the Mediterranean. Staniscia describes an eclectic atlas of the Middle Sea drawn through the forms of processes that give a sense to the water, as in the Platonic image of the pond and the frogs — an immense central public space of the continuous city that overlooks it. As in the project by Sörgel, in Staniscia's insular atlas the Mediterranean is the place where landscape and the intensity of relations induces development and produces a city, one where the sea is the principal infrastructure and personal relations establish the rules of social cohabitation. A city where many move to live is the object of our research campaign.

Local research and projects are the most important interpreting tools of the Med Net Atlas initiative. We began by studying the changing processes in the European territory, particularly along the Italian coastline in that part of the linear urban settlement that identifies the western seafront of the Liguria region.[15]

Devices

In Europe, the change in form that urban settlements have undergone in recent years, due to their increased density and expansion, similar to the experience of the industrial city in past centuries, marks a profound transformation in the way one thinks about the territory, the landscape, and the city. In Italy, cities have exploded. Large-scale mobility infrastructures are catalyzing these processes. It is increasingly evident that new economies are enlivened by means of connection and exchange. The introduction of infrastructural corridors in the European territories has modified the appeal of urban areas and introduced competition for previously untapped resources. The growth in mobility and the development of transport and communication networks is generating a sudden acceleration in the mutation processes of the urban scene. The new dimensions of physical, economic, and social landscapes call into question the concept of territory as a measurable space and of landscape as a frame or entity. Cities tend to lose a precise physical connotation, increasingly becoming fields of relations. Perhaps, as the geographer Franco Farinelli suggests,[15] we no longer need territories in which to move and communicate, but the necessity of landscapes and spaces in which to live and identify ourselves has become more evident.

All of this decisively changes how we think about the future and its forms. The new speed of change underscores the need to reconsider the use and quality of both urban and nonurban spaces. New regimes linked to economic, occupational, and social transformations have induced new ways of using the territory, as the expression of different populations using the instruments and resources at their disposal. One can read the consequences of mobility in the territory, densely inhabited and traversed, assuming the form of an "archipelago" of places and connections that reveal a need of being stable rather than nomadic. The bond to the place of residence prevails. Adjacency and vicinity are not alternatives. The direct relation between places and activities is no longer a necessary condition. Measuring physical distances makes less and less sense. We live in contexts in which one more or less manages to determine a personal lifestyle, and time prevails on space. The "never-ending city" that designs the way one lives in the European Mediterranean area in the new millennium is the result of a myriad of autonomous decisions that condition the shape and structure of everything. A continuous urban landscape that aggregates in new metropolitan formations or in identity constellations is capable of competing in the global market. Cities that were once dominant now see their importance reduced, and others gain new centrality and enhanced

14   Judith Schalansky, *Atlas of Remote Islands* (London: Penguin, 2010).

15   Franco Farinelli, *L'invenzione della Terra* (Palermo: Sellerio, 2007).

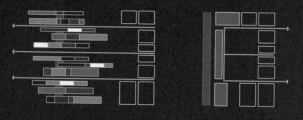

SUSTAINABLE VS FORMALIST

Multiple Connections
(Savona Central Park)

No Connection
(Mario Botta masterplan)

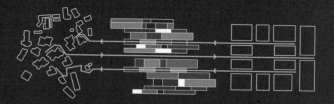

ECOLOGICAL VS METROPOLITAN

Urban Sprawl
(Savona
Oltreletimbro)

Landscape Matrix
(Savona Central
Park)

Urban Tissue
(Savona Old
Town)

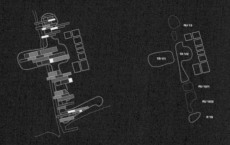

LANDSCAPE SENSIBLE VS GENERIC

Eco-cluster
(Savona Central Park)

Zoning
(Savona P.U.C.)

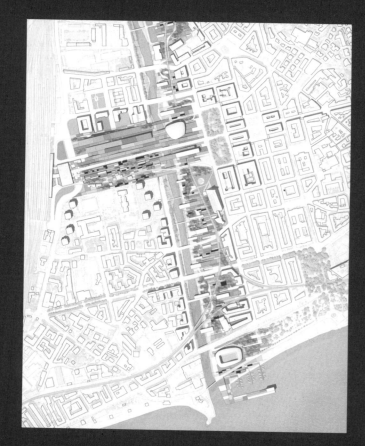

NETSCAPES:
Central Park Savona

territorial roles in relation to long and short network nodes. Urban geography marked by the velocity of interconnections promotes some territories while marginalizing others.

The quality of this never-ending city is the problem, not its form. This is no longer controllable; it has already exploded. The urban dispersion and the city's globalization is manifested in ways that we are well acquainted with as consumers of urban spaces, but that we are not able to describe or interpret with traditional planning tools. Today its possible to produce an idea of urban form on a landscape scale if, going back to Farinelli's suggestion, the territory loses meaning since it is no longer important to measure it, and distances can be rendered unimportant by artificial adjacency tools and immaterial networks.

In this framework, both the urban plan and the traditional urban project struggle as tools to govern transformations. They are tools that can pursue spatial order (as a point of equilibrium between revenue and public interest, with an aesthetic-therapeutic intent), become a form of process (in an interpretation centered on the active role of the local society), or serve as the meeting point between strategy and opportunity (in a perspective driven by the dance of power). In any case, the outcome of these urban practices leaves many questions unanswered. The lack of quality in the territory seems to express the crisis of traditional urbanism, which is no longer capable of managing relations with new urban landscapes. Often renouncing an interpretation of the new spaces of the contemporary city (infrastructures, shopping centers, parking lots, abandoned terrains, voids, places of social integration and conflict), urban projects tend to reproduce in other contexts — different from the real ones — carrying the seeds of alienation and impracticality.

The only way left to describe and interpret the space in which we live is to think of it as landscape, made up of relations, stories, gazes — of worlds that are inside each individual, made up of environmental efficiency and material products. Its aesthetics cannot depend on a superimposed measurement. It becomes a complex project construction. How many times have we heard that an architecture measures the city, defines its relations? The aesthetics of landscape is held in its images, in the way in which a place is lived, mythologized, or narrated. A landscape is the emerging form of a cultural, economic, and social context, before being a physical one. In the contemporary condition, even spatial projects can be conceived not so much as the will to give (or reinstate) form to a given place but as the capacity of giving form to processes, ways of life, using physical spaces that are in some way already active, or could be activated, in a determined context.

Changing the nature of the project proposal also means conceiving of a flexible tool that proposes the image of change as a better and possible future. With this vision it is then possible to measure effects and impacts on the physical space, on the environment, on those who become managers of these transformations, on the local society. Instead of trying to impose conflicts on a program, one can attempt to do this on a project, on a vision of change. The vision exercise represents a concrete alternative to common practices that tend to work in line with urban quality and instead attempt to conceive the definition of spaces in the field of interactions between living spaces, lifestyles, economies, and values. Through this vision, in brief, one attempts to give form to local development processes and objectives exploring change. The images of the future are useful for focusing on strategic questions, framing settlement choices, and moving beyond traditional planning methods that rarely succeed in managing the processes of change and always suffer from its consequences and effects.

The visions represent quality objectives. They are points of no return for the management of change in urban spaces, and they offer a complementary strategy of development that doesn't fear process accelerations, because in these images the future has already started. You just need to know how to see it.

PICity

PICity (The *Ponente Ligure*[16] Intelligent City) is a 25–kilometer linear urban coastal system developed between Savona and Genoa that includes eight municipalities of the *ponente ligure riviera*: Arenzano, Cogoleto, Varazze, Celle Ligure, Albisola Superiore, Albissola Marina, Savona, and Vado Ligure. It is part of the *Arco Latino* (Latin Arch), a conurbation that occupies the northwestern coast of the Mediterranean from Barcelona to Florence, where internal relations are of such an intensity and speed as of those of a single urban environment.

Investigating the nature of this city and the quality of its potential transformations is the object of the research project funded by the regional public actors.[17] From these financers we obtained the research project title. "Intelligent city" reflects the aim to investigate the

16 Western part of the Liguria region in the north of Italy.

17 Ponente Intelligent Coast City Lungoilmare, "Continuity, Modifications, and Permanence: A Hypothesis for the Development of the 25-kilometer Waterfront in Western Liguria." The research is funded and developed for Regione Liguria, Provincia di Savona, and the Municipalities of Vado Ligure Savona, Albisola Marina, Albisola Superiore, Celle Ligure, Varazze, Cogoleto, and Arenzano. Research team: Franz Prati, Gianluca Peluffo, Mosè Ricci, with Riccardo Miselli, Paola De Lucia, Simonetta Cenci, Eleonora Burlando, Gianluca Grasso, Jacopo Avenoso, Tomaso Boano, Sara Favargiotti, Sara Grignani, Cinzia Loiacono, Mathilde Marengo, Beatrice Moretti, Gianluca Motto, Chiara Olivastri, Alessandro Parodi, Fabrizio Polimone, and Emanuele Sommariva. University of Genoa, School of Architecture, 2008–2010.

future of this city, referencing the Intelligent Coast Master Course run by Manuel Gausa in Barcelona. The study takes into consideration territorial dynamics and explores developing trends within the 25-kilometer linear urban system between Arenzano and Vado Ligure. The general objective is to build an interpretative city model no longer tied to the administrative limits of each center inside the 25 kilometers but related to a broader conurbation in which the urban logics of the never-ending city come into conflict with weaker and more unstable realities. The specific objectives are to give visibility to current transformation processes and build active participation scenarios hand in hand with local administrations, leading to an integrated program of intervention toward quality change.

The urban system between Savona and Genoa, as in other Ligurian parts of the Arco Latino, is a mixed-type built heritage compressed by the steep mountains in proximity to the coastline. The historical centers of these areas, with their own diverse and innate identities, expanded so much as to penetrate one another, first as an effect of the implantation of manufacturing (mainly chemical, nautical, and steel industries), and then, from the 1960s, with the development of tourism. Today urban conditions have changed again and new inhabitants are now forced to deal with both industrial leftover and tourist settlements "stocks." The decline in manufacturing has left the landscape scarred by deindustrialization. For example, the former Stoppani chemical plant, on the seafront between Arenzano and Cogoleto, is one of the places with the highest rate of hexavalent chromium pollution in the world. Many of the tourist lodgings built in the last forty to fifty years have become residences for elderly people who have left their homes in the city to their children, retired foreigners fleeing the Northern European metropolis, and young couples who prefer a low-cost house in a nice place close enough to their job in the city. Ultimately everyone finds it more convenient to live where housing costs are contained, where facilities are efficient, where the climate is temperate, where the seaside landscape offers generous open spaces for free time and sport, and where social relations are more easygoing. The new urban conditions and lifestyles have transformed the eight municipalities between Savona and Genoa into a mainly residential and touristic cohesive linear city.

The focus of the research project is the conversion of the obsolete railway bed along the coastline into a bicycle path, a slow infrastructure capable of generating opportunities for social aggregation in the existing fabric of the linear city. The research investigates the relationship of the site with the population, the urban fabric, and the natural landscape, as well as that between the current economic activities — especially the nautical sector — and the city itself; the relation between inhabitants and infrastructure–travel time–destination and the accessibility to workplaces, beaches, and other tourist venues; and the relations between the coast and the hinterland. A central role in the research is dedicated to the investigation of public space as a significant element of connection, at both urban and territorial scales.

The research project is organized in two phases. The scientific hypothesis for the first phase is based on knowledge of the quality and intensity of internal relations in the urban coastal system and addresses the conurbation of the eight municipalities as a single continuous and polycentric city. This means putting together territorial data, building a mosaic of development expectations (approved plans and projects), and identifying strategic areas for interventions of territorial cohesion. In this framework the marginal contexts, peripheral and border areas, and urban voids and obsolete areas become important opportunities for the sustainable development of the territory.

The results of the first phase of the research project is the description of a system of territorial considerations on which to build — not predefined intervention modalities but visions of possible futures that can be integrated with one another or as alternatives. We followed a method consisting of exploring different scenarios, building four probable yet provocatively extreme hypotheses of transformation for the physical space of *PICity*. We wanted to give form to aspirations and already started processes in this urban space, sustained by the local population and groups of economic interests.

The new environmental conscience, the aspiration to metropolitan efficiency, the continuous growth in building development, the creation of tourism and leisure facilities — these are the most recurrent urban transformation policies in the plans and projects approved by the different municipalities. Some of these are in contradiction with one another, such as the growth in building development and environmental concerns, while others are easier to integrate. Although in real life it doesn't make sense to think that one of these policies will decidedly prevail over another, as an experiment we decided to create alternative and monodirectional visions, as if a particular future-oriented choice toward a single defined horizon could gain the upper hand on the territory.

The visions extend a complementary development strategy based on transformations already under way. The built heritage and sustainability (greencity), the development of infrastructural connection networks and nodes, both material and virtual (metro-city), the unstoppable building development (brick-city), or the creation of a touristic and leisure-based city (leisurecity) represent the four extreme scenarios that the research explored without preconceptions.

We were not interested in favoring any particular development hypothesis in this phase of the research. The interest was to focus on the recomposition of the needs for the future and demonstrate the possibility of an ecological vision that could hold together the expectations of the diverse social and economic groups against a horizon of a comprehensive, sustainable, and localized transformation framework in the physical space of the city.

Through comparison of the four development visions, the geography — or the map of strategic points and change "hot spots" — clearly emerges, where for all four of the future scenarios, the more important spatial transformations should be concentrated. In these areas, and based on the overall sustainability (economic, environmental, and social) of the transformation projects, the second phase of the research is developed. For the most part we are dealing with urban voids, obsolete or border areas, and valley systems. In each of these areas, the research works through exploratory projects at the most appropriate scale.

The foundation of the project is an adherence to the real situation. The objective of this phase is to demonstrate how the quality of the project, not the quantity, can make the difference. In other words, we wish to demonstrate that the construction of an ecological transformation hypothesis — in which all of the aspirations of change and sustainability criteria are respected — essentially depends on the paradigms adopted to interpret the context conditions (that is, to what one attributes value) and on the quality delivered by the project of change.

The research results concerning development opportunities of the Ponente Ligure Intelligent City tend to demonstrate three crucial theses on quality change in Mediterranean cities.

The first is the necessity of a visionary methodology in the study and ecological reframing of trends already operative in the intervention context. The second thesis regards the need for a strategy of recycling obsolete infrastructure, and in particular how this approach can represent an important opportunity to give new life to urban contexts undergoing rapid transformation. The third thesis is about the urgency of "osmotic" urban devices. The innate quality of the relation between infrastructure and the traversed territory is the capacity that these infrastructures, recycled and not, have in losing their connotation as a segment of a network and opening themselves to the wider context through a process of osmosis that ecological urbanism projects somehow activate.

Sample Projects

NETSCAPES:
Central Park Savona[18]
Savona represents an emblematic case study: a heterogeneous urban context, not free of contradictions, where recycling abandoned railway remains and urban voids, both closely related to the Letimbro River, becomes a strategic choice for the entire city-center regeneration. The expansion of interest in the urban "drosscape," as coined by Alan Berger, emerged from the European Landscape Convention and has promoted a new, balanced vision between collective interests, participation forms, and environmental compensations, leading to solutions that can foster a better quality of life.

Starting in the 1980s, the downturn in the local steel industry and port activities, related to the disuse of the old rail tracks, made the central areas of Savona attractive to the real-estate market. However, interventions within the old harbor and Piazza del Popolo, and subsequently the master plans designed by Ricardo Bofill (2003) and Mario Botta (2008), do not offer long-term answers in terms of regeneration programs as provided by the Urban Regeneration and Sustainable Territorial Development Programme (PRUSST 1998). The new Urban Plan (PUC 2009) reiterates the need for a radical change, despite confirming the structure of the previous plan (PRG 1990), which was organized into homogeneous areas, whose rules promote more private initiatives or public-private partnerships, nowadays considered the trigger for urban development.

The necessity of reconnecting the two edges of the Letimbro River, an opportunity provided by the lack of definition of these areas, represents a significant environmental enhancement for the city. In this context, "Savona Central Park" is structured as a green system that defines a new connective matrix for the

18 Research and master graduation project by Emanuele Sommariva, University of Genoa, School of Architecture, 2010.

nineteenth century urban grid and extends it beyond the river. The project creates an area of new urban centrality that reduces the gap between the historical compact city and urban sprawl, working as a landscape-sensitive layer arranged orthogonally to the river. It is an eco-logical park that contains riverfront residences, offices, and commercial spaces, which ensure the park's accessibility all day. It is an archi-tectural park, as it contains important urban facilities in Piazza del Popolo, such as a sports center, an auditorium, and a library, giving new value to the existing buildings such as the law court designed by Leonardo Ricci and the train station by Pier Luigi Nervi, now isolated in the context of Savona. It is a technological park, because thanks to the new topography, two large underground parking facilities accommo-date 2,000 vehicles, relieving the city center from vehicular traffic and converting the city's public transport service with a light tramway, which also provides fast connection with the towns of Vado Ligure and Albisola. And finally, it is a sustainable park that contains public open spaces, green areas for recreation, community gardens, and organic agriculture, connected by a wide promenade and a bike path along the river.

To fulfill these public needs, the project also coincides with the main Urban Plan ob-jectives: designing an urban park that includes the Letimbro River and connects the train sta-tion with the city center through the nineteenth century urban perspective of Via Paleocapa. Therefore the strength of the proposal is not in the form assumed by the plan but in its pro-cessual interventions that can be implemented with full respect of the existing urban program.

NETSCAPES 2:
Sansobbia Crossing[19]
The project "Crossing Sansobbia: The Ceramic Park and Contemporary Museum" proposed the regeneration of the area dividing the mu-nicipalities of Albissola Marina and Albisola Superiore. The banks of the river Sansobbia are the natural boundaries between the two municipalities. The Sansobbia valley is a gap between Albissola Marina and Albisola Superiore. It is possible to cross only at a few points. The artificial lines of the infrastructures (highway, railway) cross the valley with a huge amount of traffic. They allow the connection of the infrastructures, but they produce an isolat-ed area surrounded by a historical and natural landscape (Roman Villa, Villa Faraggiana, Villa Gavotti). The two coastal cities have funda-mentally different characters: one sustains

itself with seasonal tourism and the other is developed through agriculture. Both have a long ceramics tradition. The project has three aspects: the museum as a node; the riverside promenade; the urban park. The objective is to transform this unused area from an obsolete and desolate land on the periphery of two cities into an urban park, the new heart of one city.

WASTESCAPES:
Stoppani[20]
The former chemical plant Stoppani is among the top-ten environmental disasters in relation to an industrial site. The ground beneath the industrial site (1,251,868 cubic meters) is pol-luted by hexavalent chromium, a highly toxic and carcenogenic substance. The reclamation program, following a landscape urbanism fra-mework, offers the possibility of identifying the undervalued landscapes and reorienting them toward new processes. The polluted ground is removed and the site remodeled according to a new program, transforming the chromium fac-tory into a "landscape factory," guaranteeing environmental renewal to the two contiguous municipalities of Cogoleto and Arenzano.

19   Research and master graduation project by Sara Favargiotti, University of Genoa, School of Architecture, 2010. This project was selected for the graduation thesis competition "Archiprix Italy — Naples — 2010."

20   Research and master graduation project by Jacopo Avenoso and Sara Grignani, University of Genoa, School of Architecture, 2010.

The (PIC)ITY Ponente Intelligent Coast research was presented at the Biennale d'Architettura 2010 in Venice and at the Biennale of Landscape in Barcelona in 2012. All material produced is being published by List Lab BCN-Trento.

The Island Paradigm and the Mediterranean
Stefania Staniscia

An island is a device able to condense a multiplicity of meanings, both physical and metaphorical; islands echo material forms and mental models. An island is a paradigm in a Platonic sense: an ideal reality conceived as a model for existing realities. Scholars and researchers have made use of the island's evocative power, its exemplary nature, and its capacity to become a tool for interpreting complex urban and territorial phenomena that are intrinsic to the contemporary city.

The Island as Paradigm

Islands are often understood as analogical models. For Alessandro Petti (2007), islands and archipelagos represent a spatial model "dictated by the paradigm of safety and control." Similarly, Mark Lee (2011) envisions islands and archipelagos as a potential generative model for the contemporary city, one that sees distance as a means to generate alternative connectivity. The European landscape "appears as Archipelago, an irreducible plurality where single elements coexist insofar as they are inevitably separate. And the islands of this Archipelago are Europe's *declensions*" (Cacciari 1997). Francesco Indovina's metropolitan archipelago (2009) is the new territorial structure toward which metropolises, urbanized territories, and urban sprawl are evolving; this structure is composed of several realities — the islands — linked by strong relationships, and by virtue of these relationships they form a unity.

Islands are metaphors. In her novel/illustrated atlas, Judith Schalansky explores the histories, origins, local traditions, and physical characteristics of fifty islands. Their being isolated, so distant from the mainland and surrounded by water, have earned islands the role of idyllic places in the continental imagination, an idea that coexists with the fear of being forever confined, forced into captivity. For Schalansky, "Paradise is an island. So is hell." For Matvejević, islands are sensors of the Mediterranean situation: "Nothing reveals the Mediterranean's destiny better than its islands" (1998).

Islands are heterotopias: according to Foucault (1998), in their relationship with the mainland they are "in relation with all the other sites, but in such a way as to suspect, neutralize, or invert the set of relations that [heterotopian spaces] happen to designate, mirror, or reflect." They open up on other spaces: such as the mainland or the sea itself, the medium that makes islands and the mainland communicate. Foucault's fifth principle states that heterotopias "presuppose a system of opening and closing that both isolates them and makes them penetrable." An island lives through its opening and closing, depending on each route.

Islands are synecdoches. As significant fragments of a continent, they are a part that represents the whole. "A fragment of Europe," writes Ricci (2011), "each of them revealing a catastrophe or sparkling hope." Whether it came to life through separation or recreation, derived or original, an island is an accurately measurable

Stefania Staniscia is an architect and holds a Ph.D. in Architecture, as well as a Master of Landscape Architecture from the Technical University of Catalonia at Barcelona. She has taught in the faculties of Architecture (Genoa) and Engineering and Architecture (Ancona). She is currently a research fellow and lecturer at the faculty of Civil Engineering and Architecture at the University of Trento.

The Island Paradigm and the Mediterranean

spatial entity whose borders are neatly traced; it is a miniature world, the mainland's symbol and synthesis.

Islandness as Hermeneutic Method

Even though "approaches to the islands are characterized by various paradoxes [...] underlin[ing] a kind of singularity or irregularity" (Matvejević 1998), it is possible to consider islands as representative samples or magnifiers. Isolation is a necessary condition to better define and analyze changes and complex phenomena happening on the mainland. Islands mean to geographers and urban and landscape planners what cells mean to biologists: they are elementary units endowed with common properties that can be analyzed to identify causes, modes, and outcomes of changing processes.

For instance, the Galápagos Islands in the Pacific Ocean had a crucial role in the development of Darwinism. Long-term fieldwork conducted by Charles Darwin and other researchers encouraged them to think they had been working in a "natural laboratory." Darwin himself was active in promoting islands, uncorrupted by human impact and sufficiently isolated from the rest of the world, as the ideal environment where survival techniques and differences among species could be observed.

Thus islandness may become a hermeneutical method to comprehend changing processes involving European territory and landscape. It is also a way to predict future developments on the mainland, as islands are their mirror. It is in fact possible to affirm that:

> **Island knowledge and experience do not apply just to themselves. Analogies and parallels appear with non-islands. Mountain villages can be as isolated while cities comprising islands such as Stockholm and New York are themselves worthy of island-related study. Deltas and Arctic communities display multiple island characteristics as well. (Kelman 2010)**

Indeed, the importance that certain issues (such as mobility and tourism) acquire in the islands along with some intrinsic characteristics (controllable dimensions, a sensitive context, dependence on external support) make islands ideal places to conduct "punctual samplings," allowing architects and planners to "locally test laws and rules that regulate large portions of territory" (Boeri 2003).

The Periphery of Empire

Looking at maps that interpret aggregate demographic data referring to the European population, night views from a satellite, maps of natural areas, and maps showing spatial concentration or population density, it is immediately possible to recognize a familiar shape. One easily identifies Koolhaas's "Blueurope" (2001), Datar's Blue Banana (Brunet 1989), the great natural regions, the huge compact cities and urban-metropolitan agglomerations, and extended urban sprawl. These are all easily recognizable territorial patterns, the geographical continuum that characterizes European space.

Nevertheless, there is an ample region at the outskirts of Europe, a peripheral area whose shape appears only to those who are aware of its presence. These peripheral spaces are the frontier with Eastern Europe, the northern landscapes of high natural value, the fringes of the Mediterranean, the southern intangible limit of Europe's territorial waters. These are not merely geographical peripheries but also economic and social ones. And islands, in a way, are distillations of these regions.

Islands are often peripheral frontier-regions. They look inactive at first sight, and unconcerned by the processes at work in the metropolises. Yet to the contrary, they frequently act like sensors, intercepting innovative organizational modes and territorial developments. This is due to the little resistance they put up against change, whereas central regions and consolidated territories tend to preserve their roles, hardly contemplating the possibility of inventing new ones. In comparison with consolidated landscapes, marginal ones have a greater ability to mutate and adapt to stimuli that change over time and differ from those that originally shaped these landscapes.

Globalization, in the manifest form of intensive human mobility, determined a recentralization of the islands in Europe's new spatial structure and in the Mediterranean Basin. They became the center of a route that elevated them to a superior territorial rank, depending on neither demography nor settlement, but almost exclusively on position and strong functional specialization.

Mediterranean Islands

Intensive human mobility in the Mediterranean — migrations, diasporas, tourism — represents one of its major cultural and socioeconomic characteristics. Due to its privileged geographical position, the Mediterranean is exposed to migratory flows of diverse origin, destination, and nature. Islands are witnesses of such mobility, registering how people, driven by different needs, move across the Mediterranean in opposite directions. Europeans seeking to improve the quality of their lives, either permanently or temporarily, travel from North to South, tracing a new geography of desire. People from poor countries — jobless immigrants or political refugees — travel from South to North, along the routes of desperation, searching for an "elsewhere" and a better future: islands are their final or intermediate destinations. Illegal routes add up to official ones, "as the years go by, the Mediterranean has become a 'solid sea,' crossed by pre-established, rigid routes of monocultural, 'specialized' people: illegal immigrants, soldiers, sailors, tourists... their routes intersect without ever meeting, as they often allow their passengers no cultural exchange, no dialogue, no real interaction" (La Cecla et al. 2003).

Small and minor islands, more so than the large ones, are "extremely frail textures in the contemporary world,

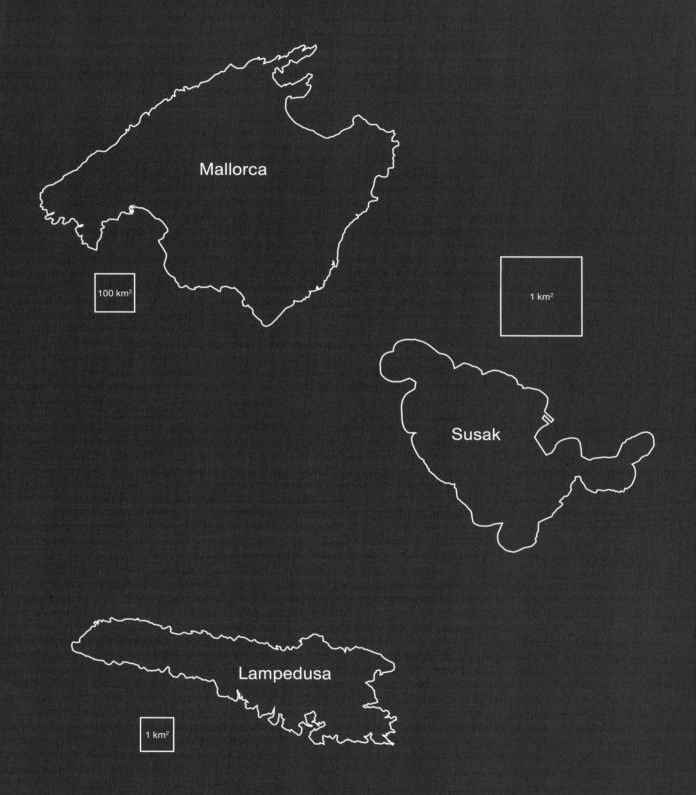

Mallorca

100 km²

1 km²

Susak

Lampedusa

1 km²

characterized by phenomena of urban and industrial concentration"; for them, "the principal factors of space modeling have always been the relationships with the outside world" (Ciaccio 1984). Small islands fall back into a state of isolation every time their relationships with the mainland and with the outside world, for a variety of reasons, happen to be interrupted. In the islands, exchanges and isolation mark alternate phases of decay and progress. These relationships are made possible by an intricate net of routes that, on the one hand, represent a danger to territorial sustainability and to the very condition of insularity, and, on the other, offer a rapid solution to the forms of economic and social decline that the islands are facing. Three examples will demonstrate how islands can represent the dynamics of change, and which phenomena they are able to register.

Majorca, Susak, and Lampedusa are local samples that display three "elementary" mechanisms of spatial construction connected to the phenomenon of human mobility. These territorial forms have been shaped by three driving principles: pressure, abandonment, and conflict. Islands often suffer from pressure produced by tourism, loading a limited territory beyond its carrying capacity; abandonment affects those territories whose main resources are still agriculture and fishing; whereas conflict develops on the frontier between profoundly discrepant realities and cultures. These examples have been selected as highly representative of the phenomenon of human mobility in the forms of tourism, emigration, and immigration.

Majorca — Archipelago Island

Pere A. Salvà i Tomàs (2005), professor of geography at the Universitat de les Illes Balears, uses food metaphors to describe how Spanish Majorca's territory has transformed under the pressure of tourism. The island's territory before the boom in tourism could have been explained through the fried-egg model (inhabited areas were concentrated in the island's internal areas). The first tourist boom brought about a territorial organization based on the donut model (internal areas depopulated, with residents and tourist settlements concentrated on the coast). The current territorial configuration can be represented by the ensaimada (a typical Majorcan dessert) model, in which differences between coastal and internal areas have disappeared, and residences (first, second, and holiday houses) are spread out over the entire territory, especially in the internal agricultural areas.

"Rurbanization" is tightly connected to the so-called sixth invasion (Llano 1999). After the Romans, the vandals, the Byzantines, the French, the Arabs, the Aragonese Catalans, and the Spanish immigrants, the 1990s saw a German influx. Northern European tourists "colonized" the forgotten and scarcely populated regions of Southern Europe, searching for a new Arcadia. Majorca scaled up and became part of a larger territorial system: the European extracontinental. Tourist areas during the first (1950s) and second (1960s–1980s) tourist booms were appendixes of far-removed settlements, authentic islands inside the host island. The barrier between the touristic and the nontouristic was neatly defined. With the third boom, the two structures began to blend, the dual settlement model melting in one territorial magma.

Residential sprawl coexists with the high level of functional specialization of some areas. The island appears as a metropolitan archipelago (Indovina 2003), as this functional specialization tends to be articulated on the territory through a system of specialized micro-poles (dedicated to free time, commerce, living, education, etc.) whose development is not strictly local but of metropolitan character. The territory becomes a support, and the multiple polarities trigger spatial integration, made possible by the intensification of functional, economic, and social relationships. Thus the current configuration transcends the two dichotomies — urban/rural and coastal/inland — that are typical of a classic territorial model of tourism. The whole island undergoes a process of "touristization," becoming able to provide a highly articulated tourist offering. Tourists are presented with a "package" including the entire island, with its beaches, natural reservations, archeological areas, rural areas, wine itineraries, theme parks, and art cities — a range of resources aimed to satisfy all kinds of tourists, discarding the stereotypical image of sol y playa tourism.

The urban pressure on agricultural areas did not encounter strong resistance, especially on extensive farming lots that did not need irrigation; therefore a high number of small fields measuring less than a hectare have been turned into urban lots. Terrains subject to more dynamic farming practices put up greater resistance. Therefore some areas maintained an exclusively rural character, whereas others became predominantly urban. In the latter, a part-time, "recreational" agriculture has been introduced, limited to the weekends, aimed at personal consumption only. The concept of decorative agriculture is increasing in popularity: "es la transformació de la pagesia en Jardiners d'Europa" [it is the transformation of farmers into European gardeners] (Salvà i Tomàs 1994).

Rural spaces transform into the connective tissue of this archipelago island, becoming a multifunctional space where rural and urban habits and functions coexist, or rather a space where new urban habits relegate traditional rural habits to interstitial spaces. From productive resources, rural spaces are thus converted into tourist and landscape resources that must be preserved, as they represent a necessary scenario for an alternative tourist product aiming to diversify tourism and extend it to all seasons. Rural landscape becomes stereotypical, picturesque, and logics of representation replace those of productivity.

Some places have resisted the spread of tourism, some have been overwhelmed by it, and yet others have been left out as an effect of planning and for financial reasons; these can be called "refractory" spaces. If we were to represent them in a map, we would see scattered, isolated "black holes" in an urban continuum with different gradients, produced by the strain tourist development puts on the territory.

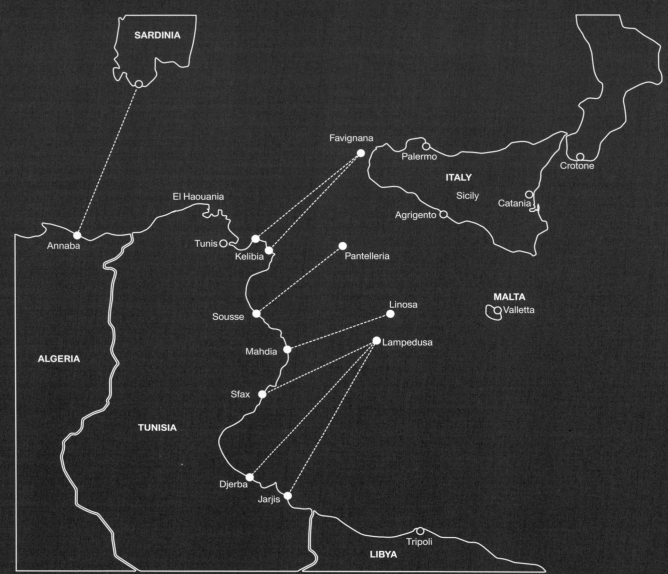

Main migration routes toward Italy during the first months of 2011

The Island Paradigm and the Mediterranean

Susak — A Resort Island

Susak is a paradigmatic example of the strong interdependence between economy and geographic/territorial structure in islands. Being based on nature, an island's economy is generally simple, and its structure appears primitive if compared to that of the mainland. On islands, economic oscillation partly depends on periodic changes in natural conditions, but especially on the progress of commerce and infrastructure, which, in their growth and expansion, create ever more efficient connections between the islands and the mainland. The history of Susak, a Croatian island, is instructive. Factors like demographic increase, the development of settlements and their decay, and nature's luxuriance and abandonment are tightly connected to the prevalent economic activity in the history of the island: wine making. New tourist trends are also bound to this activity.

Susak is part of the Cres-Lošinj archipelago, in the Gulf of Kvarner. Vineyards have long covered almost the entire surface of the island (88 percent in 1903), strongly characterizing its landscape. A stable market corresponded to a continuous demographic increase, and when the island's only economic activity could no longer sustain the number of inhabitants, this led to migratory flows, especially toward North America. Between 1961 and 1971 the population dropped from 1,200 to 300. The demographic crisis had a disastrous impact on the insular settlement: many buildings were abandoned, and the vineyards disappeared, replaced by pastures, cane thickets, and weeds. In 1953 land under cultivation constituted 30 percent of the island's territory, but only 4.6 percent by 1993.

A real-estate market for houses abandoned by the emigrants slowly started to develop in the 1970s. Local and foreign weekenders bought the largest ones, rescuing them from decay. They were the pioneers of tourism on the island. According to data provided by the town of Mali Lošinj, in 2006 in Susak 246 residences of 684 were holiday houses. According to the Tourist Board, 7,713 tourists visited the island that year. The largely family-owned tourism business evolved, in the first years of the twenty-first century, into a form of Total Leisure Experience. Responsible for this evolution was Francesco Cosulich, a wine entrepreneur of Istriot origins who was asked by the mayor of Mali Lošinj to revive the wine business on the island. Cosulich started out by planting 30 hectares of vines and founding the Cosulich Wine Cellar. According to Cosulich, wine is a "message of culture" and represents a cultural as well as an economic investment. Through the reintroduction of viniculture, the rural, cultural landscape was recreated in accordance with the traditional activities that had shaped it in the past.

But this was only the beginning. Well aware of the island's tourist potential, Cosulich and his project grew ambitious: he planned on extending the vineyard to 100 hectares and transforming the island into an exclusive resort by buying and restoring uninhabited buildings and creating an *albergo diffuso*, with a heliport and a golf course. These ideas are in line with typical urban planning guidelines, aiming to both protect the environment and promote the development of infrastructures that may improve the

territory's accessibility and appeal, with the goal of making the island attractive to the tourism market. Viniculture thus emerges as a vehicle to encourage tourism, which appears to be the only practicable way to return Susak to its ancient prosperity.

Lampedusa — A Liminal Island, Hotspot of Change

Lampedusa is located on an imaginary line linking a sequence of islands in the southern Mediterranean, a line that currently defines the European Union's third great frontier, the line between development and underdevelopment. Because of its position, Lampedusa has always been a theater of conflict. The island has hosted a penal colony, an advanced military stronghold, and a NATO base, all of which have left material marks on the territory and a heritage of buildings and sites. Lampedusa is the space of misunderstanding: "the space where cultures unfold and confront, realizing they are different," writes La Cecla (1994).

Yet in Lampedusa the conflicts that naturally affect frontier regions do not find a neutral territory but one that has been profoundly mutated by real-estate interests generated by tourism. It is not by mere coincidence that the Strategic Plan for the Sustainable Development of the Pelagian Islands (2006) "aims to tackle the impacts of tourism and the flow of migration." According to the plan, the island's territory presents an environmental threat that increases with seasonal tourism, peaking during the tourist high season, when the land surface needed to cover all uses would be 4.5 times bigger than the island itself (Strategic Plan 2006). With the addition of migrant flows, the imbalance grows remarkably.

What is at stake is not merely a delicate environmental balance; what is happening in Lampedusa today is in fact typical of what is happening all along the Mediterranean in terms of population movements. Due to ongoing conflicts, 2011 was characterized by intense migratory flows. Lampedusa, on the migrants' travel itinerary, is the closest landing place in the journey across the Mediterranean, the remotest outpost of the European fortress. Lampedusa thus functions as a sensitive register, recording the passing of populations migrating from South to North. Its role as Europe's gate has been confirmed, but this time Lampedusa is no longer a place of transit, a way in, a passage leading somewhere else, but a detention basin holding the flow of refugees, a parking lot for human transit (Liberti 2008), where traffic does not flow so quickly, to disappear without a trace.

Yet the classic "Lampedusa model" includes only rapid transfer procedures and delegates the remaining administrative procedures to other institutions located elsewhere in the country. In 2009, in addition to the reception center, a new identification and expulsion center opened in Lampedusa, where all migrants and refugees on the island are forced to remain until their cases have been decided. The daily arrival of hundreds of migrants in the first months of 2011 triggered a state of emergency. The arrivals-to-transfers ratio remains negative. Migrants are kept on the islands for an average of eight days. The situation is critical for migrants and residents, as in a few days the number of the former reaches that of the latter. In the climactic phase, a total of 13,000 people are present on the island's 20 square kilometers: 6,000 residents, as many Tunisians, and 1,000 soldiers, making for a population density of 650 people per square kilometer (Amisnet 2011).

Migrants waiting to be transferred elsewhere have to find accommodation on the island. All public buildings have been made available and were immediately occupied. Yet, these spaces, besides not being adequate to the purpose, were not large enough to accommodate all immigrants. At that point two official camps were set up, but these too proved inadequate. Some immigrants, especially the newcomers, station themselves at the harbor, on the dock, or on the hill above it, patching together improvised camps and shantytowns. The whole island became an enormous improvised refugee camp. Lampedusa is a prison-island, a Mediterranean Alcatraz (Ricci 2011), a situation made possible by its total geographic isolation and restricted territory.

This condition is the effect of a policy implemented by the European Union and many of its member states, externalizing the problem of frontier control. Migration routes are controlled and blocked elsewhere to limit the ability of migrants to penetrate the European fortress. Europe's frontiers thicken until they create a gray zone that is often an area of uncertain jurisdiction. A "topography of transit" (Liberti 2008) emerges in this gray area, along the migrants' routes. It is punctuated by many heterotopias: ghettos, detention camps, shantytowns, parallel cities — invisible, precarious, formal, and informal places where thousands of migrants are forced to stay and where they are trapped before they can resume their journey toward Europe or back to their countries of origin. Lampedusa itself becomes a heterotopia: an internal externalization of a border.

Back to Islandness

Islands have always been considered nodes of contact and exchange within the flows that characterize a communication system, with the sea as a solid element, a "liquid plain" (Braudel 1997) to cross. Islands are stations of longer journeys, privileged witnesses to the existence of an intricate net of routes whose physical traces they retain more effectively than the mainland. Yet today islands represent much more than that. They reflect the most conflictual and contemporary dynamics of ongoing changes. Islands are hotspots of territorial mutations capable of anticipating what will happen on the mainland, although in different times and modes and to different extents. Islandness reveals itself to be a hermeneutic method to comprehend processes of change, and islands emerge as "critical control points" (Ricci 2003), able to anticipate places and conditions of crises and, at the same, to test new development opportunities.

References:

Amisnet. 2011. "Le strade della fuga." *Carta*. Accessed April 08. http://www.carta.org/.
Boeri, Stefano. 2003. "Atlanti Eclettici." In *USE uncertain states of Europe*, edited by Multiplicity. Geneva, Milan: Skira.
Braudel, Fernand. 1997. *Il Mediterraneo. Lo spazio la storia gli uomini le tradizioni*. Milan: Bompiani.
Brunet, Roger. 1989. *Les villes europeénnes: Rapport pour la DATAR*. Montpellier: RECLUS.
Cacciari, Massimo. 1997. *L'arcipelago*. Milan: Adelphi Edizioni.
Ciaccio, Candida. 1984. *Turismo e microinsularità. Le isole minori della Sicilia*. Bologna: Patron Editore.
Foucault, Michel. 1998. *Archivio Foucault*. Milan: Feltrinelli.
Indovina, Francesco. 2003. "La pianificazione per l'arcipelago metropolitano. I casi di Barcellona e Bologna," *Area Vasta* 8/9.
Kelman, Ilan. 2010. Foreword to *Sustainable Tourism in Island Destinations*, by Sonya Graci and Rachel Dodds. London: Earthscan.
Koolhaas, Rem, quoted in *Brussels, Capital of Europe*, by GOPA (Group of Policy Advisors). 2001. Brussels: European Commission.
La Cecla, Franco. 1994. "Il malinteso," *Volontà* 2/3.
La Cecla, Franco, Stefano Savona, and Ilaria Sposito. 2003. "Una frontiera di specchi." In *USE uncertain states of Europe*, edited by Multiplicity. Geneva, Milan: Skira.
Lee, Mark. 2011. "Two Deserted Islands," *San Rocco* 1.
Liberti, Stefano. 2008. *A sud di Lampedusa. Cinque anni di viaggi sulle rotte dei migranti*. Rome: Minimum fax.
Llano, Rafael. 1999. *La sexta invasión. Alemanes en Mallorca*. Palma de Mallorca: José J. de Olañeta Editor.
Matvejević, Predrag. *Il Mediterraneo e l'Europa*. Milan: Garzanti, 1998.
Petti, Alessandro. 2007. *Arcipelaghi e enclave*. Milan: Bruno Mondadori.
Ricci, Manila. 2011. "Lampedusa, Alkatraz del Mediterraneo." March 26. Accessed March 27, 2011. http://www.meltingpot.org/articolo16543.html
Ricci, Mosè. 2011. Foreword to *Islands*, by Stefania Staniscia. Trento, Barcelona: LISt Lab.
Ricci, Mosè. 2003. "Dinamiche del mutamento e rischio di paesaggio." In *Rischiopaesaggio*, edited by Mosè Ricci. Rome: Meltemi.
Salvà i Tomàs, Pere. 1994. "Impactes del turisme sobre la mar Mediterranea." Congres Jornades d'Estudis Historics Locals, *El desenvolupament turistic a la Mediterrania durant el segle XX*. Palma de Mallorca: Institut d'Estudis Balearics.
Salvà i Tomàs, Pere. 2005. Interview with the author.
Schalansky, Judith. 2010. *Atlas of Remote Islands: Fifty Islands I Have Not Visited and Never Will*. London: Penguin Group.
Strategic Plan for the Sustainable Development of the Pelagian Islands. 2006. A project promoted by the Department for Development and Cohesion of the Italian Ministry of Economy and Finance. Coordinator: Alberto Versace. Project undertaken by Studiare Sviluppo s.r.l.. Project Manager: Lorenzo Canova. Developed by IUAV University of Venice, Urban Planning Department. Scientific supervisor: Giuseppe Longhi.

Ex-Murus
Escaping Gaze
Karim Basbous

Captive View

Ever since Virgil, authors have celebrated the grandeur of the Earth. The painters who introduced Nature in their vision, first in the backdrop — Giotto, Van Eyck — subsequently afforded it an expanding presence in the space of the canvas, until eventually giving it, with Patinir and Poussin, the status of subject. Literary genres (the bucolic, the arcadian, travel literature) as well as pictorial genres (the picturesque, the pastoral) evolved over time in a similar fashion; all were inspired by *locus amoenus*, the "pleasant place," the desire that the Mediterranean instills in us. Whereas architecture, a situated art — in fact surrounded by beautiful scenery that it does not have to create — has long turned its gaze away from the landscape. It is as if architecture was more preoccupied with observing itself, with self-referencing, than with looking at the world; the building and the landscape, two realities that stand alongside each other, have rarely been represented together in Western architectural conceptual work. The type of drawing that we are examining here fully supports that argument: indeed sketches that depict interior spaces have rarely integrated a view of the surroundings. The function of "opening a window" — the famous metaphor coined by Leon Battista Alberti to describe the inception of a work of art[1] — long pertained to painting. Ever since, painters have played with the theme of the "window" in a recursive manner, by painting scenes of interiors that contain windows. But what about the outward view in conceptual architectural sketches, and by extension, in buildings? The stories of houses, texts, and drawings hold keys for answering this question.

    The thematic of the villa unveils the relation between the building and the vast landscape. Throughout both antiquity and the Renaissance, while the geographical quality of the site dictates the location of high society's spaces of leisure, the visual enjoyment of the surroundings — one of the major activities of *otium*, the roman word for "free time" — appears, however, to be restricted to exterior promenades, porticos, and loggias.

1   Leon Battista Alberti, *De Pictura*, 1436.

Karim Basbous   received his architectural degree from the Ecole Nationale Supérieure d'Architecture, Paris-Belleville, and his Ph.D. from EHESS in Paris (under the directorship of Daniel Arasse) on the relationship between design and thought in architectural conception. He is the author of *Avant l'oeuvre, essai sur l'invention architecturale*(2005), and numerous articles (in *Le Visiteur, Faces, Les Cahiers de l'Ecole de Blois*). He has taught in Lebanon (USEK) and Switzerland (University of Geneva). He is a tenured Professor at the Ecole Nationale Supérieure d'Architecture de Normandie and Professor at the Ecole Polytechnique. He is also Editor of *Le Visiteur*(a critical journal of architecture fully translated in English) and in charge of cultural activities of the Société Française des Architectes in Paris. Basbous is also a practicing architect.

Representation of the site is conspicuously absent from renderings of interior spaces, which is precisely the type of representation that is of interest to us.[2] Windows appear as scotomas (blind spots), visually "closing in" the representation in the very places where wall openings should open up to the outside and offer depth. Seen from the inside, walls enclose not only the space but also the view. Openings are blind "hiatuses" in the overall plane of the wall. The prevalence of vertical windows (as a mode of aperture), the lavish ornaments on the walls' surface (trumeau, transom), take hold of the occupant's gaze and keep it busy, turning the "room" into a small totality, a finite place, eventually closed off. Alberti described the building in a similar fashion, as a body composed of smaller edifices.[3] For when the building embodies a world in itself, it no longer needs to find, in the outside world, the reason for its own composition.

Drawing on Renaissance literature, one may attest to the lack of consideration given to the act of seeing (le regard) in the conception of windows (of their locations, of their dimensions). Renaissance theorists rank sight high above all the other senses; what is more, the invention of perspective brings representation closer to the human eye, although its use is restricted to painting.[4] Anthropomorphism, on which architectural theory relies, denotes a consideration given to humankind, but one in which the human is seen as a harmonic model, as a metaphor. The human here is not seen, in principle, as the individual; even less so as an occupant that the building must take in. It must also be noted that the human figure is absent from the renderings of interiors, a testimony of the building's independence — indifference, even — toward the body that inhabits it.[5]

In his architectural treatise, Palladio dedicates one chapter to the window, but does not mention what it opens onto. He defines a minimal ratio and a maximal ratio for fenestration within a room. The former is based on the acceptable level of darkness, the latter, on the acceptable level of ambient temperature.[6] In classical language, the window does not exist in itself; rather the window belongs to the wall, to which it must give rhythm. As much as possible, the window is kept away from the edges, to ensure the soundness of the structure.[7] Incidentally, the opening represents a breach in the safety of the dwelling. Among Michelangelo's many sketches, only those of fortification projects reveal the use of cones of vision, oriented outward, in the conception of the plan itself. Except for such security considerations — keeping watch of the surroundings of bastions — the human gaze is not intended to stray to the outside. In later periods, typical buildings such as the baroque pavilion with its large glass doors, or the eighteenth-century château with its projecting rounded salon, denote a certain amount of openness toward the territory. And yet, their plans still conform to principles of ordonnance, whose function is to maintain the closed character of the architectural composition.[8] The window lets the light in, but does not let the gaze out.

In Quatremère de Quincy's Dictionary, the definition of "window" makes no allusion to vision: "general name given to any opening whose main function is to let daylight inside buildings."[9] Considered as a module of mural composition, the window is afforded its dimensions in function of the balance between empty space and built space. In dimensioning the trumeau's width (which de facto determines that of the window), sketches grapple with a range of variations, bound on the lower end by constructive requirements (excessively narrow trumeau would threaten the solidity of the structure) and, on the higher end, by aesthetic and moral requirements.[10] None of the Dictionary's other entries[11] discusses the pleasure of the eye.

In the classical tradition, the building shows its face through its external façade; but it is a face that does not have eyes. The gaze is held hostage by a plethora of decorative elements — moldings, frescoes, motifs — all mobilized to distract the eye. And openings are hazy planes. It is normal for us today to associate windowpanes with transparency. And yet, only since the nineteenth century have glass-casting techniques enabled control over the flatness of the glass surface, thus allowing perfect transparency, that is, the casting of a surface devoid of warps (any distortion in the glass would entail a distortion of whatever is seen through it). Indeed, the use of this exceptional material long remained limited to mirrors and bay windows, while

2   See Wolfgang Lotz, "The Rendering of the Interior in Architectural Drawing of the Renaissance," in Studies in Italian Renaissance Architecture (Cambridge, MA: MIT Press, 1977), 1–65.

3   Leon Battista Alberti De re aedificatoria, Florence, 1485, I, 2. Edition: L'art d'édifier (Paris: Seuil, 2004), 58. Translated into French by Pierre Caye and Françoise Choay.

4   Ibid., II, 2, 99.

5   See Lotz, "The Rendering of the Interior in Architectural Drawing of the Renaissance."

6   "Delle misure delle porte e delle finestre," Andrea Palladio, I Quattro libri dell'architettura (Venice: Domenoco de'Franceschi, 1570), I, 25; Paris: Flammarion, 1997), translated into French by Roland Fréart de Chambray, 74.

7   Ibid., I, XXV (76).

8   See the chapter "l'ordre fermé" in Jacques Lucan, Composition, non-compositions (Lausanne: Presses Polytechniques et universitaires romandes, 2009).

9   Antoine-Chrysostome Quatremère de Quincy, Dictionnaire historique d'architecture (Paris: Joseph Gibert, 1832), I, 618.

10   From the outside, overly wide trumeaux would bring about a sense of heaviness, and from the inside, they would make the room excessively dark.

11   Neither "Paysage (Landscape)" nor "Cadrage (frame)" are featured. The article on "Extérieur (Exterior)" only mentions the external aspect of a building, and not what may be seen from the inside (ibid., I, 619, article "Fenêtre (Window)"); whereas the article on "Vue (Vision)" is divided into two large sections: one deals with views in drawing, while the other, beginning with the following quote "Sous son acceptation ordinaire dans l'art de bâtir les maisons, ce mot signifie une ouverture par laquelle on reçoit le jour," briefly mentions a condition stemming for the orientation of the building in the urban context (a house with a view on a yard, on the street). Ibid., II, article "Vue (Vision)". Quatremère goes on with a list of views (vue de prospect, vue dérobée, vue enfilée), but it is still a matter of defining a practical function or a mode of distribution. Finally, the article on "Ouverture (Opening)" makes no mention of the relation with the exterior.

[39]

[13]

Villa Savoie

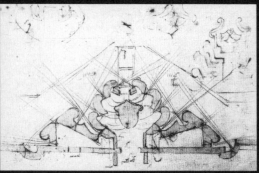
Michel-Ange: projet de fortification d'une porte

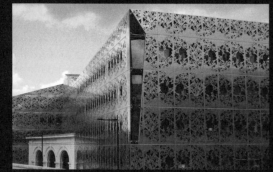
Agence Forma6: Conseil général de Loire-Atlantique, Nantes (2012)

Corseaux

Francis Soler: logements rue Durkheim à Paris (1996)

common windowpanes mostly used "window glass" ("*verre à vitre*"), whose surface was less flat, since it was neither polished, abraded, or buffed.[12]

Exoscopy

The invention of a material does not determine the invention of a new type of space, it merely renders it possible; one must wait for the advent of an imaginative mind to transform a technical event into architecture. Le Corbusier makes his appearance when the fruits of the industrial revolution are already ripe, yet still idle in terms of their architectural potential. He exploits the technical progress achieved in glass fabrication to support an ambitious, "existential" project: to reorient the occupant's gaze, toward the outside and offer him the vanishing point and the horizon line that had traditionally been restricted to painting. But the Corbusian project goes even further: the outside is not merely observed; it is absorbed, captured by the opening.

The dwelling place of humans is no longer the house itself but the landscape. The Mediterranean, which had abundantly inspired poets and painters, enters the architectural imaginary through the intervention of one of its greatest and most fervent devotees. Because of its balmy climate, its curves and hills, its fragrant flora, the Mediterranean is assimilated as a representation of the Garden of Eden, in other words, to a place where notions of interior and exterior coalesce. Contrary to transalpine lands where nature had long been perceived as hostile — threatening even, to the point that building ought to protect us from it — the Mediterranean offers inhabitable nooks, a welcoming and nurturing environment that recalls the maternal womb, and with which the building may freely interact. Recapturing the inhabitable outside thus becomes the principal theme of a Modern movement obsessed with the Virgilian dream. For Le Corbusier, the drawing is a testimony of this quest. Sketches do not show a "face-to-face" between an observer and an observed scene; rather, they show one global scene, compact, rescaled, akin to a "summary" of the world. In so doing, the Corbusian gesture recalls Matisse's own quest, in which the "windows" painted in Collioure or Tangiers do more than looking toward the outside. Matisse. These windows use color to amalgamate hills, roofs, sailboats, and domestic objects. Color captures, and windows invite, faraway objects into the privacy of the room, which they come to share, on the equal terms, with the vase, the flowerpot, and the chair. That which can be grasped by the eyes has the same color swatches as that which can be grasped by the hand. In this way, Matisse reestablishes the eye's propensity to unite objects — objects that would otherwise be dispersed, separate, on both a cartographic and three-dimensional level. "I feel that, from the horizon to the interior of my room, Matisse says, the space is but one; and that the passing boat and the familiar objects around me all dwell within the same space; the wall and the window do not create two different worlds."[13] The quality of a place — in this case, of the interior — is measured from a standpoint oblivious to systems of spatial coordinates; its aim is to procure, within the plane of the canvas, a confusion that alludes to the enigma of appearance. Whereas perspective dealt with the representation of depth, Fauvism deals, for its part, with the "constriction" of the world. The Corbusian sketch betrays a similar obsession, as if the architect wanted to achieve the same objective, although, this time, through constructed space, making use of the three-dimensionality of the built form, in the service of a pictorial contemplation of the world.[14] Privacy no longer requires enclosure; hills, oceans, and horizons are domesticated.

The convergence of architecture and landscape on the sketchbook represents, for the history of the project, more that the mere evolution of a "mode." It signals a new age for the architectural "subject."[15] The appearance of landscape within the sketches of interior spaces breaks the room's and the building's monotony. It draws on the transformation of the very foundations of conceptual drawing. The "free façade," one of the "five points" of a new architecture, symbolizes more than the envelope's liberation from the supporting wall's constructive constraints. Through the "free façade," the function of drawing is no longer limited to giving order to material lines (edges, outlines, contours) in the hope to achieve proportional harmony; rather

12   It is only since the introduction of float glass, made by floating molten glass on a bath of molten tin, around 1960, that the distinction between sheet glass and flat glass was abolished, in favor of a single technique. I thank Maurice Hamon and the "*Entreprise Saint-Gobain*" for having enlightened me on the subject.

13   Radio interview, 1942, cited in French in *Ecrits et propos sur l'art* (Paris: Hermann, 1989), 100.

14   On the pictorial quality of Corbusian architecture, see Judith Rotbart and Laurent Salomon, "N'être qu'un peintre égaré dans l'architecture," *Le Visiteur* 13, Paris, Société Française des Architectes et Infolio, 2009.

15   Here, the use of the term "subject" refers to the thinking being (*l'être pensant*).

its role is to compose with a novel agent of the plan: the landscape. The plan that Le Corbusier designs for a small house on the banks of Lake Léman in 1923 is based on the foundational choice of placing an 11-meter-long window, which plays the role of the "house's principal agent"[16] ("*l'acteur primordial*"). Corseaux Croquis. One sketch depicts a scene where the window unites the lake with the interior space. The foreground and the background coexist; the interior sill underlines the horizon and bears the weight of the faraway mountains it frames — a weight that is felt through the scene of high, distant, crests. A ledge is positioned and dimensioned so that it may conceal the immediate contours of the house: the aim is to reel in the lake and dramatize the view. The drawing seizes and interprets the landscape: it excludes, selects, and accentuates such and such an element. As a result, all lines are treated equally, etched from the same stroke, because they all pertain to the same, indivisible, event. Style and substance are interchanged: new aims in the drawing support new graphical methods. In comparison with those of architects from the Beaux-Arts, the sketches that Le Corbusier produces in the 1920s display more of a childish quality, of an enchanting quality even. The drawing no longer exhibits that academic knowledge solely preoccupied with the layout and rendering of ornaments. It becomes concerned with the edges of volumes, the smoothness of bare surfaces, all reflecting the external spectacle. Although it exists in the foreground, the architectural enclosure strives to act as a backdrop highlighting the Nature-canvas.

From now on, the building needs the landscape to be complete, since it no longer resides in a confined self-sufficient order but in the creative realm of a "successful interdependency" with the outside. This interdependency relies on the tension created when the gaze is alternately retained by the opaque surface and set free by the opening. The walls' layout procures for the visitor moments of visual and cognitive apnea, succeeded by moments of breathing. While modern construction techniques allow for the exclusive use of glass in façades, Le Corbusier notes that revealing everything at once actually dissolves the emotion: "[…] for the ever-present and overpowering scenery on all sides has a tiring effect in the long run. […] To lend significance to the scenery one has to restrict it and give it proportion; the view must be blocked by walls which are only pierced at certain strategic points and there permit an unhindered view."[17] The wall that hides the landscape creates a longing for the view and causes astonishment to happen when the landscape is revealed again. Opening the plan does not amount to a constructive performance aimed at literal transparency (the glass pavilion); rather it performs an *economics of vision* (*une* économie *du visible*). The appearance of the horizon inside the built frame is made all the more intense because it has been orchestrated and staged via an itinerary, whose conception could be equated with that of scenario: "The eye should not always be stimulated in the same manner, or it becomes tired; but give it the necessary 'rotation' and change of scene and your walks will be neither tiring nor drowsy."[18] This quote explains the "Romanesque" in Corbusian space, as it composes an eventful, contrasting journey where the element of surprise governs the spatiotemporal narrative. The sketched-out perspective becomes a draft representation, which can determine the plan.

The building no longer competes with Nature; instead, it becomes a platform from which to contemplate it. Seen from the inside, the house preciously encases the landscape.[19] Awakened, the eye begins to crave the outside, a craving both satisfied and sustained by architecture. Le Corbusier writes, "[Loos] once said to me, 'No intelligent man ever looks out of his window; his window is made of ground glass; its only function is to let light in, not to look out of.'"[20] Loos appears to be the last maker of interiors,[21] while Le Corbusier becomes the first architect to institute claustrophobia as a fundamental condition of architectural conception.[22] Extending the viewer's gaze as far as possible becomes an obsessive task. The landscape must be seized by any means necessary. And thus, altitude, which goes hand in hand with open view, becomes a preferred theme in both the Theorist's writings and the Designer's sketches:

"And in proportion as the horizon widens more and more, one's thought seems to take on a larger and more comprehensive cast: similarly, if everything in the physical sphere widens out, if the lungs expand more fully and the eye takes in vast

16   Le Corbusier, *Une petite maison* (Zurich: Artemis, 1954; consulted edition, Zurich: Artemis, 1993, 30–31) and Le Corbusier *Œuvres Complètes* (Zurich: Artémis, 1964), vol. 1, 74–75. Slender iron stems support the window's reinforced concrete lintel. The house was built in 1924. It must be specified that the sketch referred to here is dated to 1945 (it was produced a posteriori for demonstrative purposes).

17   Le Corbusier, *Une petite maison* (French, German, and English edition; Zurich: Éditions d'architecture, 1993), 23–24.

18   Le Corbusier, "The City of To-morrow and Its Planning," translated from the eighth French edition of *Urbanisme* with an introduction by Frederick Etchells (New York: Dover Publications, Inc., 1987), 62. Original French quote by Le Corbusier, *Urbanisme* (Paris: G. Crès et Cie, 1925; edition consulted, Paris: Arthaud), 58. We note that the French etymology of "scenario" is "décor" and "scene."

19   In French: "La maison devient l'écrin du paysage." The author borrows the expression from Edith Girard.

20   Le Corbusier, "Urbanisme." Translation taken from "The City of To-morrow and Its Planning," 184. In the published book in English, "Loos" has been replaced by "a friend."

21   In Loos's houses, the furniture, although positioned at the periphery, is nevertheless oriented inward. See Beatriz Colomina, "The Split Wall: Domestic Voyeurism," in *Sexuality & Space* (New York: Princeton Architectural Press, 1992).

distances, so too the spirit is roused to a vital activity. Optimism fills the mind. For a wide horizontal perspective can deeply influence us at the expense of little actual trouble."[23] The far-reaching sight develops into something other than an aesthetical value; it is equated with therapy, as if the eye and the mind were breathing together. Here, Le Corbusier formulates the spatial conditions of the mind. Architecture practically becomes an extension of medicine.

The elevation of the viewpoint — as in the Villa Savoye, a few meters are sufficient — is accompanied by a centrifugal motion, as if caused by a magnetic attraction. Contemplating the landscape prompts the desire to get closer to it. The vertical window, precisely because of its proportions, reduces the width of the angle of outward vision, especially when the viewer positions himself a few steps away from the opening. Because panes open inward, no furniture may be placed before the window. The horizontal opening, however, is easily coupled with a ledge, by which the viewer is invited to sit.[24] En série: Savoir Cuisine + Savoir Terrasse + Corseaux Jardin. While drawing views to the very core of the plan, the horizontal window also achieves a peripheral occupation of space, as illustrated by the layout of the kitchen in the Villa Savoye. The body can sit at its edge, at the threshold, from where he may look into the distance. The body is placed precisely where the cone of vision projects outward, precisely where the angle of view is at its widest. The ledge replaces the erstwhile fireplace and the periphery becomes the core, so to speak. In Poissy, the chimney is part of the peripheral storage space, and in the Jaoul House, the arches are supported by a multifunctional wall. The building's envelope is no longer a mask — as in Loos's houses — but a border that hosts an ensemble of outposts (offices, balconies, integrated shelves) and that tip the gaze toward the outside. Unlike in the salons of the Enlightenment, the perception of the surroundings — garden or landscape — occurs here in a more solitary manner: the plan distributes private spaces, corners, in such a way as to suggest that the occupant ought to be alone to appreciate the landscape. Savoie Bureau. Occupying the periphery of the plan means not only seeing the landscape but inhabiting it as well. Paysage Rio. In a lecture in 1929, Le Corbusier says: "I perceive that the project we are designing is neither alone nor isolated; that the air around it constitutes other surfaces, other grounds, other ceilings […] A project is not made only of itself: its surroundings exist. The surroundings envelop me in their totality as in a room."[25] Architecture claims the exterior and turns it into an interior. If the classical building enclosure used to sequester the gaze, the modern opening sets it free, all the while "internalizing" the landscape.[26] Indeed, most of the "five points of a new architecture" may be read as a tribute to Nature.[27] For the occupant, the building becomes a means to see rather than an object to look at: the viewer looks through it as if it were a lens.

But what has become today of the eye's desires, of its eagerness to see the world through architecture? Many buildings, emblematic of contemporary architectural production, reorient the occupant's gaze toward the inside. The effect of opacity, specific to volumes whose skin is uniform, stems not from constructive constraints, nor from defensive necessities, as was the case before. Soler + CGLA. Today the occupant's gaze is caught in a flood of pixels, disenchanted, and often devoid of critical thought about the inhabitable space. As if it was content with the voluntary confinement that many buildings bestow upon it.[28] The success of silk-screened glass and perforated sheeting "armors" — surfaces that come between the occupant's eye and the exterior — is symptomatic of a desire to confiscate the outside and subsequently produce ersatz landscapes, as if revamping the forsaken wallpaper in a high-tech disguise. Indeed, contemporary architectural production is buttressed by intellectual impoverishment, technological trickery, façade fetishism, and, let us say it, by the ostrich mentality infused into numerous signature buildings. As a result, it deliberately closes the eyes that architecture, through a lengthy evolution that freed the interior space of fortresses and walls, had just opened. It does so as one would close the eyes of the dead.

Translated from French by Marianne Potvin. Originally published as « Le regard hors les murs, » in *Cahiers de l'Ecole de Blois* no. 10 (« Lire le paysage »), Paris, Editions de la Villette, 2012.

22 We note here that the roots of "window" are "wind" and "eye."

23 Le Corbusier, "The City of To-morrow and Its Planning," 186.

24 On the debate opposing Le Corbusier and Auguste Perret on the issue of the horizontal window and the vertical window, see Le Corbusier, "Etude d'une fenêtre moderne," in *Almanach d'architecture moderne*, Paris, 1925, 97.

25 Le Corbusier, "Architecture in Everything, City Planning in Everything," third conference, October 8, 1929, at the Faculty of Exact Sciences of Buenos Aires, translated by Edith Schreiber Aujame in *Precisions on the Present State of Architecture and City Planning* (Cambridge, MA: MIT Press, 1991), 77. French quote published in Le Corbusier, *Précisions sur un état présent de l'architecture et de l'urbanisme* (Paris: G. Crès et Cie, 1930; edition consulted, Paris: Altamira, 1994), 78.

26 "The site is the 'plate' where architectural composition occurs. Outside, architecture adds to the site. But inside, architecture integrate the site." Le Corbusier, *Entretien avec les étudiants des écoles d'architecture* (Paris: Minuit, 1957; edition consulted, Paris: Minuit, 1987).

27 I should like to specify that this refers to nature, and not garden, which would mean a nature that has been transformed. From the Villa Savoie (Poissy) to the Jaoul houses (Neuilly), Le Corbusier always favored natural grounds, left unattended, over landscaped grounds.

28 See Karim Basbous, "Au nom du 'concept,'" *Le Visiteur* 17, Paris, SFA, 2011.

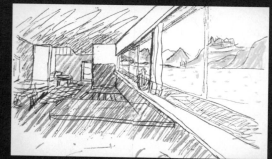

Le Corbusier, croquis du projet pour une petite maison au bord du lac Léman (1923)

Le Corbusier, extrait d'un croquis de la baie de Rio

Henri Matisse, fenêtre à Collioure, 1905

North versus South
The Mediterranean and the Histories of Modern Architecture[1]
Michelangelo Sabatino

The aim of this essay is to situate Mediterranean modernism and the vernacular tradition in relation to often-times volatile discourses on regionalism, nationalism, internationalism, critical regionalism, and postmodernism. Although a renewed interest in classicism, spurred by the rise of nationalist ideologies, helped shape modernism in the Mediterranean and beyond during the early twentieth century, this was only one side of the story.[2] Equally implicated in the history of modernism was a parallel appropriation of the forms and materiality of vernacular buildings that shape the rural and urban landscapes of the Mediterranean. The rediscovery and appropriation of the vernacular — no less tied to political events of the time — is a less well understood aspect of the history of Mediterranean modernism. By exploring the impact of the vernacular on the rise and diffusion of modernism, this essay takes a fresh look at the moment when professionally trained architects began to go beyond the academy for instruction and inspiration, and projected modern values onto anonymous building traditions that flourished for millennia among the pre-industrial agrarian cultures of the Mediterranean Basin. Paralleling the rise of modernity during the interwar years to its revision starting in the 1960s, architects working in Spain, France, Italy, Greece, Turkey, and North Africa began to discover in the built forms of "organic" and "spontaneous" villages and settlements an antidote to the style-driven eclecticism of nineteenth-century historicism. The rediscovery of the vernacular was taken as an opportunity to deeply engage elements of the local context — climate, geography, materials, and tradition — in the search for solutions for a number of building types ranging from multifamily units to villas and civic buildings.

Some of the best-known works of Mediterranean modernism — Le Corbusier's Villa Mandrot in Le Pradet, France (1931), Adalberto Libera's Casa Malaparte in Capri, Italy (1938–42), Josep Lluís Sert's Fondation Maeght in Saint-Paul de Vence (1959–64), and Alvaro Siza's Bouça Housing Estate (1973–77) in Porto, Portugal — exempli-

1   This essay draws from the introduction to Jean-François Lejeune and Michelangelo Sabatino, eds., *Modern Architecture and the Mediterranean: Vernacular Dialogues and Contested Identities* (London: Routledge, 2009), 1–12. Its contents also draw from Michelangelo Sabatino, *Pride in Modesty: Modernist Architecture and the Vernacular Tradition in Italy* (Toronto and Buffalo: University of Toronto Press, 2010).

2   Several overviews have been published that explore the impact of classicism on modern architecture. See Wolf Tegethoff, "From 'Modern' Classicism to Classic Modernism: Methods and Objectives of Architecture in the First Half of the Twentieth Century," in Gottfried Boehm, Ulrich Mosch, and Katharina Schmidt, eds., *Canto d'Amore — Classicism in Modern Art and Music, 1914–1935* (Basel: Paul Sacher Foundation, 1996), 442–451; Asko Salokorpi, ed., *Classical Tradition and the Modern Movement* (Helsinki: Museum of Finnish Architecture, 1985); Robert A. M. Stern (with Raymond W. Gastil), *Modern Classicism* (New York: Rizzoli, 1988).

Michelangelo Sabatino (Ph.D.) was trained as an architect and architectural historian in Italy, Canada, and the United States. His scholarship and teaching explore architecture and the allied arts by drawing from cultural and material history as well as anthropology and human geography.

After completing a postdoctoral fellowship at Harvard University's Department of the History of Art and Architecture and teaching at Yale University's School of Architecture, he was appointed at the Gerald D. Hines College of Architecture, where he now serves as Associate Professor and Director of the History, Theory, and Criticism program.

His book *Pride in Modesty: Modernist Architecture and the Vernacular Tradition in Italy* (2010) has won four national awards including the 2012 Alice Davis Hitchcock Book Award from the Society of Architectural Historians. Sabatino's collected volume *Modern Architecture and the Mediterranean: Vernacular Dialogues and Contested Identities* (coedited with Jean-François Lejeune, 2010) received a commendation from the UIA's International Committee of Architectural Critics. His scholarly publications are available in Italian, German, and French.

fy the breadth and diversity of this phenomenon. Yet they have rarely been brought together and examined through the lens of their shared debt to vernacular sources. Viewed as part of a collective phenomenon, they bring into relief the specificity of Mediterranean modernism, calling to mind Fernand Braudel's description of the Mediterranean as a place of many disparate voices within a climate that has "imposed its uniformity on both landscape and ways of life."[3] Architects, critics and historians such as Nikolaus Pevsner, Philip Johnson, and Henry-Russell Hitchcock stressed the contribution of the vernacular buildings of the northern countries to the work of Arts and Crafts "pioneers" like William Morris, but overlooked the equally compelling contribution of the Mediterranean vernacular to the modernism that flourished on its shores. And even though studies of the late 1940s and early 1950s brought forth new perspectives that expanded the canon of "modern" buildings and ideals, the work of tracing and attempting to understand the sources of Mediterranean modernism and the operations of appropriation it entailed have been neglected.

3   Fernand Braudel, *The Mediterranean and the Mediterranean World in the Age of Philip II* (London: Collins, 1972 [first published in French in 1949]): "Nevertheless it is significant that at the heart of this human unit, occupying an area smaller than the whole, there should be a source of physical unity, a climate, which has imposed its uniformity on both landscape and ways of life. Its significance is demonstrated by contrast with the Atlantic."

Across national borders, like-minded architects in the Mediterranean Basin subscribed to a "lyrical" Rationalism that rejected "naïve functionalism," patently dismissed academic historicism while embracing the vernacular tradition; the subtle differentiation between history (i.e., historicism) and, which was perceived as a living tradition (vernacular) generated tension and resistance on the part of critics whose vision of modernity precluded any dialogue with the spaces and places of the past. With all the risks that such generalizations entail, the essay argues that avant-garde architects and critics working in England, Germany, Holland, and Switzerland, for example, tended to associate modernity with new materials and industrial building technologies, while their counterparts in countries surrounding the Mediterranean Sea, though equally utopian, also found inspiration in the quotidian reality of the timeless buildings of landscapes drenched with sun and often shaped with "low-tech" traditional construction methods. Not by coincidence, Mediterranean modernists tended to prefer the stereotomic and shade-enhancing qualities of load-bearing walls of "liquid stone" (i.e., reinforced concrete) to the post-and-beam tectonics of glass and steel.

One of the motivations for appropriating vernacular forms from the turn of the century well into the 1940s, at least, was the quest for "authentic" national identity. Ethnographers and geographers who drew public attention to vernacular architecture during the nineteenth and early twentieth centuries furthered the ideologically driven pursuit of national identity. Their activity played a leading role in the transformation of architectural practice at precisely the moment when industrialization began to radically alter relationships between countryside and city. The growing awareness of shared origins among agrarian cultures helped shape national identity in the arts. Whereas the relationship between nationalism and modern architecture has been closely studied, the pan-regional, transnational phenomenon of Mediterranean modernism has been neglected in monographic studies of individual architects as well as comprehensive surveys of twentieth-century architecture and urbanism. There have been exceptions. In his *Encyclopédie de l'architecture nouvelle* (1948–57), a three-volume overview in which climate and geography were the framework for presenting the development of modern architecture, Italo-Swiss architect and critic

[20]

Alvaro Siza. Bouça Housing
Estate in Porto, Portugal
(1973–77)

José Luis Sert. Fondation
Maeght in Saint-Paul de Vence,
France (1959–64)

[12]

Luis Barragán. House and
Studio, Mexico City, Mexico
(1948)

[48]

Lúcio Costa, Oscar Niemeyer,
Affonso Reidy, Jorge Moreira,
et.al. Ministry of Education and
Public Health. Rio de Janeiro,
Brazil (1936–43)

[24]

Moshe Safdie. Habitat '67
Housing, Montréal

Alberto Sartoris distinguished between the Mediterranean climate and order (Ordre et climat méditerranees, vol. 1, 1948), that of the northern countries (Ordre et climat nordiques, vol. 2, 1957), and that of the Americas (Ordre et climat américains, vol. 3, 1954):

> **There can be no doubt that, through the different eras, the spirit has revealed itself in Mediterranean order and climate. Modern architecture has been bathed in the most beautiful light and we may follow, step by step, its progress through the places and nations that border the sea.**[4]

Some recent overviews of world architecture have taken up where Sartoris left off to explore how geography shaped twentieth-century architecture and urbanism.[5] For the most part, these studies stand as isolated instances, and while surveys of twentieth-century architecture tend to address nationalism, they rarely address the transnational phenomenon of Mediterranean modernism that existed within and not in opposition to modernism.

Origins of Mediterranean Modernism

The origins of the Mediterranean modernism phenomenon can be traced to the 1920s and 1930s. Writing just before the outbreak of the Spanish Civil War, Josep Lluís Sert, a founding member of Grupo de Artistas y Técnicos Españoles Para la Arquitectura Contemporánea (GATEPAC), asserted:

> **Technically, modern architecture is in part the result of the contribution of Northern countries. But spiritually, it is the style of Mediterranean architecture that influences the new architecture. Modern architecture is a return to the pure and traditional forms of the Mediterranean. It is the victory of the Latin sea!**[6]

Sert identified a number of issues central to Mediterranean modernism. He drew attention to competing approaches to the *Neues Bauen* or New Architecture among architects working in Germany, Holland, and Switzerland, the pioneering centers of industrialization, on the one hand, and those working in southern Mediterranean countries where predominantly agrarian economies were less industrialized. Although Sert's differentiation between technology (an achievement of northern countries) and spirituality (a southern aptitude) was somewhat stereotypical, at its core was a critique of the materialist and functionalist strain of the New Architecture. Taking his cue from Le Corbusier's observations on industrialization and "*l'art paysan*" or peasant art, Sert identified the influence of "pure and traditional forms" (i.e. vernacular) in Mediterranean modernism.[7]

Architects in Italy, France, and Greece during those years were anxious to show how the latent "modernism" of extant vernaculars did not preclude a critical engagement with national identity. For reform-minded architects working in Fascist Italy, the "Italian-ness" and modernity of the extant vernacular was used to undermine the bombastic monumentality of classicism.[8] For example, although identity issues related to nationalism no doubt factored heavily in Sert and Libera's work and writings, their primary concern was that the New Architecture achieve a transnational character as Mediterranean. Sert expressed his interest in "standard" Mediterranean vernacular architecture while comparing extant row houses to J.J.P. Oud's Stuttgart housing estate for the Weissenhofsiedlung (1927). Commenting on indigenous, pre-industrial standardized dwelling units in Spain's San Pol de Mar, Sert welcomed "the absence of all aesthetic concerns: fantasy, originality, historical styles, scholastic culture, individualism,"[9] and went on to show how Oud's architecture reinvented the Mediterranean vernacular using new materials and building technologies.

Decades later, the debate continued to unfold even across the Atlantic in the context of postwar challenges to modernism. Following on Bernard Rudofsky's 1964 exhibition Architecture Without Architects at the Museum of Modern Art, Myron Goldfinger's publication Villages in the Sun: Mediterranean Community Architecture (1969) stressed how Mediterranean vernacular builders prefigured the efficiency of industrially produced housing by engaging with the qualities of the specific locale or site:

4 Alberto Sartoris, *Encyclopédie de l'architecture nouvelle. Ordre et climat méditerranéens*, vol. 1 (Milan, Ulrico Hoepli, 1948) (vol. 2. *Ordre et climat nordiques*, 1957; vol. 3. *Ordre et climat américains*, 1954). My translation.

5 Kenneth Frampton, ed., *World Architecture, 1900–2000: A Critical Mosaic* (Vienna, New York: Springer, 1999–2000), and in particular, Vittorio Magnago Lampugnani, ed., *Mediterranean Basin*, vol. 4.

6 José Luis Sert, *Raices Mediterráneas de la arquitectura moderna*, in *A.C.* 18, 1935, 31-33. Reprinted in Antonio Pizza, ed., *J. LL. Sert and Mediterranean Culture* (Barcelona, Colegio de Arquitectos de Cataluña, 1997), 217–219. On Sert's Mediterranean, see Jan Birksted, *Modernism and the Mediterranean: The Maeght Foundation* (Burlington, VT: Ashgate, 2004).

7 Francesco Passanti, "The Vernacular, Modernism, and Le Corbusier," in *Journal of the Society of Architectural Historians* 4, 1997: 438–451.

8 Michelangelo Sabatino, "Space of Criticism: Exhibitions and the Vernacular in Italian Modernism," in *Journal of Architectural Education* 62, 2, February, 2009.

9 Jose Luis Sert, *Raices Mediterráneas de la arquitectura moderna,*, 25.

[18]

Le Corbusier. Villa Mandrot in Le Pradet, France, 1931

[19]

André Lurçat. *Hotel Nord-Sud* (Hotel North-South), Calvi (1931)

[10]

Charles W. Moore, Site Plan, Kresge College at the University of California, Santa Cruz (1974)

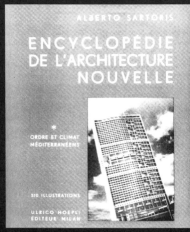

Alberto Sartoris, Cover of *Encyclopédie de l'architecture nouvelle: Ordre et climat méditerranéens*

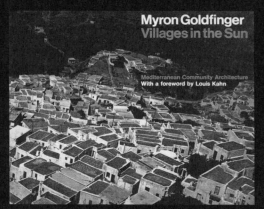

Myron Goldfinger, *Villages in the Sun – Mediterranean Community Architecture*

Since population demands will soon force the rapid development of buildings systems, we can return to the spirit of the Mediterranean village not through imitation or romantic interpretation, but through our productive capacity to develop the unit additive form out of advanced technology and thorough our belated concern for man's spiritual and spatial needs. Repetition without monotony was characteristic of the earliest human settlements.[10]

Goldfinger's study drew attention to examples of modern architecture that he claimed were inspired by Mediterranean vernacular buildings: examples shown range from José Luis Fernández del Amo's Franco-era housing estate in Vegaviana (1954-59) to Israeli-born Moshe Safdie's Habitat '67 for Montreal. Even though authors like Goldfinger and Rudofsky credit this tradition as influential form givers, to the extent that vernacular forms were appropriated by signature architects throughout the twentieth century to address issues of identity and program, site, and context, the "authors" have not been adequately recognized. For example, rarely are the builders actually credited for their work. And, since the vernacular builders were not typically identified by name and rarely recorded their own works, the question of authorship has been rarely addressed.[11] This is partly because these architects viewed anonymity as one of the most modern aspects of extant vernacular and even if this wasn't true (i.e., builders could actually be identified), they still insisted on not actually crediting individuals.

Like Goldfinger, Rudofsky stressed anonymity when he promoted "the idea that the philosophy and know-how of the anonymous builders presents the largest un-tapped source of architectural inspiration for industrial man."[12] Although Rudofsky's examples were not drawn exclusively from the Mediterranean region and included works in Asia and Africa, what is worthy of note is the fact that he almost totally ignores Northern European countries like Germany, Switzerland, and England, sig-naling a shift away from the assumption of a modernism rooted in the Anglo-German context. Despite his strong interest in the anthropological dimension of the extant vernaculars he studied, Rudofsky's focus on visual comparisons led many to dismiss the book on the grounds of its lack of scholarly rigor.[13] Jean-Louis Cohen offers a more nuanced comment on this exhibition:

"Bernard Rudofsky's Architecture Without Architects, a stunning sequence of photographs shown over a period of ten years in scores of institutions after opening at the Museum of Modern Art (1964), nourished the defiance of architecture students in the face of profession's triumphalist discourse. By presenting a kind of trans-historical vernacular continuum, Rudofsky's installation stimulated the latent populism of the 1960s."[14]

The issue of "repetition without monotony," implying type and serial production in the studies of Goldfinger (and Rudofsky), was key to designers whose identity as architects was heavily invested in Mediterranean modernism. Although they were not averse to exploiting the economic advantages of new modes of production and building materials, they sought to activate the poetics of dwelling by introducing types that were appropriate to various geographic and climatic regions. Terraces, open-air roof gardens, and balconies were common architectural elements within Mediterranean modernism. Most avant-garde critics viewed any engagement with traditional types and spatial configurations as a throwback to nineteenth-century historicism. While Mediterranean modernists and architects from northern countries who did not share the same climate and geography held many of the same ideals regarding Rationalism, and the moral impetus to provide good design to the work-ing-class masses, they did not agree on how this should be achieved. Rather than view extant vernacular as a model with which to temper the generic qualities of mod-ernism with regional context, Walter Gropius, Sigfried Giedion, and Konrad Wachs-mann celebrated the universal qualities of the anonymous architecture of American wood construction such as the balloon or platform frame. This post-and-beam wood-based vernacular was at odds with the stone and masonry, wall-centered building tradition that inspired Mediterranean modernists. Giedion authored his seminal Mechanization Takes Command: A Contribution to Anonymous History (1948) while

10   Myron Goldfinger, *Villages in the Sun, Mediterranean Community Architecture* (New York, Washington, D.C.: Praeger, 1969).

11   The dialogue between professional and "amateur" practices has been recently addressed by Gerry Beegan and Paul Atkinson, eds., "The Ghosts of the Profession: Amateur, Vernacular and Dilettante Practices and Modern Design," in *The Journal of Design History* 21, 4, Dec. 2008.

12   Bernard Rudofsky, *Architecture Without Architects: A Short Introduction to Non-Pedigreed Architecture* (New York: Museum of Modern Art, 1964).

13   Paul Oliver chastised the book (and exhibition) for it "emphasis on the visual"; see Paul Oliver, "Attitudes in the Modern Movement," in Paul Oliver, ed., *Shelter and Society* (New York: Praeger, 1969), 16–21; Enrico Guidoni dismissed it on the grounds of its "formalism"; see Enrico Guidoni, *Primitive Architecture* (Milan: Electa, 1978), 10.

14   Jean-Louis Cohen, "Exhibitionist Revisionism — Exposing Architectural History," in *The Journal of the Society of Architectural Historians* 58, 3, September 1999, 316–325.

Gropius and Wachsmann pursued their dream of the prefabricated house.[15] The Mediterranean modernists, on the other hand, sought to reconcile universal with regional and national values. In certain ways they anticipated the concept of "Critical Regionalism" developed by Kenneth Frampton, Anthony Alofsin, Alexander Tzonis and Liane Lefaivre in the late 1970s early 1980s.[16]

New Objectivity (Neue-Sachlichkeit) and anonymous design was viewed favorably by some Anglo-German critics in opposition to nineteenth-century historicism as well as expressionist modernism. As such it was key to emergent notions of affordable (and "anonymous") design formulated by the German Werkbund or Peter Behrens's concept of Industriekultur. During the first decades of the twentieth century the Anglophone world was torn between the reform-driven yet elite ethos espoused by William Morris's Arts and Crafts and the Werkbund ideals that filtered into Herbert Read's influential book *Art and Industry: The Principles of Industrial Design* (1934). In one illustration, Read compared Gropius's Dammerstock housing estate in Karlsruhe (1928–29) with an electronic circuit board, implying monotony and repetition were viewed in positive terms. Other influential Anglophone critics like James M. Richards asserted that industrial vernacular could provide the basis of much-needed "greater unity of purpose":

> Such a unity of purpose allows the establishment of a unity of cultural language — the widespread vernacular, in the case of architecture, already referred to. The existence of this vernacular might be alternatively described as the acceptance of a settled anonymity in architectural design; and it is worthwhile examining the occurrence of an anonymous tradition in the periods of live architecture. We may prove to ourselves the necessity of recovering some such anonymous tradition (deriving from a greater unity of purpose) in this age, if we are to establish an architecture of cultural value.[17]

Building on these debates regarding the virtue of anonymity viewed as a counter to self-indulgence "artistry," Reyner Banham dedicated a considerable amount of energy to the study of industrial vernacular types such as grain elevators and factory buildings in the United States and Europe.[18]

Most Mediterranean modernists who practiced in predominantly Catholic countries did not want to forego shared cultural or spiritual values for mere efficiency. These tensions that pitted functional against cultural priorities paralleled a world of hybrid identities that submitted to a process of symbiosis, of migration and dialogue.[19] Within this framework of hybridity, geography has been used to define arts as well as culture.[20] Colonialism was equally instrumental in strategically perpetuating these stereotypes. To be sure, postcolonial studies have subsequently worked to deconstruct these stereotypes to show the underlying power structures that generated them. As Edward Said has argued in his Orientalist critique and Antonio Gramsci espoused in his concept of the so-called Southern Question ("la questione meridionale") geography can perpetuate stereotype and power struggles.[21] Furthermore, as Jared Diamond has suggested, geography has been used to explain the fates of human societies.[22]

In the nineteenth century, English artist and critic John Ruskin distinguished between what he believed to be the active and contemplative dispositions of northern and southern artists of the past: "So that, in the twelfth century, while the Northern art was only in need of direction, the Southern was in need of life. The North was indeed spending its valor and virtue on ignoble objects; but the South disgracing the noblest objects by its want of valor and virtue."[23] More recently, critics and historians have used the concept of North to define Scandinavian architecture.[24] In the introduction to his *Nightlands — Nordic Building*, Christian Norberg-Schulz writes:

> The book's subtitle, *Nordic Building,* has been chosen to emphasize that architecture is primarily something built, and that built form becomes an art when it gathers and represents the world to which it belongs. The Nordic art of building thus manifests what it means to "live poetically" under Nordic conditions, whereby the word *poetic* acknowledges the qualitative identity of the environment.[25]

Although some parallels do exist with regard to the American Southwest and the

15   Gilbert Herbert, *The Dream of the Factory-Made House: Walter Gropius and Konrad Wachsmann* (Cambridge, MA: MIT Press, 1984).

16   Kenneth Frampton, "Towards a Critical Regionalism: Six Points for an Architecture of Resistance," in Hal Foster, ed., *The Anti-Aesthetic: Essays on Postmodern Culture* (New York: New Press, 1998), 16–30; Liane Lefaivre and Alexander Tzonis, *Critical Regionalism: Architecture and Identity in a Globalized World* (Munich-New York: Prestel, 2003), 24–55.

17   James Maude Richards, "The Condition of Architecture and the Principle of Anonymity," in J. L. Martin, Ben Nicholson, and Naum Gabo, eds., *Circle: International Survey of Constructive Art* (London: Faber and Faber, 1937; reprinted New York: Praeger, 1971), 184–189.

18   Reyner Banham, *A concrete Atlantis: U.S. Industrial Building and European Modern Architecture* (Cambridge, MA: MIT Press, 1986).

19   Néstor García Canclini, *Hybrid Cultures: Strategies for Entering and Leaving Modernity* (Minneapolis: University of Minnesota Press, 1995).

20   Thomas Da Costa Kaufmann, *Toward a Geography of Art* (Chicago, London: University of Chicago Press, 2004).
21   Edward Said, *Orientalism* (London, Routledge and Kegan Paul, 1978); Antonio Gramsci, *The Southern Question* (Toronto, Buffalo: Guernica Editions, 2005).

22   Jared Diamond, *Guns, Germs, and Steel — The Fates of Human Societies* (New York, London: W. W. Norton,1999).
23   John Ruskin, *Mornings in Florence: Being Simple Studies of Christian Art for English Travelers* (London, G. Allen, 1899), 32.

24   Neil Kent, *The Soul of the North: A Social, Architectural, and Cultural History of the Nordic Countries, 1700–1940* (London: Reaktion, 2000); Nils-Ole Lund, *Nordic Architecture* (Copenhagen, Danish Architectural Press, 2007).

25   Christian Norberg-Schulz, *Nightlands: Nordic Building* (Cambridge, MA: MIT Press, 1996), vii–ix.

West, few critics and historians have actually discussed the South as it relates to architecture. Lewis Mumford's *The South in Architecture* (1941) is an exception. Mumford identifies adaptation to climate as a key aspect to determining appropriate types:

> **Take for example a capital matter: adaptation to our trying American climate, with the extremes of temperature that prevail in the North and the sub-tropical conditions that exist in large portions of the South. [...] The forms of building that prevail in any region reflect the degree of social discovery and self-awareness that prevails there.[26]**

Taking his cue from Mumford, Charles W. Moore defined "Southerness" as "a kind of scaled-down urbanity that seems to me, a Northerner, the most powerful southern image."[27] Shortly after writing his book on the South in architecture, Mumford found himself defending regionalism in the midst of heated debate and controversy at the Museum of Modern Art. Moore led the turn from modernism to postmodernism by vindicating the importance of place.[28] The Piazza d'Italia in New Orleans (1976) and Kresge College at the University of California, Santa Cruz (1974), evoked public spaces of Mediterranean hill towns and cities and represented a continuation of the spatial configurations typical of extant Mediterranean vernacular.

Historiography and Criticism

Although the vernacular, considered as building traditions that hark back to pre-industrial agrarian society has been the subject of much debate by architects working in countries of the South most affected by the phenomenon of Mediterranean modernism, it was overlooked by Anglo-German militant critics up to the 1950s and 1960s, for reasons cited earlier. In fact, until the 1950s and 1960s most of the major overviews of modern architecture were written by German, British, Swiss, or American scholars.[29] In Nikolaus Pevsner's *Pioneers of the Modern Movement* published in 1936,[30] although he acknowledged the contribution of the vernacular of the English countryside in William Morris's Arts and Crafts movement, the German émigré historian ignored similar experiences among those architects who looked to vernaculars of the Mediterranean Basin. As Maiken Umbach has pointed out, "Even traditional scholars such as Nicholas Pevsner acknowledged that the English and American Arts and Crafts movements in particular helped wipe away the aesthetic 'clutter' of historicist revival styles of the nineteen century, and thus prepared the ground for modern functionalism."[31] In recent years, scholars have shown that the modern movement and vernacular-inspired national romanticism in the Scandinavian countries, for example, were not as much at odds with each other as was first thought.[32]

Shortly before Pevsner's Pioneers was published, the Franco-Swiss architect Le Corbusier had already completed his rubble-wall flat-roof villa for Congrès internationaux d'architecture moderne (CIAM) patron Madame H. de Mandrot.[33] Realized on the French shores of the Mediterranean only three years after Villa Savoye, the De Mandrot Villa posed a serious challenge to militant critics who sought to undermine the complexity of Le Corbusier's modernity by reducing it to his five points. In place of the pilotis that lifted the Villa Savoye from the ground, the villa at Le Pradet was anchored with the weight of rubble walls, serving as a reminder of the role that the vernacular could still play in an organic modernism.[34] In place of the Villa Savoye's smooth surfaces and ribbon windows, the De Mandrot villa introduced the "primitive" texture of the Provençal *genius loci*.[35] More than any other Mediterranean modernist, Le Corbusier's complex oeuvre posed serious challenges to the Anglo-German axis. In a letter of 1933 to the mayor of Algiers, Le Corbusier wrote:

> **The economy of the world is upset; it is dominated by the incoherence of arbitrary and harmful groups. New groupings, and regroupings, new units of importance must come into being which will give the world an arrangement that is less arbitrary and less dangerous. The Mediterranean will form the link of one of these groupings, whose creation is imminent. Races, tongues, a culture reaching back a thousand years — truly a**

26 Lewis Mumford, *The South in Architecture — The Dancy Lectures, Alabama College 1941* (New York: Harcourt, Brace and Co., 1941), 3–41.

27 2Charles W. Moore, "Southerness: A Regional Dimension," in *Perspecta* 15, 1975, 9–17. Republished in Robert A. M. Stern, Peggy Deamer, and Alan Plattus, eds., *Re-reading Perspecta: The First Fifty Years of the Yale Architectural Journal* (Cambridge, MA: MIT Press, 2004), 328–331.

28 For a discussion on Moore's insistence on "place" versus "space," see Michelangelo Sabatino, "The Poetics of the Ordinary: The American Places of Charles W. Moore," *Places — Forum of Design for the Public Realm* 19, no. 2, Summer 2007, 62–71.

29 Panayotis Tournikiotis, *The Historiography of Modern Architecture* (Cambridge, MA: MIT Press, 1999); Maria Luisa Scalvini and Maria Grazia Sandri, *L'immagine storiografica dell'architettura contemporanea da Platz a Giedion* (Rome: Officina, 1984).

30 Nikolaus Pevsner, *Pioneers of the Modern Movement from William Morris to Walter Gropius* (London: Faber and Faber, 1936). Subsequently republished as: Nikolaus Pevsner, *Pioneers of Modern Design: From William Morris to Walter Gropius* (New Haven, London: Yale University Press, 2005).

31 Maiken Umbach and Bernd Hüppauf, eds., *Vernacular Modernism: Heimat, Globalization, and the Built Environment* (Stanford, CA: Stanford University Press, 2005), 1–23.

32 Barbara Miller Lane, *National Romanticism and Modern Architecture in Germany and the Scandinavian Countries* (New York: Cambridge University Press, 2000); and Nicola Gordon Bowe, ed., *Art and the National Dream: The Search for Vernacular Expression in Turn-of-the-Century Design* (Dublin: Irish Academic Press, 1993); Ákos Moravánszky, *Competing Visions: Aesthetic Invention and Social Imagination in Central European Architecture, 1867–1918* (Cambridge, MA: MIT Press, 1998); and Anthony Alofsin, *When Buildings Speak: Architecture as Language in the Habsburg Empire and Its Aftermath, 1867–1933* (Chicago: University of Chicago Press, 2006).

33 For a discussion on Pevsner's attitude toward Le Corbusier, see Alina Payne, "Pioneers of the Modern Movement from William Morris to Walter Gropius," in *Harvard Design Magazine* 16, 2002, 66–70.

34 The Hungarian émigré architect Marcel Breuer employed rubble-stone walls as his trademark in many of his postwar domestic designs in America: Chamberlain Cottage (Wayland, 1940); Robinson House (Williamstown, 1946); Wolfson House (New York, 1950); Hanson House (Lloyd Harbor, 1950); Cesare Cottage (Lakeville, 1951); Neumann House (Croton-on-Hudson, 1953). David Masello, *Architecture without Rules: The Houses of Marcel Breuer and Herbert Beckhard* (New York: W. W. Norton, 1993).

whole. **An impartial research group has already, this year, through the organ Prélude, shown the principle of one of these new units. It is summed up in four letters, laid out like the cardinal points: Paris, Barcelona, Rome, Algiers.**[36]

Within these new geographical coordinates the North-South axis occupied by Berlin and London (center of modernity since Karl Friedrich Schinkel redesigned the former Prussian capital and Joseph Paxton completed the Crystal Palace) were conspicuously missing.

Some have argued that the anticlassical bias of Arts and Crafts architects in England and Germany generated a backlash against the Mediterranean and its traditions.[37] One such anticlassical stance was Charles Rennie Macintosh's description of his Hill House on the outskirts of Glasgow (1903): "Here is the house. It is not an Italian villa, or English Mansion House, Swiss Chalet, or a Scotch Castle. It is a Dwelling House."[38] The anticlassical attitude of the Arts and Crafts movement inverted a pluri-secular exchange between architects of the North and South that flourished from the Renaissance through to the Grand Tour years.[39] Only grudgingly did militant critics like Sigfried Giedion make concessions to the classical tradition:

Tony Garnier felt an attraction to the classical, as the modeling of his buildings shows. He broke through this attachment, however, in many details of his *Cité Industrielle*. Its houses, with its terraces and the gardens on their flat roofs are a sound combination of modern construction and the old tradition of the Mediterranean culture.[40]

Mediterranean modernism was eclipsed not only in Pevsner's *Pioneers* but in other influential narratives of the 1930s. Philip Johnson and Henry-Russell Hitchcock's exhibition and catalogue *The International Style: Architecture Since 1922* (1932) is a major case in point. Although Johnson and Hitchcock published André Lurçat's Hotel Nord-Sud in Calvi (1931) (along with Le Corbusier's De Mandrot villa), they failed to acknowledge the architect's explicit engagement with a Mediterranean vernacular tradition characterized by whitewashed "pure" volumes replete with flat roofs.[41] Contemporary commentators in Italy like the architect and critic Gio Ponti were quick to notice the "perfect Mediterranean character" of André Lurçat's Hotel Nord-Sud.[42] In Ponti's estimation, Lurçat's embrace of the Mediterranean was not at odds with the "*schietto stile moderno* (straightforward modern style)" of the work. Another misreading by Johnson and Hitchcock can be seen in the inclusion of Luigi Figini and Gino Pollini's Electric House (*Casa Elettrica*), realized as a temporary pavilion for the IV Triennale held in Monza in 1930.[43] When compared with a hand-drawn perspective rendering of the house replete with Pompeian red exterior walls and nautical detailing against the backdrop of Mediterranean pines, the black and white photograph in Johnson and Hitchcock's book reveals how the photographic medium falls short of conveying the Mediterranean qualities of the building. To be sure, Johnson and Hitchcock's glossing over the Mediterranean qualities of these works is not surprising in light of the fact that they were not really interested in recognizing the regional or national iterations of modernism because it would have weakened their curatorial argument geared toward the promotion of an international style. What they failed to understand is how the shared heritage of the vernacular helped Mediterranean modernists identify with a pan-regional and collective ethos without forgoing their national identities.

With the completion of two Mediterranean modern masterpieces during the postwar period, Le Corbusier's Chapel of Notre-Dame-du-Haut at Ronchamp (1956) and Sert's Maeght Foundation in Saint-Paul (1964), controversy arose and prompted substantial revisions to orthodox modernism. Both buildings convey a sense of weight and cavernousness that runs counter to a modernity in thrall to transparency. The Mediterranean modernism of Le Corbusier's Ronchamp is characterized by the use of stereotomic walls that convey stability and irregularity. The vault and wall are not exclusive to the Mediterranean vernacular and can also be found in the rural farmsteads of Germany and Switzerland or the Scottish baronial castles that inspired Macintosh. Although vernacular farmhouses typical of countries of the North are not whitewashed in the manner typical of Mediterranean countries, they are often clad with white stucco. In Germany, rural structures built of stone and wood inspired the

35 Bruno Reichlin, "'Cette belle pierre de Provence,' La Villa De Mandrot," in *Le Corbusier et la Méditerranée* (Marseilles: Parenthèses, 1987), 131–136. On Corbusier and the vernacular, see Gerard Monnier, "L'architecture vernaculaire, Le Corbusier et les autres," in *La Méditerranée de Le Corbusier* (Aix-en-Provence: Publications de l'Université de Provence, 1991), 139–155.

36 Cited in Mary McLeod, "Le Corbusier and Algiers," in *Oppositions* 19–20, Winter/Spring 1980, 55–85; "Le Corbusier — L'appel de la Méditerranée," in Jacques Lucan, ed., *Le Corbusier: une Encyclopédie* (Paris: Éditions du Centre Pompidou/CCI, 1987), 26–31.

37 Julius Posener, "Häring, Scharoun, Mies, and Le Corbusier," *From Schinkel to the Bauhaus* (New York: George Wittenborn, 1972), 32-41.

38 James Macaulay, *Hill House — Charles Rennie Mackintosh* (London: Phaidon, 1994), 15. Originally cited in Walter W. Blackie, "Memories of Charles Rennie Mackintosh — II" *Scottish Art Review* 4, 1968, p. 6.

39 Guido Beltramini, ed., *Palladio nel Nord Europe: Libri, Viaggiatori, Architetti* (Milan: Skira, 1999).

40 Sigfried Giedion, *Space, Time and Architecture: The Growth of a New Tradition* (Cambridge, MA: Harvard University Press, 1941), 693.

41 See Jean-Louis Cohen, *André Lurçat: 1894–1970: Autocritique d'un moderne* (Liège: Mardaga, 1995), 110–120.

42 Gio Ponti, "Esempi da fuori per le case da Riviera — una interessante costruzione mediterranea a Calvi in Corsica" in *Domus*, November 1932, 654–655.

43 Giacomo Polin, *La Casa elettrica di Figini e Pollini, 1930* (Rome: Officina, 1982).

cavernous expressionist and organic architecture of Hans Poelzig and Hugo Häring. Beyond the Mediterranean Basin, but still within its sphere of influence, Mexican architect Luis Barragán preferred the reassuring weightiness of stereotomic walls and appropriated cues from the form and color of pre-industrial vernacular buildings of Mexico to achieve his distinct brand of modernism from the 1930s through the 1970s. Writing in response to banal functionalism and in defense of the spirituality in modern architecture that he echoed in the design of his own home, completed in 1948, Barragán asserted: "All architecture which does not express serenity fails in its spiritual mission. Thus it has been a mistake to abandon the shelter of walls for the inclemency of large areas of glass."[44] To be sure, the thick sheltering walls that gave Barragán's architecture its spiritual dimension also played an important functional role in cooling, compared to glass enclosures.

Operative interest in the culture and arts of the Mediterranean Basin was alive in the Americas since the 1930s. One such example is the Mediterranean modernist qualities of Irving Gill's simple yet sophisticated stucco-clad Walter L. Dodge House in West Hollywood, completed in 1916, or George Washington Smith's Spanish Colonial Revival domestic architecture, also in California.[45] During the late 1920s, Louis I. Kahn traveled to Italy, visiting Capri, the Amalfi Coast, Siena, and Rome, and produced a number of watercolors and drawings of vernacular and classical sites that left a lasting impression on his design practice, especially during the 1950s.[46] Sert's appointment as Dean of the Harvard University Graduate School of Design in 1953 brought the Mediterranean discourse across the Atlantic to an important center of American architectural discourse.[47] During the postwar years, the United States began to promote Pan-Americanism, and so too Central and South America contributed significantly to help bring a Mediterranean modernity to the forefront and to challenge the hegemony of northern architects. The *Brazil Builds* exhibition at the Museum of Modern Art in 1943 was the first to promote architects Lucio Costa and Oscar Niemeyer, both of whom were already known in the United States for of their 1939 World's Fair building in New York. Their reinforced concrete Ministry of Education building in Rio de Janeiro, completed in 1942, was the first to employ, for a new architectural type such as the tower, the *brise soleil* common to vernacular buildings in sunny climates.[48] (figs. 11-12) If architects of the North like Walter Gropius stressed transparency, architects of the South stressed the poetics of shadows. For those architects in thrall to Mediterranean modernism, inhabiting space and place was based on the desire to activate the poetic qualities of geography and climate through architecture. Rather than view the phenomenon as an "other modern," I would argue that these protagonists of the Mediterranean helped reform the modern from within. As Maiken Umbach and Bernd Hüppauf put it: "It is, rather, the negotiation between, and the interdependence of, the regional and the global, concrete locality and border-devouring abstraction, that can generate a new and more complex narrative of the modern."[49]

44   Clive Bamford Smith, *Builders in the Sun: Five Mexican Architects* (New York: Architectural Books, 1967).

45   Thomas S. Hines, *Irving Gill and the Architecture of Reform — A Study of Modernist Architecture Culture* (New York: Monacelli Press, 2000); Patricia Gebhard, *George Washington Smith: Architect of the Spanish Revival* (Salt Lake City: Gibbs Smith, 2005). For a summary of the Mediterranean influence on architecture and urbanism, also see Jean-François Lejeune, "The Other Modern: Between the Machine and the Mediterranean," Jean-François Lejeune and Allan Shulman, *The Making of Miami Beach, 1933–1942: The Architecture of Lawrence Murray Dixon* (New York: Rizzoli, 2000), 200–224. On "Mediterranean urbanism" in the twentieth century, see Jean-François Lejeune, ed., *The New City: Modern Cities*, vol. 3, Fall 1996.

46   Vincent Scully, "Introduction," in Jan Hochstim, *The Paintings and Sketches of Louis I. Kahn* (New York, Rizzoli, 1991), 15–17; Vincent Scully, "Marvelous Fountainheads: Louis I. Kahn: Travel Drawings" *Lotus International* 68, 1991, 48–63.

47   On Sert at Harvard, see Anthony Alofsin, *The Struggle for Modernism: Architecture, Landscape Architecture, and City Planning at Harvard* (New York-London: W. W. Norton, 2002), 248–269.

48   Philip Goodwin, *Brazil Builds: Architecture New and Old, 1652–1942* (New York: Museum of Modern Art, 1943).

49   Umbach and Hüppauf, eds., *Vernacular Modernism*, 1–23.

Rewriting the Mediterranean City
Geography of Transformation
Ludovico Micara

Our ability to speak of Mediterranean cities today is due to the extraordinary capacity of these urban organisms to survive the many natural and historical challenges that they have faced over time. Survival and adaptation to changing conditions indeed characterizes the cities along the borders of the Mediterranean Sea. But if we question the reasons for this capacity, if we want to go beyond a simply descriptive phenomenology, the analysis becomes more complex and open to different answers.

A first element that could be emphasized is the fragility of these urban structures, relating to: construction with poor local materials, insufficiently elaborated and refined, such as stone, wood, and earth; different populations living over time in the same places, even if only for short periods, with heterogeneous building traditions; the geological fragility of the soils, due to inadequate conservation and destructive earthquakes; and weak regulations that have preserved current building practices rather than imposing more demanding alternatives.

These fragilities generated specific survival strategies that characterized the historical development of many Mediterranean cities. Sometimes new urban centers were created by adding elements to existing urban structures. A typical case is reuse and transformation, which the Arab invaders did with Hellenic-Roman cities such as Damascus and Aleppo, and with their monumental buildings and spaces.[1] Thus the bays of the ancient columned roads of the classical city became the covered suq's of the Arab-Islamic city, and the large spaces of the agora and the temples were used for building new public spaces and new mosques.

Another frequent strategy was to recycle the building materials of cities destroyed by wars, occupations, or earthquakes. The tendency toward the reuse or transformation of the built heritage, rather than its demolition and rebuilding, gave rise to the common practice of transforming even religious buildings as cultural dominance shifted: churches became mosques or mosques became churches. We must also consider people's ability to benefit from commercial relations, exchanges, and religious pilgrimages within the Mediterranean area. Such exchanges of people, information, technologies, and building methods created that particular Mediterranean koiné common to many urban centers.

1   C. Watzinger and K. Wulzinger, *Damaskus, die antike Stadt* (Berlin and Leipzig, 1921); J. Sauvaget, *Alep, éssai sur le développement d'une grande ville syrienne dès origines au milieu du XIXème siècle* (Paris, 1941).

Ludovico Micara is an architect and a Full Professor of Architecture and Urban Design in the Faculty of Architecture of the University G. D'Annunzio (Pescara), and is deeply involved in publications, projects, and research on Mediterranean and Islamic cities and landscapes. In 1982, he was responsible for the Venice Biennale exhibition "Architettura nei paesi islamici" and subsequently published *Architettura e spazi dell'Islam: le istituzioni collettive e la vita urbana.*

As scientific director (1996–) of the Italian Mission for the Study of the Architectural and Urban Heritage of the Islamic Period in Libya (sponsored by the Italian Ministry of Foreign Affairs and by the Libyan Department of Antiquities), he coordinated and published research on the Medina of Tripoli and the town–oasis of Ghadames. He has participated in many national and international architectural competitions, with significant distinctions. Among his built works are the Houshmand House in Tehran, a housing complex with eleven apartments, the rehabilitation and scientific restoration of the Municipal Theatre of Monterotondo (Rome), and the new building for classrooms and laboratories of the Faculty of Architecture of the University G. D'Annunzio, among others.

If we had to synthesize, by means of an image, a survival strategy reflected in these early urban fabrics, we would select the extraordinary aerial view of the ancient Palmyra that André Poidebard took at the end of the 1920s, during his mission to trace the Roman limes in Syria.[2] The village built in the palm oasis that gave the city its name stands next to the immense base of the temple of Bel, as if seeking protection. The powerful stone walls of the temple are both a strong support for the sun-dried earth buildings of the village and an insuperable but reassuring border for an urban fabric still precariously in progress. Presumably a large portion of the building materials of the village were appropriated as spolia from the ancient ruins of the temple, which provided an important stock for future buildings of the settlement. This image permits a comparison of two sizes and scales of the settlement: against the big, territorial, and almost geographical scale of the ancient urban structure and its infrastructures, such as the columned road of the Decumanus, the oasis village, with its reduced local scale, has to rely on the food, water, and building resources of the oasis for its survival.

The changing sizes of the settlements across time characterize the history of the Mediterranean cities that undergo periods of expansion and contraction. When the city opens to the great Mediterranean Basin and activates reciprocal exchanges and relations, it benefits from periods of great liveliness and expansion. When the city is obliged to rely on itself and on its limited environment, for various political, military, and international reasons, its horizons become necessarily narrower, and it tries to survive an unfavorable moment with appropriate strategies.

The purpose of the present study is to attempt to read these dynamics in history and in the recent evolutions of urban and territorial realities such as the Medina of Tripoli, the landscapes of oases, and archeological sites.

Tripoli, a Mediterranean Medina

At the start of the twentieth century, the Medina of Tripoli exhibited many of the admirable qualities of the Mediterranean cities of the Maghreb, namely a successful synthesis between features typical of Arab-Islamic cities and other characteristics deriving from the intense commercial, demographic, religious, and diplomatic exchanges with the countries that face the Mediterranean Basin.[3] Alongside the mosques with their tall, slender minarets that emphasize the cultural and religious

identity of the city, within the dense, compact fabric made of both courtyard houses and narrow alleys or cul-de-sacs, some elements differing from the local urban tradition emerge: houses overlooking the street through windows and balconies, quite uncommon in this area; the fifteenth-century castle and its bastions, built by the Spanish emperor Charles V; the unusual regular plan of some streets, that, on closer inspection, appear as traces of the Roman fabric of Oea, the old Tripoli; the size and airiness of the houses near the harbor, which recall the wide dimensions of the Roman *domus*; or the presence of the church of S. Maria degli Angeli, with its bell tower, and the many synagogues, recently transformed into mosques, showing the multi-ethnic and multi-religious dimensions of the former Medina. The prevailing orientation of the fabric toward the harbor confirms the Mediterranean character of the built-up area.[4]

The present Medina is the result of recurrent rewritings of the traditional urban pattern, starting from the Roman, going on to the Arab Islamic, then the Ottoman, the colonial, up to contemporary times. These rewritings transformed an ancient settlement based on the commercial trades of a harbor located in a large bay into the current living core of a metropolis of 1.7 million people. This new dimension completely changed the relations between the various sectors of the city. The reuse of the land base of demolished parts of the city walls for new streets, during the Italian occupation of Libya, integrated the previous Medina with the Italian city of the 1930s. This period generated a revised historical center, characterized by easily recognizable urban fabrics such as the Arab-Islamic, based on courtyard houses, and the Italian nineteenth-century mode, based on the relationship between the road layout and the resulting blocks. Today this historical core, wider than the traditional Medina, is still easily recognizable in the urban structure, with its traditional Arab-Islamic architectures, ancient Roman monuments, nineteenth-century porticos, and the "new" institutions of the colonial city.

From this first rewriting, resulting from the integration between the Medina and the Italian city, some urban transformations emerged that were connected to the new dimensions of the built area. Whereas the attention of the colonizers was focused on the so-called Italian city, where the buildings of the new institutions of the colonial power were located, the labyrinthine urban fabric of the Medina was left in the background in relation to the new geometries created by the Italian urban axes. This was a background that the

2   A. Poidebard, *La trace de Rome dans le désert de Syrie* (Paris, 1934).

3   L. Micara, "The Ottoman Tripoli: A Mediterranean Medina," in S.K. Jayyusi, R. Holod, A. Petruccioli, and A. Raymond, eds., *The City in the Islamic World* (Leiden: Brill, 2008), 383–406.

4   L. Micara, "The Model of the Medina of Tripoli: A Unique Contribution to the Understanding of the Mediterranean Cities," in Ludovico Micara, A. Petruccioli, and E. Vadini, eds., *The Mediterranean Medina* (Rome: Gangemi Editore, 2009), 440–446.

[2]

Palmyra, Syria: aerial view

[11]

Figuig: plan of a sector of the urban fabric of the *ksar* Zenaga

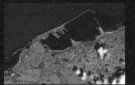

[5]

Tripoli, Libya: satellite view

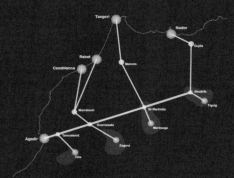

Morocco: the connections between the oases system and the main Moroccan cities

Tripoli: satellite view of the Medina

[26]

[3]

Tripoli: plan of the urban voids in the present fabric of the Medina

[29]

Umm al-Jimal, Jordan: view of the archaeological remains

[16]

Ghadames: view of a covered passageway

colonizers themselves hardly knew and was left to its mysteries, its social and religious customs, which fed the twentieth-century fascination with the Oriental city.

It is in the areas of contact between the two urban systems, coincident with the borders of the Medina, that the most relevant transformations were generated. With the demolition of some of the old walls, the construction of new roads and public buildings was allowed in their place, while parts of the fabric near the borders were "normalized" by the colonial administration. The issue of the borders of the Medina is still unsolved today, further complicated by the presence of new buildings, such as the high-rise hotels in the northwestern area of the city, or of new infrastructures, such as the great highway between the Medina and the port. This highway, created to connect the port to the main city's arteries, has taken on the role of a great beltway that avoids the city and runs along the waterfront. The beltway heavily affects the Medina. What was originally created as an urban fabric oriented toward the port does not find an access to the sea today and is enclosed within a barrier constituted by a highway that cannot easily be crossed.[5] One of the original features of the urban fabric of the Medina is thus obliterated, and this makes it much more difficult to rehabilitate the area. The move of the commercial port to the east, where greater lands and infrastructural facilities are available, may induce the displacement of the beltway, the creation of a touristic port, and an overall residential rehabilitation of the Medina. The Medina could thus rediscover one of its distinctive features by enhancing its links with the sea.

The neglect of the fabric of the Medina, even after the colonial period, produced an increasing urban decay leading to the collapse and ruin of wide sectors of the historical city, such as the small and great ghettos (hara es-saghira and hara el-kebira), which were abandoned by the Jewish population during the Arab-Israeli war in 1956. Uninhabited houses decayed and fell down, producing great voids and a progressive decline in the compact fabric. This transformation did not affect single houses; it was rather a general phenomenon that modified the original character of the residential fabric, and this produced, across time, a deep mutation in the relationship between housing type and urban morphology. The issues of Tripoli's central area remain unresolved, transforming a big metropolis into a huge, amorphous urban aggregate.

Looking at the city from a satellite view, we can imagine the pentagonal area in the northern end of the harbor increasingly empty, therefore open to new urban rewritings. Today the urban problems of Tripoli do not affect just the Medina but heavily concern the new metropolitan dimension. If we analyze the satellite image, we notice disordered development that has lost the connections that were so clear in the traditional Medina between residential fabric and public spaces.

The only ruling elements of greater Tripoli are road infrastructures that to a great extent retrace the old tracks that connected the Medina to the other centers on the coast and inland, and try to define the new urban dimension through wider and wider ring roads.

As it is impossible to approach the metropolitan dimension of greater Tripoli by means of separate projects, we need a new strategic vision to interpret the present geographical scale of the city. French landscape architect Gilles Clément intends to demolish some decayed residential fabric, called délaissés by Clément, which would integrate the resulting empty areas with other leftover spaces to establish a large metropolitan greenbelt formed by gardens, public spaces, and facilities.[6] Such a belt, following Clément's suggestions, would reach the seaside, integrating the present harbor lands in a linear system and enriching these lands with urban services. This would recreate, at metropolitan scale, the connection between residential districts and public spaces that was so relevant for the quality of the urban fabric of Mediterranean Medinas.

Today Tripoli's expansion, observed at geographical scale, fills up the territory along the Tripoli coast to the east and west of the Medina, getting close to the archeological areas of Sabratha and Leptis Magna, the ancient Roman cities that, together with Oea, the precursor of the present Medina, constituted the ancient Tripolis ("three towns"). These important areas were excavated by Italian archeologists at the beginning of the last century. What is now visible is less than the original built area and consists mainly of monumental buildings, temples and basilicas, fora, theaters and amphitheaters, thermae, and residential insulae. The increasing and amorphous urban expansion of the city overlaps with the wide, scattered archeological fabrics, partly unexcavated and formed by suburban villas, houses, and tombs. Touristic concerns and the strong appeal of the seacoasts is a further feature likely to bring new settlements near or in contact with the archeological areas.

The case of Tripoli is quite particular, as the archeological site is the Medina itself. It is still possible to recognize the cardo, the two

5   L. Micara, "Tripoli: l'affaccio a mare di una medina mediterranea," in *Portus*, 16, 2008, 78–85;

6   L. Micara and E. Vadini, "Tripoli e il suo fronte a mare (Tripoli and Its Seafront)," in *Città di Pietra (Cities of Stone)* (Venice: Venice Biennale, Marsilio, 2006), 184–189.

decumani and the series of domus as traces in the present urban fabric. The magnificent tetrapylon of Marcus Aurelius and Lucius Verus is still standing in the Medina, at the crossing point of the cardo and decumanus maximus. But the current decayed conditions of the Medina, which includes many empty and destroyed areas, could allow the excavation of these areas to bring to light the plan and the remains of the ancient city. In the new metropolitan and geographical scale it would be possible to reestablish the urban sodality that once produced the ancient Tripolis, where the archeological areas could play the role of big public spaces. This would empower an urban structure that is currently too extended, weak, and inadequate for contemporary dwelling.

The Landscapes of the Oases

The many oases scattered along the inner southern border of the Mediterranean Basin form an environmental system connected to specific natural and geographical contexts, where the presence of water is fundamental. This system is hard to transform into something different because it depends on natural conditions that are, by definition, not easy to change. Equally important for the survival of the oases and their inhabitants are the relations that were established, through caravan routes, with other oases and with the crossroads of commercial exchanges in the Mediterranean area, by land or sea.

For these reasons, some oases that were no longer crossed by these routes because of changes in the geography of commercial exchanges quickly declined and were abandoned by their inhabitants. In other cases, the oasis system adapted to the new conditions and found a way to survive and develop.

The "oasis model" is a relevant test for checking the level of transformability and survival of environmental systems that are nearly unchanged over the course of time and suffer from being highly constrained. How does such a model react to the challenge of time, to new relations with political and administrative centers of relatively recent nation-states, and to the anthropological mutation of today's inhabitants and their new living needs?

Some city-oases of the pre-desert lands of the Maghreb, such as Ghadames in Libya and Figuig in Morocco, represent interesting settlement models, both for environmental sustainability and for spatial and architectural quality. [7] These share many features with other city-oases at the edge of the Sahara: the compactness of the residential fabric, the growth of houses on several levels, the covering of passageways. The reason for such a morphological similarity resides in a series of conditions suggested by the rational and sustainable use of oasis resources. The growing height of the buildings is due to the necessity of occupying the irrigable and therefore cultivable fields as little as possible. At the same time, the compactness of the urban fabric, with its reduced open spaces and narrow, mazelike passageways, offers good protection from extreme climates in summer and a more effective water distribution in the channels along the covered paths. The building technology, adobe or pisé, drew on the building materials in situ: bricks of sun-dried earth for walls and palm wood for horizontal structures. Furthermore, such a technology permits good environmental comfort due to the high level of passive protection from day-night temperature fluctuations. Specific characteristics deriving from local situations or traditions make the fabrics of Ghadames and Figuig different: for instance, houses have courtyards in Figuig but not in Ghadames.

These urban fabrics are in a deep crisis today for various reasons. Aside from economic, anthropological, and social causes that point toward the loss of important cultural identity, other problems threaten the physical permanence of the oases settlements. First, building technologies are particularly fragile, and their efficacy in preserving the urban fabric relies on accuracy in execution and continuous maintenance. Frequently the rehabilitation of these structures is implemented with extraneous technologies, such as reinforced concrete, that does not fit with the original earth masonries, producing further damage and increasing settlement decay. Some transformations of the original housing typologies, such as the addition of new volumes in the courtyards, in galleries and terraces, or their covering or screening, worsen structural conditions and buildings' responsiveness to climate. This in turn requires new artificial and unsustainable technologies, like air-conditioning, for improving heat control and environmental comfort.

The progressive abandonment of houses by people unable to stop the decay of a compact and well-organized urban fabric is both the reason and the result of such a process. The abandonment of houses and the consequent loss of maintenance caused the collapse of these houses and increasingly produced empty spaces in a fabric characterized by

7   G. Clément, *Manifesto del terzo paesaggio* (Macerata, 2005; Editions Sujet Objet, 2004).

compactness and structural cohesion of the buildings. This became the final stage of the transformation and the main reason for the deterioration of the whole settlement. In fact, in this type of urban fabric each building is linked to the adjacent one through a structural and functional continuity that is impossible to eliminate without compromising the survival of the system. The presence of a void in the continuous fabric produces other voids around it and thus propagates and amplifies the pathology.

Could such a crisis be solved through conservation? Or is it a symptom of unexpressed attitudes that tend to devalue the traditional habitat? To address these transformations clearly requires an effort to adapt traditional typologies to changing economic and social realities, from the decrease in family size to new requirements for residential space. To simply impose conservation and restoration could be problematic. Indeed, such a prescriptive attitude basically reinforces nostalgia for the past, ignores emerging demands for change, and maintains outdated social relationships. Expert knowledge of urban fabrics, spaces, and architectural forms helps us, as architects, understand the long duration and the intrinsic flexibility of these architectures that are able to keep their identity unaltered and to absorb new transformations.

Nevertheless, it is necessary to define the new urban context where such transformations will occur. With the achievement of independence by former colonial states and the formation of new nations, "the local governance system that was intimately tied to the value of water was dismantled and remote government control introduced; the value of water eroded as society changed, institutions were dissolved, and immigrants returned to the oasis with disproportional buying power, new attitudes, a disconnect with tradition, and knowledge of technology."[8]

Water resources management moved from an integrative and sustainable system, devised to meet the long-lasting periods of resource conservation, to a supply management system. Administrators are often insensitive to the need to strike an appropriate balance between nature and society. In addition, individuals who spent many years outside of the oasis lost the sense of history and tradition that supported the community values of conservation and sustainability.[9]

Moreover, the political and social isolation of many oases, due to the reorganization of the states and regional districts, undermines the historical ties that connected them with similar oasis communities. This new situation challenges the balanced relationships between the oasis and the built area; all of the elements of the system take on different roles, searching for a new and more advanced equilibrium.

The increasing occupation of the interstitial spaces with typologies no longer based on the compactness of the fabric but on isolated buildings inside building plots diminishes the cultivable lands of the oasis. At the same time, the development of the road network creates new relations between the ksour.[10] Certainly, those new built areas that tend to fill wider and wider surfaces of the oasis should be discouraged, and new value should be conferred on the relationships between the parts, to the voids separating them, and to the public spaces organizing them

In such a transformed urban area, there should be no neat hierarchy between the most important urban elements such as new institutions and commercial centers and less important ones such as the old center, the medina with its traditional institutions, the mosque, the madrasa, and the hammam. We should return to the egalitarian character of the ancient medinas that the city-oases often preserved across centuries and that it is still possible to appreciate in some urban fabric of North Africa "physically, sociologically, historically, and ideologically defined and determined by its walls."[11] The walls constitute the raw material with which the medina is built. They define its essential and continuous character. The wall of a house is not only an element in common with the contiguous house but something that defines the adjacent street and public space. The mosque, as a public institution, was not an isolated building in the urban fabric but an organism that adjusted itself to the layout of the walls of contiguous houses and was located at the crossing of the public paths of the medina. Such an egalitarian character of the medina was gradually lost in the course of its urban development and later differentiation, creating strong inequalities in the urban fabric.[12] It rather remains an aim to pursue: to implement a well-balanced settlement given the current conditions and dimensions of the city-oases.

The Archeological Heritage and New Mediterranean Landscapes

Archeological sites have always been an essential feature of the Mediterranean landscape. Archeology, whether in the form of traces imprinted on the urban fabric and territorial network, discovered architectural

8   L. Micara, "The Town Oases of Ghadames (Libya) and Figuig (Morocco): Architectural Heritage and Sustainable Development," in Future Intermediate Sustainable Cities: A Message to Future Generations, BUE British University of Egypt, 23–25 November 2010 (Cairo: Elain Publishing Company, 2010), 500–511.

9   G. Meszoely, Water Resources Management in a Saharian Oasis, Ph.D. dissertation, Northeastern University, Boston, Massachusetts, 2006, 195.

10   Ibid.

11   Ksour, plural of the Turkish word ksar, from the Arab qasr, meaning castle or palace; indicates a fortified village in the Maghreb.

12   S. O'Meara, Space and Muslim Urban Life: At the Limits of the Labyrinth of Fez (New York: Routledge, 2007), 70.

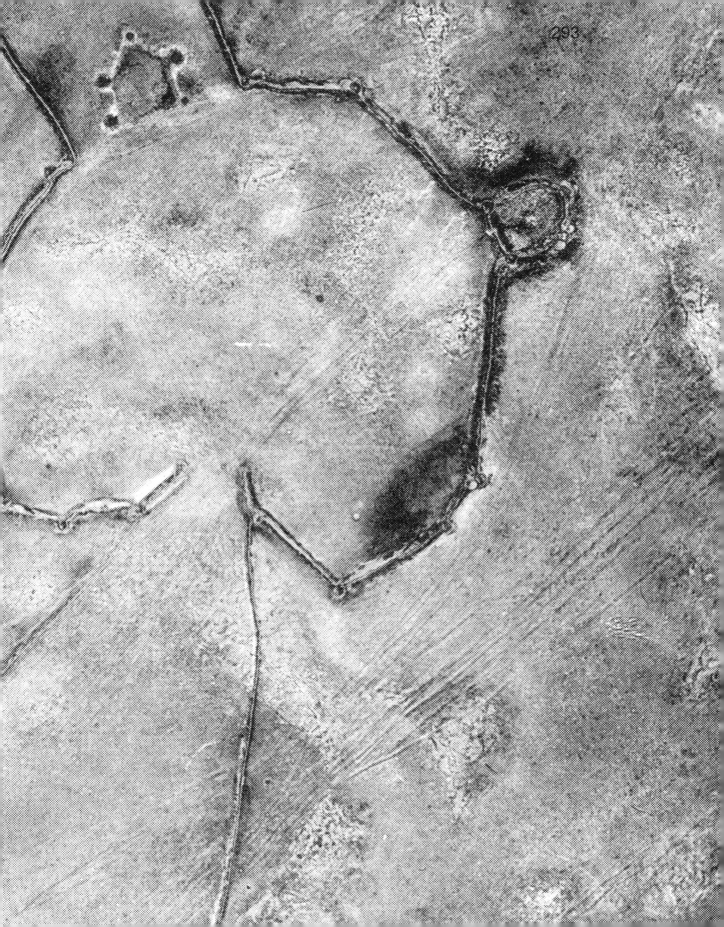

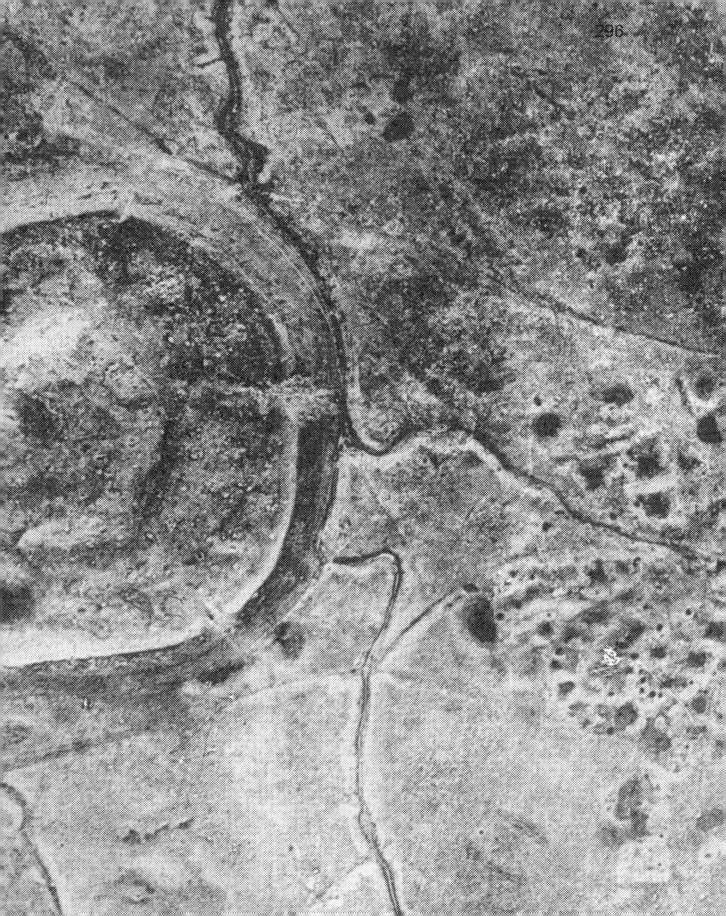

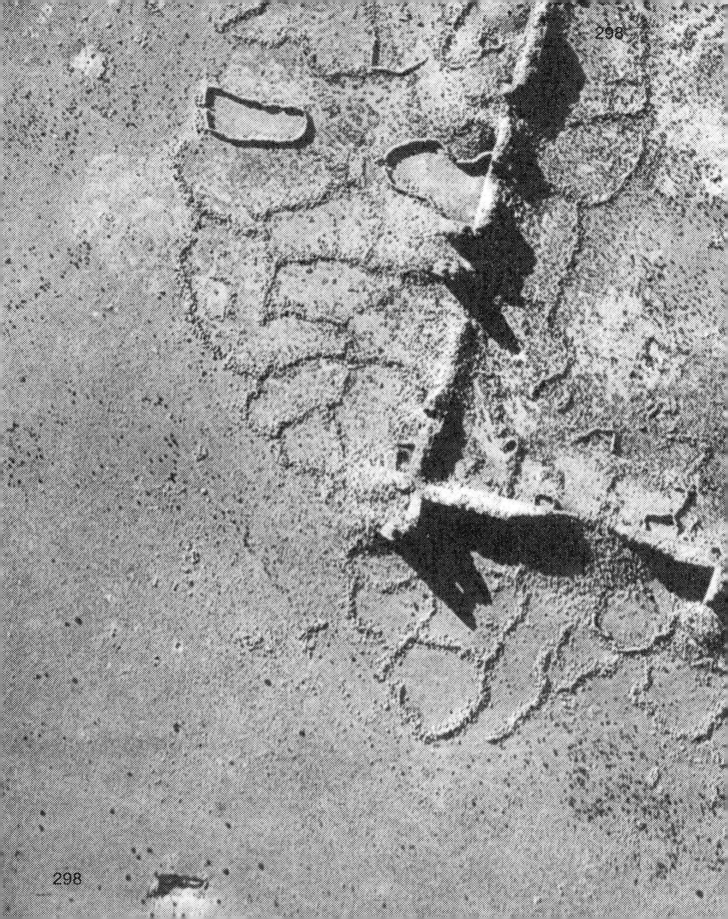

298

298

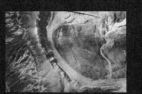

[9]

Dam of Harbaqa, Syrian Desert:
aerial view

[292]

Syrian Desert: aerial view of
a Bedouin hunting enclosure

[32]

Doura Europos, Syria:
aerial view

[294]

Syrian Desert: aerial view of
a Roman road

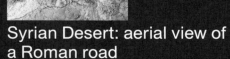

[296]

Tell Muezzar, Syrian Desert:
aerial view

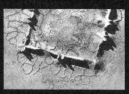

[298]

Han al-Mançoura, Syrian
Desert: aerial view

Source: A. Poidebard, *La trace de Rome dans le désert de Syrie*, Paris 1934

remains, or *spolia* reused in later buildings, is a basic component of the multifaceted identity of the Mediterranean city. Very often, however, such an important heritage does not find its place in urban systems, where it could serve as a precious cultural and environmental resource.

The main features that mark the archeological sites of the Mediterranean regions are their aesthetic quality and the historical and cultural density of the landscape in which they are located, in addition to the monumental importance of the sites themselves. Therefore protecting and valorizing them does not concern only the archeological site but its environmental context and landscape as well. Economic development further increases pressure on the areas adjacent to the sites.

These issues have been faced separately until today, but a conception of the landscape in its entirety, including its historical, cultural, physical, and perceptual dimensions, should prevail. Whereas archeological research was traditionally concerned with the centers of the ancient cities, now that these centers have been excavated and studied, the work has extended to their borders, which overlap with modern urban areas. Archeological research at a territorial and regional level is attempting to reconstruct the network that connected the scattered remains into a consistent whole. Familiarity with the ancient past is increasingly becoming an essential part of the project of Mediterranean landscapes.

The emerging concept of heritage is not necessarily associated with the idea of pure conservation. The strength of a heritage is revealed by its impact on the setting and the landscape. Indeed, the Mediterranean landscape and urban culture are shaped by this dynamic and living idea of heritage. The case of Jordan is particularly interesting because the typology of the archeological areas is very diversified, spanning from sites belonging to the ancient Nabateans, to Roman and later civilizations, to the early Islamic sites of the Ummayad Caliphate, such as the Desert Castles, to more recent sites. The peculiarity of Jordan archeological sites lies in their being prevailingly distributed along a linear system that retraces the ancient Roman Via Traiana, parallel to the Jordan River, and the eastern limes of the Roman Empire, which in turn is a settlement system. The coincidence between these two linear systems leads urban centers to develop near the archeological areas, a tendency that creates interference and mutual disturbance rather than well-balanced integration. The most common case is represented

by those contexts where the two systems just overlap, without adequate reciprocal relationships. But other cases also exist. For instance, in Jerash the two cities, the archeological and the contemporary, are placed nearly side-by-side, creating a single urban center that integrates the Roman cardo-decuman fabric with the modern one, and in Amman archeological remains are successfully included within the urban context. Other archeological sites — such as Umm al-Jimal, structurally very different from the Roman sites, although Umm al-Jimal was originally one of the many stations of the eastern Roman limes — are just as important for the quality of the remains in that they exhibit a stone building technology. The diversified territorial context within which Umm al-Jimal is located, with its cultivated fields, medium-sized urban centers of the metropolitan area of Amman, such as al-Mafraq (its poor spontaneous settlements next to archeological remains), is similar to the context of so many other sites in Jordan. The Desert Castles, much visited by tourists, are isolated in the eastern desert, once connected by trans-desert tracks and today by fast, modern roads. But the meaning of the word "desert" must be understood adequately. If we look at the satellite views of the Syrian Desert, a series of traces imprinted in the soil appear. Some are natural traces, like watercourses, whereas others are artificial signs that can be distinguished by basic geometric layouts and reveal the presence of abandoned cities, enclosures for animals, nomadic tents or camps, ancient defensive structures, and roads or hydraulic systems such as dams, moats, or tanks. This is why the word "desert" is not a synonym for absence, void, or death. On the contrary, it displays a density of past and present uses that highlight a living structure that is made available as a great environmental and landscape resource. The photographic images of the traces and remains of the Roman limes in Syria by André Poidebard, a forerunner of aerial archeology, give evidence of abundant and diverse archeological presences still unexplored.[13]

The modern Mediterranean city should therefore be reconsidered at this novel and geographically enlarged scale, defined by both contemporary urban realities and still neglected local identities. Archeological sites, with their services, facilities, and surrounding cultural landscapes, should take on the role of public spaces. The Mediterranean Medina, with its long and stratified history, can be viewed as a fascinating reference for a novel, diversified urban structure where it is possible to recognize the relationship between a

13 The parallel between the development of urban structures and of human society, in relation to what Jean-Jacques Rousseau affirmed in *Discours sur l'origine et les fondements de l'inégalité parmi les hommes*, in 1755, metaphorically highlights the loss of the egalitarian character of the original settlements in response to the progressive growth and complexity of urban centers.

compact urban fabric and the informal and
generous availability of public spaces that
once characterized the urban koiné of ancient
Mediterranean cities. [14]

14 Poidebard, *La trace de Rome dans le désert de Syrie*.

Between Mobility and Control
The Mediterranean at the Borders of Europe
Lorenzo Pezzani

Moments of rupture often have the ability to offer, in a condensed timeframe, a penetrating view of complex situations. The crisis that unfolded in the aftermath of the Arab revolts and the NATO attack on Libya brought into sharper focus the underlying technologies of power, the discourses, and the strategies that have been shaping the Southern European border regime over the past twenty years.[1] The events of 2011 offered a unique cross section of the "structured chaos" that has been trying to regulate the movement of people across the Mediterranean countries, transforming the Mediterranean into an extended order zone, at once front line and frontier.[2]

After the revolts that overthrew the regimes of Ben Ali and Qaddafi — and with them the agreements that they had signed with the European Union and with single European states to limit people's mobility — several thousand people tried to enter Italy by sea. But despite the impressive number of naval and aerial assets deployed in the Mediterranean following the international military intervention in Libya, no form of protection was guaranteed to migrants at sea. Within a few months, more than 1,800 people died in attempts to cross the stretch of sea that separates Europe from Northern Africa, making 2011 the deadliest year in the Mediterranean, according to the United Nations High Commission for Refugees.[3]

The effects of this crisis, however, did not manifest themselves only at sea but had repercussions across a wide geographical area.[4] At the end of April 2011, when a few thousand of the migrants who had arrived on Italian shores tried to reach France, a short but severe diplomatic row escalated between the French and Italian governments over the principle of free movement within the European Union. The prime ministers of Italy and France sent a joint letter to the EU leadership asking it to review substantial parts of the Schengen agreement. Denmark also reintroduced, for a short time, controls at its borders with Sweden and Germany.[5] For the first time since its integration into European law in 1997, the principle of free movement within the Schengen Area was strongly challenged.

1   On the notion of border regime, see Tsianos and Karakayali, "Transnational Migration and the Emergence of the European Border Regime: An Ethnographic Analysis," *European Journal of Social Theory* 13, no. 3 (August 2010): 373–387.

2   Eyal Weizman, Hollow Land: Israel's Architecture of Occupation (London, New York: Verso, 2007).

3   "Fortress Europe," March 2012, http://fortresseurope.blogspot.co.uk/2006/02/nel-canale-di-sicilia.html. This estimate considers only documented cases of death at sea and does not take into account all those boats that have disappeared without leaving traces. The death toll is therefore likely to be much higher.

4   Federica Sossi, *Spazi in migrazione. Cartoline di una rivoluzione* (Verona: Ombre Corte, 2012).

5   Judy Dempsey, "Denmark Reintroduces Border Controls," NYTimes.com, May 12, 2011, http://www.nytimes.com/2011/05/13/world/europe/13iht-border13.html?_r=1.

Lorenzo Pezzani is a researcher based
in London. His work focuses on the spatial
politics and visual cultures of migration,
human rights, and media. After having studied
architecture and worked as assistant curator
for Manifesta 7, he obtained a Master of
Arts at the Center for Research Architecture
(Goldsmiths, University of London, 2008)
where he is currently a Ph.D. candidate.
He was a resident at the Decolonizing
Architecture Art Residency in Bethlehem
(2010) and is now a research fellow on the
ERC project "Forensic Oceanography" and a
contributor to the ongoing body of work "Model
Court." His practice-based research projects,
moving across diverse disciplines and media,
have been presented in exhibitions and talks
at, among others, the Fourth International
Architecture Biennale in Rotterdam (2009),
the Tate Modern (2010) and Chisenhale Gallery
(2011) in London, Henie Onstad Art Centre in
Oslo (2011), and HEAD in Geneva (2012)

At the same time, the great majority of migrants who had fled Libya sought refuge in neighboring African countries, where similar spatial upheavals occurred.[6] French President Nicolas Sarkozy called for the creation of "North African 'humanitarian zones' to 'control the migration flows', thus pinning the humanitarian banner to the desire for political control over human mobility."[7] The management of the displaced required the creation of refugee camps in neighboring countries and the repatriation of some of the migrant workers coming from Libya to places as far as Sub-Saharan Africa or Bangladesh, while many today remain confined in the Choucha camp in Southern Tunisia.

These few examples suggest how the observation of the Mediterranean Basin from the vantage point of the patterns of migration and the ensemble of practices that have been deployed to contain it unsettles established definitions. It offers another image of the Mediterranean as a complex force field that organizes system of movement across vast geographical scales but requires us to rethink both geographical (sea/land) and political (interior/exterior) spatial binaries.

Since the colonial occupation of the North African rim by European states, the interplay of various systems of movement and devices of containment have been redrawing the geography of the Southern European border regime across the Mediterranean area. Colonial conquest and occupation, war, trade patterns, political affiliations, migration, and economic partnerships have connected and at the same time disconnected the different sides of the Mediterranean in a constant process of spatial reorganization. Channels for the transit of goods, raw materials, financial investments, and certain categories of people have been opened, while zones of exclusion and confinement have been created. Although exchanges and restrictions of movement have of course always taken place, the rise of colonialism marked the introduction of a new paradigm of control that is still structurally embedded within this complex ecology today. It is thus from colonialism that we have to start to track the genealogy of the contemporary border regime.

What distinguished the colonial project from other forms of domination was its effort to constantly reproduce difference by fostering the "proliferation of juridically and hierarchically differentiated zones, territories, populations and subjects" and by trying to regulate the flows between these internally homogeneous, externally differentiated areas.[8] As historian Frederick Cooper reminds us in speaking about Africa, "Colonization itself, far from just imposing a high degree of connectivity on an isolated continent, at the same time connected and disconnected, created new networks and severed ancient bonds." To study colonization, he writes, ""is to study the reorganization of space, the forging and unforging of linkages."[9]

Italy and its former African colonies, especially Libya, have been at the forefront in the redefinition of this composite economy of movement, both in recent times and during the colonial period. The 2011 revolt and the NATO intervention, in which Italy actively participated, were just one of the most recent chapters of a long history initiated with the Italian occupation of the Ottoman provinces now known as Libya exactly one century before. Retracing the history of colonial penetration into Libya and of the events that followed allows me to track the emergence of geo-historical lines of attrition and connection that developed further after the end of the colonial occupation and are still at work today.

On a symbolic level, the Mediterranean Sea played an important role in the Italian colonization of Northern Africa. Italian leaders presented the conquest of Libya as a return to a place that because of the ancient Roman presence "naturally" belonged to Italy. Roman traces, so fervently hunted by Italian archeologists, were but a confirmation of the indissoluble tie that linked the young nation to its glorious past. Italian sailors climbing ashore in Northern Africa were depicted in propaganda as taking up their ancestors' claim to possessions that had been occupied by uncivilized people. Most important, the invasion of Libya was presented as a way to regain control over the Mediterranean, the sea that the Romans had dubbed Mare Nostrum. Italian colonialism, well before Fascist times, made this imperial trope one of the cornerstones of its project of territorial expansion and presented the move into Northern Africa as the reconquest of the "fourth shore," the missing seaboard of Italian territory. And even if the reality on the ground was very different, and Italy

6 According to the International Organization for Migration, of the 721,772 people who fled Libya, only 25,932 reached Italy, while the others reached neighboring countries by land. See http://www.iom.int/jahia/webdav/shared/shared/mainsite/media/docs/reports/IOM-sitrep-MENA.pdf .

7 Michel Agier, "The Undesirables of the World and How Universality Changed ACamp," www.opendemocracy.net, May 16, 2011, http://www.opendemocracy.net/michel-agier/undesirables-of-world-and-how-universality-changed-camp.

8 Miguel Mellino, "De-provincializing Italy: Notes on Race, Racialization, and Italy's Coloniality" (forthcoming); Alessandro Petti, Arcipelaghi e enclave: architettura dell'ordinamento spaziale contemporaneo (Milan: B. Mondadori, 2007).

9 Frederick Cooper, "What Is the Concept of Globalization Good For? An African Historian's Perspective," African Affairs 100, no. 399 (April 2001): 189–213 (25).

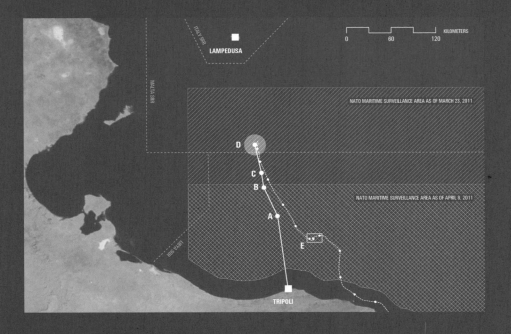

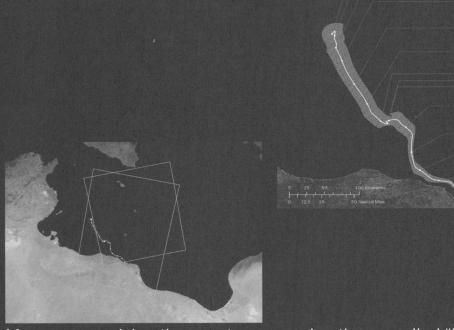

Maps summarizing the events concerning the so-called "Left-to-die boat" case, during which 63 out of 72 migrants fleeing Tripoli on a small rubber boat died while drifting for 14 days at sea. The map reconstructs the trajectory of the ship across NATO's maritime surveillance area, closely monitored in the frame of the 2011 military operations in Libya, and indicates the different Search and Rescue Regions of various coastal states. More than 1.500 migrants died in 2011 in the Central Mediterranean.

Excerpt from the report on the "Left-to-die boat" realized by Forensic Oceanography: Charles

was able to exercise effective control over the sea only in limited areas and for short periods of time, the Mediterranean was constantly presented as an internal sea finally connecting again the shores that had been separated after the fall of the Romans.

Italy seized the area that now is known as Libya from the Ottoman Empire in 1912, but the establishment of real military control was long and difficult, especially in Cyrenaica. At the time of the first Italian invasion, Cyrenaica was controlled by the Sanussi, an Islamic brotherhood strongly rooted there since the beginning of the nineteenth century. Against the Italian invaders, Sanussi and its charismatic leader, Omar Al-Muktar, waged a strenuous guerrilla war that was crushed by General Graziani only in the early 1930s, after almost half of the population had died in concentration camps built on the coast. To enhance political and military control over the areas that had been occupied, the Italian government committed vast resources to the construction of several *villaggi agricoli,* new agricultural towns built on the coastal areas of Tripolitiania and Cyrenaica.[10] While several thousand Italian farmers crossed the Mediterranean Sea to take possession of their new colonial houses, Libyan anticolonial leaders were carried in the opposite direction, to be confined on small prison islands in Southern Italy.

The connection with the sea did not have only a symbolic value but was reflected in the spatial arrangement of the colonial occupation. Although military outposts were also established in the internal, desert regions, the colonial occupation of Libya focused almost exclusively on the control of the cities and villages on the coast and in its immediate hinterland, reflecting similar patterns of colonial penetration into the countries situated between the Sahara and the sea.[11] Achille Mbembe has explained how the importance of the coast in African states "goes back to the period of the trading-post economy, when Europeans set up agencies on the coasts and began to trade with the natives. The establishment of this economy explains, in part, some of the physical characteristics of African states, and first of all the distinction between the littoral areas and the hinterland that so deeply marks the geographical structure of various countries."[12]

It was only after the end of colonialism and, more specifically, the revolution in 1969 that ousted the king backed by the British government, that the penetration into the interior of the country took on a new impetus. Shortly after coming to power, Qaddafi started to build the infrastructures that enabled the discovery and exploitation of large oil resources located in the internal regions.

The "rediscovery" of the inland desert areas reflected larger developments happening across the Sahara. After decolonization, the Sahara started to emerge from a latency period to which it had been relegated by the opening of transoceanic routes and by colonial powers. This new geography of the desert has been shaped by precise historical events that have contributed to its urbanization and to the development of a frontier economy.[13] "It [was] paradoxically the desire [by the newly established African states] to clearly demarcate borders and to institutionalize them that generate[d] flows and activate[d] circulation."[14] From this renewed connection many migrants profited as well, arriving mainly from other Arab countries, attracted by the wealth generated by Qaddafi's decision to nationalize several foreign oil companies in the early 1970s. Unlike other poorer Northern African countries such as Tunisia and Morocco, the presence of vast numbers of migrants has been crucial to economic development in Libya since decolonization. The fall of oil prices in the middle of the 1980s as well as the 1992 UN sanctions that marginalized Libya on the international scene caused an economic crisis to which Qaddafi responded with the progressive privatization of the Libyan economy.[15] This reform has required the influx of an even larger and cheaper workforce since the beginning of the 1990s. This demand was met by a large number of Sub-Saharan and South Asians migrants, who before last year's uprising made up 25 percent of the working population and whose arrival was also encouraged by the markedly pan-African orientation that Qaddafi's foreign policy had assumed since 1997.[16]

In the same years, the whole Maghreb region underwent deep socioeconomic changes that modified its relation with both Europe and Sub-Saharan Africa. At the end of the 1980s and beginning of the 1990s, it was mainly Moroccans and Tunisians who

10   Mia Fuller, *Moderns Abroad: Architecture, Cities and Italian Imperialism* (London and New York: Routledge, 2007).

11   Nicola Labanca, *Oltremare: storia dell'espansione coloniale italiana* (Bologna: il Mulino, 2002).

12   Achille Mbembe, "At the Edge of the World: Boundaries, Territoriality, and Sovereignty in Africa," *Public Culture* 12, no. 1 (January 1, 2000): 284.

13   Hein de Haas, "Trans-Saharan Migration to North Africa and the EU: Historical Roots and Current Trends," *Migration Information Source,* November 2006, http://www.migrationinformation.org/feature/display.cfm?id=484.

14   Ali Bensaâd, "Les migrations trans-sahariennes. une mondialisation par le marge," *Maghreb-Machrek* 185, Fall (October 7, 2005): 13–36.

15   Olivier Pliez, *La nouvelle Libye: sociétés, espaces et géopolitique au lendemain de l'embargo* (Paris: Karthala Editions, 2004).

16   Delphine Perrin, "Aspects juridiques de la migration circulaire dans l'espace euro-méditerranéen. Le cas de la Libye," series "CARIM AS," 2008-23, Robert Schuman Center for Advanced Studies, San Domenico di Fiesole (FI): Institut universitaire européen, 2008.

attempted to cross the Mediterranean to reach Spain and Italy; in more recent years the number of Sub-Saharan migrants who have transited through Maghreb countries on their way to Europe has increased dramatically. From an area in which migration flows emerged, the Maghreb has been transformed in recent years into a relay of movements that plunge deeper into Sub-Saharan Africa and propel intercontinental connections. "It has become," as geographer Ali Bensaâd has written, "a multifunctional migration space that amplifies and renews the modalities of its connection with the world and becomes thus in its turn affected by migration in its social and spatial foundations."[17]

The new lines of connection that have been drawn across the Mediterranean by the emigration of Northern Africans toward Europe have been mirrored in the reactivation of trans-Saharan circulations and by the progressive rapprochement of the two "shores" of the desert. The Sahara thus progressively becomes the core of an important migratory system that started to connect Libya, as well as other Northern African countries, with Sub-Saharan Africa, becoming somehow the mirror of the other sea, the Mediterranean.[18] Sahelian cities located at the point of junction of paved roads with the dirt roads that run into the desert transformed into veritable gateways to the desert. In places like Timbuktu, Gao, Kidal in Mali, Agadez in Niger, Dongola in Sudan, and Abéché in Chad, the crossing of the migrants was (and in several cases still is) organized and managed, as the condition of borderland became a resource harnessed by different actors, be it migrants, traders, pastoral communities, rebels and terrorist groups, or humanitarian personnel.[19] The desert, "the spatial archetype of the periphery," was thus transformed into a functional crossroads connecting and disconnecting spaces at an intercontinental scale. "It spins out and weaves together the threads of a system of mobility that it simultaneously channels and injects with its own specificities, thus becoming a space which is both a conduit and a creator of globalization."[20]

It is in this sociopolitical context that the construction of a European border in the Mediterranean Basin has started. As new lines of connection have been drawn, new spaces of confinement have arisen. Since the beginning of the 1990s, the consolidation of freedom of movement within the EU for its citizens resulted in increasing restrictions on the entry of non-European migrants. European states responded to the increasing influx of Northern and Sub-Saharan African migrants not only by intensifying "traditional" border controls but also by devising new technologies of control, trying to externalize onto Maghreb countries the control and surveillance of migrants and transform the Northern rim of the African continent in a sort of "buffer zone" protecting Europe.[21] The EU and single European states have been progressively negotiating a role for Northern African countries as guardians and advanced sentinels, similar to what had happened on the Eastern European border a decade before. The introduction of Schengen visas, the opening of camps in North Africa financed by European countries,[22] initiatives in police cooperation, readmission agreements, and push-backs in the open seas are some of the measures that have been taken to externalize the control of migrants and the processing of asylum requests outside of EU territory.

Linear borders have at the same time shrunk into discrete points that follow certain bodies — those of migrants — and at the same time multiplied and spread all along several division lines between Southern Europe and Northern Africa.[23] Migrants trying to reach Europe have been refused visas in the consulates of their countries of "origin," intercepted by national police in the frontier towns of the Sahel, surveilled by satellites when entering Northern African countries, detained in camps financed by EU countries along the Mediterranean coast and in the desert itself, repatriated with flights and trucks leaving from the Maghreb and European capitals, and pushed back or left to die at sea. Under the influence of European externalization policies, the Sahara has become not only a crossroads, where both outgoing migrants and those who have been intercepted at sea or during raids in the coastal cities are brought back to the border of the country from which they are supposed to have come, but also a refuge, a waiting area and a prison, where people spend months or years recovering from previous trips, trying to gather enough money to continue to travel or just awaiting better opportunities.

The stemming of migrant mobility has also been, in the last decade, one of the most important clauses on which many cooperation treaties have been based. Northern

17   Ali Bensaâd, Le Maghreb à l'épreuve des migrations subsahariennes: immigration sur émigration (Paris: Karthala Editions, 2009): 5 (my translation from the French original).

18   Bensaâd, "Les migrations trans-sahariennes. une mondialisation par le marge"; Ali Bensaâd, "The Militarization of Migration Frontiers in the Mediterranean," in Ursula Biemann and Brian Holmes, eds., The Maghreb Connection: Movements of Life across North Africa (Barcelona: Actar, 2007); Bensaâd, Le Maghreb à l'épreuve des migrations subsahariennes; Sylvie Bredeloup and Olivier Pliez, eds., Autrepart, 36, 2005: Migrations entre les deux rives du Sahara (Armand Colin, 2006); Delphine Perrin, "Immigration et création juridique au Maghreb. la fragmentation des mondes et des droits," in Le Maghreb à l'épreuve des migrations subsahariennes: immigration sur émigration , 245–265.

19   Biemann and Holmes, eds., The Maghreb Connection.

20   Bensaâd, "Les migrations transsahari ennes. une mondialisation par le marge," 14.

21   Externalization can be defined as a practice "which involves the displacement of border control and its technologies beyond the territorial edges of formally unified po-litical spaces. Whether this involves the es-tablishment of offshore detention facilities, the interception and diversion of vessels, co-operation in deportation procedures, or the surveillance of routes and so-called carriers of migration, the defining aspect of externalisation is the involvement of third countries in the creation and management of the border regime." (Brett Neilson, "Between Governance and Sovereignty: Remaking the Borderscape to Australia's North," Local-Global Journal 8 (2010): 126, http://mams.rmit.edu.au/56k3qh2kfcx1. pdf). Externalization policies have been often criticized for being used by those societies that define themselves as liberal and democratic to justify the imposition of violent forms of control on a large number of unwanted people.

22   For a general overview of the practices of externalization in the European context, see Thomas Gammeltoft-Hansen, "The Externalisation of European Migration Control and the Reach of International Refugee Law," in Elspeth Guild and Paul Minderhoud, eds., The First Decade of EU Migration and Asylum Law (Leiden: Martinus Nijhoff Publishers, 2010): 273–298. For specific info on detention facilities financed by European states in Northern Africa, see Miriam Ticktin, "The Offshore Camps of the European Union: At the Border of Humanity" (International Affairs at The New School, 2009). On the practice of push-backs at sea, recently condemned by the European Court of Human Rights (Case of Hirsi Jamaa and others v. Italy), see Human Rights Watch, Pushed Back, Pushed Around (New York, 2009).

23   Paolo Cuttitta, "Points and Lines: A Topography of Borders in the Global Space," Ephemera 6, no. 1 (2006): 27–39; Paolo Cuttitta, Segnali di confine. Il controllo dell'immigrazione nel mondo-frontiera (Milan: Mimesis Edizioni, 2007).

African leaders (Quaddafi above all) have often promised, in exchange for financial, military, or political support, to crack down on "illegal" immigration and impose tighter control on both the boats leaving from their coasts and the Saharan land borders. Several European states and the EU itself have been fostering Euro-Mediterranean integration through a plethora of political and economic initiatives, partnerships, and framework agreements, which have tried to extend the liberalization of the economies across North Africa and limit migration at the same time. The neoliberal penetration of Europe into North Africa has thus been tightly tied to the issue of migration. The case of Libya provides again a paradigmatic example.[24] Through a long series of multilateral (EU-Maghreb) or bilateral (Libya-Italy) political negotiations, Libya has been requesting and obtaining political and economic concessions by raising the specter of "invasion" by the hundreds of thousands (almost 2 million according to some estimates) of "transit" Sub-Saharan migrants present in Libya.[25] Despite the extensive presence of migrants in Libya since decolonization, it was within the context of Euro-Mediterranean partnership and mounting internal racism that Libya (as along with all other countries of the Maghreb) introduced restrictions on the presence of immigrants, signed readmission agreements with other African countries, and tightened controls at their Southern border.

The effects of this increasing militarization of borders has been dramatic, forcing migrants to resort to clandestine, precarious means to enter EU territory. Aboard unsafe vessels, migrants have taken increasingly dangerous trajectories to cross the Mediterranean Sea. European states have often refused to disembark migrants rescued at sea on their territory, and even criminalized those seafarers who carried out rescue operations, accusing them of smuggling.[26] This situation has made the conditions and trajectories of the crossing increasingly dangerous, causing the deaths of at least 13,417 people at the maritime borders of the EU since the end of the 1980s.[27]

And yet thousands of migrants enter Europe every year; most of them do not enter by boat, but simply overstay the duration of their visa. The movement of people is always in excess of the systems of control that try to regulate it. Those migrants who manage to enter European territory remain there as illegal non-citizens and "end up carrying with [themselves their] individual border on this side of the linear border, a mobile border in the shape of a point that will differentiate [their] 'reduced' status of 'clandestine' from those of the other people living in that territory."[28] The border that separates the northern and southern sides of the Mediterranean thus gets reproduced by the racialized borders that crisscross European cities. In this sense it is clear that the border's function "is not simply to keep out those who are perceived as 'trespassers' but, first and foremost, to govern populations both inside and outside the territory."[29]

This account shows that what is at stake here is a redefinition of what the Mediterranean region is, and what are its characteristics. Traditionally, there have been "two principal ways in which Mediterranean unity has been characterized: by reference either to ease of communications, which we may conveniently label the interactionist approach, or to common physical features, the ecologizing approach."[30] The observation of the Mediterranean Basin from the perspective of the management of migrations[31] provides another model that displaces these approaches and moves them beyond the pitfalls of both social constructivism and ecological determinism. While it is clear that the physical characteristics of both desert and sea have created the opportunity to establish tragically effective borderlines, the complex economy of movement that I have described takes place across an area that does not have clear territorial limits but exists as a shifting, elastic zone. In this sense, the Mediterranean as Southern European border could be defined as a space that encompasses the whole territory extending between and including Europe and Sub-Saharan Africa and "whose contours are continuously negotiated by the movement of people and things, new forms of surveillance technology, and new processes of sovereign and supranational government."[32]

In 2002, the Milan-based collective Multiplicity looking at the changing geography of the Mediterranean, highlighting some of the emerging features of this area. In a research project titled "Solid Sea," these architects and artists tried, perhaps for the first time, to reflect critically on the spatial phenomena that had transformed this sea into a border zone, abandoning the tired rhetoric of the

24 Pliez, "La nouvelle Libye"; Claire Rodier, "Externalisation des frontières au sud de l'Europe. L'alliance Union européenne-Libye," in Bensaâd, ed., *Le Maghreb à l'épreuve des migrations subsahariennes* ; Sylvie Bredeloup and Olivier Pliez, "The Libyan Migration Corridor" (Robert Schuman Center for Advanced Studies, EUI (2011).

25 The most famous of these treaties remains the "Treaty on Friendship, Partnership, and Cooperation" signed between Italy and Libya on 30 August 2008. "As part of the agreement, Italy has pledged 5 billion US dollars over a period of 20 years for infrastructure projects in Libya. In return, Libya has agreed to take back intercepted migrants, allow joint migration control patrols inside Libyan territorial waters and for Libyan authorities themselves to help prevent irregular migrants from both entering Libya and moving on towards Europe." Gammeltoft-Hansen, "The Externalisation of European Migration Control and the Reach of International Refugee Law,"273.

26 See for example, Statewatch, 2007, "Italy—Criminalising Solidarity—Cap Anamur Trial Underway," http://www.statewatch.org/news/2007/apr/03italy-cape-anamur.htm; and Fortress Europe, 9 August 2007, "Lampedusa: Fishermen Arrested Having Saved 44 Shipwrecked Migrants," http://fortresseurope.blogspot.com/2006/01/lampedusa-fishermen-arrested-having.html.

27 "Fortress Europe," March 2012, http://fortresseurope.blogspot.com/2006/02/immigrants-dead-at-frontiers-of-europe_16.html.

28 Cuttitta, *Segnali di confine. Il controllo dell'immigrazione nel mondo-frontiera*, 46 (my translation from the Italian original).

29 Enrica Rigo, "Citizenship at Europe's Borders: Some Reflections on the Post-colonial Condition of Europe in the Context of EU Enlargement," *Citizenship Studies* 9, no. 1 (February 1, 2005), 11.

30 Peregrine Horden and Nicholas Purcell, *The Corrupting Sea* (Oxford: Blackwell, 2000), 10.

31 Migration management is new catch-phrase often employed by various governmental and non-governmental organizations concerned with migration to describe a new approach toward the cross-border movements of people. Within this framework, the issue is not whether migration should be stopped or not, but rather how it is to be "managed" to optimize its impact on the global labor market. It is defined as a new form of "softer, post-control spirit" that tries to regulate the porosity of borders rather than seal them, but has also been often criticized for having no less deadly effects than more traditional forms of border control. On migration management, see Martin Geiger and Antoine Pécoud, *The Politics of International Migration Management* (Basingstoke: Palgrave Macmillan, 2010).

32 Ticktin, "The Offshore Camps of the European Union," 3.

[7]

Aerial photograph of the colonial settlement called Gioda, one of the thirty-one "agricultural villages" built for Italian farmers on the coastal areas of Tripolitania and Cyrenaica in the 1930s

The original caption reads: "Marching in thick rows, the Twenty-thousand set out to Piazza Castello in Tripoli"

Image taken from the book I Ventimila, the photo story of the first

Mediterranean Sea as cradle of civilization and prototype of cultural encounter.
"The Mediterranean," they wrote, "is turning into a large continent interposed between Europe, Asia Minor and Africa…, a liquid continent cut to differing depths by impenetrable corridors and subdivided by high barriers in which specialized enclosures and vast, uninhabited plains alternate. Its borders are perforated by funnels of entry and exit that increasingly respond to the logic of exclusion and separation. It is a new continent, the map of which we are still unfamiliar with."[33]

The analysis they put forward complicates two opposite but interconnected visions: the rhetoric of flow — often used by globalization enthusiasts — which sees in a frictionless sea the medium of circulation par excellence; and the image of the "Fortress Europe," evoked in campaigns against the increasing violence of European anti-immigration policies, which regards the Mediterranean as an insurmountable fence. The sea is described by Multiplicity as an increasingly jellylike, tri-dimensional mass that "can oscillate between states of fluidity, enabling the passage of people, forms and ideas and states of solidity, blocking passage under given political and historical circumstances."[34] It thus seems to respond to the characteristics that Foucault ascribes to the concept of apparatus. "An apparatus of security," he writes "cannot operate well except on condition that it is given freedom, in the modern sense [the word] acquires in the eighteenth century: no longer the exemptions and privileges attached to a person, but the possibility of movement, change of place, and processes of circulation of both people and things."[35] Liberal societies, Foucault argues, try to enhance circulation and movement by "maximizing the positive elements, for which one provides the best possible circulation, and [by] minimizing what is risky and inconvenient, like theft and disease, while knowing that they will never be completely suppressed."[36] It is precisely by putting to work these mobilities and making them productive that the apparatus of border management functions. Within this complex and conflictual geography, connection and division, intervention and segregation, are no longer opposites. Both can become instruments of an apparatus of border management that is both brutal and sophisticated; that works by stopping as much as by delaying and sifting; and that excludes as much as it includes. What we have seen operating in the Mediterranean is a differential form of control, which aims to sift flows by making borders harder and softer at the same time.[37]

Understanding the Southern European border as an apparatus allows me to take into account the interconnection of several types of flows. As I have tried to show, the mobility of people is structurally connected to other forms of movement that cross borders and with other forms of social, political, and economic relations that have been created around them. Transnational flows of global capital in the form of development aid, private investments, remittances, and reparation for colonialism; the extraction of raw materials like oil, gas, and uranium, and their transportation; the pillage of cultural artifacts during colonial times and their restitution; the economies of war and refugee camps on both sides and within the Sahara — all of these elements are part of the same economy of movement that is governed by a multiplicity of actors and rationalities that operate at the border.[38]

But acknowledging that the sea is becoming increasingly solid, as Multiplicity has done, has another important consequence. It means that the traditional binary on which geopolitics has been predicated for a long time — the fixed division between a solid land where territories can be clearly demarcated and a free sea where borders cannot be maintained — is no longer valid.[39]

Carl Schmitt famously described the sea as an anarchic space in which the impossibility of drawing long-standing and identifiable boundaries made it untenable for European states to establish any durable legal order or found any claim of sovereignty.[40] Far from being a sign of commonality, however, the concept of the "free seas" has been used during the centuries both by established and emerging powers to assert freedom of competition and the right to dispose of a space of commerce. It was, in this sense, a problematic but effective notion that had to be maintained thought active intervention of the various powers that claimed it. "Freedom requires policing and mobility requires fixity, and both of these activities require continual efforts to striate the ideally smooth ocean."[41] One of the most famous examples is probably Hugo Grotius's treatise *Mare*

33   Multiplicity, "Around a Solid Sea," *Archis*, 2002, 5 (191): 22–33.

34   Vyjayanthi Rao, "Speculative Seas," in Güven Incirlioglu and Hakan Topal, eds., *The Sea-Image: Visual Manifestations of Port Cities and Global Waters*, (New York: Newgray, 2011),124.

35   Michel Foucault, *Security, Territory, Population: Lectures at the Collège de France, 1977–78* (New York: Palgrave Macmillan, 2007), 71.

36   Ibid., 34.

37   This situation is closely reminiscent of Foucault's analysis of the political spaces of modernity, which were determined for him by the overlapping of two distinct paradigms of control. On the one hand, the paradigm of leprosy, based on a program of outright exclusion—the treatment of the disease in which the sick were placed outside the city; and on the other hand, the model of the plague, in which complete separation was impossible. The latter works by dividing the city into quadrants and placing each section under the surveillance of an attendant. Such sovereign exclusion and disciplinary techniques of filtering were to become, in what Deleuze has called a "society of control," parts of a same apparatus. See Foucault, *Security, Territory, Population*, and Gilles Deleuze, "Postscript on the Societies of Control," *October* 59 (1992): 3.

38   In analyzing the instruments of government that had been developed in the eighteenth century in response to the disorder introduced by liberal politics, Foucault identifies the target of government in a complex composed of men and things. "The things with which in this sense government is to be concerned are in fact men," he wrote, "but men in their relations, their links, their imbrication with those other things which are wealth resources, means of subsistence, the territory with its specific qualities, climate, irrigation, fertility, etc.; men in their relation to that other kind of things, customs, habits, way of acting and thinking, etc.; lastly men in their relation to that other kind of things, accidents and misfortunes such as famine, epidemic, death, etc." Foucault, *Security, Territory, Population*.

39   Paul Hirst has already remarked how "land and sea do differ in certain basic ways [but] neither is a constant: the salience of both and their relative value alter through time with changing technology, cultures and institutions […]. In this sense, we can only talk about spaces like the sea historically and specifically." Paul Hirst, *Space and Power: Politics, War, and Architecture* (Cambridge and Malden, MA: Polity Press, 2005). Carl Schmitt had recognized how new spatial dimensions introduced by technological advancements like air travel and radio communication had already made the land-sea binary obsolete. Carl Schmitt, *Land and See*, retrieved at http://www.counter-currents.com/2011/03/carl-schmitts-land-sea-part-1/, 2011.

40   Carl Schmitt, "The Nomos of the Earth," in *International Law of the Jus Publicum Europaeum* (New York: Telos Press, 2003).

Liberum, written with the specific aim of justifying the Dutch right to trade with the East Indies without being attacked by the Portuguese Navy.

With increasing interaction across oceans and with the growing drive to consider maritime areas themselves as resources, the sea has been increasingly divided by various forms of legal and spatial enclosure. This process has been also closely related to the technological and scientific possibility to "know" the oceans, such as the current interest in mapping the extent of continental shelves to determine states' jurisdictions over Arctic resources. As a result of this drive to subdivide the ocean, partial boundaries have been established to delimitate areas of decreasing sovereignty, hydrocarbon exploration fields, fishing regions, zones of responsibility for the search and rescue of persons in danger at sea, etc.

The already mentioned arguments that have arisen among Mediterranean states over the responsibility for rescuing migrants in distress at sea, as well as over the duty to disembark rescued migrants, show how the sea itself, far from being a lawless, empty expanse, is crisscrossed by multiple lines that delimit contested areas of responsibility.[42] The paradox here is that within the malleable framework of international law, it is not the lack of regulations but rather their conflictual nature that spans many actors and legal rationalities, that supports divergent interpretations. These have been often used as a means to evade responsibility and have made any attempt to identify and prosecute those responsible for the deaths of migrants at sea an extremely difficult task.[43]

What the above scenario demonstrates is the fundamental role that migrations have had in reshaping the Mediterranean. Sandro Mezzadra claims that

the friction between a 'politics of migration' and a 'politics of control' lives at the very heart of capitalism's history. […] Capitalism [is in fact] marked by a structural tension between the ensemble of subjective practices in which the mobility of labour expresses itself […], and the attempt by capital to impose a 'despotic' control over them by means of the fundamental mediation of the state. Struggles over mobility crisscross the whole history of capitalism, from the moment when the first enclosure in England mobilized the local rural population as well as from the moment when the first slave ship crossed the Atlantic.[44]

Certainly, the battle over mobility has marked the recent history of the Mediterranean in such a profound way that it seems impossible to think about this region without considering the new spatial configurations that have arisen from the clash between systems of mobility and apparatuses of containment.

The revolts that have swept the Maghreb and Mashrek have been just the latest in a series of challenges that have been brought to this border regime. Mainstream Western media have tried to read these events through Orientalist and racist conceptions that tend to confine non-Western politics to the past. And the same European leaders who cheered the "discovery" of democracy on the southern side of the Mediterranean (thus ignoring decades of battles that workers, students, and activists have been waging against exploitation, pauperization, and oppression) have been in the past months keen on renegotiating similar agreements for the containment of human mobility. Nevertheless, these uprisings can and should be read as well as a challenge to this apparatus that seeks to limit the mobility of people. They have opened up new scenarios and new possibilities for struggle, whose full consequences are for the moment still unknown.

41   Phil Steinberg, "Free Sea," in Stephen Legg, ed., *Spatiality, Sovereignty, and Carl Schmitt: Geographies of the Nomos* (London and New York: Routledge, 2011), 271.

42   One event that attracted international media attention became the emblem of paradox. In 2004 the *Cap Anamur*, a cargo freighter converted into a "humanitarian boat" by a German NGO, rescued in the Mediterranean thirty-seven African migrants who had come into distress during their sea crossing to Europe. The ship was later denied permission to enter Italian territorial waters and was kept off the coast of Sicily during a legal and diplomatic standoff in which the fate of the asylum seekers bounced between competing claims and denials by the governments of Italy, Germany, and Malta, and the EU and the UNHCR.

43   The Dutch Senator Tineke Strik was appointed by the Parliamentary Assembly of the Council of Europe to investigate into the deaths of migrants at sea that occurred in 2011. In April 2012 a coalition of NGOs filed a legal case for non-assistance of migrants at sea.

44   Sandro Mezzadra, "The Gaze of Autonomy: Capitalism, Migration, and Social Struggles," in Vicki Squire, ed., *The Contested Politics of Mobility,*. (London: Routledge, 2010), 124.

—

Although this essay is largely based on an unpublished draft, several of the issues under consideration have been developed during long and stimulating discussions with Charles Heller, whom I would like to thank. With him and the New York–based architectural practice Situ Studio, I have developed "Forensic Oceanography" (http://www.forensic-architecture.org/investigations/forensic-oceanography/), a research project funded by the European Research Council that uses new tools of spatial analysis to produce evidence of the violation of the rights of migrants at sea.

Algeria's Colonial Geography
Shifting Visions of Mediterranean Space
Muriam Haleh Davis

Algeria should be the keystone of a Maghreb associated with Europe by France, the opening of Europe in the Sahara and Africa, the protection of free passage in the Western Mediterranean. For these reasons, we should make sure that it remains in our economic and political system.[1]

— French colonial administrator, writing in 1960

1   *Centre historique des Archives nationales*, Paris (hereafter CHAN), F/12/11804, memo dated 11 January 1960. All translations by the author.

In 2007 French President Nicolas Sarkozy gave a much-anticipated speech in Algiers. Claiming that he sought to "construct a future of shared solidarity between [the French and Algerian] people," he asked Algerian President Abdelaziz Bouteflika to work toward a "Mediterranean Union." He explained that this partnership would benefit the security interests of the two countries and would encourage economic development and peaceful coexistence. France's relationship to Algeria, he claimed "is primarily an issue of geography: we are neighbors from two sides of a sea that has always been a point of union (*un trait d'union*) and not a barrier."[2] In this speech, he sought to revive the 1995 Barcelona Process that aimed to "[turn] the Mediterranean basin into an area of dialogue, exchange and cooperation guaranteeing peace, stability and prosperity." Yet he also appropriated a geographical unit that had been common in the 1950s: EurAfrica. According to earlier proponents of EurAfrica, Algeria and France would be joined through mutual economic interests instantiated by the European Union and the Common Market (1957). Similarly to Sarkozy's understanding, defenders of French colonialism often claimed that EurAfrica was the product of geography itself since the Mediterranean linked France with Algeria.[3]

2   A full text of the speech is available at: http://www.afrik.com/article13062.html. Accessed 24 July 2012.

Whether the Mediterranean should be considered as bridge or barrier is certainly not a new polemic. It is clear that the vision of EurAfrica highlights the Mediterranean as a link, while the thousands of individuals from North Africa who cross the sea by boat, known harragas, have a very different idea of the Mediterranean. Yet both visions posit the Mediterranean as a geographical fact rather than a spatial construction. In the nineteenth and twentieth centuries, understandings of the Mediterranean were tied to the shifting lo[gic] of economic and political space rather than a singular concept of Mediterranean identity. Thus rather than seeing the Mediterranean as either bridge or barrier, I seek here to explore the "modalities

3   See Max Liniger-Goumaz, *L'Eurafrique, Utopie ou Realité?: les métamophoses d'une idée* (Yaoundé: Editions Cle, 1972), 53.

Muriam Haleh Davis is a Ph.D. candidate in the Department of History at New York University. She holds a Master of Arts in Middle Eastern Studies from Georgetown University and a Master of Arts in Culture and Theory from the University of California, Irvine. Her dissertation looks at the intersection of European integration and development in Algeria during the War of Independence. Her academic articles have appeared in *Social Identities*, the *Journal of French and Francophone Philosophy,* and the *Review of Middle Eastern Studies*. She is a contributing editor for the *e-zine Jadaliyya* and has also written for *Al-Jazeera English*, the *Huffington Post*, and *Warscapes*.

Colonial Geography

through which a territory becomes the object of an appropriation or of the exercise of a power or a jurisdiction."[4]

As historians have argued, a stable notion of the Mediterranean as a geographical referent did not exist until the nineteenth century. Henry Laurens writes: "The concept of the 'Mediterranean' is a nineteenth-century creation similar to the rediscovery of the mountains or the sea. The image is linked to both imperial and imperialist domination, particularly France's supremacy over North Africa."[5] Iain Chambers also claims that the concept of the Mediterranean entered the European lexicon only in the early nineteenth century.[6] Given the link between colonialism and geographical construction, the French occupation of Algeria allows us to examine the shifting ways in which the Mediterranean was produced as a civilizational, territorial, and economic space. Indeed, the relationships among the racial, physical, and economic boundaries of the Mediterranean show how empire was "dependent on shifting categories and moving parts whose designated borders at any one time were not necessarily the force fields in which they operated or the limits of them.[7] "

This essay examines the attempts to consolidate Mediterranean space in the early decades of colonial rule before discussing the post–World War II notion of EurAfrica. In the nineteenth century, the Mediterranean was viewed as a space of competing civilizational logics that was articulated through the conflicting notions of the "Arab Kingdom" and the "Granary of Rome." These contradictory visions reflected the fact that French sovereignty in Algeria remained partial and uneven. To integrate Algeria with France, colonial rule introduced private property and attempted to tie the population to the land. Thus Algeria's relationship to the Mediterranean had to be formatted through the standardization of territory that would make the southern shore compatible with the economic and ideological claims of early colonization. The period after World War II, however, grappled with a very different set of problems that centered on the creation of the Common Market and need for economic development. While the organization of markets was one way of producing the spatial unit of EurAfrica, this process was predicated on a series of technical and economic logics. Moreover, the production of EurAfrica depended on an understanding of Mediterranean nature linked

an older racial discourse of the "Mediterranean Man."

In tracing these shifting visions of the Mediterranean, I hope to discuss the stakes of Sarkozy's recent invocation of EurAfrica in light of the historical processes that have fashioned our current conception of the Mediterranean. More important, my aim is to show how colonial rule produced scales of space that were tied to the writing and rewriting of nature while also constructing changing notions of racial difference. While many views of the Mediterranean have relied on a geographic determinism, this essay maintains that the two shores of the Mediterranean were linked through a set of economic, technical, and discursive practices.

Colonial Histories of the Mediterranean: From the "Granary of Rome" to the "Arab Kingdom"

In the battle over whether the Mediterranean should be thought of as bridge or barrier, dueling images of empire are often at play. On the one hand, the Mediterranean has been seen as a timeless geographic entity in which waves of colonizers — from the Romans to the French — have cultivated the land and advanced the foundations of "Western civilization." On the other hand, beginning with Napoleon's expedition to Egypt in 1798, France actively fashioned itself as a "Muslim power," using its desire to protect Islamic customs as a pretext for occupation. Edward Said, for example, saw the French invasion of Egypt as the beginning of a long process of Orientalism, through which the West tried to gain knowledge of the East to govern it more effectively. While the former vision centers on incorporation and the role of North Africa in the development of Western civilization, the latter highlights France's imperial designs and domination of its Muslim subjects.

The Mediterranean then was purely a site of neither incorporation nor domination. It reflected instead a layering of imperial sovereignty. This was especially evident in the early stages of the French occupation, when colonial administrators themselves held conflicting visions of the Mediterranean. While some highlighted and romanticized the fundamental difference of the Arab population, others looked to the legacy of Roman North Africa to frame the southern shore. Even while the ideological contours and scale of colonization remained uncertain, Algerian territory had to be made legible to French rule. As a result, the standardization of property rights and control

4   Achille Mbembe, "At the Edge of the World: Boundaries, Territoriality, and Sovereignty in Africa," *Public Culture* 12 (2000): 262.

5   Quoted in Jean-François Daguzen, "France's Mediterranean Policy: Between Myths and Strategy," *Journal of Contemporary European Studies* 17, no. 3 (2009): 387.

6   Iian Chambers, *Mediterranean Crossings: The Politics of an Interrupted Modernity* (Durham, NC: Duke University Press, 2008).

7   Anne Laura Stoler, "On Degrees of Imperial Sovereignty," *Public Culture* 18 (2002): 138.

of mobility were fundamental to the incorporation of Algeria into French empire.

France's adoption of Roman imperial ideology started well before the full pacification of Algeria was complete. From 1830 to 1871, the French administration in Algeria was split between military and civilian administrations that battled for political supremacy. In 1845, Algeria was a jumble of administrative norms; different forms of sovereignty existed in the *communes de plein exercice* (*colon* regions that elected mayors and councils for self-governing), *communes mixtes* (which had large numbers of Muslims and therefore was run by appointed officials), and the *communes indigènes* (which remained unpacified). These legal, spatial, and administrative divisions created a fractured space where pockets of European presence were surrounded by Muslim threat. Given this multiplicity of territorial arrangements and the uncertain vision for the future trajectory of French colonization, the early decades of occupation produced an uneven and contingent notion of Mediterranean space.

The legal duality between Muslim and European space began to change in 1848, when Algeria was declared to be an integral part of France. This shift necessitated an occupation of the land that would legally and physically incorporate Algerian territory into European space. As the French sought to construct a historically and geographically consistent notion of Mediterranean space, they increasingly claimed to be participating in the "reconquest" of Roman North Africa. Accordingly, they would resurrect the former glory enjoyed by North Africa as the "Granary of Rome." This vision implied an agricultural, civilizational, and economic program that sought to recover a historical trajectory that had been interrupted by the Arab occupation in the eighth century. As Diana Davis writes, the "image of the natural fertility of North Africa by the Romans was accompanied by an image of the subsequent destruction, deforestation, and desertification of the North African environments by hordes of Arab nomads and their ravenous herds."[8]

If this "return" was often understood in terms of agricultural rehabilitation and environmental resurrection, it was also a racial myth that posited the Arabs (and to a lesser extent Berbers) as fanatical and backward. Instead of having to account for a civilizational disjuncture structured by the two sides of the Mediterranean, the French could claim a historical, spatial, and racial unity. In other words, "the added bonus of being able to refer to Rome as an illustrious precursor was a way of reinforcing the spatial and ideological transition from East to West."[9] While the Mediterranean was an inchoate entity struggling to be defined in the nineteenth century, viewing the colonization of Algeria as a return to the grandeur of Rome helped inscribe the Mediterranean's southern shore as a space of Western civilization rather than colonial conflict.

A different means of achieving this was Napoleon II's 1852 declaration of an "Arab Kingdom." Proclaiming that "Algeria is not a colony… but an Arab Kingdom," Napoleon also insisted that he was "as much the emperor of the Arabs as of the French."[10] Todd Shepard describes this attempt as "an imperial fantasy, in which French rationalizing and modernizing oversight and instruction would contain and shape 'Arab' character."[11] However, it was not only a way of consolidating France's status as a Muslim power by bringing the gifts of the civilizing mission to the indigenous population; it was equally a way of inscribing colonial conquest within the geographical framework of the Mediterranean. Underpinning the idea of an Arab Kingdom was a Saint-Simonian geography, which called for "a better exploitation of the globe" (*une meilleure exploitation du globe*) that would merge the best qualities of orient and occident.[12] In fact, Ismail Urbain, one of the key figures of the Saint-Simonians, converted to Islam — allegedly because his time in Egypt provoked an explosion of sensuousness, a mystical spirituality, and an Eastern fatalism.[13] By expanding French presence to the other side of the Mediterranean, Saint-Simonians sought to improve a race that was distinct but not incommensurate with the dictates of progress and civilization.

Despite the obvious differences, both the "Granary of Rome" and the "Arab Kingdom" secured a vision of the Mediterranean through reforming relationships to mobility and property. Mobility was not only something to be controlled; ideas of circulation and settlement were also part and parcel of understandings of race and civilization. The formatting of the Mediterranean as a colonial space depended on promoting the circulation of certain figures of modernity (the évolué, the colonial administrator, the European traveler), while fixing allegedly backward subject to the land (the Algerian peasant, the destructive nomad). General Bugeaud, for example, who looked to Rome in adopting a "vision of colonization… by the sword and the plow,"[14] also established policies that sought to educate the peasantry through changes in their living conditions; the hope was that "better conditions and the introduction of European agricultural methods would reinforce the peasants' attachment to

8 Diana K. Davis, *Resurrecting the Granary of Rome: Environmental History and French Colonial Expansion in North Africa* (Athens: Ohio University Press, 2007), 3.

9 Patricia M.E. Lorcin, "Rome and France in Africa: Recovering Colonial Algeria's Latin Past," *French Historical Studies* 25, no. 2 (2002): 305.

10 Benjamin Stora, *Algeria: 1830–2000, A Short History* (Ithaca, NY: Cornell University Press, 2001), 5.

11 Todd Shepard, *The Invention of Decolonization: The Algerian War and the Remaking of France* (Ithaca, NY: Cornell University Press, 2006), 26.

12 Marcel Emerit, *Les saint-simoniens en Algérie* (Paris: Les Belles Lettres, 1941), 12.

13 Emerit, *Les saint-simoniens,* 70.

14 Lorcin, "Rome and France in Africa," 308.

the land."[15] Unsurprisingly, the fact that forms of movement serve to define subject positions in a geographic space of the Mediterranean continues to be vital in discussions about visas and migration.

Related to these concerns about mobility and physical attachments, the introduction of private property was fundamental to incorporating Algeria into a modern Mediterranean space. When the French arrived in Algeria, land holdings were split between religious land (*habous),* collectively owned land (*arsh*), private property (*melk*), and lands that had been owned by the Turkish *beylick.* This uneven spatiality was economically and politically dangerous for France's project of assimilation. In the early decades of colonization, therefore, "land transactions served to highlight the weak sovereignty claims the colonial state was able to make on Algeria."[16] The drive to confiscate land and impose private property was fundamental for creating a modern subject that could participate in a geographical and civilizational collectivity. Lisa Lowe has written that:

> **Property in oneself and in the objects one makes through will, labor, and contract — all are levels in Hegel's dialectical development that resolve in the unity of the particular will of the individual with the collective universality of the whole…the individual's possession of his own person, his own interiority, is a first sense of property.**[17]

The incorporation of Algeria was not just about ideologically inscribing Algeria as Mediterranean but modernizing its relationship to land, mobility, and nature. In the process, the French were as interested in reshaping the psychological and cultural characteristics of the Muslim population as restructuring its economic claims to the Algerian territory.

The conflicting visions of Algeria as a site of an Arab Kingdom or the Granary of Rome were transformed in the late nineteenth century as Algeria was definitively populated as a settler colony of Europeans from Spain, Italy, and Malta as well as France. Instead of maintaining the dichotomy between Western universal civilization and Arab cultural particularity, a new racial identity was formed around linguistic and cultural references that would enable these colonizers to refer to themselves as "Algerians," erasing the indigenous inhabitants in the process.[18] The resulting notion of the "Mediterranean Man" operated as a racial category that was seen to be a melting pot of various European ethnicities.

Founded in the scientific racism of the early twentieth century, the physiological features of a Mediterranean race were increasingly debated in the following decades. Giuseppe Sergi's *The Mediterranean Race,* published in 1901, saw the race as originating in Africa and coming from Eurafrican roots. Writers such as Louis Betrand wrote of an "Eternal Mediterranean" that existed under the African sun and that would retrieve Latin civilization. According to Betrand, European settlers could reconstruct this glorious past while overcoming the pernicious effects of Islamic influence. This view was the subject of much debate in the 1920s and was foundational for the *Ecole d'Alger* of Albert Camus and Gabriel Audisio in the late 1930s.

Undoubtedly these debates had wide-ranging consequences for the construction of a Mediterranean space. Paul Silverstein notes that Braudel himself "began his doctoral studies […] at the exact moment in which the racial and historical dimensions of Mediterranean unity were being fiercely debated." Later, his political commitments would be influenced by this geographical vision as Braudel "side[d] clearly with the *Ecole d'Alger's* vision of the 'Eternal Mediterranean,' maintaining its insistence of the region as an integrated geographical and historical system."[19] While this move helped consolidate the racial and economic space of a singular Mediterranean, the post–World War II period integrated the two shores of the Mediterranean based on markets and technology, thereby prompting a shift in viewing Algerian Muslims as *homo islamicus* to proclaiming them to be an example of *homo economicus.*

The Consolidation of the Mediterranean: EurAfrica, Development, and the Question of the Sahara

Prior to World War II, the notion of the Mediterranean was generally diffused through civilizational histories and symbols such as the Mediterranean sun or the heroic qualities of the *pied noir.* After 1945, however, the production of the Mediterranean would take on a new form due to the political economy of the postwar period. The rise of state Keynesianism, the specter of European integration, and the turn toward a regional logic in addressing problems of underdevelopment — all played a role in constructing the Mediterranean as an economic space known as EurAfrica. The decentralization of capital, the organization of markets, and the development of infrastructure worked in tandem with the older racial myth of

15   Zeynep Çelik, *Urban Forms and Colonial Confrontations: Algiers under French Rule* (Berkeley: University of California Press, 1997), 124.

16   Henry Sivak, "Law, Territory, and the Legal Geography of French Rule in Algeria: The Forestry Domain, 1930–1903" (PhD diss., UCLA, 2008), 67.

17   Lisa Lowe, "The Intimacies of Four Continents," in *Haunted by Empire: Geographies of Intimacy in North American History*, ed. Anne Laura Stoler (Durham: Duke University Press, 2006), 200.

18   See David Prochaska, *Making Algeria French: Colonialism in Bône, 1870–1920* (Cambridge: Cambridge University Press, 1990).

19   Paul A. Silverstein, *Algeria in France: Transpolitics, Race, and Nation* (Bloomington: Indiana University Press, 2004), 66.

the "Mediterranean Man" to naturalize a rendering of space that focused less on national sovereignty and instead advanced an expanded notion of Europe. Despite the conjuncture of social and technical processes, the discursive and economic axes that produced EurAfrica have generally remained isolated. While for Bruno Latour this conceptual partition is part of the modern contract,[20] the process of creating EurAfrica points to the simultaneous creation of spatial and racial categories. By constructing a single Mediterranean "nature" for both the inhabitants and the land, both sides of the Mediterranean could be joined in a singular spatial unit.

The conception of EurAfrica was undoubtedly a product of the postwar climate in which development theories posited the region as "an intermediate territorial level, between the state and the locality,"[21] articulating a notion of underdevelopment that contrasted with core-periphery models. As Michael Keating writes, for theorists of the regional question, "In a context of generally full employment and growth, regional economic problems were seen as a marginal issue which would be addressed by specific policies aimed at integrating depressed regions fully into national economies."[22] Working at a time when the future of France's colonial possessions was increasingly uncertain, many of these regional theorists wrote about Europe's future while casting a darting glace toward the colonies.

In the 1950s, a group of economists writing on the "regional question" interrogated the neoclassical notions of perfect competition, perfect equilibrium, and balanced growth. Albert Hirschman, Gunnar Myrdal, and François Perroux sought to foster even development by encouraging certain "poles" of development that would then enjoy a "trickle-down" or "spread-out" effect. What seemed to be a theory of economic growth was also a profoundly new way of envisioning space; Perroux's notion of "economic space" rejected the abstract conception of space that viewed it as a "container." Instead he delinked space from a bounded geographical model, defining "economic space" as a field of relations.[23] For Perroux this also entailed a transcendence of national boundaries and a reconfiguring of Europe itself: The most effective way to overcome national economies was to change their internal logic by instituting poles of development that were necessarily supranational. Perroux envisioned an enlarged Europe that pointed to a devaluing of frontiers rather than an enlargement of existing nationalisms; he claimed that in the former, Europe would seek to strengthen

its "Europeanness," but in the latter, it would display "human values." In the former, Europe would have one network of transport and one army, but in the latter, "the nations of Europe use a world money, intercontinental networks, to participate in a world army." This vision, which merged civilizational and economic links through a unified space that was dynamic rather than territorial, would be formative in formatting the colonial links between the two shores of the Mediterranean in the 1950s.

The notion of a "trickle-down" effect and "poles of development" also had important social and cultural implications that have gone largely unexamined by scholars interested in the regional question. In the context of the declining of formal empire, this was perhaps not surprising. Myrdal, for example, shunned the rejection of imperialism as a cultural force, repeatedly highlighting the danger that the colonized countries might reject the legacy of Western civilization. In line with his notion of "circular and cumulative causation," Myrdal envisioned racism in largely cultural terms; he wrote that "white prejudice and low Negro standards thus mutually 'cause' each other" so that if "either of the two factors should change, this is bound to bring a change in the other factor, too, and start a cumulative process of mutual interaction in which the change in one factor would continuously be supported by the reaction of the other factor and so on in a circular way."[24] Elsewhere he insisted that the black population was not biologically inferior and that a rise in the standard of living would help ameliorate white prejudice. Yet his conflation of poverty and morality is particularly striking; he notes that economic development would augment "wages, housing, nutrition, clothing, health education, stability in family relations, law observance, cleanliness, orderliness, trustworthiness, loyalty to society at large."[25] The circular benefits of development meant that while racial traits were no longer an impediment to economic progress, the stigma of poverty was a cultural as well as material malaise.

The implications of this economic orthodoxy for French Algeria — and the creation of EurAfrica — were profound. Françoix Perroux spent time in Algeria and became a key reference for Algerian policymakers after 1971.[26] The notions of "poles of development" served as the model for CADAT (*Caisse Algérienne D' Aménagement du Territoire*), which sought to create there main zones of industrialization along the Mediterranean coast. Moreover, the decree of 1 May 1959 attempted to attract French capital to Algeria with a series of laws

20 Bruno Latour writes that "the more the social construction of nature is calmly asserted, the more what is really happening in nature–the nature that is being abandoned to Science and the scientists–is left aside." Bruno Latour, *Politics of Nature: How to Bring the Sciences into Democracy* (Cambridge, MA: Harvard University Press, 2004), 33.

21 Michael Keating, *The New Regionalism in Western Europe: Territorial Restructuring and Political Change* (Northampton: Edward Elgar, 1998), 9.

22 Keating, *New Regionalism*, 13.

23 François Perroux, "Economic Space: Theory and Applications," *Quarterly Journal of Economics* 64 (1), 89–104. For a discussion of Perroux's thought in the context of "Spatial Keynsianism," see Neil Brenner, *New State Spaces: Urban Governance and the Rescaling of Statehood* (Oxford: Oxford University Press, 2004).

24 Gunnar Myrdal, *Rich Lands and Poor: The Road to World Prosperity* (New York: Harper and Brothers, 1958), 17.

25 Myrdal, *Rich Lands and Poor,* 22.

26 Kay Adamson goes so far as to claim that "in fact, it is only possible to make sense of Algerian industrial policy planning, and consequently its view of agriculture, if one refers back to the writings of Perroux." See Kay Adamson, *Algeria: A Study in Competing Ideologies* (London: Cassell, 1998), 10. For a discussion of the impact of De Bernis' thought on Algerian economic policy, see Stora, *Algeria, 1830–2000,* 151–152.

that offered financial incentives for their installation in Algeria and encouraged industries to settle in three zones. In these zones, known as *Zones d'Industrialisation Décentralisée*, the French administration offered financial aid to compensate for the cost of transport and other inconveniences that industrial capital would face by moving to Algeria (not the least of which was the War of Independence). Unsurprisingly, the industrialization of Algeria was viewed as part of the industrial decentralization that had been occurring in France.

Yet in trying to attract metropolitan capital, the French administration also had to account for the role that the existing Muslim population would play in this push to industrialize Algeria. One question was repeatedly invoked: Would Muslim Algerians be capable of providing efficient labor for these new factories? French administrators and economists claimed that the answer was yes. They believed that the "trickle-down" effect of the "poles of development" would be psychological as well as material.

These economic linkages that propelled Algeria into a Mediterranean orbit were also informed by ideas of racial difference. While it is now commonplace to speak of space and nature as categories produced by capitalism, the notion of race generally remains a second-order concept that results from the mode of production.[27] I maintain, however, that racial categories were fundamental in the construction of space and nature; essentialized notions of capacities, traditions, and dispositions were imbricated with the economic orthodoxies that prompted certain programs for development. Thus it is not sufficient to posit that capitalism merely invoked a preexisting category of race to divide, oppress, or "racialize" a segment of the population. Instead the markers of race itself — as religious, cultural, or biological phenomena that are globally legible — emerged in and through a particular experience of capitalist development.

The economic unit of EurAfrica sought to complete the full transformation of *homo islamicus* into *homo economicus* by creating individual property holders out of the Muslim population and dissolving extended kinship networks, which were thought to be a sign of premodern solidarities. As A. de Cambiaire, a professor at the National Academy of Agriculture in Algiers, claimed in 1956:

We will never make a "good peasant" on undivided land, no more than we will settle him on collective land. The metropole possesses a peasant population that is fiercely attached to the land and that is hard-working, but it saw a brutal dislocation of its customary structures and practices in 1789; we should not forget that the liberation of the French peasant followed the liberation of the land.[28]

Creating a parallel between the French Revolution and the "liberation" of Algerians from collective land was one way of standardizing the cultural and legal codes of Algeria and France. This legal and physical assimilation was deeply linked to the creation of a single Mediterranean space. For example, one colon argued that Algeria should be subjected to the same laws as those of the metropole since "this conforms to the policy of integration that we all want to see applied in Algeria, and which would assure the uniformity of these institutions on both sides of the Mediterranean."[29]

As late as 1961, just a year before Algeria won independence, some French administrators continued to envisage an economic system that was based on a loose confederation between North Africa and France:

The negotiations with the Algerian authorities should have as a base the constitution of a Franco-Maghrebin community, since such an association constitutes a factor of balance in the world. The Sahara and French aid are the two elements of a union between the participants. Following, one could envision a common political organization among the three countries of North Africa and France. This construction would be enlarged with the representation of the European Economic Community and the states of Black Africa; Algiers would become the political pole of EurAfrica.[30]

Algeria was the pivot through which an economically integrated Europe could maintain its African links. Yet to secure this vision of economic development, Muslims would have to be made into productive members of EurAfrica. Thus colonial administrators responsible for economic development, such as Jean Vibert, believed that development would prompt this shift: "*Homo economicus* is born. He replaced *homo Islamicus*, this man who had an extremely basic set of needs and who, as a result, was not driven to work more than that which was necessary."[31]

Agriculture was a particularly important aspect of development that was to simultaneously join the shores of the Mediterranean, raise standards of living, and alter the cultural and psychological mores of the Muslim population. Scholars have looked at the construction of an "imperial culture" though colonial products in France, underlining how colonial agricultural production was market-

27 Neil Smith, for example, manages to avoid reductive accounts by which the physical environment merely "reflects" changes in the mode of production, but he concludes that capitalism leads "to a differentiation of cultures along class lines, and of course a further differentiation on the basis of gender and race." See Neil Smith, *Uneven Development: Nature, Capital, and the Production of Space* (Athens: University of Georgia Press, 2008), 76. Similarly, David Harvey writes, "Capitalists can and do seize upon … differentiations and actively use them to divide and rule the working class–hence the importance of racism, sexism, nationalism, religious and ethnic prejudice to the circulation of capital." David Harvey, *Limits to Capital* (New York: Verso, 2007), 383.

28 *Archives Nationales d'Algérie* [hereafter ANA], Chambre de Commerce B.129 "texte de la conférence donné par M.A. de Cambiaire Maitre de conférences à l'école nationale," dated 11 May 1956.

29 ANA, Chambre de Commerce B.185 "Session Ordinaire du 20 Novembre 1958."

30 CHAN, F/12/11804, "Problèmes poses par l'aide de la France à l'Algérie indépendante: mission d'étude pour l'Algérie," dated 2 March 1961.

31 CHAN, F/12/11810, *Travail et Méthodes,* April 1961, "Questions Générales."

ed for consumption in the metropole.[32] But this phenomenon was not merely ideological. Nor was it the imposition of a "colonial consciousness." Instead, the unification of the Mediterranean through agriculture was closely tied to the organization of markets, packing of products, and shipping of goods and networks of transportation — all of which played a role in constructing the Mediterranean as a space in the postwar period. This culminated in the vision of EurAfrica whereby the two shores of the Mediterranean would be connected through markets and trade in a mutually beneficial relationship. What now seems as a "natural" indication of the unity of the Mediterranean space — the uniformity of agriculture and the production of olive oil and wine, for example — was actually produced by a series of scientific and economic reforms that defined the Mediterranean as a space of development in the 1950s.

Undoubtedly, a major component of the Mediterranean Myth had always been the mainstay crops such as wine and olive oil. The introduction of the Common Market in 1957 and the gradual adoption of the Common Agricultural Plan created a new urgency for making Algerian produce viable on the European market. Thus in the context of modernizing colonialism, new attention was also paid to agriculture as colon interests sought to make their products profitable, as French protection of the Algerian economy was increasingly untenable. Yet ironically for French *colon* in Algeria, they could not help but notice that they were seriously disadvantaged by one slight factor: the Mediterranean itself.

In contrast to the image of a seamless Mediterranean space, Laurent Shiaffinao, the President of the Chamber of Commere of Algiers, claimed that "it has often been said, and the image is correct, Algeria is an island." By this he meant that Algeria's commerce was, for the most part, obliged to pass by the sea, which increased shipping costs. Moreover, he noted that Algeria was subject to economic competition for the same products. Citing Eugène Guernier's theory of "economic zones" (*fuseaux économiques*), he noted that "international commercial relations are geographically enacted along the meridian lines and not along the parallels. The successive production that one finds in following a meridian tends to be complementary, while they tend to be in competition (*concurrent*) if one follows the same parallel."[33] In other words, it was not immediately self-evident that the Mediterranean was a boon to agricultural producers in Algeria. Nor was it clear how these efforts could be made

profitable in light of the Common Market.

Despite the Mediterranean's image of a natural space of farming and harvest, the development of agriculture in Algeria relied on a series of technical questions: How could producers remain competitive when faced with the considerable costs of shipping across the Mediterranean? What steps would need to be taken to assure the standardization and quality of products so that they would appeal to a French clientele that was more finicky than their Algerian counterparts? How could better shipping methods — refrigeration methods in particular — help make this enterprise more profitable by reducing waste? What techniques of production and purification would allow for a standardized product that would be compatible with the Common Market?

These questions were especially pressing in the case of wine, which was the colon crop par excellence. Not only did it produce the most revenue for the colon, instituting what many economists have labeled a dual economy, but it was also used as evidence of the "Frenchness" of the land itself. Pierre Berhault echoed this sentiment when he noted that "an essentially colonizing crop, wine attaches men to the soil and develops settlement."[34] This primordial attachment to the land was not merely a function of a natural disposition found in the soil of the Mediterranean, as was often claimed. Instead, the relationship between the extension of finance capital and the development of viticulture was essential. As Michel Launay writes, "The cultivation of wine [was] inseparable from the development of credit"[35] Even institutions such as the SAP (*Société Agricole de Prévoyance),* which attempted to aid the Muslim population, found themselves caught in a system whereby finance capital was the driving logic of agricultural activities. Credit not only helped circulate capital, it was also responsible for helping to cultivate and promote the crops that have been seen as a "natural" expression of the Mediterranean space. Credit and agriculture worked together to allow agricultural products to circulate from one side of the Mediterranean to the other, helping to create the spatial unit of EurAfrica.

To create the optic of agricultural unity as the basis for a Mediterranean space, the creation of a single system for the harmonization, classification, and production of these products was also vital. In the case of wine, institutions such as *la Fédération des Associations Viticoles* brought Algeria into a homogenized regional market. Similarly, the 1950s witnessed a series of international conferences that sought to standardize the classification

32 Sandrine Lemaire, for example, argues that official propaganda "sought to manipulate the habits of the French through the creation of propaganda for colonial products so that the French consumed "imperial" [products]" See Lemaire "Manipuler: À la Conquête des Goûts," in *Culture impériale 193–1961: Les colonies au Coeur de la République,* eds. Pascal Blanchard and Sandrine Lemaire (Paris: Éditions Autrement, 2004), 75.

33 ANA, Chambre de Commerce B.120, Speech given at the *Association des Officiers de Réserve de l'Armée de Mer* (ACORAM) on 8 April 1954.

34 Quoted in Amicable des anciens élèves des écoles d'agriculture d'Algérie, *L'Oeuvre Agricole Française en Algérie: 1930–1962* (Editions de l'Atlanthrope, 1990).

35 Michel Launay, *Paysans algériens: la terre, la vigne et les hommes* (Paris: Éditions du Seuil, 1963), 51.

and production of olive oil. This culminated in 1960, when the *Conseil Oléicole International* (COI) along with the *Organisation des Nations Unies pour l'alimentation et l'agriculture* (FAO) signed an international accord that fixed the rules of production for olive oil coming from Algeria as well as Europe.

The logic of standardizing olive oil and wine was at once technological, economic, cultural, and political. As the chamber of Commerce of Bougie pointed out, this stipulation also went against the local habits of Muslim olive-oil producers, who often preferred their product to have a more bitter taste.[36] This standardization tended to erase the geographical origin of a product that had once been tied to the ground; a once traditionally Algerian crop was diluted in a regional market. One expert on Algerian olive oil argues that international standardization had the effect of excluding "marginalized regions, like Algeria, which do not obey the rules of the global market and where the oil is entirely organic," thereby limiting the vast richness of flavors to a certain set of standardized characteristics.[37]

Technical, economic, and racial logics also refashioned the Sahara's role in Eurafrica during the late 1950s. While the invention of the Mediterranean in the nineteenth century invoked a body of water as its organizing principle, its southern border was often divided by another environmental feature: the desert. The Sahara, as Fernand Braudel has claimed, was seen as the "second face" of the Mediterranean, defining territorial limits while also providing a cultural space against which the Mediterranean was defined. Despite the trade routes and migrations that had historically linked North Africa with the Sahara, the two spaces were often posited as dichotomous. The desert had long been viewed as a harsh space inhospitable to settlement and resistant to colonial rule. In addition, the economic logics of colonial rule discouraged French administrators from pursuing a policy of southern expansion. The discovery of oil in the 1950s radically changed this understanding and introduced a new uncertainty regarding the geographic configuration of the limits and function of the Mediterranean.

Until this time, the Sahara had been understood through an unbridled romanticism. Travelers, explorers, and colonial administrators reveled in the aesthetic value of the desert, culminating in what Ben Brower has called the "Saharan Sublime." According to Brower: "French colonial ideology became bound in a particularly violent aesthetics of sublime" which also suggested that the "Sahara tested the representational limits of both ordinary and scientific language."[38] While in the first decade of colonization the Sahara was largely viewed as the Mediterranean's limit, by the late 1840s French administrators sought to accomplish a "peaceful penetration" (*pénétration pacifique*) to extend French sovereignty in the desert.

The discovery of natural gas in 1956 at Hassi R'Mel and Hassi Messaoud fundamentally reworked the relationship between colonization and territory with regard to the southern edge of the EurAfrica. Where the Sahara had been comprised of four *territories du Sud* since 1902, on 7 August 1957 it became two Saharan departments of *les Oasis* and *la Saoura*. The redrawing of borders was not without controversy, as the territories included parts of Chad, Mauritainia, Niger, and current-day Mali, all unhappy with the prospect of surrendering their sovereign rights to the *Organisation commune des regions sahariennes* (OCRS). The fact that the geography of oil did not fit neatly into existing borders created a profusion of legal, technical, and administrative issues that would need to be overcome. This also prompted a question unthinkable just fifty years prior: Was the Sahara really Algeria?

Rather than embodying the eternally heroic spirit of the Algerian desert, the Sahara became a pivot for the French community and was included in the image of EurAfrica. Instead of the timeless noble savage, the Sahara became a place of technological progress fundamental for a reconception of EurAfrica. As Jacques Soustelle (director of the OCRS) wrote: "These apparently inert conduits that tie the young Sahara to old Europe trace the guiding principles (*les lignes de force*), the veritable nervous system of EurAfrica that is on the road towards its achievement."[39]

To remake the Sahara along these lines, the OCRS had to create a new unit of geographical and administrative space that was fundamentally depoliticized. In 1961 the OCRS Bulletin included this statement: "The new fact, the important fact, is that, by the separation of functions…one has 'depoliticized,' and also 'dis-administered' (*désadministrativé*) … an organization which had appeared to be unable to fully play its technical, economic, and cooperative role."[40] Rather than discussing the political valence of the *mise en valeur* of the Sahara, the OCRS concentrated on informing the public of the technical questions that the organization faced in the desert. Besides tackling the problems of hydraulics, communication, investment, and transportation, the OCRS embarked on agricultural and educational programs and set out to remake Saharan space.

36   ANA, Chambre de Commerce B.136, Letter from the Chamber of Commerce of Bougie to the Chamber of Commerce of Algiers, dated 7 March 1960.

37   Rachid Oulebsir, *L'Olivier en Kabylie entre mythes et réalités* (Paris: L'Harmattan, 2008), 85.

38   Benjamin Claude Brower, *A Desert Named Peace: The Violence of France's Empire in the Algerian Sahara, 1844–1902* (New York: Columbia University Press, 2009), 216.

39   CHAN, F/12/1108, Jacques Soustelle, "Sahara Nouveaux: Victoire des hommes pour les homes," in *Revue Économique Fanco-Suisse* 5 (1959).

40   *Bibliothèque Nationale Française* NF, 4-FW-6704, *Bulletin O.C.R.S* 1, January 1961, 10.

This remaking of the Sahara also called for an ethnographic redefinition of the existing population. Who were the people in the south, and what would their role be in the new Sahara? Given the violence of the war, how should colonial administrators, international investors, and French engineers view ethnic and tribal divisions? These questions were vital, and the oil community showed a keen interest in the ethnological information that might provide a response. Publications such as *Petrol Progrès* ran pieces trying to classify the people of the Sahara. Interestingly, two main trends emerged. First, these ethnological classifications defined these populations in terms of their capacity to work, defining the Harrantine as a population that "would adopt to industrial labor."[41] Second, while the conception of EurAfrique often invoked the conception of the Mediterranean Man that fused both sides of the Mediterranean, the "Saharan Man" was now emerging as a ethnically, sociologically, and politically distinct entity. The Saharan population would be integrated with EurAfrica not by producing and consuming goods for the Common Market but by taking part in the shared project of industrialization and progress. One brochure spelled this out by portraying Algerian and French workers working in the oil fields with the subtitle "A fraternity of labor: Europeans and Algerians unified around their machines."[42] Other works stressed the social consequences of industrialization, emphasizing that the development of the Sahara was not only about economic prosperity but would provoke a veritable social transformation.

Non-Mediterranean Spaces: Opposing Visions of Algeria's Geography

The official history of EurAfrica ended in 1962 when the FLN (*Front de liberation nationale*) led the Algerian people to a bloody independence that was a model for Third World struggle. As Matt Connelly has written, the victory of the FLN was largely due to a diplomatic — and symbolic — battle waged against a regime of colonial domination.[43] Yet an important part of this process was also a geographical, economic, and civilizational reinscription of Algeria. Rather than looking toward EurAfrica to provide a sense of historical continuity, the FLN posited a dramatic rupture by emphasizing the nation-state even while appealing to a regional logic that looked not toward the Mediterranean but to its North African neighbors. Rather than EurAfrica's pan-Mediterranen space, the FLN propagated a pan-African and pan-Maghreb identity that reshaped its Mediterranean

imaginary for the coming decades. In the face of neocolonialism, the FLN looked to a United Arab Maghreb rather than to a singular Mediterranean space.

This legacy was shaped by a number of contradictions. Even while political independence claimed the nation-state as the form of liberation, its economic ties remained deeply transnational. One of the main criticisms of the Evian Accords, which ended the Algerian war, was that it enabled a form of neocolonialism by maintaining French economic and financial interests under the rubric of cooperation. The development of Saharan resources by a joint Franco-Algerian organization was viewed with particular suspicion. That the founding document of independence is replete with guaranties of transnational cooperation is a contradiction that remains relevant for contemporary Mediterranean discourse.

These ambiguities have continued to mark Algeria's political and economic spatial imaginary. The Algerian regime has both been a singularly important — and especially reticent — partner with its European neighbors. According to a 2011 report by the European Council on Foreign Relations, "Algeria has had the reputation of being the EU's most difficult partner in the central Maghreb," with reference to Algeria's hesitation or refusal to participate in the bilateral cooperation agreements of the 1960s to the Global Mediterranean Policy of the 1970s and the more recent European Neighborhood Policy and the Union for the Mediterranean (UfM).[44] Yet even as Bouteflika has repeatedly called for a North African Economic Union[45] and advocated the opening of the border with Morocco despite the ongoing conflict over the Western Sahara, the dominance of the cultural and economic links with Europe are undeniable. Algerians' fraught identification with people from the South is evident not only in daily racism against people with darker skin, but with the government's injunction, repeated during the May 2012 legislative elections, that people from the South are less patriotic.[46]

The production of the Mediterranean then is not merely a colonial discourse imposed on Algerians but a spatial frame that is contested and called upon by both European and North African actors. By denaturalizing the geographic and political import of this spatial unit, we see that the question is not merely that Algeria does — or does not — have a place in a Mediterranean community. Rather, it is to see the Mediterranean space as produced by a series of political, economic, and racial logics instead of pointing to a natural geographic logic on which to cast the unfolding of history.

41   CHAN, F/12/11810. "Les hommes au Sahara," *Petrol Progrès* 47, October 1960.

42   CHAN, F/12/11810, "Le Sahara," published 27 December 1957.

43   See Matthew Connelly, *A Diplomatic Revolution: Algeria's Fight for Independence and the Origins of the Post-Cold War Era* (Oxford: Oxford University Press, 2002).

44   Hakim Barbouche and Susi Dennison, "A 'Reset' with Algeria: The Russia to the EU's South," *European Council on Foreign Relations* 46 (2011).

45   See "Bouteflika: 'La realisation de l'unité maghrébine arabe est un impératif vital et present,'" *Algérie 1* news, 18 February 2012, http://www.algerie1.com/actualite/bouteflika-«la-realisation-de-lunite-maghrebine-arabe-est-un-imperatif-vital-et-pressant»/. Accessed 13 August 2012.

46   Prime Minister Dahou Ould Kablia's speech can be seen at: http://maghreb.minutebuzz.com/2012/05/12/algeriens-sud-nord/. Accessed 13 August 2012.

Mediterranean Cosmopolitanism and its Contemporary Revivals
A Critical Approach
Nora Lafi

The idea of cosmopolitanism today is often an exercise in regressive nostalgia, harking back to a time when Muslims and Jews, or Greeks and Turks, lived together in Mediterranean cities, mostly within the Ottoman Empire. The link between what is perceived as a form of cosmopolitanism and the philosophical idea of cosmopolitanism that developed in Europe during the age of Enlightenment is, however, often indistinct, and the only certainty is that this era concluded with the emergence of a new world order, composed of nationalisms and colonialisms.

In this essay, I argue that, in spite of the difficulty of articulating cosmopolitanism in distinction with the cosmopolitan idea developed in European philosophy — a theoretical obstacle on which many readings of the actual content of the cosmopolitan idea have foundered — the Ottoman experience of governance of diversity represented a form of cosmopolitanism. I will try to compare this manifestation with its possible equivalents on the Northern shores of the Mediterranean and consider the substance of various contemporary revivals. I propose here to examine how this feature of Ottoman imperial belonging — with of course its fundamental limits and lasting ambiguities — was confronted with a form of modernity that challenged not only cosmopolitanism as a constructed form of coexistence and shared governance but also urban diversity. On the basis of such reflections, I try, in the final part of the essay, to critically examine contemporary revivals of the notion, arguing that, although such revivals sometimes using the imagery, rhetoric, and vocabulary of cosmopolitanism, they rarely encompass a genuine cosmopolitan dimension, in the sense of participatory governance of diversity in which different groups have access to the civic sphere.

The difficulty when studying cosmopolitanism in Mediterranean cities is that the notion is often held prisoner to two implicit referential horizons: the European concept of cosmopolitanism as developed in philosophy, and the situation of some cities of the region in which diversity was a fundamental fact. Reflecting on the notion without clearing the effects of such possible misunderstandings is a source of confusion, the relationship between, let us say, Kant and colonial Alexandria being difficult to absorb in a single theoretical package. That is why it is important to clear both sides of this implicit horizon before trying to examine another situation, the imperial Ottoman regime, in light of the concept of cosmopolitanism.

Understanding if and why the philosophical concept of cosmopolitanism has relevance in the Mediterranean urban context is indeed a prerequisite, as is addressing the ambiguities of what is often perceived as a kind of cosmopolitan golden age. This journey through the history of the notion of cosmopolitanism seems necessary to avoid the dangers of Eurocentrism, anachronism, and confusion between the presence of a diverse population and the existence of a civic sphere allowing minorities to participate in urban governance. The aim is also to take

Nora Lafi   is a researcher with the Zentrum Moderner Orient (ZMO) in Berlin (BMBF). She graduated from Aix-en-Provence University in 1999 (Urban Studies and Mediterranean Studies) and then moved to Berlin. She is a specialist in the urban history of the Ottoman Empire and specifically of Arab towns in North Africa and the Middle East. She chairs (with Ulrike Freitag) the research field, "Cities Compared: Cosmopolitanism in the Mediterranean and Beyond," part of the EUME program at Wissenschaftskolleg Berlin (Forum Transregional Studies). She is cofounder and editor of H-Mediterranean (H-Net, Michigan State University) and serves as review editor for the Middle East for the journal *Planning Perspectives*. Her current research program is on urban violence in Aleppo, Cairo, and Tunis in Ottoman and colonial times. Among her latest publications, she coedited *The City in the Ottoman Empire: Migration and the Making of Urban Modernity* (2010).

part in contemporary debates about cosmopolitanism (Vertovec and Cohen 2003, Breckenridge 2002), using the urban Ottoman regime case study as an alternative to existing visions of the notion and as a way to go beyond the theoretical dichotomy between philosophy and the description of post-Ottoman colonial societies.

Cosmopolitanism in Philosophy and the Governance of Urban Diversity: A Legacy of Confusion

The first use of the term cosmopolitanism comes from the Cynic tradition in ancient Greece. The concept was later used by Stoics and is, in its very essence, a Mediterranean idea. It matured with the decline of the model of the Greek city and its form of governance, which had been promoted in the entire ancient world. At the time of the imperial domination of Alexander, the Cynics introduced the idea of an egalitarian morality, based on the individual and his right to access governance for what he is and not for the group he belongs to. The Stoics developed the idea of the world as a big city, with citizens of the world being given the rights that citizens had in Greek cities.

Lisa Hill, in an attempt to examine the relevance in present debates on citizenship of the Greek cosmopolitan philosophy and its Roman imperial interpretations, illustrated the relationship between the Stoic moment and ideas of republic, government, and cosmopolitanism (Hill 2000). Cosmopolitanism as a concept was an answer to the limits of citizenship in a Mediterranean world where diversity was common. It was from the beginning a notion situated at the articulation between the government of the world and its differences and urban government, with of course the specificity that the Greek city was not limited to an urban reality and that reflections on imperial citizenship in Roman times was by definition global. After a series of reforms the Roman Empire acquired, at the scale of imperial citizenship, a certain cosmopolitan dimension, as people from the entire Mediterranean were progressively granted access to the civic sphere (Mathisen 2006). Ancient cosmopolitanism — with of course its limits, such as the presence of slaves, prisoners of war, and people without rights, and of course the issue of gender — refers to the political and civic sphere, and not only to the presence of a diverse population.

This ancient concept of cosmopolitanism has also been elaborated in the context of Hellenistic philosophy — Socratic, Stoic, and Epicurean (Brown 2012). Some cities of the ancient Greek world were known for the diversity of their populations, and it is believed that the development of the notion in philosophy has something to do with the adaptation of the Greek city, as a political form giving exclusive rights only to its native citizens (generally a narrow group)

to such diversity. The problem was how to give access to the urban civic sphere to Greek merchants from the wider Greek world living in port cities, and sometimes even to merchants from other Mediterranean horizons. Delos is the most studied among these port cities; it is presented as an emporium open to people from the entire Mediterranean (Malacrino 2007).

Cosmopolitanism having been used and reinterpreted throughout history, this Greek origin of the term is to be remembered, as along with some founding ambiguities, such as the difficult articulation between urban citizenship and imperial citizenship, both realities encompassing significant limits. What seems most interesting, however, is to discuss the evolution of the meaning of the concept from the Greek idea of government of the world as an extended city (the political entity) and to a certain extent of the city (the urban reality) as a little-world, a microcosm, to the social situation of Mediterranean towns 1,000 years later, and to present debates about world governance, urban governance, and life in the cities.

But for the sake of this discussion, an understanding of what happened to the notion in between is necessary: cosmopolitanism today is not just a metaphor of what it was in ancient times, for the concept was deeply re-elaborated in the eighteenth and nineteenth centuries. Debates today can't simply rely on a theoretical bridge between cities of the Mediterranean in the nineteenth or twentieth century and Delos in Hellenistic times. In a way, cosmopolitanism became less Mediterranean when European philosophers began to appropriate it and accommodate it to debates of a different kind. The fact that the history of the concept now relates mostly to European political philosophy must be taken into account in discussions about the Mediterranean nature of urban diversity. Taking this approach is not the promotion of a possible Eurocentric vision but instead represents a clarification of the renewed origins and connotations of a concept whose circulation is at the center of present discussions.

From the beginning, the cosmopolitan idea included a tension between the universal and the individual, between the idea of the possible coexistence of different identities of the individual and a need for an egalitarian-individualist attitude of indifference regarding men as citizens of the world or as participating entities in social life, including urban life. The concept of cosmopolitanism is also born at the intersection of ethics and the concrete governance of diversity. During the European Enlightenment, the concept was reinterpreted, mostly in the context of German philosophical debates, far from the practice of governance of diversity in Mediterranean cities. That is why an examination of its pertinence today cannot do without a renewed discussion of Kant's ideas on cosmopolitanism, world government, and the role of the individual in society (Slomp 2005, Pojman 2005, Nussbaum 1997). Martine Prange also illustrated how until Nietzsche at least, Kantian cosmopolitanism was a reference for a new definition of the concept (Prange 2007).

This new cosmopolitanism, taking various forms until the nineteenth century, was key in the definition of the European self in philosophy and in the maturation of modern political thought in Europe, in the context of the emergence of the national idea (Rosenfeld 2002). Throughout its journey in European philosophy, cosmopolitanism became an argument in discussions about the ontological dimension of nations and about the relationship between ethnicity and nation building. The later second circulation of the concept of cosmopolitanism must be read in the context of the nineteenth-and-twentieth-century exchange of ideas between Europe and the Middle East, in a new complex relationship in which many things had changed and ideas such as Orientalism, influence, imperialism, and Eurocentrism had become key. The new philosophy of cosmopolitanism was a mirror, sometimes absorbing, of the growing nationalism (Meineke 1970, Bowden 2003). This has to be remembered when studying the stakes of nationalism in Europe and the Mediterranean and the challenge to diversity that they represented.

From the tension during the French Revolution and its impact on nation building and the promotion of universal values (Dédéyan 1976) to the ambiguity generated by considerations of race and ethnicity in European nation-building processes (Gikandi 2002, Holton 2002), discussions on cosmopolitanism have since the nineteenth century been characterized by a new dimension: they expose the philosophical ambiguity of the European process of nation building and a definition of citizenship based on an often ethnicized vision of the self. Such discussions became matters of even greater relevance when this tradition was confronted with diversity and complexity in a region that had experienced a different path toward the governance of diversity, and where the impact of the European tradition was accompanied by domination and colonialism. The effect of the new European conception of cosmopolitanism on the Mediterranean not a mere revival of ancient philosophical ideals but rather part of a more complex process of reading societies that had been subjected to domination.

The fact that cosmopolitanism as a concept became multilayered in this period must thus be kept in mind before making any further use of it. As Terry Cochran argues, there is indeed a linguistic economy of cosmopolitanism in present debates that has to be made explicit (Cochran 1999). And it is sometimes difficult to be sure that various people using the concept are in fact dealing with the same thing. Pheng Cheah's warnings might be very useful in this regard. He doesn't believe in one of the first assumptions made by many users of the concept of cosmopolitanism — that is, that there would be something to understand in the relationship between cosmopolitanism as an Enlightenment idea and cosmopolitanism as a tool to analyze societies with a component of diversity: "Any contemporary revival of cosmopolitanism must take a critical distance from the older style cosmopolitanism of philosophical modernity" (Cheah 1997). For him, what he calls "ancestor cosmopolitanism" is something else entirely. But then, his aim is to confront contemporary societies with the modern idea of the nation and its roots, as if cosmopolitanism as a theoretical creation for the contemporary world was only indirectly related to its ancestor.

One of the aims of the present essay, based on an examination of the Ottoman urban situation, is instead to explore the possibility of a more complex relationship. Of course, the nature of the concept has changed, but as part of a phenomenon that is precisely the one under study: the evolution of the idea of nation in Europe and the impact of the spread toward the East and the South of such a conception in the context of a biased modernity. For Cheah, "The history of colonialism has disproven Kant's benign view of the unifying power of international commerce" (Cheah 1999; see also Cheah and Robbins 1998), and for him, contemporary reflections on cosmopolitanism are aimed at explaining what he calls the present neocolonial globalization, so the discussion seems closed. But one could argue that, to the contrary, it offers a good basis for discussion, though commerce and global exchanges are not the right focus and that instead, the urban governance of diversity in Mediterranean cities might be. We'll see here that the Ottoman case might suggest at least partially reopening this discussion. As for the responsibility of universalism in imperialism, the discussion is also open, as arguments by Pratap Bhanu Mehta illustrate (Bhanu Mehta 2000).

Cheah also contradicts the various theories on hybridity, such as developed by Bhabha and Clifford, and their use of the cosmopolitan context: "I argue that the accounts of radical cosmopolitan agency offered by hybridity theory obscure the material dynamics of nationalism in neo-colonial globalization" (Cheah 1997). For him, contemporary cosmopolitanism is a constant renegotiation of the postcolonial nation-state, in the framework of complex forces of both resistance and accommodation. But for the historian, the impression is that in Cheah's account, several steps are missing. The sequence "Kant, colonial, postcolonial" cannot be more satisfactory than the "diversity equals cosmopolitanism" postulate, and situations like the old regime Ottoman might help clarify the picture and reevaluate the concept.

The Ottoman Old Regime Urban Form of Cosmopolitanism

Studies on Mediterranean cosmopolitanism have mostly focused on the situation in port cities of the Ottoman Empire (or formerly Ottoman, in some cases): Alexandria, Izmir, Salonica, and Beirut, for example (Driessen 2005). But most of these studies do consider the Ottoman form of cosmopolitanism only at the moment of its impact with modernity, nationalisms, and European colonialism. Robert Ilbert's study on Alexandria, which remains the most valuable book in Mediterranean cosmopolitanism studies, focuses, for example, on the period of reforms of the Ottoman old regime and the creation of new municipal institutions in which not only confessional communities (Greek, Jews) were represented, but also European merchants and entrepreneurs (Ilbert 1996). Cosmopolitanism, conceived as participation in urban politics extended to minorities (if only the notables), was ephemeral in such cities. Reimer has underlined how this situation could also be seen as a colonial bridgehead (Reimer 1997).

The common feature of such cosmopolitan situations, during the time of the Ottoman reforms of the 1850s to 1900s, is formalized access to the reformed municipal institutions for notables from various communities, and in many cases for foreign merchants (Lafi 2005). From Beirut (Hanssen 2005) to Izmir (Georgelin 2005) and Salonica (Darques 2000), the cosmopolitan situation in such cities is rather ambiguous, however, if its consideration begins only in the middle of the nineteenth century. Such a perspective, though fascinating for understanding the logics at work in late Ottoman cities and the nature of Ottoman urban modernity, has the drawback of viewing cosmopolitanism only in the context of a relationship between an "oriental" society in the process of modernization and influxes seen as coming from Europe. In this situation, the late Ottoman cosmopolitanism is ambiguous by nature (Fuhrman 2003).

Recent studies on late Ottoman urban societies have shown that modernity was not the mere importation of solutions from Europe into a vacuum, but rather the modernization — in the framework of a rational imperial Ottoman project, with expertise found on the international scene, and sometimes bought on the international market — of a complex existing situation of old regime urban governance. What I argue here is that the understanding of this Ottoman urban old regime is also a way of exiting the impasse of cosmopolitanism seen only in its late Ottoman form, an instant before its colonial and/or national negation. Outside of the ephemeral and ambiguous late Ottoman moment, modernity in Mediterranean cities promoted segregation and separation and not cosmopolitanism, from French-occupied Algiers to ethnically homogenized Salonica or Izmir. The Ottoman old regime instead had been in many cases a negotiated form of urban balance based on the coexistence of communities.

One must of course not have a naïve or irenicist vision of this social form: it was not democracy, but an old regime unequal in its very nature and organizing different layers of inequalities; it was not general harmony but rather a constantly renegotiated balance, with moments of crisis and sometimes violence. But it was also an expression of plural civic participation in urban governance, in the context of an empire that granted the general framework for these local urban declensions of the *Pax Ottomana*. This framework was progressively built on different heritages, among which the imperial Byzantine, itself related to Roman roots, and the Islamic are the most relevant. In a medieval Islamic context, the governance of diversity had been dealt with both at the theoretical philosophical level and at the level of the practical organization of daily life in cities. The issue of the regime of difference has been treated in medieval Islamic philosophy by authors such as al-Farabi, with his *al-madîna al-fâdila* — the ideal city (Muhsin 2001) — or Ibn Khaldun (Baali 1988). They proposed visions of urban society in which the Greek philosophical heritage, local traditions, and of course the precepts of Islam were combined to make an original creation, which contributed to framing urban governance in the Middle East.

Minorities were granted access to the urban sphere through the authorization of communal representation, the participation in guilds, and the right to petition. Among the central notions in Islamic medieval thought, the *Hisba,* or good governance, integrated such dimensions. Representatives of communal institutions were generally inserted, though often with a minor role, into the institutions of urban government. This scheme was extended by the Ottomans and made part of the general functioning of the Empire. On the basis of the medieval Islamic heritage and the Byzantine imperial heritage, confessional communities were granted the right to have local councils, of which the notables were members. Such institutions did not only deal with religious communal affairs — Jewish, Armenian, Greek Orthodox, for example, according to the city — but also had fiscal, judicial, and urban jurisdictions. The chief of each community was a generally a member of the council of the notables of the city, the form and composition of which was a result of negotiations with the empire. This system can be seen as a form of cosmopolitanism, as diversity was not only a demographic fact but was translated into a system of governance. Of course Muslims had a dominant position, and not all public offices were open to members of all communities. But such communities were recognized as collective civic bodies and were granted access to the urban and imperial civic sphere. Even nomads and the Roma in the Balkans were given a collective civic existence.

The petitioning system in the Ottoman Empire, during the old regime, was also more than an appeal against bad administration: it was an institutionalized dialogue between individuals or collective bodies (communal or professional) and the empire. There was an administrative system established to handle petitions, and most decisions in the empire were taken in response to a petition (Lafi 2011). Another hint of the existence of a form of cosmopolitanism in old regime Ottoman cities is the fact that the urban habitat was not fully segregated, and people from different communities had common daily lives and even common civic activities. There were of course quarters with a given communal identity, from the Greek quarters in Istanbul to the Jewish quarters in Tripoli or the different neighborhoods of Sarajevo (Gudelj 2007). But in all cities there were also mixed quarters, and in many cities, guilds could also be multi-confessional. And it was not rare, as the archives of the office of petitions in Istanbul illustrate, to have "notables" from different communities sign common petitions to the empire, embodying in this process a single civic body.

Cities of the empire were also the theater of the development of a kind a cosmopolitanism of the subaltern (Bayat 2010), as daily life was made of common experiences between people from various communities and as mobilization often happened according to shared needs and claims. All of these features, which participated in the negotiated construction of a kind of Ottoman *Pax Urbana,* were of course subject to growing tensions with the decline of the empire and with the impact of nationalisms and the modern definitions of politics, participation, and citizenship. But they constitute, from the fifteenth to the early nineteenth centuries, an original feature of cosmopolitan coexistence and governance. The specific characteristics, as locally negotiated with the empire (an entity that recent historiography invites us to read not as merely external but entangled with local societies) differed from city to city, just as layers of historical heritage and the local population composition differed. The Ottoman equilibrium, as in all old regime societies, was also regularly challenged, either by external events or internal rebels, or even more often by an alliance between both. Cosmopolitanism in Ottoman cities was in no way a perfect world, but an old regime configuration in which diversity, and inequality, were accommodated by (limited) participation and negotiation.

The existence of this system prompts a comparison with what happened in cities of the Northern shore of the Mediterranean in the early modern period. In places where the construction of kingdoms encouraged ethnic and religious homogenization, urban cosmopolitanism, which had medieval roots there too, had little chance to survive. And indeed, Ottoman Salonica, Tunis, Algiers, or Istanbul became safe havens for Jewish refugees from Christian Spain. In only a few European cities a certain form of urban cosmopolitanism — here again seen as the possibility of access to the civic sphere for minorities, and not just toleration of their existence — seems to have developed (Bottin and Calabi 1999). It is the case in Venice, a city-state that managed to avoid empires and kingdoms, and whose main source of wealth was commerce with the orient. In Venice, Jews, Muslims (Bosnians, Turks, Tunisians, Albanians), and non-Catholic Christians (Greeks, Armenians, Albanians) were granted the right to petition and designate the representatives of their communities, who were allowed to negotiate affairs regarding the community with the authorities of the Republic (Pedani 2010). In 1575 the Fondaco dei Turchi was created on the model of the institutions of the Jewish community. Such communal institutions had mandates much broader than the organization of confessional life. It was also the case in Livorno, a Tuscan harbor city where Mediterranean Jews were invited to settle by the Florentine power. Historical studies have illustrated how Jewish merchants in this city took part in a form of cosmopolitan urban governance (Fettah 2003, LoRomer 1987). But in many other cities of Europe, such developments were limited.

As for the Ottoman Empire, the modernization of the old regime did not include the development of an innovative tool for the generalization of equality without the explosion of the common civic sphere. Given growing frictions between Ottoman urban societies, nationalisms of various sorts, and European influence and colonialism, situations of cosmopolitanism disappeared in most cities.

Contemporary Urban Cosmopolitan Revivals: Between Place Marketing and Inauthenticity

In present-day Mediterranean cities, cosmopolitanism, with diverse specific meanings, is again a word that carries positive connotations. It is often used in the context of strategies of place marketing, presented as a fashionable feature of global cities of the region. It rarely, however, signals a new form of political cosmopolitanism, in which minorities

would be associated with urban government and the general governance framework would reflect a common civic sphere shared by members of various minorities. This idea of cosmopolitanism is more a form of coexistence of people of diverse origins, sometimes with positive effects on the image of the cities, than a mode of cosmopolitan urban government and governance of diversity. Indeed, Mediterranean cities are struggling with the limits of their models of integration and participation: from the banlieues of Marseille to the Roma camps of Naples, the neighborhoods with a dense migrant population in Athens or Barcelona, the Arab neighborhoods of Haifa or Jaffa, the camps of Palestinian refugees in Beirut or the camps of African migrants in Tripoli — all situations being diverse in their nature but sharing the common feature of exposing the limits of the cosmopolitan political sphere.

Cities of the Mediterranean exhibit more shortcomings in cosmopolitan governance than innovative and harmonious solutions. Very often, of course, local situations depend more on the ambiguities of state policies and even on geopolitical stakes than on the urban political ideal. But in spite of the broad diffusion of municipal democracy (though not all Mediterranean cities are part of this municipal democratic sphere), and in spite of the opening of this municipal democracy to migrants or their children or to members of minorities in many cities of the region, the Mediterranean does not seem to be the place for the construction of a new cosmopolitan ideal, in the philosophical and political science meaning of the term. The new Mediterranean cosmopolitanism we often hear about is definitely not mainly made of a general participation in urban affairs, which would reflect the diversity of urban societies. It is more a matter of urban identity, culture, marketing, and sometimes hiding (more or less deliberately) situations of exclusion. This new form of Mediterranean cosmopolitanism is characterized by extreme contradictions: the fashionable surface sometimes tells narratives that strongly contrast with the general context.

This is the case, for example, in Alexandria, a city that was until the 1950s an example of cosmopolitan society, though with many internal contradictions related to the colonial nature of cosmopolitan rule (Reimer 1997). Since the 1990s, the city has been the object of a program of cultural revitalization with strong cosmopolitan accents. Cosmopolitanism in Alexandria even became the focus of a marketing strategy (Starr 2005). But the paradox is that in this former cosmopolitan city, Greeks and Jews have mostly disappeared due to the tensions of the late twentieth century and the impact of decolonization, nationalism, and Zionism on urban coexistence. Alexandria is now a stronghold of radical Islam, a fact that does not prevent the city from playing on the image of a cosmopolitan past. This cosmopolitan myth has little to do with the actual evolution of the local urban society, in which sectarian polarization is stronger than ever (Iskander 2012) and urban space is marked by tensions that are in many respects a negation of cosmopolitanism (Tadroz 2011).

In post Civil War Beirut, cosmopolitanism is also, since 1990s, the theme of the construction of place marketing. The reconstruction of the city played on the image of a cosmopolitan city center, albeit in the context of polarized sectarian politics (Nagel 2002). Cosmopolitanism was both an object of real-estate marketing for developers and a brand to be sold to investors and visitors. Speculation, evictions, and corruption were also part of the process (Adwan 2004). Cosmopolitanism largely functioned as an accessory to gentrification and to the privatization of public space, with little echo in the governance sphere, where sectarian politics continued to divide communities. In another way, however, Beirut might be, in spite of all these limits, one of the rare Mediterranean cities where diversity is still part of the governance pact, and political alliances between sectarian parties, beyond their sometimes caricatural and ambiguous nature, might be a form of social consensus.

In Istanbul too, cosmopolitanism has been a key word in recent narratives of the city's cultural revival (Asu and Robins 2010, Thelen 2008). But in a city where profound demographic changes, with a massive immigration from Anatolia, and the Turkish national idea have both deeply challenged the very concept and reality of cosmopolitanism, the contradictions within the present revival of something that Benton Jay Komins called a "depopulated cosmopolitanism" (Komins 2002) are strong. This revival, made of both Islamist discourses on diversity, which often model themselves on a vision of the Ottoman past (Yavuz 1998), and cultural expressions of a fashionable Istanbul made of art galleries, discos, bars, and gay neighborhoods (Öktem 2008) — two cosmopolitan expressions with little in common (Potuoğlu-Cook 2006) — also takes place in the context of often unresolved questions on the relationship between the nation and the heritage of diversity (Mills 2008). The opening of the ruling Islamist party toward Greek and Armenian minorities can be interpreted as both a challenge to the Turkish idea of nation and a revival of an Islamic vision of tolerance, but also as a political maneuver with few consequences for daily patterns of interaction (Ter-Matevosyan 2010). Incidents during the Istanbul Cultural Capital of Europe 2010 season, when radical Islamists raided art galleries where alcohol was being served during *vernissages*, also illustrate the limits of coexistence in Istanbul between a cosmopolitan cultural elite and other trends on the local political and social scene, as well as the tensions that gentrification with a cosmopolitan image bring to popular neighborhoods (Pehlivan 2011).

In Marseille, cosmopolitanism has also been used as a tool of cultural marketing during the last ten years, with a process of Mediterraneanization of several major cultural projects, and in general of the narrative of the city (Bullen 2012). From the project of a Museum of the Civilizations of Europe and the Mediterranean (Bromberger 2007) to the content of the season of Marseille as the Cultural Capital of Europe 2013, Marseille has been using the Mediterranean as a brand for its own urban positioning, a process that has led some scholars to call Marseille's Mediterranean an "artificial product" (Gastaut 2003). In a city with a very diverse population, with serious issues of segregation and postcolonialism (Nasiali 2012), the cosmopolitan idea of the Mediterranean has nothing to do with local governance of diversity; it is rather a marketing product aimed at bringing back investors to a harbor city that has experienced a serious decline since the end of the colonial era.

In Salonica, present uses of the cosmopolitan past are also strategic. They developed on the occasion of its turn as the Cultural Capital of Europe in 1997, in the context of the emergence of a postnationalist narrative of the city's past. But they tend to focus on a static vision of the multicultural past, with little opening toward the multicultural present (Hatziprokopiou 2012). Even if the architectural heritage of the Ottoman past has been better protected, and if the Jewish history of the city has received renewed attention, one cannot say that this new vision of cosmopolitanism is really cosmopolite.

In Israel too, appropriations of the Mediterranean identity have been criticized as examples of place marketing with strong ideological inconsistencies, rather than expressions of what would be a postnationalist (or post-Zionist, in that case) form of cosmopolitanism (Locke 2009). In Tel Aviv/Jaffa, such contradictions have been denounced in real-estate projects whose narratives are intercultural and seek to develop the idea of a cosmopolitan city, but in reality often segregate populations and reinforce not only gentrification but the eviction of Arab populations (Goldhaber 2010). It is a process that Hadar Livne has called the creation of a "mythical Mediterranean space" made of Orientalist fake authenticity and provoking the "devalorization and erasure of the local urban space and its long neglected Arab population, and consequently in the creation of an alienated, exclusive Jewish gated community which ignores its social and physical surroundings" (Livne 2008). In such a process, cosmopolitanism is often used a marketing tool that masks practices of eviction (with strong colonial connotations), resulting in a reinforcement of the ethnic homogenization of the urban space. The situation in Haifa, where cosmopolitanism tends to be reduced to a folkloric vision of the orient (Kallus and Kolodney 2010) and has nothing to do with the invention of a new cosmopolitan governance, is comparable.

Such cosmopolitan façades have also been denounced in Morocco, and specifically the city of Marrakesh, where the vision of a cosmopolitan society tends to be limited to the attraction of foreign investors on the real-estate market and results in a violent gentrification of urban space, with a clear postcolonial dimension (Escher et al. 2001). The positive effect on the cosmopolitan scene of the return of Moroccan Jews, now mostly French, does not seem to have consequences for the true cosmopolitan dimension and seems to be part of a broader phenomenon of eviction of the poor under the effect of gentrification and control of the real-estate market by foreign investors.

Mediterranean cities do not seem to be places sponsoring the invention of a new cosmopolitan ideal. The present situation, in which uses of cosmopolitanism are more often ideological decoys than genuine innovations in terms of governance of diversity, draws on a limited vision of the cosmopolitan past of some cities of the region. They also often relate to rewritings of the narratives of nationalism and colonization. What is selected is the presence, and sometimes coexistence, of various communities, but rarely the model of a governance of diversity that, in some situations, was innovative (but of course should not be mythologized). Both new forms of diversity in Mediterranean cities (Meijer 1999), resulting from new migrations and the persistence of old injustices and segregations, call for the invention of a new Mediterranean cosmopolitanism, of which migrants to Mediterranean cities of Europe, Roma minorities from Naples to Istanbul, Chinese migrants in Algiers, or Sub-Saharan African migrants in Tripoli could be the beneficiaries. But until now, the effects of globalization on Mediterranean cities and on the uses and interpretations of the cosmopolitan idea have supported trends toward segregation rather than incentives for a true cosmopolitan revival, which would be something more than empty Ottoman (or sometimes Habsburg, per Ballinger 2003) imperial nostalgia or a caricatural and folkloristic vision of the past. But at least in debates about cosmopolitanism in other regions of the world (Cartier 1999), the Mediterranean can be used for the contrasted richness of its cosmopolitan history: a first step, perhaps, toward the invention of a new model.

References:

Adwan, Charles. 2004. "Corruption in Reconstruction: The Cost of 'National Consensus' in Post-War Lebanon." Center for International Private Enterprise.
Asu, Aksoy, and Kevin Robins. 2010. "Changing Urban Cultural Governance in Istanbul: The Beyoglu Plan."*KPY Working Paper 1*.
Baali, Fuad. 1988. *Society, State, and Urbanism: Ibn Khaldun's Political Thought*. Albany: State University of New York Press. 175.
Ballinger, P. 2003. "Imperial Nostalgia: Mythologizing Habsburg Trieste." *Journal of Modern Italian Studies* 8: 84–101.
Bayat, Asef. 2010. *Life as Politics: How Ordinary People Change the Middle East*. Stanford: Stanford University Press. 304.
Bhanu Mehta, Bratap. 2000. "Cosmopolitanism and the Circle of Reason." *Political Theory* 28-5: 619–639.
Bottin, Hervé, and Donatella Calabi, eds. 1999. *Les étrangers dans la ville*. Paris: MSH. 486.
Bowden, B. 2003. "Nationalism and Cosmopolitanism: Irreconcilable Differences or Possible Bedfellows?" *National Identities* 5: 235–249.
Breckenridge, Carol. 2002. *Cosmopolitanism*. Durham: Duke University Press. 241.
Bromberger, Christian. 2007. "D'un musée... l'autre." *Etnografica* 11-2 : 407–420.
Brown, Eric. 2012. "Hellenistic Cosmopolitanism." In Marie-Louse Gill and Pierre Pellegrin, eds. *A Companion to Ancient Philosophy*. London: Wiley. 549–558.
Bullen, Claire. 2012. "Marseille, ville méditerranéenne? Les enjeux de pouvoir dans la construction des identités urbaines.' *Rives Méditerranéennes* 42: 157–171.
Cartier, Carolyn. 1999. "Cosmopolitics and the Maritime World City." *Geographical Review* 99-2: 278–289.
Cheah, Pheng. 1997. "Given culture: Rethinking Cosmopolitical Freedom in Transnationalism." *Boundary* 2: 157–197.
Cheah, Pheng, and Bruce Robbins, eds. 1998. *Cosmopolitics: Thinking Beyond the Nation*. Minneapolis: University of Minnesota Press. 385.
Cochran, Terry. 1999. "The Linguistic Economy of the Cosmopolitical." *Boundary* 26-2: 59–72.
Darques, Régis. 2000. *Salonique au XXe siècle: de la cité ottomane à la métropole grecque*. Paris: CNRS. 390.
Dédéyan, Charles. 1976. *Le cosmopolitisme européen sous la Révolution et l'Empire*. Paris: SEES. 641.
Driessen, Henk. 2005. "Mediterranean Port Cities: Cosmopolitanism Reconsidered." *History and Anthropology* 16: 129–141.
Escher, Anton, Sandra Petermann, and Brigitte Clos. 2001. "Gentrification in der Medina von Marrakech." *GR*: 24–31.
Fettah, Samuel. 2003. « Le cosmopolitisme livournais: représentations et institutions (XVIIe-XIXe s.). » *Cahiers de la Méditerranée* 67.

Fuhrmann, Malte. 2003. «Cosmopolitan Imperialists and the Ottoman Port Cities: Conflicting Logics in the Urban Social Fabric." *Cahiers de la Méditerranée* 2003, 67.
Gastaut, Yvan. 2003. « Marseille cosmopolite après les décolonisations : un enjeu identitaire. » *Cahiers de la Méditerranée* 2003, 67.
Georgelin, Hervé. 2005. *La fin de Smyrne: du cosmopolitisme aux nationalismes*. Paris: CNRS. 254.
Gikandi, Simon. 2002. "Race and Cosmopolitanism." *American Literary History* 14: 593–615.
Goldhaber, Ravit. 2010. "The 'Jaffa Slope Project': An Analysis of 'Jaffaesque' Narratives in the New Millenium." *Makan: Adalah's Journal for Land, Planning and Justice* 2: 47–69.
Gudelj, Jasenka. 2007. "Sarajevo, la città cosmopolita 'alla turca.'" *Città & Storia* 2-1: 33–44.
Hanssen, Jens. 2005. *Fin de Siècle Beirut: The Making of an Ottoman Provincial Capital*. Oxford: Oxford University Press. 340.
Hatziprokopiou, Panos. 2012. "Haunted by the Past and the Ambivalences of the Present: Immigrations and Thessalonica's Second Path to Cosmopolitanism." In Caroline Humphrey and Vera Skvirskaja, eds. *Post-Cosmopolitan Cities: Explorations of Urban Coexistence*. New York, Oxford: Berghahn. 194–216.
Hill, Lisa. 2000. "The Two Republicae of the Roman Stoics: Can a Cosmopolite Be a Patriot?" *Citizenship Studies* 4: 65–79.
Holton, R. G. 2002. "Cosmopolitanism or Cosmopolitanisms? The Universal Races Congress of 1911." *Global Networks: A Journal of Transnational Affairs* 2: 153–170.
Ilbert, Robert. 1996. *Alexandrie 1830–1930: Histoire d'une communauté citadine*. Cairo: IFAO. 879.
Iskander, Elizabeth. *Sectarian Conflict in Egypt. Coptic Media, Identity, and Representation*. London: Routledge. 227.
Kallus, Rachel, and Ziva Kolodney. 2010. "Politics of Urban Space in an Ethno-Nationally Contested City: Negotiating (Co)Existence in Wadi Nisnas." *Journal of Urban Design* 15-3: 403–422.
Komins, Benton Jay. 2002. "Depopulated Cosmopolitanism: The Culture of Integration, Concealment, and Evacuation in Istanbul." *Comparative Literature Studies* 39-4, 360–385.
Lafi, Nora, ed. 2005. *Municipalités méditerranéennes: les réformes municipales ottomanes au miroir d'une histoire comparée*. Berlin: Schwarz. 365.
Lafi, Nora. 2011. "Petitions and Accommodating Urban Change in the Ottoman Empire." In *Istanbul as Seen from a Distance: Centre and Provinces in the Ottoman Empire*. Elisabeth Özdalga, Sait Özervarlı, and Feryal Tansuğ, eds. Istanbul: Swedish Research Institute. 73–82.
Livne, Hadar. 2008. "Being There and Away: Globalization and Gentrification in Andromeda Hill Project, Jaffa, Israel." *Territorio* 47: 150–158.
LoRomer, David. 1987. *Merchants and Reform in Livorno*. Berkeley: UCLA. 389.
Malacrino, C. 2007. "Cosmopolitismo e architettura a Delo in età ellenistica." *Città e Storia* 2-1: 11–32.
Mathisen, Ralf. 2006. "Peregrini, Barbari, and Cives Romani: Concept of Citizenship and the Legal Identity of Barbarians in the Later Roman Empire." American Historical Review 111-4: 1011–1040.
Meijer, Roel. 1999. *Cosmopolitanism, Identity, and Authenticity in the Middle East*. Richmond: Curzon. 196.
Meinecke, Friedrich. 1970. *Cosmopolitanism and the National State*. Princeton: Princeton University Press. 403.
Mills, Amy. 2008. "The Place of Locality for Identity in the Nation: Minority Narratives of Cosmopolitan Istanbul." *International Journal of Middle East Studies* 40-3: 383–401.
Muhsin, Mahdi. 2001. *Alfarabi and the Foundation of Islamic Political Philosophy*. Chicago: University of Chicago Press. 264.
Nagel, C. 2002. "Reconstructing Space, Re-Creating Memory: Sectarian Politics and Urban Development in Post-War Beirut." *Political Geography* 21-5: 717–725.
Nasiali, Minayo. 2012. "Ordering the Disorderly Slum: 'Standardizing' Quality of Life in Marseille Tenements and Bidonvilles." *Journal of Urban History* 38-6: 1021–1035.
Nocke, Alexandra. 2009. *The Place of the Mediterranean in Contemporary Israeli Identity*. Leiden: Brill. 298.
Nussbaum, M.C. 1997. "Kant and Stoic Cosmopolitanism." *Journal of Political Philosophy* 5: 1–25.
Öktem, Kerem. 2008. "Another Struggle: Sexual Identity Politics in Unsettled Turkey." Middle East Research and Information Project.
Pedani, Maria Pia. 2010. *Venezia Porte d'Oriente*. Bologna: Il Mulino. 350.
Pehlivan, Behice. 2011. "Rethinking Gentrification: The Analysis of Artistic Space and Violence in Istanbul." Masters thesis, Central European University, Budapest. 37.
Pojman, Louis. 2005. "Kant's Perpetual Peace and Cosmopolitanism." *Journal of Social Philosophy* 36: 62–71.

Potuoğlu-Cook, Öykü. 2006. "Beyond the Glitter: Belly Dance and Neoliberal Gentrification in Istanbul." *Cultural Anthropology* 21-4: 633–660.

Prange, Martine. 2007. "Cosmopolitan Road to Culture and the Festival Road to Humanity: The Cosmopolitan Praxis of Nietzsche's Good European againt Kantian Cosmopolitanism." *Ethical Perspectives* 14-3: 269–286.

Reimer, Michael. 1997. *Colonial Bridgehead: Government and Society in Alexandria (1807–1882).* Cairo: AUP. 251.

Rosenfeld, S. 2002. "Citizens of Nowhere in Particular: Cosmopolitanism, Writing, and Political Engagement in Eighteenth-Century Europe." *National Identities* 4: 25–43.

Slomp, Gabriella. 2005. "Kant's Critique of Hobbes: Sovereignty and Cosmopolitanism." *Contemporary Political Philosophy* 4, 83–85.

Starr, Deborah. 2005. "Recuperating Cosmopolitan Alexandria: Circulation of Narratives and Narratives of Circulation." *Cities* 22-3: 217–228.

Tadroz, Mariz. 2011. "A State of Sectarian Denial." Middle East Research and Information Project.

Ter-Matevosyan, Varham. 2010. "The Armenian Community and the AK Party: Finding Trust under the Crescent." *Insight Turkey* 12-4: 93–111.

Thelen, Sibylle. 2008. *Istanbul, Stadt under Strom.* Freiburg: Herder. 192.

Vertovec, Steven, and Robin Cohen, eds. 2003. *Conceiving Cosmopolitanism: Theory, Context, and Practice.* Oxford: Oxford University Press. 314.

Yavuz, Hakan. 1998. "Turkish Identity and Foreign Policy in Flux: The Rise of Neo-Ottomanism." *Critique: Critical Middle Eastern Studies* 12-7: 19–41.

New Geographies 05
The Mediterranean

Editor-in-Chief
Antonio Petrov

Editorial Board
Gareth Doherty
Rania Ghosn
El Hadi Jazairy
Stephen Ramos
Neyran Turan

Advisory Board
Neil Brenner
Bruno Latour
Mohsen Mostafavi
Antoine Picon
Hashim Sarkis
Charles Waldheim

Editorial Advisor
Melissa Vaughn

Editorial Team
Nikolaos Katsikis
Jarrad Morgan
Savina Romanos
Farida Farag

Design Labs Administrator
Edna van Saun

Graphic Design
Tomas Celizna & Daniel Harding

Printed in the Netherlands by Lecturis
Logo Design by Jean Wilcox

Distributed by Harvard University Press
ISBN 978-1-934510-33-9
gsd.harvard.edu/newgeographies

**Harvard University
Graduate School of Design**

New Geographies is the journal produced by
doctoral candidates in the New Geographies
Lab of the Aga Khan Program at the
Graduate School of Design. It presents the
geographic as a design paradigm that links
physical, representational, and political
attributes of space and articulates a synthetic
scalar practice. It extracts its themes from
contemporary challenges facing urbanization
in the contemporary Muslim world and casts
them in a comparative perspective with themes
and challenges from other parts of the world.
Through critical essays and projects, the
journal seeks to position design's agency amid
concerns about infrastructure, technology,
ecology, and globalization.

The Mediterranean has been made possible
by grants from the Graham Foundation for
Advanced Studies in the Fine Arts and the
Aga Khan Program at the Harvard University
Graduate School of Design (GSD).

All attempts have been made to trace and
acknowledge the sources of images.
Regarding any omissions or errors, please
contact: New Geographies, c/o Publications,
Harvard University Graduate School of Design,
48 Quincy Street, Cambridge, Massachusetts,
02138.